Rusty Young grew up in Sydney, Australia. He studied Finance and Law at the University of New South Wales and currently lives in Colombia, where he teaches English.

Marching Powder

A true story
of friendship,
cocaine and
South America's
strangest jail

RUSTY YOUNG

MACMILLAN
Pan Macmillan Australia

To Sylvia, Simone and the backpackers

First published 2003 in Macmillan by Pan Macmillan Australia Pty Limited
1 Market Street, Sydney

Reprinted 2003 (five times), 2004 (four times), 2005 (three times), 2006 (twice),
2007 (twice), 2008 (three times), 2009 (twice), 2010 (three times)

National Library of Australia
Cataloguing-in-Publication data:

Young, Rusty, 1975– .
Marching powder: a true story of friendship, cocaine
and South America's strangest jail.

ISBN 978-0-7329-1180-5

1. Young, Rusty, 1975 – Imprisonment. 2. Penitenciaria Nacional San Pedro
(La Paz, Bolivia). 3. Prisons – Bolivia – La Paz. 4. Cocaine industry –
Bolivia – La Paz. 5. Prisoners – Bolivia – La Paz.
6. Smugglers – Bolivia. I. Title.

365.98412

Set in 12/14pt Adobe Garamond by Midland Typesetters Pty Ltd
Printed in Australia by McPherson's Printing Group

Papers used by Pan Macmillan Australia Pty Ltd are natural, recyclable products made
from wood grown in sustainable forests. The manufacturing processes conform to the
environmental regulations of the country of origin.

Contents

PART ONE
RUSTY

卌 ||

Three days before I was arrested and ordered to leave the Republic of Bolivia, guards at San Pedro prison in La Paz caught me with several micro-cassettes hidden down my pants. I was on my way out of the main gates when they conducted the search. They were looking for cocaine, which is what most visitors smuggled out of San Pedro, and were slightly confused by what they found in its stead.

At the time, I believed I had got away with it by convincing the guards that the cassettes were the latest in Western music technology. However, three days later I was arrested on an unrelated charge. To this day, I do not know whether the police had found out about the book I was writing for Thomas McFadden, the prison's most famous inmate, or whether they thought I was a spy of some description. Either way, they were extremely suspicious as to why a foreign lawyer on a tourist visa had been staying voluntarily in Bolivia's main penitentiary facility for three months.

During the first month of my stay in the prison I had told the guards at the gate that I was Thomas's cousin. For the second month, the guards probably assumed I was there in order to do drugs, like the other Western tourists who arrived at San Pedro carrying their guide-books and departed wearing their sunglasses. By the third month, the guards let me in and out without question. Provided I paid them enough money, they believed whatever I told them.

Then they arrested me. Ironically, the arresting officer chose bribery as the pretext. He was the same major I had been bribing every week since I had been there. I slipped him the customary twenty bolivianos as we shook hands on my way in, but on that occasion he looked at me as if we had never met before.

'Give me your passport,' he said, glaring incredulously at the folded note that had appeared in his hand. I did as I was told. 'Now follow me.'

It was a Saturday morning when they arrested me. They placed me in the police holding cells to stew for a while. Monday was a public holiday. The tourist police would not be able to process my crime until Tuesday, they said. I would have to wait for three days. No, I could not leave my passport as collateral and come back on Tuesday. No, I could not have any food – I was under investigation. No, I could not make a phone call – this was not a Hollywood movie.

Having spent three months in the prison, I wasn't particularly rattled by any of this. I had been listening to Thomas's stories about the Bolivian police for long enough to know that it would end up in a bribe. When they asked which hotel I was staying at and hinted that they would search my room and find drugs, I gave them a phoney address. When they left me alone in the cell, I went through my wallet and found the card of the hostel where one of my traveller friends was staying. They would not have needed to plant anything there; he had smuggled ten grams of cocaine out of the prison in a book the day before. I ripped the hostel card to shreds and then chewed it into a soggy ball, just like Thomas had done nearly five years earlier after he was busted at La Paz's airport with five kilos of cocaine concealed in his luggage.

Four hours later, I heard the police coming for me. I thought about my dead cat in order to induce some tears and continued to pretend not to speak much Spanish. Now that he had 'cracked' me, the captain at the police station offered me a deal.

'You have fallen badly, *señor gringo*. Bribery is a very serious crime in this country. You will have to pay.' I nodded solemnly. My tears of 'fear' mixed with tears of gratitude and irony, but I tried not to smile.

I managed to bargain the captain down by emptying my pockets and showing him all the money I had on me. The rest of my money was hidden in my socks in three rolls. I knew how much was in each roll in the event that the negotiation skills I had developed while in San Pedro required greater reserves. The captain had one more condition before he would make my charge sheet disappear: I had to agree to leave the country and never return. That would mean the end of work on the book that Thomas and I were writing.

'If I see you in San Pedro prison again,' the captain threatened, 'I'll send you to jail. *¿Comprende?*

I nodded. Despite its paradoxical phraseology, I knew this threat was serious. The police wanted to scare me off from whatever it was I was doing with the micro-cassettes. I left immediately for the dirty town of Desaguadero, on the Peruvian border. As soon as I arrived, I got stamps in my passport as proof to show the captain that I had at least obeyed the first part of his instructions. Peruvian immigration laws prevented me from officially leaving the country on the same day as I entered it, but that did not stop me from walking back across the border to get a hotel for the night on the Bolivian side, which was cheaper.

I rang Thomas in prison. I had to call his mobile phone, since the inmates in the four-star section of San Pedro where Thomas had his apartment were not allowed land lines. I had not told him about the guards finding the micro-cassettes, which we were using to record our interviews, because I knew he would have been angry.

'This isn't a game, Rusty,' he had lectured me on numerous occasions. 'This is my *life* you're playing with here. These people are not joking, man.'

When he answered the phone, Thomas was unsympathetic.

'Where were you, man? I waited all day.'

I told him I'd been arrested.

'Thanks a lot, man. You ruined my life,' he said, before hanging up on me.

I knew he would want me to call again, so I waited half an hour before buying another phone card. I didn't even need to say who was calling.

'You is a stupid kid, Rusty,' Thomas said, as soon as he picked up the phone. I could tell by his voice that he had taken a few lines of coke. 'I told you this would happen if you wasn't careful.' The coke seemed to have calmed him down a little.

'So, what am I going to do?' I asked him.

'We have to bribe them again. We'll have to call the governor of the whole prison. That's going to be an expensive bribe, man.'

When Thomas said 'we' in reference to spending money, he always meant that it would be *my* money we would spend.

I got my Peruvian exit stamp the following morning and then returned to San Pedro prison. Thomas had already arranged for me to bribe the governor. It cost us one hundred US dollars. I continued to make flippant remarks until a week later when the police tortured

Thomas's friend Samir to death, then left him hanging in his prison cell by a bed sheet in order to make it look like suicide. Samir had been threatening to write a letter to parliament exposing high-level corruption in the police force. Imagine if they knew what Thomas and I were doing. I had not taken the danger seriously until then.

The story of Samir's death was front-page news. When I showed the article to Thomas, he didn't look at it.

'I told you these people are not joking, man. You didn't believe me.'

卌ll

I had heard about Thomas McFadden long before I met him. A group of Israelis I met while trekking to the ancient Incan ruins of Machu Picchu had spoken of him with reverence. An Australian couple had told me about him during an Amazon jungle tour out of Rurrenabaque. Indeed, his fame had spread all the way along the South American backpacking circuit affectionately dubbed by travellers 'the *gringo* trail', which extends from Tierra del Fuego in Argentina up to Santa Marta in Colombia.

The jail in which Thomas was housed was even more famous than he was. I had heard of it as far back as Mexico, even before I'd heard of Thomas.

'When you're in Bolivia, you have to visit the prison,' a blonde Canadian traveller had advised me in all seriousness.

'What for?' I asked.

'It's unbelievable. The inmates have jacuzzis and the Internet, and they grow marijuana on the rooftop.'

When I looked at him quizzically, he added, 'It's listed in all the guidebooks. Look it up.'

As soon as no one was watching, I pulled out my *Lonely Planet* guidebook from the bottom of my backpack where it was wrapped in a T-shirt along with my moisturising cream. 'The prison' was el Penal de San Pedro; by all accounts, the world's craziest penitentiary system – where wealthy inmates lived in luxury apartments with their wives and children and ate at restaurants inside the prison. And, as I later learned, Thomas McFadden was its tour guide.

As I approached the city of La Paz, talk of Thomas and San Pedro intensified. There were flyers on the noticeboards in the Hostal Austria and Hotel Torino advertising prison tours. The foreign travellers I met talked of almost nothing else. Among their ranks, the best informed was Uri, a German backpacker with an unkempt beard who had made the dilapidated El Carretero hostel his new home.

Uri was an expert on anything to do with South America. His attire was an eclectic assortment of local apparel picked up during his travels: a scarf from Chile, a Peruvian poncho, an imitation Ché Guevara beret and necklaces made from rainforest seeds sold by Brazilian street hippies. He was too tall and skinny for any of it to look right, but somehow he carried it off. The truth was, all these fashion accessories lent him a certain kudos among the other travellers.

When I talked to Uri, the basis of Thomas's fame became more apparent: not only was he the prison's tour guide, he was also its resident cocaine dealer.

'The best coke in the world comes from Bolivia,' Uri informed me, sitting up on his stained dormitory mattress in order to light his second joint of the morning. He deliberately directed a stream of smoke my way.

'And the best coke in Bolivia comes from inside San Pedro prison. The inmates manufacture it in laboratories inside.'

The fact that convicted drug traffickers could continue their trade from prison would have struck me as ironical in any other country. In Bolivia, it didn't warrant comment.

'So, you know this guy Thomas who does the tours, then?' I asked.

'Of course. He's my main supplier. Why? How much coke do you need?'

I liked the way Uri said *need* instead of *want*. 'So, how do I get to the prison?' I asked, ignoring his offer. 'And how do I find Thomas?'

'Just catch a taxi,' he answered, making his way towards the door that hung tentatively by its remaining hinge. 'But don't worry about finding Thomas. He'll find you.'

卌||

I set out that very afternoon. Chilly air blanketed the city of La Paz even though the day was beautifully clear and the sun abnormally brilliant. At three thousand, six hundred metres above sea level, the thinner atmosphere imbued the light with a slightly surreal quality. The sky emanated a rarefied, crystalline blue, and everything looked sharper and more in focus. Above the city basin, the snow-capped peaks of Mount Illimani loomed unrealistically close.

According to the map, the prison was within walking distance, but I hailed a taxi so as to make no mistake.

'To San Pedro prison,' I ordered the driver in my best Spanish.

'*Sí, señor.*' He nodded nonchalantly and headed off into the chaotic La Paz traffic with the obligatory dangling plaster statuette of Jesus swinging erratically from his rearview mirror. I wondered whether I had pronounced the destination correctly. Did he not think it a trifle odd that a foreigner would want to visit the prison?

We crossed the Prado and, almost immediately, found ourselves hemmed in by traffic. My gaze roamed aimlessly out the window and over the scenes in the street where hawkers threaded through rows of cars, offering bananas, cigarettes and fake leather mobile phone covers to motorists. A stout old woman sat on an upturned box beside her hotplate that milked its power from an illegal cable running down a nearby electricity pole. A young indigenous girl was slowly making her way up the steep hill carrying a baby on her back wrapped in colourful cloth. In her arms she held a heavy bundle of potatoes. She was stooped forward with their weight, but didn't stop to catch her breath. If she lost her momentum, I sensed it might be forever.

Through the other window I saw a malnourished young boy, dressed in dirty jeans and rubber sandals made from old tyres, weaving his way lazily around the maze of traffic, half-heartedly offering to wash windscreens. The drivers ignored him, but before the lights changed, he had tipped dirty detergent water on someone's window and begun wiping it without being asked. The driver must have felt guilty and started to search for a few coins just as the lights turned green. A dark-skinned policeman blew his whistle, trying to advance the cars, but none of them could move because the front driver was busy looking for coins for the boy. The policeman kept blowing his whistle and commanding the cars forward. Still, nothing happened. By the time the driver had found some coins, the lights were red again. My driver breathed heavily through his nose.

We continued through the traffic. Only a block further up the hill, we rounded a plaza and the driver braked suddenly, interrupting my reverie.

'*Aquí no más,*' he said, pointing to a large metal gate set in a high, yellow wall. It did not look at all like a prison. We were still in the middle of town. There were no bars, no barbed wire and no signs.

'Are you sure?' I frowned.

'*Sí, seguro,*' he replied, pointing once more at the building and then holding out his hand to receive payment. 'Fifteen bolivianos, please.' It seemed he now spoke English. I shook my head and smiled to show I had been in the country long enough to know the cost of a taxi ride.

'Six.'

'OK. Thirteen.' Eventually, he dropped his price a further two bolivianos, but he couldn't go any lower than that. Cost cutting in Bolivian schools has resulted in generations of taxi drivers who do not know the numbers one to ten. They learn to count from eleven upwards. I paid him the correct fare and he laughed good-naturedly and then drove off.

I was still dubious about whether this was the right place. Apart from two uniformed policemen leaning idly against a metal railing, there was no indication that there was a jail behind those walls. Besides, many buildings in La Paz, even apartment blocks and private businesses, could afford to have state-paid policemen stationed outside. As it turned out, the driver was correct; this *was* the prison.

It was inexplicably situated on prime real estate, occupying an entire block in the city centre and fronting on to the beautiful San Pedro Plaza. As I looked up at the enormous walls again, deliberating on my next move, one of the policemen appeared beside me.

'Tour, yes? You Eengleesh. You American. Prison tour?' He motioned that I should approach the gates. It seemed I was in the right place. However, I baulked until he said something that caught my attention:

'*¿Necesita a Thomas?*'

'*Sí,* Thomas,' I confirmed, still at a safe distance. He became even more excited and beckoned frantically for me to accompany him.

'*Sí.* Thomas! No cameras, *señor*! *No fotos,*' he advised, leading me inside.

The outer gateway opened up into a high-ceilinged, spacious passageway and there, directly in front of me, was another set of gates, this one consisting of vertical bars. On my side of the divide was a wooden table manned by several indolent guards in green uniforms. On the other side, pressed tightly against the metal gate, jostling each other and vying for optimal viewing positions, was a sea of expectant Bolivian prisoners.

Scarcely had I time to take in this initial spectacle, before my appearance generated a clamorous uproar. Voices bellowed from all directions:

'Tours!'

'Mister. Hey mister!'

'*¡Señor!*'

'Cocaine?'

'Marijuana?'

'Tour!'

'*Una moneda.*'

Prisoners also called out from the wings that branched out to the left and right of this main chamber. They were like frenzied monkeys, screeching and rattling their cages and clambering over the top of one another to capture my attention. Hands gripped the bars and others extended through them, waving and offering drugs or appealing for coins. I stared back at them. At the same time, my policeman was tugging at my sleeve with *his* hand out. As I gave him some coins, I heard someone call the name 'Thomas.'

The speaker this time was a diminutive inmate with dark skin and a shock of white hair at the front. I nodded to him and the din subsided instantly. The other prisoners resumed their intense vigil over the entrance, waiting for the next visitor, while the prisoner who had spoken yelled excitedly, '*Thomas! Thomas. ¿Quiere que le traiga a Thomas?*' When he smiled, I saw that he was missing a tooth.

I nodded again and he whispered something to one of the officers through the bars. The officer stood up, opened the gate using a set of keys chained to his belt and nodded for me to go through. It was the gateway into the strangest place I have ever visited.

卌‖

A group of about five or six Westerners was already waiting just inside the gate. A young man of medium height, dressed in a freshly ironed designer shirt and cream-coloured jeans, noticed me looking around uncertainly.

'Hi. I'm Thomas.' He smiled warmly, extending his hand to shake mine. He had a chubby face with intelligent eyes that engaged my attention immediately. 'What's your name, man?'

'Rusty,' I answered hesitantly.

'*Rusty*,' he said, still clasping my hand between both of his: 'That is nice name, man. I like a lot. Strong name.'

This was not at all the Thomas I had expected.

First, he was black. Uri had told me Thomas was from Liverpool, in England, so I had expected him to be white. Second, he was charming and courteous in a way that I would not have expected of a prisoner. When four more tourists arrived, he shook hands with each of them in turn, looking them squarely in the eyes and repeating their names. Over the next hour and a half, he didn't get a single name wrong.

Thomas had a strange accent for an Englishman. He called everyone 'man' and sometimes mixed up his words and tenses. But that didn't matter. Thomas had a magical way of drawing you right in. He had an energy I have encountered in very few people in the world. There were nine of us in the tour group, but I never doubted for a moment that Thomas was speaking only to me. The tour itself was fascinating, but it did not end there. When the other visitors left, Thomas invited me back to his 'cell', which was more like a student room in a fraternity house. He had cable television, a refrigerator and said he had once owned a computer.

Without another word, Thomas produced a small wrap of cocaine and started chopping its contents into lines on a CD case. I looked at the door, which he had locked. Thomas sensed what I was thinking.

'My prison cell is the safest place in the world to take cocaine,' he assured me, laughing to himself. 'I won't get busted, man. I can have the police fired if they give me any trouble.'

He sniffed a line, slid the CD case over to me and then started talking. Soon, I did not want him to stop.

It is impossible to convey adequately the way in which Thomas related the events of his life to me. He did not simply narrate them; he acted them out as if he were reliving the entire experience. From the moment he started talking, I did not shift from my chair. Thomas, on the other hand, stood or moved around almost the entire time. As new people entered the story, he played their various roles. He imitated their voices, their mannerisms – even their facial expressions. He used objects and furniture in order to tell his stories. He even tapped himself on the shoulder when describing how two policemen had approached him in the customs queue at La Paz's airport four-and-a-half years earlier.

Thomas's experiences in San Pedro and his life beforehand were the stuff of books – the types of true stories that are so bizarre they seem like fiction – and when he finally paused for breath, I told him so. He said that it had always been his intention to write a book, but he was yet to find someone to whom he could entrust the telling of his life story. He did another line of cocaine and then continued his narrative.

I was completely mesmerised for another hour until a bell sounded. All visitors were now supposed to leave. However, there was something the official guidebooks had failed to mention: for a small bribe, tourists could also spend the night in San Pedro.

That evening, Thomas took me into the dangerous sections deep inside the prison. Some of the things I saw there made me cry with laughter; others utterly repulsed me. I saw a side of life that I had never seen before. Many of the inmates were addicted to drugs – some so severely that they cut themselves deliberately in order to come down or because they were paranoid. I even made the acquaintance of a cat that was addicted to smoking cocaine. It was the craziest night of my life and the most fascinating. I do not know what possessed me to take the risks I did. I think it was Thomas. In the few hours since I had met him at the gate, I had come to trust him almost completely. As long as he was there, I felt certain that no harm would come to me in San Pedro.

By the end of the night, I understood why Thomas McFadden was so famous. With Thomas holding court, the entire evening was bathed in magic. It was also powdered with cocaine. However, that was only part of the experience. The coke he dispensed that night was of the quality that Uri, the German backpacker, had boasted, but it was used in the same manner as the furniture and other objects in his room; it was merely another prop to help him narrate. His life story was also as fascinating as the Israelis on the Inca trail had described. But it was not that, either. It was Thomas himself. I had never met anyone like him in my life, and I doubt I ever will again.

Something clicked between us that night. We talked non-stop until daybreak and then I decided to stay another night. Around four o'clock in the morning of the following day, it was decided: I was going to write his book for him. We hugged and Thomas told me I was his white brother. He bought a dozen bottles of beer to celebrate.

The next day I had a hangover and a vague recollection of having made a very serious pact. I was now Thomas's brother and I had to stick to our agreement. It would be a risky undertaking; if the prison administration or other prisoners were to discover our intention of exposing the corruption in San Pedro, there would be grave repercussions. There was also a catch that Thomas had neglected to mention: I would have to live in San Pedro with him. Otherwise, I would never genuinely understand what it was like to be a prisoner there.

'The tourists only see the easy side of prison life for an hour when they do a tour,' he told me. 'But there is a lot of suffering here, man. A *lot* of suffering.'

⊞⏐⏐

I went back to Australia for six months in order to work and save up money, before returning to Bolivia. For the next four months, I spent time with Thomas in San Pedro every day. It was not long before I discovered that Thomas was right – it seemed like a relaxed place for a prison, but it was a prison nonetheless. Fortunately, he had obtained permission in writing for me to come and go as I pleased. Unlike the real prisoners, I could take a cheap room in a hotel on the outside for the night whenever things became too much.

In taking on this project, I knew from the outset that Thomas McFadden was no angel. Very few foreigners end up in prison in South America for no reason. Thomas was a convicted cocaine trafficker, but he was also one the most magnetic people I have ever met. However, I will allow you to discover that for yourself.

This is Thomas McFadden's story.

PART TWO
THOMAS

ﾌﾟﾟﾟﾟﾟ II

1
EL ALTO AIRPORT

When I stepped through the automatic sliding doors into La Paz's El Alto Airport carrying five kilograms of pure cocaine concealed in my luggage, I got a shock. There were police everywhere. Some were ordinary policemen dressed in green, but many others wore the blue uniforms of Bolivia's main drug squad, the FELCN. As soon as I walked into the terminal, every single one of them looked up. It was as if they had been waiting for me.

Normally, whenever I walk into an airport anywhere in the world carrying merchandise, I treat everything as a game. I try to see the funny side of things. If you think too much about the risk you're taking, it makes you nervous and you make bad decisions. Of course, you're always going to be a bit nervous, but thinking of the whole thing as a game stops those nerves from showing on your face.

It took me a while to slip into game mode this time because there were so many police and because the terminal was so small. La Paz is the biggest city in Bolivia, so I had expected its airport to be truly international. But it wasn't. It was tiny. However, now that I was inside, it was too late to turn around.

I chased after my porter. He had slowed down a few metres inside the door, waiting for me to catch up and tell him which airline I was with. I pulled out my ticket and pretended to be flustered because I had arrived so late. We studied the ticket together and then searched for the correct counter. All the while I was looking around in order to make a more thorough assessment of the airport's security system. Because it was so small, I could have got all the necessary information in a single sweep, but I took my time and made all my observations very openly. That's the first mistake amateur traffickers make: they think the less they look around, the less attention they will attract. But that's exactly the opposite of what you should do. If you've got nothing to hide, then why wouldn't you look around? A typical passenger walks into a terminal and stops, looks at the departures board, goes the wrong way and then asks directions of people, all the while searching for the right counter and looking around them. They might even look up at the ceiling and notice the security cameras.

Gradually, I began to relax and slip into proper game mode. The police had stopped staring at me by then, and everything I observed confirmed my previous experience of Bolivian security: the system was going to be easy to get through. Apart from its size, the airport layout was standard, with the floor covered in those shiny, off-white tiles you get in all airports. The roof was the typical painted-cement variety. It looked like they hadn't renovated it in years. I knew straight away that there were no hidden cameras up there. It was the same with the walls. There were no observation rooms hidden behind advertising posters, that I could make out. Along the far wall was the row of check-in counters. The most obvious airline was the national airline, Lloyd Aero Boliviano.

Even though it was early in the day, you would have expected an international airport such as La Paz to be reasonably busy. There should have been airline staff behind all the counters and other employees rushing about all over the place. However, there was a total of four staff waiting to check people in. But I wasn't worried because I had already seen that there were no specialists around.

'Specialists' is the name I give to the security personnel in airports whose job it is to specifically target drug traffickers. You never really know for sure who might be a specialist or who the specialists might have helping them. It could be anyone from a Drug Enforcement Administration agent posing as a passenger, to an airline employee at the check-in counter or an innocent-looking cleaner. I have even heard of an airline flight attendant who was paid by a specialist to take note of people who didn't eat during a flight, because that can indicate they have swallowed merchandise. However, not eating during a flight may also say something about the quality of airline food, and the attendant pointed the finger at hundreds of innocent people until the specialist stopped paying her.

The regular police and army officials never worry me in the

slightest, no matter how many there are. In fact, the more the better. When there are a lot of them, they relax, thinking that someone else will cover for them. But you do have to look out for the specialists; they never rely on the support of a lazy and incompetent team. They work alone and take all the credit themselves. Even when they get you, they don't like to reveal themselves; they stay undercover and keep working until they catch the next one, and the next one after that. A lot of traffickers who get caught never even find out that it was a specialist who got them. They think it was a sniffer dog, or a lucky customs search or a tip-off, when actually it was a specialist who pegged them in the terminal.

The normal police and customs people are there just to earn a living, but the specialists are properly trained and actually *enjoy* their jobs. It's like a challenge to them and they really like busting traffickers. They have discipline and that's how they get to the top of their field. In fact, many of them are as passionate about and dedicated to their jobs as I am. We're in exactly the same business, just on different sides. I think of the specialist as my direct enemy in the airport, like the opposing number on a sports field: to beat him, you have to know who you are up against and how to outsmart him, because you can't be successful at anything unless you are better than your opponent. The best specialists and drug traffickers think alike. They are looking out for me, and I'm looking out for them. Luckily, I'm smarter than they are and have never been caught by one. Well, there was that one time they got me in Nairobi with the heroin, but I still don't know to this day if it was a specialist who got me. I eventually got out of that one anyway.

Usually, I can see through their disguises easily, although some of them are very good. I often know who the specialists are because they are *too* casual; they are trying *too* hard to blend in. But just knowing who the specialists are doesn't mean you have won; they can still get you. In fact, if they catch you catching them, then you've lost, because only a trafficker would be looking out for a specialist. At the same time, not looking around at all when you are in an airport is also suspicious behaviour.

With all my knowledge of the way this business works, I was thinking about becoming a specialist after I retired, just to keep myself in touch with the industry. I think the best disguise for a specialist would be as a drug trafficker. Or they should at least wear bright clothes and be more extroverted. No one would suspect them then – who ever heard of an attention-seeking undercover agent?

I'm only joking, of course, but that's my point. When I'm working, I treat the whole job as a game and I like to play with them. And in a game, you have to laugh. Whether it's the drugs game, or any other game. But the only thing the specialists don't have is a sense of humour. They take things way too seriously. That's why I'm smarter than them and why I elude them every time. But there was no need to worry about them this time. There were no specialists in La Paz airport.

卌||

I paid the porter and checked in my suitcases at the airline counter without any problems.

'You'll have to hurry, sir,' said the girl, pointing to the departure gates. 'You're running very late.'

'I know. There were protestors blocking the highway.'

'Yes, sir. I understand. We've been informed of that and take-off has been delayed slightly. But you must hurry, please.'

In order to reduce the time the customs police would have to ask me questions, I wasted a few more minutes buying some cigarettes in the duty-free shop. I got my passport stamped and cleared customs easily. I was completely relaxed as I joined the queue for the departure lounge. It was when I was waiting in line that the real trouble started.

Suddenly, I heard someone call my name. From out of the corner of my eye I saw two policemen approaching me quickly.

'Thomas McFadden!' they called again.

Once more I pretended not to have heard. I continued studying my boarding pass. But when one of the policemen tapped me on the shoulder, I couldn't ignore it.

'¿Es usted Thomas McFadden?' he asked. I hardly spoke any Spanish at that time, but I couldn't pretend not to know my own name.

'Yes,' I nodded. 'Why?'

'Sígame, señor,' he said, indicating with his hand that I should follow him. I thought about arguing, but the other passengers in the line were beginning to look around. I wasn't sure what was going on yet, but I kept my cool.

I followed the policeman who had spoken to me, and the other one walked behind me. There was no point in trying to escape; I wouldn't have made it to the terminal door. Besides, I had only just checked in my bags. There was no way that they could have found the drugs already and then traced them to me. As we walked along, I asked them what the problem was, but they couldn't speak English. They kept repeating the word '*perros*' and touching their noses.

I was still quite relaxed at that stage. I didn't yet know what '*perros*' meant, but I had dealt with airport police before and had always outsmarted them. I had been doing this drug business since I was a boy. When I was younger, I was like an action man – I could go anywhere in the world with merchandise and never get caught. Sometimes I worked out of India with hashish or heroin, sometimes from Pakistan, but the last few times had been out of South America with cocaine. I would fly over, buy a few kilos through my Bolivian contacts, and then fly back and sell to my contacts in Europe. I never got caught, because I was smart. This time would be no different. I also had a friend in a high place in case things went wrong.

The two policemen led me through a door, down a set of stairs and then along a dimly lit corridor that ran under the airport terminal. Finally, we stopped outside an office and the policeman in front knocked. A plaque on the door read, 'Colonel Toro Lanza'.

'*Pase*,' ordered a voice from inside. The policeman opened the door. Behind a large desk sat a stern-looking officer with a well-decorated uniform indicating his rank of colonel. He had a commanding presence, and the policemen who had escorted me were obviously afraid of him. They pushed me forward. The colonel looked at me fiercely.

'*Siéntese, señor*,' he demanded, indicating the seat in front of his desk. '*Su pasaporte, por favor.*' I handed him my passport. He inspected my photo and then looked back at me to make sure it matched.

'*¿Señor Thomas McFadden, sí?*' he asked, reading my name from the passport.

I nodded.

'Do you speak Spanish, *Señor* McFadden?'

'No. Only English.'

I waited for an explanation of what was going on, but the colonel didn't look up. He continued flipping through the pages of my passport. I looked at my watch. It was ten minutes before my flight had originally been due to leave. I knew it wouldn't leave without me – there is a security rule that planes cannot take off with the passenger's luggage onboard if the passenger isn't also on the plane. I asked the colonel what was going on, but he ignored me. He began writing down some of the details from my passport on some kind of report.

The colonel's office was only partly underground – at the top of the back wall was a window that was just above ground level. Through it, I could hear a plane engine starting up outside. I wasn't sure if it was my plane, but I started to feel a little worried.

'Please, *señor*. Is something wrong?' I asked, and finally, he answered.

'They have found something in your bags, *Señor* McFadden.'

'Who has?'

'*Los perros,*' he said.

'I don't understand.'

'The dogs. They have detected something in your suitcases.' I felt my heart sink. But I didn't panic.

Just then, the other officers left the room. I leaned forward and put my hands on the colonel's desk.

'What's going on, Mario?' I asked.

2
CHANGE OF PLANS

The colonel's full name was Colonel Mario Toro Lanza. I had met him through a friend of mind named Tito in Santa Cruz, a city in Bolivia where I had a lot of contacts in the trafficking business. Tito was my best contact – he worked in customs at Santa Cruz Airport. He was an expensive friend, but he always got me through airport security without any problems. Before I did this last run, we met up at our usual spot – the bar at the Continental in Santa Cruz.

Tito looked exactly the same as when we had been introduced years before. Out of work, he always wore loose-fitting casual clothes because of the tropical heat, as well as gold bracelets and a nice watch. However, you could still tell that he was a cop by his short hair and moustache, which made him look slightly Arabic. All the cops in Santa Cruz had moustaches and wore gold in those days. It was almost part of the uniform. You could spot them a mile away.

'What you are doing back in Santa Cruz again?' he asked me in his broken English, which was still better than my terrible Spanish. I signalled to the barman to pour a beer for Tito.

'I'm working,' I answered, refusing a beer myself. Tito raised his eyebrows and smiled. 'No. I'm serious.'

The barman stayed out of earshot while I gave Tito my routine about the new fruit juice company I was managing. The previous time I had done a run out of Santa Cruz, I had a lot of spare cash and was looking for ways to expand my operations. I set up a fruit juice business as a front. As company manager, I would be required to travel in and out of South America frequently. The Bolivian Fruit Juice Company S.A. never sold so much as a glass of orange juice. Nevertheless, I had an office, a temporary secretary and faxes from all over the world to prove that it was a very successful business. Tito probably guessed it was a front – he knew I hadn't called him out to our meeting spot to discuss pineapples and papayas – but that was the way you had to talk to these people. It was all a game; I gave him some nice stories and he pretended to go along with them.

'Show me your passport, please,' he requested when I'd finished my sales pitch. He flipped through the pages and then said something I hadn't expected after all the deals we had done together: he wouldn't be able to help me this time.

'Why not?'

'The *yanquis.*'

'The what?' The way he pronounced the word made it sound like 'junkies', but he meant the Yankees. Tito explained that the US government was now heavily involved in fighting its 'war on drugs' in Bolivia. It had finally decided to clean up Santa Cruz Airport, which had a very bad reputation for trafficking because of people like himself and me.

'Too many stamps in your passport, my friend. You understand?' Apparently, things were now a lot stricter and Tito couldn't guarantee that I would get through safely when customs agents saw how many times I'd been in and out of the country that year.

At first I thought this was Tito's way of asking for more money. I offered him an extra fifty per cent. Then I offered him double. When he refused again, I knew it wasn't about the money. There must have been a real problem with the Americans. I felt my stomach starting to float. Without Tito's help I was lost. I had already bought the stuff, packed it, pre-sold it and was ready to fly.

The coke had been sealed up and hidden using a technique that I had thought of myself and that no one else was using at the time. You have to be smart and creative in this business, because whatever new way to smuggle drugs you might hear about, the drug police have already seen it a year ago. They have specially trained personnel whose job it is to think about these things all day, and they have technology for detecting drugs that the public don't even know about yet, so the only way to get through is to be smarter than they are. The three most important factors in transporting merchandise are the amount you take, disguising the smell, and where you hide it.

You should never strap it to your body; that went out in the 1980s.

It's very obvious, even to the untrained eye, when people are loaded up with drugs under their clothes. As soon as an official suspects something, or even if the police do a standard security pat down for weapons, they'll catch you straight away. If that happens, there's no way that you can deny the drugs are yours. What judge is going to believe that you don't know how ten bags of cocaine got taped around your body?

Swallowing the stuff, known as body packing, is still OK. All sorts of stories go around about the horrible death you die in the airport if one of the capsules bursts in your stomach or gets caught in your intestines, but if the job is done properly, then there's almost no chance of that happening. If you don't know how to do it yourself, there are people in the industry who specialise in compressing the cocaine into tight balls and wrapping them so that there's no way they will accidentally break open. The bigger operators even have special industrial machines that do the job perfectly – a hydraulic press that compacts the merchandise into a cylindrical mould and another machine to seal the product with several layers of the latest-technology plastics that aren't affected by stomach acid.

The optimal-size package for swallowing is ten grams. It's not a pleasant task, but you get used to it after a while. It can take several hours to get the whole lot done – the first few go down OK, but once your stomach starts to get full, it becomes more and more difficult. If you force yourself, then you want to vomit. The packets can be swallowed with water to make it easier, but that also fills your stomach up faster. The best thing to do is to prepare your body by eating lots of fibre in the days before. After swallowing the packets, you mustn't eat anything that might raise the acid levels in your digestive system or push the packets through too quickly.

Obviously, as with body strapping, if the police find merchandise inside your body there is no way to deny it's yours. But there is a lot less chance of the authorities finding it in the first place. The first check they do at an airport, if they suspect that you are body packing, is to press your stomach with their hands. They can usually feel any hard objects with their fingers, so it's best to swallow the packets two days before flying so that by the time you reach the terminal they are in your intestines, where they are more difficult to detect. The packets will still show up on an X-ray machine, or the police can detain you until your body expels them, but they have to be pretty certain for it to get to that point. Aside from the physical discomfort, the main disadvantage of swallowing is that you can only transport a small amount; six or seven hundred grams each run, or a kilogram at the very most.

At the same time, you shouldn't get too greedy in this business; the more stuff you carry, the more space it takes up and the harder it is to hide. I learned that lesson the hard way when I lost forty-five kilos of cocaine in Brazil. But for this run I had exactly five kilos, which was the perfect amount; it was enough to make good money, but I had compressed it so that it was very small and almost impossible to find.

I had done this by dividing the five kilos into four equally sized lots and wrapping them in a layer of cling plastic – the type people use for keeping sandwiches fresh. I then placed each of these bundles in a friend's machine press, which had a handle that you turned in order to screw the top down against the base. I tightened it with all my strength, and then re-tightened it at five-minute intervals. The press completely flattened everything in between, so that the cocaine was as thin as cardboard. After half an hour, I unscrewed the press and folded these sheets over a few times and trimmed them with a knife so that the dimensions were exactly right for the compartments they would go into. Then I pressed them for another half an hour. There were about seventy grams left over at the end. I decided to make them into balls for swallowing. It wasn't much of an insurance policy – that amount would hardly cover the expenses of my trip, let alone the cost of the five kilos – but if I got caught and was sent to prison, I figured I could use it to bribe my way out.

The next thing to consider is the smell. Sniffer dogs have a sense of smell a hundred thousand times stronger than humans do. And not only are they taught how to find the merchandise, they actually *want* to find it. The way they train those dogs in South America is by getting them addicted to cocaine. Dogs aren't used in every airport, and there aren't enough of them to check every single bag on every single flight in every single hour, but if there is a coke-addicted hound with a big, sensitive nose anywhere near your merchandise, you can be sure it will smell even a tiny molecule of the stuff. So, you have to do absolutely everything you can to stop the smell getting out, just in case.

After the first layer of plastic cling wrapping, I added a thick coating of chilli powder. Chilli has a powerful smell that throws the dogs off the scent. Then I added another layer of cling film and then another thin layer of chilli powder. The next layer was the completely airtight one made by placing each package between two plastic sheets, which were then melted together along the edges. I did this using my friend's special machine that they use in Bolivian restaurants for making meat-filled pastries called *salteñas*. All those layers should have been enough, but for good measure, I wrapped one more layer around, with ground coffee underneath. I mixed the coffee granules with a little water first. When it dries, it sticks evenly around the outside of the plastic like strong glue, forming another airtight layer. Coffee also has a very strong smell that confuses the dogs if they happen to get close enough.

The final question was where to hide the packages. I now had four compressed, airtight loads of slightly less than one-and-a-quarter kilograms. I hid them very cleverly in my two custom-designed suitcases. You should never use the false-bottom suitcases that you can buy in any flea market in South America; they also went out in the '80s. I had my cases manufactured in England to my own specifications. They had cost me a lot of money, but they were worth it.

The secret compartments were in the actual spines of the suitcases, next to the hinges. The spines of the suitcases were so thin that no one would ever think of looking there. The packages fitted exactly, with not an inch to spare. If the police searched me, they would be too busy tapping other parts of the suitcase listening for the hollow sounds that indicate a false bottom to even think that the merchandise might be hidden in the spine. My suitcases could be used only once. After the merchandise had been wedged into place and the spine glued down, no one could get to it without damaging the case. The cops would need to be one hundred per cent certain that they would find something, if they were going to start destroying my luggage.

As always, I took special care to leave no traces whatsoever when handling the merchandise and the suitcases. The whole operation was performed wearing rubber gloves, and I also wore a shower cap to stop any stray hairs falling into the cases. Afterwards, I threw away the clothes I was wearing. Even a single fibre from your sweater can be matched to you.

I usually packed and hid the coke so well that I didn't need to worry about getting caught. I simply paid Tito as an extra precaution. He always put my suitcases on the plane for me so that I didn't have to check them in or even touch them. And if ever anything were to go wrong, he would have sorted it out for me. However, this time Tito scared me with his talk of the *yanquis* and by refusing to accept my money. After what he had said, I was convinced that inside help wasn't merely an extra precaution; it was an absolute necessity.

'I very sorry, my friend,' Tito repeated. 'Is too dangerous for both of us. The Americans catch a lot of people with their new drug law *Mil Ocho*.'

When he saw my expression, I knew he felt bad for me. He took a long sip of his beer. Tito always did that when he was trying to decide on something. Then he nodded slowly to himself and put down the beer. I knew he had made a decision. 'OK, wait. There could be solution. But you must go to La Paz.'

I waited for Tito to continue.

'I have a good *contacto* for you there. He is colonel. He is head of airport security in El Alto Airport. Good *amigo*. We make business together many times. I can call to him. He will help you. Is good, no?'

I hesitated before answering. As a rule, I never worked with people I didn't know. It's too risky. Also, I didn't know the layout of the airport at La Paz. In fact, I'd never even been to La Paz. However, I had no choice, really. If there were US agents everywhere, I couldn't do anything without inside help.

'How much would I need to pay him?'

'Is better you decide yourself. That way to avoid the problems.'

Eventually, I nodded my agreement. Tito patted me on the back when he saw that I was still anxious.

'*Tranquilo*, Thomas,' he said, writing down the colonel's number on the back of one of his business cards. He ran a car dealership on the side with his brother. 'I am ringing him tonight. He will expect you when you have arrived.'

Tito had never let me down before and it was a good sign that he knew the colonel's number by heart, but I was still uncertain. He continued to reassure me. 'No problem, Thomas. *No pasa nada*. This is Bolivia. OK?'

卌‖

I caught a bus that night. The journey to La Paz was seventeen hours and the first part, to the city of Cochabamba, was over a dirt road filled with potholes. During the night, we stopped at several military checkpoints. At one of them, armed soldiers led sniffer dogs through the cabin and over the luggage stowed in the compartments beneath. I pretended to be asleep. My baggage-claim tickets were screwed up tightly in my pocket. There was nothing else linking me to the suitcases; however, I was still a little worried that the dogs might find my merchandise. But they didn't; the job was perfect.

After dawn, the bus began its ascent towards La Paz. As we climbed higher and higher up the Andean mountain range, the windows steamed up and the other passengers pulled out blankets they had brought with them. I sat there shivering until we arrived at the terminal just before midday.

La Paz was a shock to my system after Santa Cruz. Apart from the cold, the first thing I noticed was the altitude. When I stepped off the bus, I couldn't breathe properly because of the lack of oxygen. I had to get the taxi driver to help me carry my suitcases because I felt like I was going to faint. The whole look and feel of the city was also completely different. Santa Cruz is flat and spread out and its roads are wide. The buildings are only a few storeys high, even in the business centre. However, the streets in La Paz are narrow and winding and blocked with traffic. I was now surrounded by multi-storey office blocks and billboards. It didn't seem like I was in Bolivia anymore. Even the people looked and dressed differently.

I checked into a cheap hotel on Avenida Pando then rang the colonel from a telephone booth down the street. He must have been expecting the call because he answered the phone in English.

'Hello?'

'Um. *Aló*,' I said. 'Colonel Lanza, *por favor*.' The colonel recognised my accent immediately.

'Ah, Mr Thomas. You must call me Mario, please. How are you?' He had a pleasant voice and spoke firmly.

'OK, then. Mario. I'm fine, thank you.'

We spoke briefly and arranged for him to pick me up from my hotel at eight o'clock in order to eat a meal together.

꜡꜡꜡꜡꜡꜡

You can tell a lot about people when you first meet them. I liked Colonel Lanza as soon as I saw him open the hotel door and stride confidently into the reception area where I was waiting. He was about forty years old, of medium height with broad shoulders, and he was dressed smartly in pants and a jacket with no tie.

'Good evening, Mr Thomas,' he said, looking me straight in the eye and shaking my hand very firmly. He had a forceful way about him – which I had expected, since he was a colonel – but he was also friendly and extremely polite. When we went out to his four-wheel drive, he walked around and opened the passenger's side door for me.

'So. How you like La Paz, Mr Thomas?' the colonel asked as we drove off. 'Very cold, no?'

I didn't feel comfortable enough just yet to tell him he had my name wrong.

'Freezing,' I said, looking over at him. Now that I could see him up close, I noticed that his cheeks had been scarred by acne and the sides of his mouth drooped down whenever he stopped smiling. He looked at me sideways when he noticed me studying him. 'But it's nice,' I added.

During the drive to the restaurant, we talked mainly about Santa Cruz, which was where Colonel Lanza was originally from. He told me he had brought his wife and two young children to La Paz when he had been transferred.

'How old are your children, Mario?' I asked, trying to keep the conversation flowing.

'Mario junior has eight years and Catalina has six years. They are very beautiful. You must meet them.' The way he talked about his children made me think this was a man I could trust. We also talked about Tito, but by the time we were seated in the restaurant, we seemed to be running out of things to discuss.

'Do you like a beer?' he asked in order to break an awkward silence that had settled upon us. I didn't want one, but I didn't want to risk offending him on our first meeting.

'Yes, thank you. I'd love one.'

'Have you tried the beer of La Paz? Is called Paceña.'

'Not yet.'

'Is not like beer of Santa Cruz. You will see.'

He was right. For a start, it was impossible to pour.

'Slowly,' the colonel warned when he saw the glass filling with froth. 'You see. That is the altitude.' I tried again with the glass tilted almost horizontally, but it still didn't work.

'The beer is like the woman,' he instructed me, snatching the bottle from my hand and demonstrating how it should be poured. 'You must treat it very nice. The woman from La Paz is also called *paceña*, like the beer. You must treat them with same respect.'

After the first beer, Colonel Lanza seemed to relax a bit. However, I still had the impression that he didn't fully trust me. He was polite, but I think he was trying to work out whether I was an undercover American agent. He kept asking me questions about England. His suspicion made me trust him more.

'*Salud,*' we said at the same time, clinking our glasses after I had successfully poured the next round of Paceña. I was already feeling a bit light-headed.

'That's strong beer,' I said.

'Yes. That is the effect of the altitude also. You know, many people have died from drinking too much and taking cocaine on their first night in La Paz.'

This was the first time drugs had been mentioned and he made it sound like a passing comment only. However, I knew that he had thrown it in to test me. I took a small sip of my beer and didn't react.

'I'd better have only one glass more then,' I said when the critical moment had passed. 'Normally, I don't drink when I'm on a business trip.' He didn't react either and I sensed we were beginning to reach an understanding.

When the waitress brought our desserts, we finally got around to the real reason behind our meeting. It was Colonel Lanza who brought up the subject.

'I understand you have hurry to catch your flight, no?'

Without mentioning specifics, we agreed that I would fly the day after next. When I asked him how much I could give him for his assistance, he asked for double what I normally paid Tito. Added to the cost of the flight, it would use up most of my remaining money. However, I didn't want to bargain with him in case it caused problems later. We shook hands and agreed that I would come to his house the following day to meet his family.

|||| ||

The next day was Tuesday and much of the city was out shopping because it was Easter week. I purchased an Apex ticket from a travel agent on the main road, known as the Prado. The flight was for the following day at 7.15 am. The date couldn't be changed and the ticket was non-refundable, but it was the cheapest available. Afterwards, I returned to my hotel room and swallowed the seventy grams of cocaine balls.

The colonel picked me up in his four-wheel drive again. I handed him the money immediately. We hadn't finalised the details of our arrangement yet, but I wanted to pay him beforehand as a show of faith. Colonel Lanza liked this.

'Yes. It is good idea to get business out of the way first, I think. After we can enjoy the nice meal my wife will cook.'

On the way to his house we stopped at the markets so that I could buy the food.

'Come with me,' he said, 'I show you where the poor people buy everything cheap.'

We dodged our way around the crowds of people wandering through the busy market. I had to stand aside as old men carrying heavy sacks ran through the spaces between the tiny stalls calling, '*Permiso. Permiso.*' Everything was for sale in those markets, from electrical goods to strange vegetables I had never seen before.

'What's that?' I asked, when I saw some kind of meat bubbling away in a pot.

'Believe me. You do not want to know,' answered the colonel. 'These people are Indians. That is the Aymara and Quechua languages they are speaking. These people are not educated, you see.' He motioned around him and spat on the ground. 'You know, some of the people does not even know Spanish.'

After I had paid for the food, we continued walking through the markets, discussing as we went how we would get the merchandise on to the plane. Colonel Lanza was to come to my hotel that evening to pick up my suitcases. He would take them to the airport in the morning and personally ensure that they were placed safely onboard.

'After that, is not my problem,' he said. 'Anything happen, is your problem, OK?'

I nodded. 'OK, but I can definitely get on the plane without touching the suitcases?'

'*Exacto*. There will be no problem in Bolivia. You get on the plane, the plane flies to Europe and then is not my problem. You say nothing about me. I deny everything.' We shook hands.

Before we returned to Colonel Lanza's four-wheel drive, I bought a bottle of wine for his wife and a tricycle for each of his children.

'You are very kind, Mr Thomas,' said the colonel, putting his arm around my shoulder. 'My children will like you a lot. Maybe one day my family will come to visit you in England.'

Bolivia is a very poor country, but I could tell there was money in the south of La Paz – *La Zona Sur* – where Colonel Lanza's house was located. You could almost smell it. Everything was bigger and cleaner and more modern. As we drove south, the dirty, cramped apartment buildings in the city centre gave way to freshly painted houses that were surrounded by high walls with private security guards patrolling outside. The cars were newer, and the traffic flowed more quickly along wider roads that were lined with trees. Even the people looked different. There were no colourful Indian markets. I saw only boutiques and modern shopping arcades with big window displays set up for Easter. The few people on the sidewalks looked taller and thinner and whiter. They wore imported jeans and designer T-shirts. It was almost as if a little piece of the United States had been transplanted into the heart of South America. Even the sun seemed to be shining more brightly.

We arrived at the colonel's house, which was one of the smaller ones on the block but tastefully decorated inside. I got along very well with his family. I didn't get to know his wife very well because she couldn't speak English and spent most of the time in the kitchen cooking. However, Mario junior and Catalina played with me the whole afternoon. They were very well behaved at first and I could tell that the colonel was strict with them. After lunch, I taught them how to count in English and we played chasings around the small garden. Colonel Lanza watched us from the door and laughed.

'You see. They like you.'

Now that I had met his family, our trust in each other grew. He even mentioned doing some more business together after this run.

By the end of the afternoon the children were climbing all over me, squealing in delight.

'*¡Basta!*' roared the colonel suddenly when Catalina put her feet on his sofa. Her lip started to quiver and she looked like she was about to cry. Luckily, her mother came into the room and sent both children outside to play. There were a few difficult moments when neither Colonel Lanza nor I knew what to say.

'Another cup of tea, Mr Thomas?' he asked, pretending nothing had happened. He was obsessed with the idea that Englishmen drank a lot of tea.

'Yes. Thanks a lot.'

Through the open window we could hear Mario and Catalina's screams as they raced around on their new tricycles. We drank three more cups of tea. The colonel smiled as he watched his children pedalling up and down the driveway. One time, when I looked over at the colonel, I noticed that he had stopped smiling. The corners of his mouth were drooping and I saw him glaring at the children with a look that was something like resentment or jealousy.

卌||

I finalised everything that night. I rang my buyers in Europe and then my contact who worked in customs at Charles de Gaulle Airport in Paris. I would leave the suitcases on the baggage-claim carousel and, when no one claimed them, they would be placed in the lost luggage room. My customs contact would then switch them with the two identical suitcases he had. From there, it was simply a matter of him getting them out of the airport which, for a trusted customs official, would not be difficult. While I waited for Colonel Lanza to collect the suitcases, I did one final check over my luggage and ran through the timetable for the following morning.

I had everything carefully planned. I had booked a wake-up call from reception. I'd also set my alarm clock as a backup. I'd estimated the time it would take to get to the airport, with an allowance for traffic. Officially, passengers were supposed to arrive at the airport two hours before take-off for international flights. However, I had booked the taxi to pick me up so that I would arrive about fifty minutes beforehand. This isn't so late that it raises suspicion, but it doesn't give customs much time to do a proper search. I also had two industrial hair machines with me – a steamer and a dryer. I had bought them in Paris as a present for a hairdresser friend of mine in Holland who wanted to start her own salon. They were heavy to carry around, but they would also provide a good distraction at the airport. If the police were suspicious, that's the first place they would look.

As it got later and later, I began to worry. The colonel still hadn't called. After another half an hour, I went out and called his house from the phone booth down the street. No one answered. I called his work number. No answer. The hotel receptionist shook his head when I asked if there had been any calls while I was out. After another half an hour, I went out and phoned again. There was still no answer. Finally, at 11.30, I heard the phone ringing in reception. I ran downstairs. It was for me.

'Hello.'

'Mr Thomas, hello. There has been a small change in the plans. Nothing big.'

My heart started thumping, but I didn't say anything. I hoped it wasn't bad news.

'Hello. Mr Thomas?'

'Yes.'

'We change one thing only. I cannot come to take the bags on to the plane. But everything else is the same, OK?'

'What do you mean?'

'Is too suspicious, if I arrive to my work with two big bags. People might see.'

'What do we do, then?'

'Is OK. You just take the suitcases to the airport yourself. Check the bags in at the counter, then get on the plane and fly to Europe. You understand?'

As soon as he said that, I wanted to call the whole thing off. I never liked to change my plans. But I was locked in. I'd swallowed the stuff and I'd set up everything at the other end. I'd paid the money to the colonel. I'd paid for the flight and couldn't change it.

'Mr Thomas, are you there?'

'Yes.'

'You understand how we going to do it now?'

'Yes, I understand.'

35

卌ll

I had trouble getting to sleep that night. I was angry with the colonel for changing everything at the last minute. Why was I paying him so much money if he couldn't put the suitcases onboard? Finally, I managed to settle myself down. I went through the situation logically and decided I didn't really need the colonel to take the bags on, anyway.

For a start, I was confident of the job I had done in packing the coke. But even if police found the drugs, there was nothing linking me to the suitcases. A false name was written on the identification tags of the two suitcases containing the coke. As an extra precaution, I had packed these two suitcases with women's clothing. My own possessions were in a third suitcase that I originally intended to check in on its own and that looked nothing like the other two. I also had my briefcase as carry-on luggage. Nothing would go wrong, but if it did, at least I could rely on the colonel's help to get me out of it. I wiped the luggage for fingerprints one more time and then went back to bed.

In the morning, I followed my usual routine. I had a shower, then slowly dressed myself in my best suit and tie. I put on my gold watch and the special gold ring that had always brought me good luck. I did my hair using the steamer and dryer. Then I stared at myself in the mirror for a long time. By the time the taxi sounded its horn, I had forgotten that I was transporting cocaine. I was a successful businessman.

The taxi driver was an old, wiry man with tattoos. So as not to get my fingerprints on the suitcases, I got him to carry the two bags containing the cocaine for me. The driver looked at me curiously in the rearview mirror and tried to make conversation as he drove. I didn't understand what he was saying and went back to studying the business faxes I kept in my briefcase. Halfway up the main highway that led to the airport, we stopped and the driver got out. There was a roadblock and flashing lights up ahead. Suddenly, I heard sirens. I looked out the window and saw three police cars speeding up the wrong side of the road towards us. I panicked and grabbed the door handle, ready to jump out of the taxi and run. But the cars flew past us and continued up the highway. My driver looked at me strangely through the window.

When I looked more closely, I saw that the roadblock was caused by a demonstration. Hundreds of protesters were marching down the street waving banners that read '*Cocaleros*'. They were Bolivian coca farmers and they were protesting against government restrictions on growing coca and against pressure by the US government to fumigate their crops. The delay was throwing out my timetable, but there was no way that I could tell the protestors they should let me pass because I was one of their best customers and had a plane to catch.

My driver didn't think there would be much of a delay. He seemed prepared to wait for the police to clear the *cocaleros* off the road. However, as the protesters dispersed down the hill towards us, we noticed that they were carrying planks of wood. They began throwing rocks and the windscreen of the car next to us was smashed. My driver quickly started his engine and did a U-turn.

'To the hotel,' I instructed him.

I had decided to call the whole thing off. There had been too many bad omens: first, Tito not being able to help me; then the colonel changing the plan; and now the protest. Someone was trying to tell me not to get on that plane. However, the driver was determined to earn the full fare and must have known a different route.

'*Sí, señor. Vamos al aeropuerto,*' he said, turning up a side street.

The back streets that went up towards El Alto Airport were steep and unsealed. Several times the tyres skidded on rubbish as we sped our way up the hill. We passed through poor neighbourhood after poor neighbourhood where the houses had no windows and were made of mud bricks. Every now and then, I caught a glimpse of the highway that we should have been on. The route we were taking was a lot longer and I didn't think we'd make it in time, but the driver pretended not to understand when I told him to turn back.

Finally, we arrived at the airport and he held out his hand for payment. As soon as I got out, a swarm of porters surrounded me. The driver dumped my three suitcases on the pavement and one of the porters loaded them onto his trolley without being asked. He started racing ahead to the check-in counter. It was too late now to back out.

3
LOS PERROS

'What's going on, Mario?' I asked him again. 'Colonel Lanza?'
Now that there were only the two of us in the room, I expected
that he would drop the pretense of not knowing me, but he didn't.

'*Los perros han encontrado una sustancia controlada,*' he answered,
pretending not to know how poor my Spanish was.

He was behaving strangely, but at that stage I still believed it was in
case someone overheard us talking. I assumed that it was customs
agents who had found something and that the colonel had called me
down to his office to save me. I asked him what we were going to do,
but he continued writing his report. He wouldn't tell me anything
more.

For the next ten minutes, police and customs officials entered and
left the office. The colonel's telephone rang a few times. I couldn't
understand what was being said, but I kept hearing '*positivo*' and '*los
perros*'. Whenever anyone came in, I pretended not to know the
colonel. But we were running out of time. I looked at my watch again.
It was now five minutes after my original take-off time.

'How much money do you need?' I asked. Colonel Lanza looked
like he was about to answer, but there was another knock on the door.
This time the police brought in all my luggage and placed it on the
desk, saying '*Positivo.*' Outside, the sound of a plane's engines warming
up became louder.

As his men started to open my bags, I continued trying to persuade
the colonel to help me. By that point, I didn't care if his men worked
out that we knew each other. There was no time left to play games.
I now suspected that the colonel might be the one setting me up, but
I still thought there was a chance I could get out of it, if I played it

right. Sometimes these officials get greedy and want more money at the last minute. I knew I had a bit of extra time before take-off, because of the delay, but it wouldn't be much. I pulled out all my remaining cash and put it on his desk. I told him he could take the lot; I just needed two hundred pounds to pay for my hotel and taxi when I got to Europe. The colonel took all the money and put it in his drawer, then nodded to his men to proceed with the search.

When I saw the way his men were searching for the merchandise, I knew for certain that there were no dogs. They clearly didn't know which piece of luggage the drugs were hidden in. They began by opening my briefcase and the three suitcases. When the policemen discovered women's clothing in two of them, they looked at each other in complete confusion. They held up some bras and underwear to show the colonel.

'Are these your suitcases, *Señor* McFadden?' he asked me, trying not to let on that he might have made a mistake.

I shook my head and pointed to the case with my clothes in it. 'Only that one.'

The colonel frowned and inspected my plane ticket again. I had removed two of the luggage stickers, only leaving the one that matched the suitcase containing my clothes. When we'd made our agreement the previous day, I hadn't told him how many suitcases I would bring, but he had obviously been expecting there would only be one. He was also confused by the hair dryer and steamer.

I knew it wouldn't take too much effort for the colonel to confirm how many pieces of luggage I'd checked in, but in the meantime he told his men to start searching the suitcase with my clothing in it. They began by placing my clothes in a pile and inspecting the pockets and lining of each item. Next they took apart the hair dryer and steamer with a screwdriver. Although there was still confusion about whether the two suitcases with women's clothing were mine, they eventually searched through them as well. Once more, they found nothing. Then they started tapping the bottoms of all three suitcases, trying to find secret compartments.

There was no longer any doubt that Colonel Lanza was behind the whole thing. I still didn't get angry. There might still be time. I promised to send him more money when I got to Europe. I could send him any amount he wanted. I could give him half the profits.

I became desperate. I could give him *all* the profits. Colonel Lanza continued writing his report while his men continued searching. But they couldn't find the merchandise. It was too well hidden. The only way the colonel knew there was anything was because I had told him in the first place.

When the policemen produced knives and looked like they were about to cut my suitcase open, I got angry and told the colonel that it was very expensive. I would call my embassy and he would have to pay for any damage caused. I pretended not to care about the other two cases. He hesitated and then ordered his men to search everything all over again.

Eventually, the colonel nodded his head and gave the order to start breaking open the suitcase that had had my clothes in it. Outside, the plane engines increased to a deafening pitch. The policemen completely destroyed the lining of my suitcase, but found nothing. The colonel looked worried. He hesitated before nodding to his men to do the same to the other two cases. The noise of the plane engines gradually faded as the plane ferried out onto the tarmac for take-off.

'*¡Mira! Aquí está. ¡Mira!*' called one of the police excitedly. He had broken one of the spines and was holding up a package. The search had taken over half an hour. He licked the knife and pushed it through the plastic, then tasted the tip.

'*Sí, sí. Positivo.*' His colleague took the knife to test for himself and then confirmed the result to the colonel. In the distance, I heard the distinctive sound of the plane taking off. I finally accepted that I was busted.

I knew that the colonel must have been pleased to have finally found the merchandise. However, he didn't allow himself even so much as a smile. He sat there writing his report with the packets of cocaine on the desk in front of him. I sat in my chair, staring at him with absolute hatred. Any remaining chance that he would let me go became more and more remote with each additional phone call he made and every additional policeman who came to the door to look at me.

'Mario?' Colonel Lanza looked up at me. His face gradually began to show his good mood. 'Can I go to the toilet, please?'

'Yes. You can,' he nodded to the guard who had been stationed behind my chair to escort me to the bathroom.

The guard led me down the corridor. They still hadn't handcuffed me because they knew I wouldn't get very far if I tried to escape. I would have been lucky to make it back up the stairs. There were no windows in the bathroom, but the guard insisted on accompanying me into the cubicle and watching me urinate anyway. I pulled the chain and noted that the toilet flushed properly. On the way back to Colonel Lanza's office, I counted the number of paces.

The cocaine was still on the desk in front of me when I sat back in my chair. The guard stationed himself behind me as before. I sat patiently, pretending to look casually around the room. There was another guard against the wall who was smaller. Someone knocked at the door.

At the exact moment that the colonel and the two guards looked over to see who it was, I snatched the bags of cocaine from the desk and charged towards the door. The colonel was seated behind his desk and couldn't do anything. The guard behind my chair was too slow to react; I was at least two metres ahead of him before he realised what was happening. The only guard I had to get past was the one against the wall. He was small and I threw him to the ground when he tried to stop me. But what I hadn't counted on was that the policeman who had just arrived would try to play the hero.

He grabbed hold of the doorframe and when I tried to push him out of the way, I bounced off him and into the wall. I regained my balance for another attempt, but the others were on me immediately. I was taller and stronger than they were and managed to break free. I only had to make it through the doorway to have a clear run to the bathroom where I could flush the coke. However, one of the guards locked his arms around my ankles and wouldn't let go. I couldn't kick him off, but my hands were still free. I ripped one of the packages open with my teeth and sprayed the cocaine everywhere. They tried to grab my arms, but I held the packet above my head and continued to shake it. I then ripped open the other packets and twirled them around until they were also completely empty. Suddenly, more police arrived. They knocked me to the ground and overpowered me. It was all over.

Colonel Lanza was furious. Most of his office was covered in white powder. Five kilos of cocaine doesn't seem like much when it's tightly compacted. But it's a lot when broken up. Much of the merchandise had come out in small clumps and sailed across the room, then broken up on impact with the walls or furniture or people. There was a layer of cocaine spread over everything and everyone in the room. Hardly anything had escaped the impact.

'*¡Límpien todo!*' the colonel shouted angrily at his men, pointing around at the mess I'd made. I was expecting to be beaten for what I'd done, but the police didn't harm me. They handcuffed me and lifted me back onto the chair with two guards watching me closely.

Then they brought in dustpans and brooms to begin the cleanup operation.

I had succeeded in reducing the amount of cocaine significantly. There was a lot embedded in the carpet and in the guards' clothes. None of the police had the courage to tell Colonel Lanza that his hair was completely white. He sat back down behind his desk and glared at me. I glared back at him.

'*Señor* McFadden, I thought you were intelligent. You now make things more worse for yourself.'

From then on, my file listed me as *peligroso* – a 'dangerous' prisoner, who was to be considered violent and an escape risk. I was to be hand-cuffed at all times. And, according to Colonel Lanza, the judges would take my attempted escape into account when sentencing me.

I continued staring at him long after he had gone back to writing his report. I was no longer in shock about what had happened. I was past shock. I was shaking with anger. This man had invited me to his house. I had played with his children. I had eaten lunch with his wife. He had accepted my money. And then he had betrayed me. I wanted to kill him.

When he finished writing his report, the colonel stood up and ordered his men to take me away. As they lifted me out of my seat, I felt a sudden surge of anger come over me. 'Look me in the eyes, you bastard!' I hissed angrily, 'Look me in the fucking eyes!'

The guards were holding me very tightly, so Colonel Lanza felt safe enough to come out from behind his desk. He came up quite close and raised his eyebrows.

'Yes. I'm looking you in the eyes, *Señor* McFadden,' he said sarcastically.

I lowered my voice and spoke very calmly this time. 'I'm going to kill you. It is now my mission in life to kill you. Do you understand? You are going to die.'

Then I tried to head-butt him, but the gap between us was too great and I didn't reach. It gave him a shock, though, and he jumped back. He tried not to show any fear in front of his men, but I could tell from his expression that he had taken my threat seriously. And so he should have. I *was* serious. I was going to have him killed. I didn't care what it took. Even if I had to do it myself after twenty years in jail, I would kill him.

'You're dead! Do you hear me? Dead!' I yelled again, as the police pulled me away from him and out into the corridor.

4
THIRTEEN DAYS IN HELL

I was taken to the FELCN building back down the hill in La Paz. FELCN stood for *Fuerza Especial de Lucha Contra el Narcotráfico* – Special Force in the Fight Against Drug Trafficking. There, I was introduced to the *capitán* who was to be in charge of the investigation. He undid my handcuffs, shook my hand and was very kind to me until he realised that I wasn't going to cooperate. When he asked me to sign an official statment – known as a *declaración* – admitting my guilt, I refused. I said I wanted a lawyer. The *capitán* laughed.

'This is not the United States of America. You are in Bolivia now, *Señor* McFadden.'

He asked me over and over again where I had bought the cocaine, who I'd bought it from, when, and how much it had cost. He told me he wasn't after me. He wanted the sellers. If I gave him the information he needed, he would let me go.

'I don't know what you're talking about,' I answered every time. He pointed at the suitcases, which had been placed on the desk in front of me. Most of my possessions, including my business papers, as well as the various items of women's clothing, were spread out beside them.

'But here is the evidence.'

'Those bags aren't mine,' I answered. 'I have never seen them before.'

'Who is this man, please?' he asked, holding up the business card Tito had given me. It had the colonel's phone number on the back but there was no way I could dob in the colonel without admitting my guilt and getting Tito in trouble. I had stupidly forgotten to take it out of my briefcase the night before. 'He is your *principal*, yes?'

'I don't know. It's not mine.'

44

'We will see,' he said, placing Tito's card back on top of the pile of fruit juice documents.

Eventually, the *capitán* gave up on me and began to weigh what was left of the cocaine. While he was busy balancing the scales, I leaned forward and retrieved Tito's business card, which I then slipped into my underwear without anyone noticing. Later, in the cell, I tore it into tiny pieces and swallowed them. When the scales balanced, the *capitán* read the weight out to the other officer, who wrote down the figure, and then they both signed it. The *capitán* saw that I was listening.

'Eight hundred and fifty grams,' he repeated in English for my benefit, sealing up the merchandise in an official *evidencia* bag and handing it to the other officer to take away. 'You had a lot of cocaine, no?'

'I don't know,' I said. 'It's not mine.' What was I supposed to say – 'No, there was actually five kilograms'? Anyway, I thought that being charged with a smaller amount would be to my advantage.

'Yes. Of course it is not yours, *Señor* McFadden,' the *capitán* said sarcastically. 'I understand. The police planted it in your suitcase, yes?' He nodded to the guards to take me down to the underground cell. And that cell was where I spent the next thirteen days.

卌\\

Those thirteen days were the toughest of my life. I honestly thought I was going to die. For that whole time the police fed me only a piece of bread each morning and a cup of unsweetened tea made with cold water. The bread was always stale. When I complained about being hungry, the guards just shook their heads because they were under strict instructions not to talk to prisoners.

By the third day, I was so hungry that I pounded my fists on the door all morning until the guard on duty got sick of the noise and came to quieten me down.

'Food. I am hungry. Food,' I begged him, as soon as his face appeared at the observation window in the door. He looked at me blankly, so I put my hand to my mouth and pretended to chew, then patted my stomach. He shook his head sadly and said something back to me in Spanish. When he realised that I didn't understand him, he fetched another guard who spoke a little English. This second guard had a kind face, but he also looked at me sadly.

'My friend. We no have money to buy the food for you.' He explained that prisoners under investigation were supposed to provide their own food.

'But how can I eat, then?' I asked. The other prisoners in the interrogation cells had families that could bribe the guards to give them food, but I didn't know anyone in La Paz and the police had stolen my money. The guard shrugged his shoulders.

'Sorry. No money. No eat.'

He did, however, go upstairs and find my carton of cigarettes for me. I didn't even smoke before then – I'd bought the cigarettes at the airport just to take up some time and do a final check for specialists. When I lit the first cigarette and inhaled, I could feel the smoke ripping at my lungs. I started coughing, but I forced myself to keep going; it was the only way to stop feeling hungry.

The cigarettes suppressed my appetite, but they didn't stop my body from slowly starving. I had to get food somehow. Every time I heard the guards change shifts, I banged on my cell door in the hope that one of them might feel sorry for me. The nicer ones sometimes brought me an extra piece of bread to keep me quiet. However, most of them wanted money.

'*Dólares*, my friend,' they said, rubbing their fingers together. I promised to pay them hundreds when I got out, but when they realised that I didn't have anything on me, none of them would help.

'Food,' I begged repeatedly, making gestures so they would understand.

'*No hay*,' they said, while stretching one hand out in front, palm down, and rocking it from side to side, like people do in England when they're telling a friend that a movie they have seen is only OK. I worked out very quickly what this meant in Bolivia: 'There is none.'

The seventy grams of cocaine that I had swallowed came out a few days after I was arrested. The guards always waited outside the bathroom whenever I went in, so I had no choice but to wash the balls and reswallow them.

After several days with no food and smoking a lot of cigarettes, my stomach had shrunk and I felt only a tight pain in my abdomen. Then, I didn't notice it so much. I only knew that I was weak. Besides, there was something worse than the hunger: the cold. It was colder than you could ever imagine in those FELCN cells. La Paz is the highest major city in the world. It's in a kind of valley, so the cold gets trapped at night. The walls and floors of the cell were made of concrete, and there was nothing to keep me warm. Absolutely nothing. Not even a blanket or a mattress to lie on. The police had taken everything I owned: my clothes, my jewellery, my money. Everything. The only thing I had been allowed to keep was the suit I was wearing at the airport, although they confiscated my shoelaces, socks and belt so that I couldn't hang myself.

Because of the cold, I took to sleeping during the day, when the floor was slightly warmer. I was not allowed any exercise time on account of being listed as 'peligroso'. At night I remained standing or crouching on the spot, shifting my weight from foot to foot. My muscles and joints constantly ached from remaining in the same position for hours on end. I would have paced up and down in an attempt to keep warm, but I had no energy left. I couldn't even lean against the wall for support because it was too cold. Even with my shoes on and changing feet all the time, the cold still got in. It penetrated through the leather soles of my shoes and started by attacking my toes until they were frozen. Next, I could feel the blood in my feet getting colder and the cold then travelled through my veins into my ankles, up my legs and then worked its way around my body, chilling it bit by bit. Each night I shivered so much that I didn't think I'd live to see the morning.

I complained to the *capitán* about wanting my clothes back. He shook his head. All my possessions were needed as *evidencia*, he said. He then gave me a receipt and told me that I should claim them back after my trial. There was nothing more that I could do. Apart from the guards, there was no one to complain to because during the FELCN investigation period, I was officially *incomunicado* – I wasn't allowed visitors, or even phone calls. This also meant that the interrogation police could do anything they wanted to me. If I hadn't been a foreigner, they probably would have tortured me, like they did the Bolivian prisoners. Many of them died before they even made it to court.

I wasn't completely cut off. The police did allow a stream of lawyers to visit me. In fact, they had called the lawyers themselves, hoping for a kickback when I agreed to hire one of them. The lawyers all promised to have me let off, but I had to pay them up front. When I said I had no money on me, they left their business cards and told me to call them when I did.

I eventually managed to bribe one of the guards with a full packet of cigarettes to ring the British Embassy. As soon as the embassy got word that I was there, they sent someone around. Simon Harris was a serious man with a good heart. He brought me some supplies, including orange juice, sandwiches and a few magazines to read. He asked me whether I had been tortured or mistreated. I said that I hadn't because I was worried that the police might take revenge on me if I made a complaint about being deprived of food.

However, I did complain about not having a mattress or blanket. The *capitán* pretended to be outraged when Mr Harris questioned him about this. He ordered his men to fix the problem immediately. They gave me a sack filled with straw to lie on and two blankets. But as soon as Mr Harris left, they took them away.

I thought the investigating police were treating me harshly in order to make me confess. But it wasn't that. After four or five days I made my *declaración* stating my innocence, and signed it. I thought that now the police would send me to court to be charged in front of a judge, but they just kept me imprisoned in my cell. They seemed to want to punish me because I hadn't given in and confessed.

After another week in the FELCN interrogation cells I became extremely sick. By then, even if they had let me out to exercise, I couldn't have. I was too weak to remain standing, so I spent most of the time lying down. I no longer noticed how cold the floor was. I could see my ribs poking through my skin. I had also developed a severe cough. At first I thought this was because my lungs weren't used to smoking, but when I started coughing up blood, I knew it was something more serious. I spat the blood into the corner of the cell because there was nowhere else to put it. Gradually, the wall became stained with small red and green lumps where the bloody phlegm had trickled down and dried against the cold concrete. Some mornings, after the colder nights, I noticed that little crystals had formed on them. The guards refused to call a doctor because I had no money to pay for a consultation, or even for the phone call. I knew for certain that I was dying.

On the thirteenth day, I had a fight with the guards. When it was time to return to my cell after the morning toilet break, I refused to go back in. There were two guards and they were nice about it at first.

'My friend, *por favor*,' they said, patting me on the back and pointing into the cell. But I refused to go in. I was thinking to myself, if I go back into that cell, I'm a dead man. I won't ever come out again.

'*Vamos, Enkono,*' they said, still trying to get me to cooperate voluntarily. They called me 'Enkono' because I reminded them of Thomas Enkono, a famous black goalkeeper from Cameroon who had been contracted by one of the Bolivian football clubs.

For a few minutes, they tried gently to persuade me. Then they ordered me in, and finally they tried to drag me in by force. But I wouldn't go. I was weak, but even two of them couldn't get me in there because I was so afraid that that would be the end of my life. I started panicking and thrashing about with a strength that came from fear.

'Let me go! Help! Somebody!'

A third guard arrived when he heard me yelling. Between the three of them, they got hold of me and lifted me up to carry me into the cell. However, they still couldn't get me through the doorway. Each time I got near it, I wedged my legs against either side of the doorframe and pushed back with all my remaining strength. They almost succeeded, but I went crazy, twisting around and punching out at them and yelling at the top of my voice for someone to save me. I think they were afraid because they knew that my file listed me as dangerous.

'OK. *Tranquilo. Tranquilo, Enkono.*' One of them went to call the *capitán*, while the others attempted to calm me down.

When the *capitán* came down the stairs, his face was flushed red. He was very annoyed at having been disturbed and I thought he would simply order his men to use more force on me. The sudden strength I had found when fighting with the guards had disappeared. I was now very weak and my body was trembling. I wouldn't have been able to resist them again.

'What this time?' demanded the *capitán*, looking at me angrily.

'I want to go to court, please *señor*,' I said, trying not to show him how much my muscles were twitching or that I was on the point of collapsing.

The *capitán* gave me the same excuse as every other time: I couldn't go to court until the police investigation was complete.

'But I've already made my statement,' I said.

'The judge will only send you direct to the prison. You want to go to the prison, yes?' he asked sarcastically.

'I'm sick. I need food. Can't you see? I'm dying here.'

'And you think the prison is better?'

'It can't be any worse.' The *capitán* laughed at this and translated it for the other guards, who also laughed.

'Really? You are sure?' he asked, smiling.

I already had a mental image of what a South American prison would be like. There would be fifty prisoners crammed into a single room. The small amount of food we would get would be infested with maggots. The toilets would be overflowing. Rats would crawl over my face in the middle of the night. The guards would be corrupt and violent. They would torture prisoners. And the inmates would have blunt, homemade knives with which to attack new inmates.

As a foreigner, I mightn't last long in a Bolivian jail. However, I knew that if I stayed at the FELCN, I would die anyway. Besides, there was a slight chance that I might survive in prison – they would give me some food, a blanket and a uniform that would be warmer than my suit. I might even get a bed. There would at least be a prison doctor. With a little nutritious food, I could get back enough strength to protect myself in a fight.

Two weeks before, I would have done anything to avoid being sent to a Bolivian prison. However, at that moment, I actually *wanted* to go.

'Yes,' I nodded. 'I would prefer to be in prison.'

When the *capitán* and his men had finished laughing, he looked at me sternly. 'You know what they do to the *gringos* in the prison of Bolivia, my friend?' I shook my head.

'This is what they will do to you.' He put his hands forward as though he was clutching someone's hips and started pumping his groin back and forth, making grunting noises. The three guards laughed again and joined in groaning and squealing as he thrusted. 'You still want to be in the prison?'

'Yes,' I answered determinedly, meeting his gaze. The other guards stopped laughing and waited for the *capitán*'s reaction. He made another joke in Spanish, probably saying that I would enjoy being raped. I continued to stare back at him while they laughed.

'Fine, then, my friend.' He threw his hands in the air. 'You will go to the court. Then after you will see how is the prison in Bolivia.'

5
SAN PEDRO PRISON

I put my tie back on and the FELCN guards took me up the stairs and then outside into the glare of daylight. I stopped, wanting time for my eyes to adjust after so long without seeing the sun, but the guards pushed me into a police car and drove me to the courthouse. I was placed in a holding cell that was no different from the one I had just come from, except that there was a window high up in the wall. I waited there all day, watching the light through the window gradually fade. No one brought me any food or came near my cell. I coughed blood a few times into the corner. It was no use yelling out or banging on the door; I had to conserve my energy.

'Thomas McFadden!' someone finally called from the corridor.

I patted my hair and flattened out my tie, thinking I was going to appear before a judge. I had been wearing the same suit for thirteen days. I must have smelled bad, but I no longer noticed. Two policemen unlocked the door and helped me to my feet because I was too weak to stand properly on my own. They handcuffed me and led me outside and into the street.

I was expecting to be taken to court, but the two men in charge of me waved to an unmarked car on the street. When it stopped, the shorter, bossier policeman opened the door and said, '*Suba*,' and then pointed for me to get in. '*¡Suba!*' he repeated louder, when he saw that I was hesitating.

I thought they were trying to trick me. The driver wasn't wearing a police uniform, and I could tell that the car, which was old, wasn't a police vehicle. However, I was weak from hunger and my hands were cuffed behind my back, so they simply pushed my head down and threw me in. At first I thought they were taking me somewhere to kill me, because that sometimes happens with the police in South America. People just disappear. There had been no sign on top of the car and I only realised it was a taxi when I saw a cardboard sign on the dashboard and the driver stopped in traffic to buy cigarettes, blocking the whole road. After that, I relaxed a little.

When we stopped outside the prison gates, one of the policemen guarding me in the back seat asked me something in Spanish. I didn't understand, so I just stared back at him, confused. He repeated the same phrase – 'La tarifa' – again and again. He sounded like he wanted something. Then the taxi driver became angry and the two policemen started grabbing at me. I was still handcuffed, but at first I struggled to get away because I didn't know what they were trying to do. One policeman got hold of my arms and kept me still, while the other went through my pockets. Then I worked it out: they wanted me to pay the taxi fare.

It was almost dark when I was escorted through the outer gates of San Pedro prison. I remember thinking that the building we were entering couldn't possibly be a prison, because the plaza in front of it was so beautiful. The last thing I saw of the outside world was a couple walking hand in hand along the footpath. The girl was pretty, and I thought it would be a long time before I saw a woman again.

The policemen were angry that I hadn't had any money to pay for the taxi. They dragged me roughly up the stairs to a big, important-looking office. A plaque on the door said that the office was that of a major. When we entered the office, the major didn't look up. My file was open on the desk in front of him and he continued studying it as if I wasn't there, just like the colonel had done at the airport. I sat patiently, watching him and waiting. I noticed that his uniform was perfectly ironed, although he was so fat that the buttons looked like they were about to pop off. I desperately needed food, but I decided it would be best to wait for the major to speak first. Eventually, he lifted his head and just stared at me.

When the major did finally speak, it was to ask me for money. I couldn't understand much of what he said, but I knew the numbers in Spanish, so I picked up the words 'twenty-five bolivianos'. I automatically assumed he was asking me for a bribe because I was a foreigner. At the time, one boliviano was worth about twenty US cents, so the amount he wanted was only five dollars. I wouldn't have argued with him, except that I didn't have any money.

'I haven't got any money. I'm sorry,' I said, shaking my head, frustrated that I couldn't use my hands to explain. When the major noticed that I was struggling with my handcuffs, he nodded for my police escorts to remove them. They had been done up very tightly and my hands stung as soon as the blood started to flow again.

'*Gracias, señor*,' I said respectfully, nodding to him. I wondered whether this was the right time to ask him for some food. However, first I wanted to apologise for not being able to give him any money. I turned my pockets inside out to demonstrate that I actually wanted to pay him but couldn't. I think the major misinterpreted this gesture as a refusal, because he immediately sent for a corporal who could speak English. The first thing the corporal translated was, 'But is true, my *amigo*. Everybody pay the entrance fee. Bolivia prisoners also.'

I still assumed this 'entrance fee' was just the major's polite way of asking for a bribe. But I later learned that all new prisoners were indeed required to pay an entrance fee of twenty-five bolivianos for the privilege of being imprisoned in San Pedro. They called this '*el Ingreso*' and when you paid it, the police gave you a receipt.

'But what if I can't pay?' I asked, when I realised they were serious. I was worried that the major would become angry.

'You must work in the kitchen for a period of six months to pay the money,' answered the corporal.

I promised the major that the British Embassy would pay the fee when they came to visit me. He seemed satisfied with that arrangement. Even though he now knew that I had no money, he then told me that I would have to buy a prison cell. When the corporal translated this, I looked at him blankly and said that I didn't understand. The other policemen in the room grinned when they saw the look of confusion on my face.

'*Ahora tiene que comprar su propia celda*,' the major repeated impatiently. When his men heard this the second time, they struggled to contain their laughter.

'Now you must buy your own cell,' the corporal translated again. Once more, I suspected that this was simply another way of asking for a bribe because I was a foreigner. 'OK,' I nodded, playing along with it. My plan was to stay on the major's good side and promise him some money later.

The major then sent one of the policemen out of the room to get something. While we were waiting for him to return, I told the corporal that I was hungry. He put his hand up to silence me.

'Wait. After,' he said, as the policeman came back in carrying a large blue book. The major opened the book upside down so that I could read it from my side of the desk. He motioned for me to come closer. I leaned forward in my chair and followed his finger as he ran it down the page, explaining something in Spanish as he went.

It took me some time to understand what the book was about. The pages were divided into columns that contained dates and names and descriptions. When he sensed that I was having difficulty, the corporal explained that this was a list of all the cells currently for sale that I could choose from.

Still not quite believing that any of this was real, I asked the major how much a cell cost, using one of my few Spanish expressions: '¿Cuánto cuesta?'

'Cinco mil,' he responded. I thought I knew the numbers, but I must have misheard. Five thousand was too much. I asked the translator to repeat the amount in English. He confirmed that it was five thousand.

'Dollars or bolivianos?'

'Dollars, my amigo,' he said. 'Cell prices in San Pedro are always in American dollars.'

'But I've already told you. I haven't got any money,' I said. The major said something to the corporal, who translated.

'The major say four thousand. But that is minimum. Is good price, no?'

Once the major realised that there was no money to be made out of me, our interview was terminated immediately. He nodded to his men to remove me from the office.

'Wait!' I cried out as the guards stepped forward. 'Can I have some food? Where do I sleep?' But the major had already begun shuffling the papers on his desk. 'Please,' I begged him. 'I have money. Just not here.'

The major didn't look up again, not even when I tried to struggle with the guards. That morning, I had been able to fight them, but by then I was too weak. There was no need to handcuff me this time. They took me down the stairs again, opened a big gate with metal bars and pushed me through. I felt myself collapsing from hunger and exhaustion.

𝍤𝍦‖

When I looked up, it wasn't at all what I had expected. There were no prisoners to be seen anywhere. I was in a cement-paved area that appeared to be the main prison courtyard, but the place was completely deserted. It was now night-time, and the yard was well lit by a number of naked bulbs hanging from the walls. In the centre of the courtyard were two garden beds, each with a large, healthy-looking tree. A few colourful flowers grew at their bases. I noticed a tap beside me. Underneath it was a bucket for watering the gardens with. The water was freezing cold and tasted dirty, but I was so thirsty I didn't care.

When I had finished drinking, I looked upwards. I expected to see guards patrolling the roofs with rifles slung over their shoulders, but there weren't any. Above me was a wooden balcony with two separate staircases running down into the courtyard. Over on the other side of the courtyard were three doors. Two of them were closed.

There was no way that I could sleep in the courtyard; it would be too cold. I needed to find somewhere warm to sleep. I went through the open door and felt my way down a dimly lit tunnel, with my hands stretched out in front of me for protection. The corridor led to two more passageways and, at the end of one of these, a second courtyard. Fronting onto this courtyard was a building with three storeys, each with rows of doors that seemed to open into tiny rooms.

I wandered around, looking for someone who might be able to help me. All the doors were closed, but I saw two men talking and went up to them.

'*Hola*. Can you help me, please? I need food.' They couldn't understand English and walked away when I patted my stomach. I saw another prisoner, but he disappeared before I could even talk to him. He took one look at my dirty suit and at the way I was stumbling and must have thought I was drunk. By then, I was completely out of energy. I just needed to lie down.

Eventually, I found cover in a building in the far corner of the courtyard. There were no lights on inside, but I could make out that there was no one there. There was no door, so it would be just as cold as sleeping outside, but at least I would be slightly more protected from the wind or from attackers. If I stayed alert, I might survive the night.

I sat down and leaned against the hard wall, thoroughly exhausted. The cement floor was cold and a little damp, so I couldn't lie down without getting wet. I stayed sitting there for some time, resting in the shadows where no one could see me, trying to keep my eyes open for any danger. It was an uncomfortable position, but after two weeks in the FELCN cells, I was used to it and must have fallen asleep, because the next thing I remember was feeling wet. It was the middle of the night or the early morning and foul-smelling water was seeping across the floor. My pants were saturated. I remember thinking that I should change positions, but I had no energy left to do so. I went back to sleep, sitting in a puddle of sewage, until morning when I heard a bell ringing. When I woke up I was still exhausted and delirious with hunger. I staggered to my feet and looked outside. I was so weak that my mind wasn't working properly and what I saw made me think I had gone crazy.

The first thing I noticed was a big red sign painted on the wall advertising Coca-Cola. Then I saw a number of women and children. I had expected to find myself in a horrible Bolivian prison, where I was probably going to die. Had it all been a bad dream? I didn't actually know *where* I was or how I'd gotten there, but it certainly didn't look like a jail. I looked around again and wondered if it was some kind of peasant village or city slum. Surrounding me was a deteriorating building complex of small apartments of all shapes and sizes, with their doors painted in various colours. It was three storeys high and made mostly of wood. The sun was shining and what seemed like hundreds of families were beginning to stir.

Wooden balconies creaked as the women emerged from their houses and began their daily chores. Some carried fresh market produce – fruits, vegetables and chunks of meat – in sacks slung over their shoulders. Others were setting up small stalls that sold all types of goods, from soft drinks, cigarettes and chocolate bars, to secondhand cutlery and cassette tapes. A group of women, dressed in poor but colourful rags, were scrubbing and rinsing clothes by a washbasin and then placing them out to dry on the concrete. One young woman, who could not have been more than sixteen, was seated on a bench, breast-feeding her baby.

There were also children of all ages everywhere. The older ones – dressed in their school uniforms, some wearing backpacks – were

56

enjoying the final moments before they had to leave for class. Two small girls jumped gleefully from square to square on a hopscotch grid they had drawn on a cement playing field. Around them, a group of boys was playing a noisy game of soccer. I definitely wasn't in prison. But where was I? I walked out further to investigate.

It was at that moment that I realised my pants were completely saturated and stuck to my legs. There was also a disgusting smell somewhere very close to me. When I squeezed the back of my pants to wring out some of the water, I recognised the horrible stench. My hands were covered in shit.

It all came back to me in a sudden rush – everything that had happened to me since I had gone to the airport two weeks before. It hadn't been a dream. I *was* in prison. I felt faint. Suddenly, my knees folded beneath me and I slid down against the wall to the ground. I coughed violently and saw blood splatter on the cement in front of me before I passed out.

6
RICARDO

When I came to, I knew that if I didn't find help soon I was going to die. I decided to make my way back to the main courtyard. On the way there, I came across some other prisoners. They stopped to stare at me, but none of them did anything. I must have looked a sight, stumbling along and coughing up blood.

In the corner of the courtyard, I saw a door with a red cross painted on it and the word 'MEDICO' written beneath. There were three inmates already waiting outside, so I lined up with them. When it was my turn, a short man with glasses ushered me into a tiny room and pointed to a seat. Apart from a shelf stacked with thick medical textbooks and a stethoscope on the small table, there was nothing to indicate I was in a doctor's surgery. The doctor himself was dressed in jeans and a T-shirt and looked no different from the other inmates. I later learned that he *was* an inmate, having been jailed for stabbing his wife fourteen times.

'Do you speak English?' I asked him. He shook his head.

'No. Sorry. No speak English,' he said, before launching into an explanation of some sort in Spanish.

I couldn't follow much of what he was saying except that he was asking me for a payment of twenty bolivianos. I pretended not to understand. Instead, I patted my chest and coughed so he could see how serious my condition was.

'The *costo* is twenty bolivianos, please, mister,' the doctor then said in English, ignoring my coughing. I told him I couldn't pay and showed him my empty pockets, just as I had done with the major. When he saw that I had no money, he apologised and then stood up and opened the door. 'Sorry, mister,' he said, trying to get me to leave. The next patient started to enter the room.

I took a breath that was so deep it hurt my lungs and sent me into a coughing fit. I spat the blood that came up onto the carpet. As soon as he saw me about to take another breath, the next patient turned to leave again and the doctor grabbed a roll of toilet paper. He tore off a long strip, which he put on the floor where I had spat, and then handed me the roll. He could see that I wasn't going to leave until he helped me.

We stared at one another for a moment longer. Then, without saying anything, he reached for his stethoscope and checked my breathing. I watched the reaction on his face.

'Big *infección*. Need *antibióticos*,' he concluded, writing out a script and motioning for me to follow him to the door. He pointed up the stairs and said, '*Farmacia*', then closed the door behind me in relief.

⊦⊦⊦⎜⎜

The woman in the pharmacy smiled as I entered. When she saw me up close, she noticed how sick I was and made a big fuss over me, like I was her own son. It was the first real kindness anyone had shown me in two weeks and I smiled back, thinking I was finally saved. She took the script and rushed around to find the right medicine on the shelf. She put the box on the counter and, seeing that I couldn't speak Spanish, wrote down the price on a receipt, which she showed to me. When she saw the worried look on my face, she snatched the box back off the counter. Then, when she realised how bad that had looked, she shook her head sadly and started apologising.

'*Lo siento, señor. Lo siento mucho.*'

She did look sorry, too. I was dying and the Bolivians were all very sorry. She slid my prescription back across the counter, still with the same sad expression on her face. I tore it into shreds and threw the pieces back at her before leaving. I hoped she would think of me dying while she was picking them off the floor.

I gave up completely after that. I couldn't speak the language, I had no food, no clothes, no medicine, nowhere to sleep, no money to call anyone, and I knew no one in La Paz anyway. My life was over. Once I had accepted that I was going to die, I didn't even feel that bad. I just felt kind of numb. It was almost a relief to no longer have to fight. I just remember thinking that I didn't want to die in the courtyard. I wanted to die on my own, not with everyone watching.

As I made my way back down the passage to my abandoned building, a small man appeared at my side, trying to attract my attention. One of his teeth was black and he had a patch of hair at the front that had turned completely grey. He started talking to me, but I ignored him, thinking he wanted money. He kept following me.

'*Thomas. ¿Usted es Thomas, sí?*'

I stopped and looked at him, wondering how he knew my name. When he saw my reaction, he became more excited.

'*¿Thomas, sí? El negro de Inglaterra, sí?*'

He took me lightly by the elbow and led me back up to the courtyard and through a door to the side of the main gates.

The door led into a very narrow room that was packed with prisoners. The wall in front had metal bars about chest height and on the other side of the bars was a similar room packed with women, who were speaking to the prisoners. Among the mass of women I spotted a fair-skinned, middle-aged woman waving to me. She was slightly taller than the others and had greyish hair and gentle blue eyes. My guide with the black tooth took me up to her and pointed at me.

The woman gave him a coin and then looked at me and asked, 'Thomas? You're Thomas, right?'

I nodded and she offered me her tiny hand through the bars.

'I'm Sylvia. Sylvia Venables.'

I can hardly describe the wave of joy that passed over me to hear someone speaking English with an English accent. My spirits lifted immediately. Finally, there was someone who could understand me. However, I still didn't know what to say because I was confused about how she knew about me.

When she saw my confusion, she said, 'My husband and I are with the Anglican Church in Bolivia. We're from England originally and we saw you on television. We wanted to know if you were OK.'

Then I remembered. The police had called the television stations when they arrested me, although I had refused to answer any of the journalists' questions. I kept repeating that I was innocent and that I was English and that I needed help. That had been two weeks before, so I didn't think anyone had seen it. I kept staring at her, not knowing how to thank her for coming.

'Thomas. Are you OK?'

'Yes, I'm fine,' I said automatically, although it had never been so untrue in my life.

'Anyway. I brought you some things,' she said, holding a plastic bag up to the bars. This is Tim's old pullover – it might be a bit big for you, but it's warm. And a blanket. Some antibiotics. And there's some food in there, too. We thought you might be hungry.'

'Thank you. Thank you so much. I don't know what to say . . .' I stammered as she handed me the bundle through the bars. A guard came over and wanted to inspect the contents. Sylvia said something to him and he went away.

'Thanks. Thanks so much. You don't know . . . I mean. You saved my life.' My words came out all over the place. There was so much I wanted to say but none of it came out right. 'How did you . . .? I mean . . . thanks for everything.'

Sylvia smiled kindly, but I continued to stare at her stupidly until I made her so embarrassed that she had to look away. She glanced down at my hands. The blood had drained from my fingers and the knuckles had turned white from gripping the bars so tightly. The impatient guard came back and muttered something to her again and she nodded.

'He says I have to leave now. I'll come again in a week. Well. Until next time, I suppose,' she said kindly, and both her hands came forward to touch mine. She wrapped her fingers around my fists and squeezed firmly. My hands were so cold that they had almost frozen, but hers were warm. I felt a warm energy go through me, surging slowly from my icy hands, up through my wrists and arms, then buzzing over my whole body. I remember staring at her hands and thinking how delicate and white they looked against my dark skin. Her fingers were so tiny; how could something that small have given me so much energy?

When I looked up, Sylvia had disappeared. I stayed glued to the spot, staring after her, until the guard on my side of the interview bars indicated that I, too, must leave. There were three or four chocolate bars in the bag and I ate them immediately. Again, the guard told me to leave. As I walked down the steps, still feeling slightly dazed, I looked once more at my hands. I thought that I could see the outline of Sylvia's little hands where they had gripped mine.

I had no other place to go, so I started heading back to my abandoned building. As I passed through the courtyard, I heard a voice behind me call out in English.

'Hey you! Where you from, motherfucker? You speak English?'
I turned around, wondering whether I had imagined it. Seated on the
low brick wall of the garden were three tough-looking prisoners staring
up at me.

'Me?' I pointed to myself, looking from face to face. Two of them
were definitely Bolivian, but although the thin man in the centre had
quite dark skin, his face looked slightly foreign. He had a strange
appearance; his dirty shirt hung loosely over his skinny rib cage and he
had straight, dark hair with silvery streaks, tied in a ponytail that hung
down to his shoulders. From his wrinkles and the grey hairs, I guessed
he was about forty-five or fifty, although his voice sounded younger, so
it was difficult to tell.

'Yeah! You, buddy! Who else? Where do you come from? You speak
English or what?' He had an American accent. All three of them were
staring at me menacingly, waiting for an answer.

'Yes. Hello. I speak English. My name is Thomas,' I extended my
hand to greet the speaker, but he didn't take it.

'You are not from *los Estados Unidos*, are you?' he demanded.
I looked at him blankly, feeling stupid with my outstretched arm left
dangling in the air.

'Sorry?' I took my hand back. I hoped they weren't trying to start
a fight.

'*¿De dónde viene? ¿No entiende nada? ¿Si es gringo?*' threatened the
man next to him.

I didn't understand what he had asked me, but there was no mistak-
ing that his tone was aggressive. It crossed my mind to ignore them
and walk away, but it was too late by then – I had already started
talking – so I figured it was best to be as friendly and polite as possible
in order not to give them any reason to start a fight.

'*Los Estados Unidos*. The United States. You are not a *gringo* from the
United States, are you?' said the skinny foreigner with the grey hair.

'Who me? No! No, I'm from England. From Liverpool.'

'Ahhh, *Inglaterra. Inglés*,' he translated for his companions, who
nodded and exchanged a few comments. The three men relaxed a little
and the speaker smiled kindly, then put his hand out to shake mine.
'That's OK, then. England is OK. We like England.'

I was worried that this was a trick because they knew that I was new
to the prison. At the same time, I couldn't be rude – that might be just

the excuse they were looking for – so I shook hands with him. Nothing happened.

'What is your name?' he asked.

'Thomas,' I told him again.

'Thomas, my name is Ricardo,' he shook my hand a second time and smiled like we were meeting at a party. I was more than a bit confused by this man's strange behaviour.

'Pleased to meet you, Ricardo,' I said respectfully. I didn't know whether I should also shake hands with his friends. They were both still staring at me, although not with the same hostility as before. I decided not to take the chance.

'You see. We hate *gringos* here. My friends thought you were from the States. If you had been American, they might have killed you, you know? We hate the United States. Where are you from in England? London?'

'From Liverpool,' I repeated.

'Oh, that's near to London, is it?' he asked.

'Yeah. Quite close to London.' London is usually the only English city anyone in South America has ever heard of, so I always said I lived nearby in order to avoid explanations that only make things more complicated.

Ricardo then started becoming quite friendly. I stayed alert, but I sensed that any danger had passed and tried to keep the conversation going. Maybe he could tell me where I could get some more food.

'You speak very good English,' I complimented him. 'Where did you learn to speak so well?'

'In New York. I'm from New York.'

'In America? But then you are American? Why don't they kill *you* then?' I blurted out, without thinking. Ricardo's face suddenly became serious and I immediately regretted saying anything.

'No. I am Bolivian. I am not American,' he responded angrily. 'I have a Bolivian passport. I also have an American passport, so sometimes I am American, but nobody knows that, so you don't say anything. OK?'

'OK. Sorry! I'm very sorry,' I apologised, but he was still very agitated and I readied myself in case he was going to hit me.

'That's OK, *inglés*.' Just as quickly, his angry expression was replaced by a friendly smile. '*No hay problema*, my friend. So, how do you like your new home?'

Everything Ricardo said was making me more and more disoriented; one minute he was pretending to be my best friend, the next he was making fun of me and deliberately trying to start a fight. Then he was nice again. I hadn't done anything wrong but I felt extremely uncomfortable.

'So, do you miss London much?' he asked.

'Not too much.'

'Well, you should. You really should miss your own country, don't you think? Or do you want to go back to the United States?'

I said nothing, convinced that he was playing games to test me out. I decided it was definitely time to leave. I was glad to have finally found someone in the prison who spoke English, but I felt I was being led into some kind of trap.

'Ricardo, it was very nice to meet you. Thank you.' I put out my hand to say goodbye.

'Where are you going?' He looked surprised and, once more, refused to take my hand.

'Just back down there,' I pointed towards the filthy passageway. 'I'm sorry. I'm very tired.'

'Do you have a room already?'

'No.'

'Then where do you sleep?'

'Just down there on the ground. In a building.'

'Which building?'

'The one with all the water.'

'You can't go down there. That section is dangerous. They'll kill you. Everyone thinks you are American.'

'Where else can I stay, then?'

Ricardo stared at me while he thought about this for a while.

'How much money do you have?'

'None.'

'Don't lie to me, inglés! I'm trying to help you. Your friends in the interview gave you money. That's where you got that blanket from.'

'I don't have anything. I promise you.'

'You must have some money, otherwise you can't survive. You'll die here.'

'I promise. I have nothing. The police took everything.'

'The FELCN?'

I nodded. 'And they took all my clothes and they gave me no food.' I was hoping that he would take the hint about food, but he didn't.

'Can you get money?'

'I think I can get money. Maybe that woman will come back. Maybe the British Embassy. If I can speak with some friends, they'll send me money, for sure.'

Ricardo looked me over again, then appeared to come to a decision.

'OK, *Inglaterra*. You can sleep on my floor tonight. But you have to pay.'

'Thank you, but I'm sorry. I have no money.'

'You can pay me when you get money. Two dollars per night. You can go now. I am talking with my friends. See you tonight.'

'OK, thank you,' I turned to leave and the three immediately recommenced their conversation. Then I remembered something. 'Ricardo. I'm sorry to interrupt, but how can I find you?'

'In Pinos. You see that gate with the five stars above it? Just next to the Coca-Cola sign? In there. Ask for Ricardo.' He turned back to his conversation and ignored me.

I wanted to get out of their way before Ricardo changed his mind, so I hurried back down the corridor to my abandoned building. There was now a group of four men inside, huddled together under a blanket against the opposite wall, passing a pipe around. They looked up briefly. One of them muttered something and the others laughed. I only caught the word '*gringo*'. I remembered what Ricardo had said about *gringos*. However, after that they ignored me and went back to their pipe. I sat down near the entrance, just in case. I was weak from hunger.

Night began to fall and I could feel the air getting colder. I put on the pullover Sylvia had given me, but even with the blanket it wasn't enough to keep me warm. I wanted to go to Ricardo's cell as soon as possible, but I was worried he might be annoyed if I went too early, so I decided to wait as long as possible. I pulled my knees up to my chest for warmth and waited patiently for several hours, all the time wary of the men propped against the opposite wall. Someone switched on a light outside, so I could still make out their figures. Every now and then one of them would mumble something, but mostly they stayed silent. I started shivering.

Eventually, one of them stumbled to his feet and left the building.

When he returned, they smoked more pipes and started laughing. The smoke smelled really odd, like a strange chemical burning. For five minutes the conversation started up again, then there was some kind of argument. One of the men screamed at his friend, then laughed hideously. The sound bounced off the damp walls into the empty space. Finally, they were silent and I went back to waiting and shivering.

An hour later, I was shaking so much I couldn't stand it any longer. I got weakly to my feet and made my way out through the door.

'*Chao, gringo. ¡Suerte!*' one of the men called from behind me, and all four laughed. Still wrapped in my blanket, I walked carefully back up the corridor. When a group of prisoners passed me, one of them bumped into me on purpose and the others hissed '*gringo*' at me. I hurried on through the courtyard and into the section with five stars above its entrance. I thought I might collapse at any moment. I asked the first inmate I saw if he knew Ricardo. He laughed at me.

'Which Ricardo?' he wanted to know. I shook my head.

'*¡Ricardo! Le busca. ¡Ricardo!*' he yelled up into the night air, then shrugged as if to say that was all he could do. There could have been fifty men called Ricardo in that section. How would I ever find *my* Ricardo?

'Hey, *Inglaterra*! Up here!' a voice came from above. I looked up. It was him! 'What are you doing down there? Get your sorry black arse up here!' He waved his arm to come up. 'What are you waiting for, *Inglaterra*? There's no elevator. This is a prison, for chrissakes. The stairs are right there!'

Ricardo greeted me warmly on the second-floor balcony with a firm handshake. His hair was wet and he smelled of aftershave, as if he had just stepped out of the shower.

'How was your day, Thomas? Are you well?' The way he said this made it sound like we weren't prisoners, but two good friends meeting after work, and I responded in the same way.

'Not bad, thank you.'

'Really? You don't look it,' he poked me playfully in the ribs. 'You look sick, actually. Are you sick?'

'Yes. A little bit. But I'm OK,' I responded automatically for the second time that day.

That morning I had prepared myself to die and now I was so weak that I hardly had the strength even to stay on my feet. I only had antibiotics for my illness, and the only thing I had eaten were three chocolate bars. The one thing that had changed – in fact, the only thing that was keeping me alive – was the hope that Sylvia had given me and now, added to that, the possibility that Ricardo might be able to help me.

'Are you hungry?'

'Starving, man,' I responded with a smile, trying not to sound too desperate. 'Where do we go to eat?'

'Right here in my apartment,' he pointed upwards. 'I was expecting you to come earlier for dinner. I've already eaten, but I left you some and we can heat it up in the microwave.' This confused me a little. I suspected that he was trying to trick me, like before, but I decided to ignore it.

'But isn't there a dining hall where all the prisoners go for meal times?'

Ricardo burst into peels of laughter. 'Dining hall? Thomas, this is San Pedro. You have to cook your own food. Or you can go to a restaurant.'

'Huh?'

'I know it sounds strange. Come up! You'll see what I mean.' With that, he started to climb a wooden ladder that at first seemed to lead only to the ceiling.

I followed him hesitantly up this makeshift staircase. As it turned out, the entrance to his cell was a wooden hatch in the roof, secured by a padlock that he opened with a key that was tied to a leather string around his neck. I thought it was strange that he had the key to his own cell, but I said nothing.

'I must apologise, Thomas. My apartment is a complete mess. Careful of your head!' he called down to me when I was halfway up the ladder. 'I tried to clean it up for you, but it's no use. I'm sorry.'

'That's fine. No problem,' I assured him. Above me, a light came on and I climbed up the remaining rungs into his cell.

The sight that greeted me was truly amazing. It wasn't at all like a proper prison cell should have been. I was expecting something tiny and bare, with concrete floors and a metal door, or at least metal bars, to stop him from escaping. I had imagined the only furniture would be a regulation, metal-framed bed with a thin mattress, white sheets and maybe a grey blanket. At most, there might be a shelf with a few clothes and maybe a book or two, if they were permitted. Apart from that, everything would be completely plain. I also thought there would be several inmates sharing each cell.

I was completely wrong. There were no bars, no concrete floor and no white walls. The cell, although small, was more like a studio apartment and Ricardo obviously lived there on his own, because there was only one bed. The floor was made of wooden boards that creaked wherever you trod, except in the middle, where it was protected by a faded blue carpet. The walls were painted green and covered in posters of naked women. To my right was a single bed that had a thick mattress, colourful sheets and several big, puffy pillows sitting on top. On the far side was an open window that overlooked the courtyard below, and through the left wall a narrow doorway led to a tiny kitchenette.

The biggest shock was how many personal possessions Ricardo had crammed into the cell. There was stuff absolutely everywhere. Beside his bed, a night table was littered with all sorts of items: a lava lamp, an ashtray, a few dog-eared books, a statuette of Jesus crucified on the cross and two half-finished cups of coffee. Empty cigarette packets lay everywhere. Two chairs flanked a wooden table, and from the stack of dirty plates on top, I guessed that this was where he ate. A chest of drawers was piled with books, pens and pencils, as well as toiletry items such toilet paper, skin cream, a toothbrush and toothpaste, a hairbrush and gel. Dirty clothes were strewn all over the floor, including several pairs of shoes. In the corner was a tiny electric heater. On one wall hung a large mirror. Above it, a clock marked the time. Below it was a power point, from which a messy network of electric cables ran; one up to the roof, one into the kitchenette, one to the lamp, another to a portable stereo. And most incredibly, perched on a large cardboard box at the foot of the bed, was a big-screen television.

I scanned everything again in complete confusion. It was nothing fancy, but everything was so comfortable and so normal that once more I had trouble believing that I was actually in a prison. Ricardo must have noticed my bewilderment.

'You look unhappy,' he said. 'I told you it was messy. I'm sorry.'

'It's not that, it's fine! I just never expected . . . Well . . . Is this really your cell? Is this actually where you live?'

'Yes, of course. It's small, I know, but you see, I'm not a rich man. This is the only home I've got. It doesn't please you?' he asked defensively.

'Oh, yes, I like it. It's very nice,' I rushed to reassure him, fearful that he might become angry again. 'Really nice. It's beautiful, in fact.'

'Oh, good,' Ricardo mimicked a lisp and waved his hand forward like he was a gay interior designer. 'I did the whole décor myself, you know. You don't think the colours clash?' He really was strange, this guy.

'But, it's just . . . I don't know. It's amazing. I've never seen anything like this in my life. You live here on your own? And these are all your things?' I pointed around the room, once more fixing my gaze on the television.

'All mine.' He did a pirouette and bowed.

'But it doesn't seem like a prison. Are you actually allowed to have all this? You have your own key and the guards don't say anything. They let you . . . I mean . . . they don't confiscate anything?'

'Huh. The guards!' Once more, Ricardo started laughing hysterically. It seemed to me like a reasonable question, but Ricardo had one of those high-pitched, uncontrollable laughs that made me feel stupid for having spoken.

Eventually, he stopped laughing. 'The guards never come into the prison. I will explain everything, Thomas. Just wait! I was the same on my first day. There is a lot to learn here. But right now, you must be hungry. Here! Let me take your blanket. Please sit down. You look sick. Are you hungry?' he asked again. This time I didn't even try to cover my desperation.

'Starving!' I repeated, sitting down on one of his chairs. 'I haven't eaten for two weeks. Only bread and tea.'

'Ah yes, wait right there. Don't move!' Ricardo hurried into the kitchen and came back with some food. 'I remember the FELCN. That is normal. Did you confess?'

'No.'

'No? Well done, my friend.' He congratulated me, placing a large plate of rice and fried chicken in front of me. 'The FELCN is really tough! I am sorry the food is cold. If you like, I can heat it up. Wait! I will get you a knife and fork,' he offered, heading for the kitchen.

But it was too late. I didn't care about knives and forks, or that the food was cold. I had already set upon the meal and stuffed half of it down my throat.

'Slowly, my friend. There is more. *Tranquilo*. You'll be sick,' he cautioned.

And he was right; suddenly I felt completely full and couldn't eat another mouthful. A minute later, I wanted to vomit.

'*Tranquilo*. Here! Have some water!' he said, handing me a glass. I took a few sips and the sensation passed.

After that first intake of food, I felt better immediately. Just putting something into my mouth, then feeling it reach my stomach, gave me energy. I waited five minutes before resuming the meal, eating more slowly this time. Meanwhile, Ricardo sat down with me and that made me relax even more.

I couldn't believe how kind Ricardo was being; it seemed that he was really worried about me. When I had first stepped into his room, I had been nervous and was very careful of everything I said. I had seen him snap without warning that afternoon in the courtyard and I was worried that if I said the wrong thing again, he might get offended and tell me to leave. However, from the moment he called down to me from the balcony, it was as if he was a different person from the tough inmate I had met only a few hours earlier. He still laughed at me and confused me on purpose, but it wasn't like before. He seemed nicer now and genuine in his concern – he constantly apologised for the state of his 'apartment', as he called it.

'I'm sorry for all this mess,' he kept saying. 'It doesn't worry me . . .'

He also asked me continually if I was feeling OK, if I was warm enough, or if I needed anything – anything at all – and he went out of his way to make me comfortable. While I was waiting for the food to settle, he set up a small bed on the floor using a mattress borrowed from one of his neighbours and gave me the thickest blanket from his own bed. During the course of the evening, I realised that Ricardo's behaviour that afternoon had all been an act. With none of the other prisoners around, he was completely relaxed and treated me like an old buddy. The only things that didn't change were how he laughed at me, the funny way he spoke and how he forgot what I had said all the time.

'You know, sometimes I miss speaking English. I have almost

forgotten how to speak. I am thinking in Spanish and have to translate in my head so it comes out all wrong all the time.'

'But you speak perfectly.' I complimented him. He seemed to like this.

'So I should. I am an American citizen. But sometimes I forget, so I need to practise with you, if that is OK.'

'Of course.'

I was still hungry, but my stomach had shrunk. After a few more small mouthfuls, I couldn't eat any more. Even though I had only eaten a tiny amount, as the food began to enter my system properly, I felt the strength returning to my body and I pushed the plate away.

'You need to eat more,' declared Ricardo, thrusting the half-finished plate back towards me. Moments before, he had been telling me to be careful; now he wanted me to eat until I was sick. 'Eat it! You will feel better.'

'I can't. I'm totally full.'

'Force yourself. You need to get your strength back. I'll leave it on the table. Try to eat some more during the night.'

'Thank you!'

Despite the fact that I was fighting tiredness, I already felt a hundred times better and wanted to show my gratitude, so I started to stack the dishes on the table, readying them for washing up.

'Just leave them. You need to rest. You should go to bed,' insisted Ricardo. 'I can clean those plates tomorrow.'

'It's fine. No problem.'

There was no tap in the kitchenette, but I found a bucket of water, some soap powder and a sponge, and I began to scrape the food scraps off the plates. As I did so, I looked around the small room; it was crowded with all the things a normal kitchen contains: cooking spices, knives, frying pans, a salt shaker, and many different pots. In the corner, there was even a small refrigerator and on top of it, a tiny microwave. He hadn't been lying, after all.

'You have a refrigerator!' I exclaimed. 'This place is amazing!'

'After a while you will forget you are in prison. Well, I mean, you will always know that you are in prison, but as far as prisons go, San Pedro is not bad. Just make sure you never get sent to Chonchocoro. Now, *that* is a prison,' Ricardo replied.

I finished cleaning up and returned to my seat at the table. Ricardo looked at me and smiled.

'Feeling better now?'

It was the happiest I had felt for weeks and I didn't know how to express my gratefulness, but I think he could see it in my eyes. He smiled and held out some freshly ironed pyjamas for me to change into. I suddenly remembered that I still must have smelled of sewage, but Ricardo kindly hadn't mentioned it.

'Hey, man, thanks a lot.' I smiled back at him. It was the first time I'd smiled properly in a long time; with all the misery I'd been through, I'd almost forgotten how.

Yeah, I was feeling better, all right. If you had asked me at the time, I probably would have said I'd never felt better in my life. It is impossible for anyone who has never been starved to understand the joy of having a full stomach and knowing you are no longer going to die. When you get the feeling that your life has just been saved, nothing else matters. Thirteen days in the police interrogation cells had almost killed me. So, for that moment at least, I didn't care that I was in prison or that I was still very sick.

'I'm glad. You should get some rest now,' advised Ricardo, in a fatherly voice, bending down to turn back my blankets for me.

With my body now working overtime to digest the sudden intake of food, a heavy tiredness came over my body. This time I didn't fight it. I was absolutely exhausted, but it was a happy tiredness. I swallowed three of the antibiotic pills that Sylvia had given me with a glass of water and then lay down on the bed Ricardo had made up for me. With his thick blanket, and Sylvia's blanket on top, comforting me, I instantly fell asleep.

When I woke up the following afternoon, I was still tired so I went back to sleep for a few hours more. However, each time I woke up, I still felt tired. In fact, it seemed the more I slept, the more tired I became. I had to spend the next few days in Ricardo's room, regaining my strength.

The first time I needed to go to the toilet, Ricardo showed me where they were. The toilets stank. They were cleaner than I had expected, but they were still horrible. Ricardo said they hadn't been fixed up since the prison had been built over a hundred years before. They were hosed out three or four times a day, but the sewerage system was so ancient that nothing could be done about the smell.

For urinating, there was a heavy, cement trough that was moulded into the wall, but on the wrong angle, so the urine never drained away completely and there were always a few centimetres of it collected at the bottom. A sign on the wall said you were supposed to dump a bucket of water in the trough after urinating but no one ever bothered, so the piss just sat there, bubbling and frothing and stinking the place out.

For defecating, there were five partitioned cubicles in a row, each with its own swinging door. Inside each cubicle, there was no actual toilet; just a hole in the concrete floor that you had to squat over. At first, it was a strange sensation not having a seat, but you very quickly learned where to position your feet and after a while, you got used to it. When you'd done your business, you had to throw a couple of buckets of water down the hole to wash away any spillage and to help push the waste along the open pipe that ran beneath the floor and out of the prison. For the sake of hygiene, the inmates enforced this rule, although the waste never ran freely along the pipe, so there was often a horrible build-up that no one volunteered to clear.

The second time I needed to go to the bathroom I went by myself. There were a few inmates hanging around and they hissed at me and called me 'gringo'. This time, they also spat on my back. I pretended not to notice, but when one of them started pushing me, I hurried back to Ricardo. After that, I was afraid to leave his room. When I had to go the bathroom, I did so very early in the morning before any of the prisoners were awake. I didn't even take a shower until Ricardo suggested that I smelled a bit. Even then, I tried to find an excuse not to go to the bathroom.

'But the water's too cold. I'll get sick again.'

In fact, the water in the showers wasn't just cold; it was icy, particularly in the early mornings when the temperature in La Paz could drop to below freezing. Ricardo couldn't argue with me on that one. The showers were supposed to have hot water, but at that time they weren't working properly so he usually showered after midday, when the temperature of the water in the pipes had risen a few degrees and he could sit in the sun afterwards. Instead, he brought me a bucket with soap and hot water, which is what he used himself when it was too cold for a shower.

73

It took me several days to fully catch up on all the sleep I had lost and get my stomach used to accepting normal amounts of food again.

After that initial period of tiredness, I felt a little better every day, although I still had a severe chest infection.

'You've still got a nasty cough,' Ricardo looked at me with concern. 'You'll have to get some more medicine.'

'I have to wait to get money.'

'I'll cover you. But for this week only. Then you have to find your own place and pay me back. I'm writing it all down.'

Ricardo went to the prison pharmacy and got me some more antibiotics. He also did all of the cooking those first weeks, he lent me some old clothes and, in the end, he refused to accept full payment for all the nights I slept on his floor. I am forever grateful to him for the help he gave me; without him, I would have died.

I wanted to repay him in some way as soon as I could. When I started eating properly again, I passed the seven balls of cocaine I had reswallowed at the FELCN. I washed them off and took them straight to Ricardo.

'Ricardo, I don't know how I can ever thank you enough for what you've done for me. Maybe you can help me to sell these and I can give you some of your money back.'

Ricardo looked at the packages in my hand, one of which I had cut open, and laughed. 'Is that cocaine?'

'What's wrong with it? It's good quality. I guarantee it.' I held up the open ball for him to inspect, but he just waved it away.

'There are a lot of things we miss out on in prison, *inglés*. But cocaine isn't one of them.' I looked at him curiously. 'This is where the coke comes from, my friend,' he explained casually. 'It's made in here. The best in the world.'

'What are you talking about?' I wondered whether this was another of Ricardo's jokes, but he seemed serious.

'The inmates set up laboratories at night and sell to people on the outside. The stuff in here is purer and cheaper than what you can get on the outside. This is the source, Thomas.' When he saw my disbelieving expression, he added, 'I shouldn't be telling you this just yet, so keep your mouth shut, OK?'

'You're joking!' I had guessed that the prisoners would take drugs, which is why I had swallowed the stuff as an insurance plan in case

I got caught, but I never expected that they would actually manufacture drugs inside. 'Don't the guards do anything?'

'They're in on it. How do you think the chemicals get past the gates?'

All this sounded incredible. However, after what I had been through with the Bolivian police in the past weeks, I believed anything was possible.

'But it must be worth *something*?' After all, it was still seventy grams of pure cocaine.

Ricardo shook his head. 'Sorry, *inglés*. You would have been better off smuggling bananas into prison. Or in your case, antibiotics,' he laughed.

'So, it's worth nothing?'

He looked doubtfully at my merchandise again. 'You'll get something for it. But it will be less than what you paid for it, that's for sure.'

卌||

There was a question that had been bugging me for days. Every morning when I went to the bathroom, I saw female prisoners walking around. I finally asked Ricardo after breakfast one day, as he was doing his hair.

'Isn't it dangerous to have male and female prisoners mixed in the same prison?'

'The women aren't prisoners. They just live here,' he answered in his usual casual manner, turning his face sideways to study a small patch on his neck that he had missed shaving. 'Shit. Damn razor.'

'What? What for?'

Ricardo kept checking himself in the mirror. 'To be with their husbands.'

'But why?' I couldn't believe that anyone would actually choose to live in a prison.

'There's no other choice. It's the only way the family can stay together.'

'Why can't they live outside and just come in to visit?'

'This is Bolivia, Thomas. There are no jobs on the outside. The economy is dead.' Ricardo put down the brush, applied some shaving cream to the tip of his finger and gently picked away with the razor at the whiskers he'd missed. 'How can a woman get a job if there aren't even jobs for the men? And if she gets a job, how can she afford to pay rent, look after the kids and support her husband in prison at the same time?'

'But surely there's some way? Can't the government help?'

'Don't be so stupid, *inglés*.' He turned to me in irritation. 'We're not in Europe. There is no social security. If you don't have money in this country, you starve to death. I thought you would have worked that out by now.'

'And the kids live in here, too?' I asked.

Ricardo nodded.

'But . . . don't you think . . .?' I was about to say that I thought it was unfair that children should have to grow up in a prison. The women I could sort of accept; at least they had a choice. But the kids hadn't done anything wrong. Ricardo interrupted me.

'I know what you're going to say, *inglés*. Just trust me. It's sad. But it's better this way.'

'But . . . I mean . . .'

'Just drop it, will you?' Ricardo's voice rose slightly and he snatched up the brush again. I could see he didn't want to talk about it. But I had to know.

'But isn't it dangerous?' I asked softly.

He thought for a minute. 'Sometimes.'

'What about rapists and child molesters?'

'There are no rapists or child molesters in here. They're not allowed.'

'What do you mean, "They're not allowed"?'

Ricardo looked at me sideways in the mirror and opened his mouth as if he was about to say something. Then he changed his mind. 'I'll tell you about that later. Right now, you've got more important things to worry about.'

'But –'

'Just drop it, I told you!' Ricardo snapped, slamming his brush on the bedside table and storming into the kitchen. It was the first time he had raised his voice with me since I had been staying with him and I didn't want to push him any further. I let the subject drop.

﷼|||

At first, Ricardo was like my mentor in prison, but he very quickly became my best friend. I'm sure that part of it was the situation I was in: I had no one else to turn to because all the other prisoners seemed to hate me, so it was only natural that I came to depend on him. But to this day, I have yet to meet anyone who was as kind to me as Ricardo. He became like a father to me. He was very easy-going and had only one house rule: 'No smoking base in my room. If I catch you, you're out. No questions. Straight out.'

Base was apparently what those men had been smoking in the abandoned building on my first day. It was the raw paste which they used to make cocaine powder in the prison laboratories; less refined, but cheaper and far more addictive.

'Don't worry,' I reassured him. 'I don't even take cocaine.'

He laughed. 'Oh you will, my friend. You will.'

Aside from educating me about drugs, Ricardo also took it on himself to educate me about the ways of prison life. Without his help, I don't know how I would have got through those first weeks. San Pedro was no ordinary prison; there was a lot to learn. As I recovered my health, Ricardo taught me something new each day. The first piece of real advice he gave me I remember very well: make sure that all the other prisoners know where you are from.

'You must learn the expression "*No soy americano*," he advised me, 'because it might save your life one day. This means, "I am not an American." You have to be certain that everyone knows you are English. Remember that you are *inglés*. You are from *Inglaterra*. Now repeat!'

I noticed that Ricardo always made a point of calling me '*Inglaterra*' or '*inglés*' whenever there were other people around. Apparently, it was for my own good as well as his; if people thought I was American, being friends with me might cause him problems. This was the second time Ricardo had mentioned the Americans. Although I had already been picked on for being a foreigner, I still didn't understand why the Bolivian prisoners hated Americans so much. However, it wouldn't be long before I found out how dangerous being thought a *gringo* could be.

卄卄\\

Unfortunately, my body hadn't yet fully adjusted to normal amounts of food and I got diarrhoea. The need to rush to the toilet struck without warning, at any time of the day or night. I didn't like going to the bathroom at the best of times; it was small and cramped and dirty, and there was only one door. Once you were inside, you had to go back out the same way, which meant you could be trapped. At least during the day, the door was kept open and there were people around in the court-yard. In the evenings, the bathroom was locked and you needed a key to open it from both sides. I wasn't happy about going down to the toilet after dark, and worse still, by myself, but there was no choice with diarrhoea; I couldn't do it in my pants and I couldn't ask Ricardo to hold my hand and wait outside the cubicle every time I needed to go.

Luckily, when I went to the bathroom for the first time at night it was around eight o'clock and there was no one else in there. I breathed a sigh of relief. Crouching down to the floor, I checked under the partitions for feet, just to be sure, then I shat the liquid out as quietly as possible, listening intently for the sound of anyone entering. The only noise was a shower that had been left dripping. However, when I came out of the cubicle, there were two men in the narrow passage that led to the door, blocking my way. One was bent forward at the basin, slowly washing his hands; the other was standing directly behind him, leaning against the wall, as though he was waiting to use the basin next, even though there was another one next to it. I hadn't heard them come in.

Not wanting them to hear my foreign accent, I nodded coolly to the man leaning against the wall. He didn't respond. I waited a while longer for the other man to finish washing his hands. But when he eventually did stop, he left the tap running and stood there with his hands on the rim of the basin, watching the water going down the plug hole. Neither of them showed any sign of moving.

'Perdón,' I said, but they didn't look at me. The one at the basin began rinsing his hands again and, from the corner of my eye, I saw him looking at his friend in the mirror.

I had to get to that door. There was no way around them and no other way out of the bathroom. If I hesitated any longer, they would know that I was afraid.

'Perdón,' I said more forcefully, moving forward to squeeze between them, but they stood firm and wouldn't let me pass. I took a step back and waited a few more moments, all the while readying myself in case they attacked.

Finally, the one at the basin stood up and faced me. He had mean eyes and a fresh cut across his forehead. He said something threatening to me in Spanish. I only understood the word '*gringo*', but it was obvious they wanted money.

'I don't have any,' I said, patting my clothes. Luckily, I was wearing some old, loose-fitting pyjamas with no pockets that Ricardo had loaned me, so they could see I wasn't lying. The two looked at each other and there was a brief exchange. I could tell by their facial expressions that they had decided to let me go. The one against the wall nodded to me and jerked his head towards the door, saying something about giving them money later.

'*Gracias. Perdón*,' I managed to mumble as I slipped through the small gap they had created for me, trying not to brush against them. I fumbled to insert the key in the lock. It wouldn't go in and I started panicking. It must have been Ricardo's room key, so I shakily tried the other one, but that was the wrong one, too. Eventually, I got the first key to work. '*Gracias*,' I said again as I hurried out of the bathroom. They stared after me without saying a word. Next time I would have to pay the toll.

7
RESEARCHING THE HOUSING MARKET

I stayed inside even more after that incident and was afraid to go to the bathroom at all. The part of the prison that Ricardo lived in was Pinos, the five-star section. It was one of the safest parts of the prison. However, inmates from other sections had the right to go wherever they wanted during the day, so it was difficult to stop the gangs from entering. After nine o'clock each night, the section locked its gate and Ricardo told me that that would be the safest time for me to go. I still didn't like going down when it was dark.

Fortunately, my diarrhoea was cured very quickly. Ricardo brewed me up a special concoction to settle my stomach called *maté de coca*, which was a tea made from coca leaves. The Bolivians had been using it for centuries as a remedy for every type of illness under the sun and it seemed to work. He also said that I could stay on his floor for a week more, free of charge, until I felt safer. But after that, I had to get my own room. I didn't have any idea how I was supposed to get a prison room, but Ricardo promised to help me. He began by explaining the cell arrangements in great detail. After hearing about the women and children in the prison and the cocaine laboratories, I didn't think there could be many more shocks. But there were.

Although they had tried to rip me off on the price, the police hadn't been lying to me on my first night about having to buy my own prison cell. San Pedro was comprised of eight sections – Posta, Pinos (where Ricardo lived) and Alamos, and the rundown inside sections San Martín, Prefectura, Palmar, Guanay and Cancha. After you paid the entrance fee – *el Ingreso* – to the police for the privilege of being allowed into the prison, you then paid another fee to become a member of one of these sections. And all that was before you spent more money buying your own cell and then having the cell title transferred into your name.

'And you can't just go out and buy *anything*,' Ricardo warned me. 'You have to know what you're doing. Otherwise, you're going to get completely taken for a ride.'

The system was very complicated and there was a great deal of information to take in. It took a long time for Ricardo to explain everything to me, since I kept interrupting him to express my disbelief or to ask questions. Once Ricardo started talking, it was hard to stop him, especially when it had anything to do with his favourite topics: economics and politics. The way things worked in San Pedro was astounding. Everything was about money. And I mean *everything*.

There were inmates who acted as freelance real estate agents, scouting around for potential buyers on a commission basis. There were restaurant owners who advertised lists of the various properties that were for sale, charging a small fee to the sellers. The section delegates allowed advertisements – known as '*propaganda*' – to be placed on the section noticeboards, because room sales generated income for the section. Even the police were involved, since they were in the best position to get hold of new arrivals who didn't know how things worked. Luckily, I hadn't had any money with which to buy a cell on the first night; the police usually added fifty per cent to the price as their commission.

The first step was paying the twenty-five bolivianos to the police, for which you received a receipt. Then you paid the section entrance fee. This was non-refundable and the amount varied according to which section you joined. When I found my own place, I paid one hundred and fifty bolivianos, approximately thirty US dollars. In the dangerous sections it was much cheaper. This money was placed in a fund that was used to cover section expenses such as maintenance, administration, cleaning, renovations and the occasional social event such as the Prisoners' Day party every September, when the section delegates cooked a barbecue and hired a band for the inmates.

Admission to a section was rarely refused, provided there was a vacancy and provided you had enough money to pay the entrance fee and buy a room. However, in the better sections of the prison the process was a little more selective; you often had to be invited by one of the existing members. They mainly wanted to know that you were a person of good fame and character so that they could maintain the high safety and quality of the section. This might sound strange for a prison, but there were a lot of politicians and businessmen in San Pedro and many of them were well educated. Occasionally, the section delegate even asked for personal references, although this obviously made it hard for new inmates, especially foreigners, who didn't know anyone. Luckily, Ricardo was prepared to recommend me.

Once you had decided on a section, the next step was to buy a cell. Ricardo explained that the market for prison cells operated just like any normal property market: prices went up and down according to supply and demand, and you had to pay commissions to agents and legal fees for the actual transaction. I could hardly believe it.

Each room had a legal owner who held the title to the property. The actual title was a document that contained details of the room: its number, location, a brief description, the name of previous owner and the price paid for it. The original copy of the title was held by the owner. A section property register was also kept, but it was best to hide the original well. Without it, you could have troubles proving owner-ship. It was also a good idea to keep a photocopy in the office or with someone else, just in case. The police officers had their big blue book, but that was only for sales.

The rooms that came on to the market were announced by a sign saying '*En Venta*' – 'For Sale' – on, or above, the door. The best policy, according to Ricardo, was always to negotiate directly with the owner and ignore all the other people who wanted a slice of the action. The actual sale was conducted by the buyer and seller agreeing on a price and then signing a sale–purchase contract in front of the section delegate, who signed and stamped it with the section stamp in order to make everything official. Another trusted inmate was also needed to sign as a witness. Then, after the sale price had been paid and the contract signed, the buyer had to pay the title transfer fee, which was received by the section treasurer, who also stamped and signed the title deed. This transfer fee was officially set at twenty per cent of the sale price and was another way of earning money for the section's administration fund. Finally, once that was done, the transfer was noted on the actual title and the title document was physically handed over to the new owner.

The owner then had the right to live in the room until he sold it, which usually occurred when he was leaving the prison. In the meantime, he could mortgage it if he needed to borrow money, in which case the lender would ask to hold the original title as security until the debt was fully paid. And just like in the outside world, there was no limit to how many properties you could own. So, if you had spare cash, you could buy another room and rent it out or start up a restaurant or a shop, or just keep it as an investment if you thought its value might go up.

'A shop! What do you mean a shop?' I interrupted.

'Where do you think I buy all our food from *inglés*?' he said, shaking his head at me like I was stupid.

'So, you have to pay for everything?'

'*Everything*,' Ricardo confirmed.

The authorities did provide some food. But it was usually a watery soup, served out of a large bucket twice a day. It didn't contain enough calories to last the day. Describing all this now makes it sound like a game of Monopoly. And for people who had money, it almost was – for those in the four- and five-star sections, it was like sitting on Park Lane and Mayfair. But in reality it wasn't a game; this was real money, and real people's lives were at stake.

A lot of unfairness resulted from this system, the saddest being those inmates who couldn't afford a place to stay. Some of the rooms went for only a few hundred dollars. By Bolivian standards, this was a lot, especially for those who had become involved in crime because they were poor in the first place. Even with the help of their family, some inmates couldn't get enough money together to pay rent, especially when the prison was full and prices were high. Those inmates often had to sleep outside in the cold or in a passageway or some corner, just as I had done on my first night. You could die if you slept outside.

Most people, though, managed to get by, even if they didn't have money. The poor people in Bolivia are very caring and hospitable, and since the authorities hardly helped the inmates at all, they had to look after each other as best they could. The prisoners tried not to let anyone freeze to death. In Alamos, there was even a room that was owned by the section for people in difficult situations. The room was rented out very cheaply, or sometimes without any charge, in return for working for the section – scrubbing the bathrooms, cleaning the courtyard, taking out the rubbish and running errands.

Nothing ever came for free in San Pedro, but if you were a decent person, you could usually persuade someone to help you by offering to work for them or promising to pay later. This was particularly the case when you were new, because people might think they could do you a favour and get some money out of you later.

There were inmates who did die out there, though, of starvation or exposure. Usually, they were the base addicts, who had lost all hope. They didn't have anything at all and, according to Ricardo, whenever they got their hands on something, even a few coins, they preferred to buy drugs than to sleep in a warm bed or pay back a debt.

'That's why I don't let anyone who smokes base in my room,' he said. 'It's sad. But no matter how sorry you feel for them, they'll steal everything you own.'

'But they're still people, aren't they?' I felt quietly disgusted that people could die of hunger in jail, even drug addicts, and no one would do a thing.

卌\\

A week had gone by since I arrived at San Pedro and I still had no money to buy a room. Since my insurance plan of selling the cocaine had failed, I tried to repay Ricardo in other ways: I cleaned and tidied his room every day; I did the cooking and washing up; and eventually, when I felt strong enough, I offered to go to the shop he had told me about to buy supplies for him. Having heard Ricardo talk about the dangerous inside sections where they smoked base, Pinos didn't seem so dangerous, especially during the day.

'Are you sure you're ready?' he asked sceptically.

'Why not? I'm almost better now. And it will be a good way for me to learn how to speak Spanish. You can teach me the words and I'll go down each time.'

Ricardo hesitated. 'I suppose you have to start learning about the prison one day,' he said, pulling some coins out of his pocket and handing them to me.

After explaining where the shop was, he opened the hatch for me and I climbed down the wooden ladder, repeating to myself the words he had taught me – *mantequilla, pan, espaguetis* and *tomate*.

'I'll leave the door open,' said Ricardo. 'Call out if you have any trouble.'

'I'll be fine. It's easy. Listen! *Buenas tardes. Mantequilla, pan, es-paguetis y un tomate . . . por favor.*'

Ricardo nodded. I'd even got the pronunciation right, but he still looked worried.

I never made it to the shop. I only got as far as the courtyard. Someone hissed '*¡Gringo!*', and a heavy blow to the back of my head knocked me forward. Then another hard blow landed on my neck and a whole group of prisoners attacked me. They must have been hiding, as I hadn't seen anyone. I can't even say how many there were, because it all happened so quickly and I was dizzy from that first hit. As I turned to defend myself, a fist struck my face from the side and someone kneed me in the groin, which dropped me to the ground. After that, all I could do was cover my head for protection as they kicked me from all sides.

For the first minute I yelled, '*¡No soy americano!*' each time they struck me. When one of them booted me in the head, I pretended to go limp and stopped making any noise. They thought I was unconscious and after a few more kicks, they went through my pockets and then fled. I stayed curled up like that for a while longer in case any of them had remained behind, then I made my way slowly back up to Ricardo's room.

Ricardo didn't look surprised when he saw the blood on my face and he didn't need to ask what had happened.

'Sit down there. I'll get some ice,' was his only comment.

I looked at him strangely. It was as if he had known beforehand but hadn't warned me or come down to help. I continued to stare at him and he must have sensed what I was thinking because he wouldn't look me in the eye. He suddenly threw his hands in the air and went down to the shops to get the dinner supplies himself, without even bothering to ask whether I still had the money he had given me.

When Ricardo returned, I was lying on my mattress. He still wouldn't look at me. He cooked the meal that night and we ate it in complete silence, apart from the sound of our spoons scraping against the bottom of the bowls. I watched him shovelling the final spoonful of pasta into his mouth, then he suddenly stood up.

'I'm an old man, Thomas,' he muttered, stacking the dishes loudly. 'I can't protect you in here.'

I looked at him. He was right. He was skinny and his hair was greying, and he was old enough to be my father. I was on my own for this one.

The day after the attack, Sylvia came back to visit me, just as she had promised. When she saw me come into the interview room, her hand immediately went up to cover her mouth.

'Thomas! What happened to your face?'

'I fell over when I was running down the stairs,' I answered. I didn't want her to worry, but I could tell she didn't believe me.

'That looks terrible. Here. Show me.' I moved closer to the bars and she ran her fingers over the skin next to the cuts. 'Look what they've done to you. You should report this to someone. Does the embassy know?'

I knew Sylvia meant the best for me, but there was no way someone like her could understand how things worked in a prison. If I said anything, the Bolivian authorities would only laugh. And although the British Embassy could complain, it had no power inside the prison, where it counted.

'No. It's OK. I'm fine. Really, I'm OK.'

'Are you sure?' It felt so good to be mothered again. I wished I could have been on the other side of the interview bars so that I could tell her everything that had happened to me. I wanted to tell her about the attack and what the police were like, and I wanted her to get me out of there and take me home, but I couldn't. I had to be strong.

'Well, at least be careful that those cuts don't get infected,' she said. 'It's not very hygienic in this country. I'll bring you some antiseptic cream this afternoon. Look. I brought you some more of Tim's clothes . . . are you looking after yourself in there? Do you need anything else?'

There were many things I wanted to ask her for, but I felt ashamed. Sylvia was already doing a lot just by visiting me, and if I became a burden to her, she might stop coming to see me. Besides, provided Ricardo let me stay in his room a while longer, I could probably make it through.

'I'm OK.'

'Well. Here's my phone number again. You ring me if you need help. Any time of the day or night. OK? Don't be embarrassed.'

卌〢

Ricardo pretended not to mind me staying on his floor, even after three weeks had passed. However, a few days later, he reminded me that I should try to get some money as soon as possible to pay him back what I owed him and then buy my own cell. I still had no cash at all, but I knew he was right; I couldn't stay on his floor forever. I could sense that he wanted his privacy back, or maybe he was worried about being associated with me, since I was a target. I placed some reverse-charge phone calls back to England and did my best to try and get some money in order to get out of his way. I was owed a few favours back home, but it would probably take a while to get the cash together.

A few days later, Mr Harris from the British Embassy, who had visited me in the FELCN cells, came to the prison. When I saw him, getting my own room was the main thing on my mind. I hoped that he already knew about the property system, because I didn't know how I could possibly explain it otherwise. I was called by two of the guards and escorted to a special room in the administration office that was far cleaner than the public interview room. Mr Harris had brought me a small package of supplies: some antibiotics, a toothbrush and tooth-paste, soap and some fresh fruit.

The interview was quite short, but in that time he asked me many questions. Again, he didn't comment on the crime I'd been charged with or ask whether I was innocent or guilty, and he changed the subject when I asked whether the embassy could help get me out. Unfortunately, I could tell from the questions he asked that he didn't have a clue about the corruption in the prison. He told me that the embassy's role was to ensure that I was treated fairly under the Bolivian justice system. He talked about getting lawyers for my case and asked me once more whether I had been tortured or mistreated. I said I hadn't. My cuts had almost healed by then, so he wasn't suspicious.

Finally, he asked me whether I needed anything more. I had a mental list of the things I needed – but there was one thing I needed more than anything.

'Money. I need money.'

'I'm afraid there is no provision for that in our funding, Mr McFadden. We can contact any family members or friends in England and help facilitate the transfer of any moneys they may wish to send.'

'But that could take weeks. I really need money *now*.'

'Our function at the embassy is to do all we can to protect your rights, but unfortunately there is no money we can give you,' he dutifully informed me.

I explained to Mr Harris that I needed money urgently in order to purchase a cell and to buy blankets, food and clothes because the FELCN had kept mine and only given me a receipt. I didn't explain about *el Ingreso* and the section entrance and transfer fees, because I thought that might complicate things too much.

'I beg your pardon, Mr McFadden. I do not think I quite understand you,' he said.

I explained again, this time giving him details about my first night and how I had been asked to pay a prison entry fee, and then five thousand dollars for a cell. I also explained, as best I could, that I had to pay a section entrance fee and a transfer fee for the title to a cell. At first, Mr Harris's eyes seemed to get wider and wider, but then he folded his arms, leaned back in his chair and looked at me over the top of his glasses.

'But that is preposterous, Mr McFadden! You do not mean to tell me that prisoners must pay to be incarcerated by the state and, furthermore, that they are obliged to purchase their own housing within the penitentiary facility?'

I went over the system a third time with him, explaining about the book that lists all the available properties and their registered owners. I knew it would be hard to believe so I thought that the more detail I gave, the more convincing I would be. Unfortunately, the exact opposite occurred: the further I got into the description, the more ridiculous it sounded, especially when I started talking about getting witnesses' signatures for transfers of cell titles and about how the restaurant owners could earn real estate commissions.

'I will look into this and see what I can do,' said Mr Harris in his business-like fashion. However, I could tell by his expression that he did not believe me. He wanted to call me a liar, but he didn't. Instead, he looked at his watch.

'I will come again next week when I know more about your case. We have also contacted a charity organisation in England called Prisoners Abroad. They should contact you in the near future. Legally, I cannot make representations on their behalf, but it is possible that they may be able to assist you financially. My sincerest apologies, Mr McFadden. I must leave you now.' He stood and turned to leave.

'Don't go! Please.' I grabbed his sleeve. There was no chance of convincing him that I was telling the truth, but I was desperate. It was my final chance.

'Look. I'm getting some money, I promise. Can you lend me something?' I begged him. 'I'll pay you back. I'm not lying. I promise.'

Mr Harris paused and I thought he was going to call me a liar to my face. Instead he reached into his jacket and pulled out his wallet.

'This is all I have on me,' he said, handing me some notes. It was sixty bolivianos and it came from his own pocket.

'Thank you so much. I will pay you back,' I said, slipping the cash into my sock because one of the guards had seen him give me the money. 'Thank you. You are very kind. Thank you.'

'That's fine, Mr McFadden. It is my pleasure. The embassy will be in contact. In the meantime, you have my card. Please take care of yourself.'

卌||

On my way back from the interview room, I was attacked again. Once more, it was an ambush. However, it was more serious this time.

As I rounded the corner into Pinos, I checked for anyone suspicious before climbing the stairway. When I got three-quarters of the way up, four prisoners appeared at the top. It was the same group of prisoners that had attacked me before. I spun around immediately and ran back the way I had come, leaping down three steps at a time, but another group appeared at the base of the stairwell. I was trapped between them.

There were only three men at the bottom of the steps and I was coming from above them. With the momentum I already had, I decided to keep running and try to get past them. I charged down the stairs at full speed, intending to push them out of the way until I saw something metallic. I stopped suddenly. One of the men had a knife.

I was travelling so fast that I almost fell over in my efforts to avoid the blade. I lost my footing and slipped. Slowly, they advanced on me. I scrambled to my feet. There were seven of them now and I didn't know which way to turn. One of them smiled and said, '*Gringo.*'

'Ricardo! Ricardo!' I yelled. But Ricardo was miles off and wouldn't have heard me. Even if he had, what could he have done against seven men? I was completely on my own. I had to make a decision. Up or down? There was no way I could fight them all at once.

I decided to go upwards. However, it was impossible. I was fighting uphill in a narrow stairwell against four men. As soon as I got close enough, one of them kicked me hard in the mouth. I felt my tooth go loose and the taste of blood in my mouth. They came down another step. I turned to the three below me but there was that knife again. The man held it in front of him as he advanced one more step. I turned back to the group above me and charged at them again, this time covering my face.

I didn't get very far. I managed to ram the first man out of the way but the others leapt on me immediately and pushed me to the ground. Ignoring their blows, I did all I could, using my hands as well as my feet to scramble up the steps. However, it was no use. Within a few seconds, they had me pinned. The man who had kicked me grabbed me by the throat. Two of them struck me repeatedly in the face. The one with the knife was still coming up the stairs. I struggled but I could feel myself passing out. Then a strange thing happened.

Someone hissed, '*Niña*' and suddenly the two men hitting me stopped.

'*¡Niña!*' hissed another man, louder than the first. The others loosened their grips and I struggled free. I got to my feet and turned to the group below me. The man with the knife held it in front of my face, blocking my way, but the others hissed at him angrily, '*Niña.*' Grudgingly, he put the knife behind his back. His companions dropped their hands to their sides and I was able to slip past them, down the stairs. They didn't even attempt to prevent me and fortunately, they hadn't managed to find the sixty bolivianos that Mr Harris had given me. I didn't know what had happened, but I couldn't believe my luck.

When I got to the base of the stairwell, I looked back up. The seven men were standing to one side and a small child, about five or six years old, was trotting down the stairs on her own, completely unaware of what had been occurring moments before.

Niña. Little girl.

卌\\

I didn't want to tell Ricardo about what had happened this time in case he thought I was asking him to solve my problems for me or that having me stay in his room might be too dangerous. When he asked about the interview with the embassy, I handed him thirty bolivianos to help pay for the food I'd eaten, and told him I would definitely receive more money soon to pay him for the accommodation. I used twenty-five to pay *el Ingreso* and kept the remaining five for myself. Ricardo agreed to let me stay with him a little longer, but I could tell that he wanted me out of his living space as soon as possible because he started encouraging me to look around for a room.

However, he also warned me it could take some time to find the right one. 'You can't go out and buy a room just like that. You've got to do your homework first. Research the market, my friend. Buyer beware.'

The next day, he gave me a rundown on all the sections and afterwards insisted on taking me around the prison so that I could see them for myself. I didn't want to go. I already knew where I wanted to stay: as close to Ricardo as possible. And although I couldn't tell him the reason, I was very scared of going out into the main prison, especially down to the inside sections where the gang was from.

'You should come, Thomas,' Ricardo said. 'You need to meet the people. Don't worry. Guillermo and Pedro will be with us. It's daytime. You'll be safe. Just remember you are *inglés*.'

'*No soy americano*.' I parroted the expression he had taught me. He laughed.

'That's the spirit. We'll have to work on your pronunciation, though.'

'*Soy de Inglaterra*,' I put on my jacket and a brave face, ready to go out.

'Exactly! Come on! It'll be fun.'

When I thought of those four men I had seen on my first day smoking pipes in the abandoned building, laughing and screaming at me crazily, and the gang that had attacked me, 'fun' wasn't the word that came to mind.

91

卌||

Each of the eight sections in San Pedro had a star rating, like hotels do. The best and most expensive section in the whole prison was the five-and-a-half-star section of Posta. This was where all the politicians and wealthier drug dealers stayed. Ricardo didn't take me there that day because it had a separate entrance gate and you had to get permission to leave the main prison, go outside into the street and around the corner to get in. He said I couldn't afford it, anyway.

'Beyond your budget, I'm afraid.'

The cells in Posta weren't cells at all – they were more like small hotel rooms. They had carpet, furniture, television, hi-fi equipment, proper glass windows and private bathrooms. And because the inmates there had money, they could afford to decorate and make improvements to their rooms, which increased their value even more. Ricardo had heard of one room there changing hands for fifteen thousand dollars.

'The politicians in there live better than most people in the country on the outside,' he told me. I thought he was exaggerating until months later when I saw the place myself.

The Posta inmates weren't only physically separated from the main prison population, they had a completely separate lifestyle. Most of them used their cellular phones openly and brought alcohol through the gates without any questions being asked. Many of them could pay to leave the prison during the day under police escort, and others were released before completing their sentences. Everything was run by money, and everyone involved kept very quiet. The guards in charge of Posta certainly wouldn't have said anything – they were receiving good monthly bribes in return for allowing the inmates to do virtually anything they liked. And since the section had a separate entrance and was located right next to the administration block, it was easier for the inmates to continue receiving their privileges without anyone complaining, or even knowing what went on in there.

The other sections in the main prison weren't quite as luxurious as Posta. Standing at the main gate looking across the courtyard, you could see the three passages that I had seen on my first night. On the wall to the right, just below the Coca-Cola sign, was the doorway to Pinos. On the far side, to the right of the church, was the entrance to Alamos; and to the left of the church was the dirty passageway that led to the inside sections.

The best section in the main prison was the five-star section Los Pinos – 'The Pines' – where Ricardo lived. It had a spacious courtyard and the rooms were on two levels, with a set of stairs leading up to the second-storey wooden balcony. There were also a few rooms, like Ricardo's, which sat on top of the second storey and were accessed by ladders or stairs. Parts of the construction were getting old and falling apart, but because there was money available in the administration fund, they painted over the cracks and made everything look nice.

Although the rooms weren't in the same league as those in Posta, they were still quite comfortable. Everyone had their own television and cooking facilities, although only a few rooms had private toilets. The majority of the members shared the common bathroom, which was kept clean throughout the day, although it smelled horrible.

For me, the most attractive part of the section was the garden in the centre of the courtyard. The big old pine tree gave the place a naturally peaceful atmosphere. Around the edge of the courtyard were various stands and restaurants that opened at lunchtime. Eating a nice meal outside on a clear, sunny day, you could be forgiven for forgetting you were actually in prison. Everything was *tranquilo*, as the Bolivians would say.

Alamos, with a four-star rating, was the next-best section. It had three storeys and was also quite safe, with a quiet, family atmosphere similar to that of the neighbouring Pinos. It wasn't quite as nice as Pinos – it didn't have a garden, only a concrete courtyard, and was badly in need of a paint job – but it was close. Nothing much happened in there either, everything was *tranquilo* most of the time, except when the children came back from school and started running around playing games. The section owned benches and chairs that were put out during the day, and you could usually find inmates playing chess and games of cards or just leaning against the wall, smoking cigarettes. The common areas, such as the bathrooms and dishwashing area, were hosed down and scrubbed each morning and sometimes also in the evening.

Generally speaking, the inmates in Alamos and Pinos weren't rich, but they had enough money to get by. Most could afford a reasonable lifestyle, and although everyone complained a lot, no one was dying of hunger. Many of the inmates were private people who spent a lot of time indoors. They were simply waiting for their lawyers to hurry up and get them out; in the meantime they wanted to stay out of trouble and make their stay as easy as possible. These were mainly prisoners from the Bolivian middle class; many of them had been educated and, on the whole, they were a lot more civilised than in the other sections. There was less violence and no one smoked base. Not openly, anyway. The members could kick you out for that. They did sniff cocaine, of course, although everyone was secretive about it, especially in Pinos, where no one talked about it, except with very close friends. The section had to maintain its respectability.

Both these sections were safe at night because they locked the gates after 9 pm, preventing inmates from other sections from entering. During the day, the inmates were extremely friendly. You had to say something by way of greeting whenever you passed someone, no matter how many times you had already seen them that day. At first I found this pointless and annoying, but I soon saw that it made a difference to the way people treated each other. There was more respect between the inmates in these sections, and a sense of community – of living and sharing together.

卌ll

The inside sections were where I had slept on my first night. Eventually, I was brave enough to go back there on my own, but at first I was too scared, plagued by memories of that horrible abandoned building and the haunting laughter of those four men. I didn't want to go down there at all, even though Guillermo and Pedro, Ricardo's tough-looking friends who had been with him in the courtyard on my first day, would be accompanying us. However, Ricardo made me go. I was lucky to have my companions, because everyone stared and hissed and several of them yelled out '¡Gringo!'. Guillermo was from those sections, so he was very relaxed, but I felt as if I was about to be attacked at any moment.

The difference in quality between the inside sections and Posta, Pinos and Alamos was incredible. You noticed the lack of money as soon as you entered the passageway that led down from the courtyard; it was dark and narrow and the white paint was discoloured and peeling. Further inside, everything was dirty and grimy. In fact, the whole place was falling apart and looked like no one there cared how they lived.

The cheapest of the five inside sections – Guanay, San Martín, Cancha, Prefectura and Palmar – had no star rating. Although each was officially separate, they were joined by a maze of tunnels, stairwells and damp passageways, making it difficult to tell where one section ended and the next began. It was easy to get lost because all the corridors were dark, with smashed bulbs that were never replaced.

We came out of one of these narrow passageways into the bright sunlight of a wide, open area where the air was fresh and people were sitting around relaxing. It looked like some kind of exercise yard and although I didn't feel completely safe, it was more bearable than being stuck in one of those corridors, especially with all the people around. Ricardo explained that this was the section called Cancha, which means 'playing field' in Spanish.

'This is where we have the annual football tournament. Can you play? Our section is going to win this year,' he declared proudly. 'But we really need players.'

'Yeah, a little bit,' I replied unenthusiastically. The idea of playing a game of soccer on concrete didn't much appeal to me.

Since the football field wasn't being used at the time, children were jumping along a hopscotch grid they had chalked up and were happily chasing each other everywhere. Around the perimeter, you could see inmates working on repairing and constructing furniture or making handicrafts to sell to visitors. Some prisoners lay on the ground in the sun; others simply stood watching. There were also women washing garments at the concrete basins, and others sitting around mending clothes and keeping an eye on the children. These were almost the same scenes that had greeted me on my first morning when I had woken up and didn't know where I was. Once more, I was reminded of a small village. I had only been in San Pedro three-and-a-half weeks, but so much had changed for me in that time.

In the next section, Ricardo pointed out a big, round hole in the ground with concrete steps leading down into it.

'They call that *la piscina*,' he said.

'What does that mean?'

'It means "the swimming pool".'

It was about two metres deep, but for a swimming pool, it was extremely small. I also wondered if La Paz ever got warm enough to go swimming.

'But when do they use it?' I asked.

'Um. Occasionally they fill it up, but the water gets dirty very quickly, so most of the year it stays empty.'

'But what do they use it for? It's too narrow for swimming.'

'Mainly they use it for baptisms and celebrations. You know, when a new inmate gets given his sentence or when someone has a birthday, they get thrown in the water,' he explained hurriedly before changing the subject quickly. 'Do you wanna see where they make the leather jackets?'

There was something Ricardo wasn't telling me about *la piscina*. I later learned that it had a more sinister name – '*el pozo*', which means 'the well'.

We went up some stairs and into another dark passageway. This was the section of San Martín and it was more like what I had imagined a third-world prison would be like. In some parts, there were long rows of tiny, identical concrete cells, with the same grey metal doors. Often, they had no windows and so, in some parts, there was a horrible smell that must have been there forever. These were the dirtiest areas of the prison, where the poorer prisoners and the base smokers lived, sometimes four or five crammed into a minuscule room.

'Life is cheap here,' explained Ricardo. 'People do whatever they can to survive.'

He pointed out that, unlike Pinos and Alamos, there were no gates between the various inside sections, so at night the inmates were free to wander from one section to another, making it more like a big neighbourhood in a city slum.

'And this is where all the stabbings occur,' he warned me as we came into one of the darker passages. When he saw my worried look, he re-assured me. 'It's perfectly safe during the day. At night is when you have to look out.'

This didn't make me feel any better. Although it was the middle of the day, the part we were in was so dimly lit that it could just as easily have been midnight.

We came to a corner and went down some stairs and outside again. This was where Ricardo came to buy his marijuana once a week. He didn't want to talk about it at that moment – even in English – in case someone overheard us, but he quickly mentioned that this was also where the cocaine laboratories were located. We were right near the source. 'Even the dealers in the other sections get their stuff from down here,' he whispered.

'Where?' I wanted to know. But he wouldn't answer.

I looked around, thinking that I might be able to guess behind which door they were making the cocaine. I was trying to picture small Bolivian scientists running around in white lab coats with thermometers stuck behind their ears, surrounded by bubbling beakers and smoking test tubes. However, it was the middle of the day, so it was hard to imagine that any of it was possible, especially with all the women and children nearby.

'The food in that place is quite good,' Ricardo said, changing the subject once more. He pointed to a restaurant we were passing. 'The pork is the best plate they make. The cook is from Cochabamba. Cheap, too. Five bolivianos, with corn and boiled potatoes.'

We stopped to look at the menu of the day, which was written on a chalkboard. I didn't understand any of the names, but the prices were very low, even for Bolivia.

'So, if you want to save money, this is where to come, Thomas. Everything's cheaper down here. Whatever you need.'

The main difference between these inside sections and the four- and five-star ones, however, wasn't the quality of the rooms or restaurant prices, it was the people. Immediately, I noticed that they were much poorer; their skin was dirtier and their clothes were cheaper. But that didn't worry me so much as the way some of them looked at you. I didn't feel welcome at all. One old man spat on the ground next to me and I think I heard the word '*gringo*' again. I noticed they were even a bit suspicious of Ricardo, because he obviously wasn't from around there. In fact, they seemed to be suspicious of everyone, including each other.

But the worst thing was the number of base addicts. You could usually tell them by their faces, which were sort of caved in. They were also unnaturally skinny. As soon as one of them looked at you, you could tell what he was going to say, even before he opened his mouth. In Pinos and Alamos, all of the inmates spoke to you when they walked past. They also spoke to you in these inside sections, but it wasn't to say hello. They wanted money.

At first, I felt obliged at least to acknowledge that someone was speaking to me. The first few times someone held out his hand, I said, 'Sorry. I haven't got any money. *No hay.*' But Ricardo told me just to ignore them.

'Once they get your attention, they won't leave you alone until you give them something. So it's best not even to look at them. Don't establish eye contact. OK?'

I thought he was being a bit heartless and didn't answer him. If someone is right there in front of me, I find it impossible to turn my head and pretend that he doesn't exist at all. But I suppose Ricardo had been there longer than me and knew better. He must have sensed what I was thinking.

'Look, Thomas. I know it's sad,' he said, sounding like I had just accused him of something very serious. 'Give them some money, if you want. But they'll just buy base with it. If you want to do someone a favour here, you're better off buying them a meal or giving them something they can't sell.'

When I still didn't respond, Ricardo decided to prove his point in a different way. He led me up a staircase and along another dark corridor. We stopped at the very end, where I could just make out a thin ladder that looked similar to the one that led up to Ricardo's room.

'Alonso!' he called out, banging on the trapdoor above him.

No one answered, so he called again. Eventually there was a shuffling of feet and the trapdoor opened.

The first thing that struck my senses as we climbed into Alonso's room was the overpowering smell. It was one of those horrible chemical smells that gets inside your skin and stays with you for a long time afterwards.

'That smell is base,' Ricardo whispered in English before introducing me to Alonso, a short, skinny Bolivian dressed in filthy clothes. Alonso was balding slightly and, judging by his wrinkly skin and tired face, I guessed he was about fifty years old. Ricardo later told me he was only thirty-five.

'*¿Cómo está?*' Alonso asked politely, nodding to me, although his eyes were so glazed that it seemed he was only just aware of my presence. I looked around his room.

The cell was tiny and had no windows, trapping the smell of base smoke inside. Posters of half-naked women lined the walls and where there were no posters, the paint was peeling off. The only furniture was a bed and a small bedside table, but even so, there was hardly enough space for three of us.

After a brief conversation, Ricardo handed Alonso a one-boliviano coin.

'*Gracias,*' he mumbled in response, with a faraway look still on his face. He opened the trapdoor and disappeared slowly down the ladder.

'Where's he going?' I asked.

'He's gone to buy another packet of base,' Ricardo explained, and at that moment I noticed a ginger cat curled up on the bed. I leaned forward to pat it, but Ricardo grabbed my wrist.

'Don't touch the cat!' he warned. 'It'll scratch your eyes out.' When he saw that I was slightly taken aback by his reaction, he explained: 'The cat doesn't let anyone touch him when he's in a bad mood. Wait until Alonso comes back, then you can pat him.'

'What's its name?' I asked, wondering how Ricardo knew that the cat was in a bad mood.

'I don't know his proper name, but I call him Crack Cat,' Ricardo said, chuckling to himself. 'You'll see why in a minute.'

When Alonso returned, he immediately lay down beside the cat. He then reached into his sock and produced a tiny, folded piece of paper containing the base. Next, he felt under his bed for a pipe, which he cleared by tapping against the wall. When the cat heard the tapping sound, it pricked up its ears and climbed onto its master's stomach.

Alonso packed the pipe with tobacco, sprinkled some of the off-white base crystals on top and then lit the mixture using a match. The base bubbled, liquefied and then disappeared completely. Alonso held the smoke in his lungs and his eyes glazed over even more. The cat stalked forward slightly, advancing onto Alonso's chest, looking poised to strike. I was convinced that the cat was going to scratch his face, but as Alonso exhaled a strange thing occurred: the cat craned its neck, lifting its head upwards to get closer to Alonso's mouth. Alonso blew some smoke at its face.

The cat shook its head from side to side, and then sneezed before collapsing back into a comfortable position on Alonso's stomach. It took a deep breath, as if it were sighing, and its eyelids drooped over in contentment. Alonso stroked the cat's back and I heard it purring.

'You see!' said Ricardo, laughing and scratching the cat behind the ears. 'That's why I call him Crack Cat. He's happy now so you can pat him, if you like. Crack Cat only needs a little bit, so Alonso has to be careful. That base is very strong and maybe, if the cat has a big night smoking, he might overdose.'

卌\\

A cocaine-addicted cat wasn't the only surprise Ricardo had in store for me during our tour that afternoon. We had one more stop: Julio's.

'This guy is also a base addict,' Ricardo said to me under his breath as Julio opened the door. 'Only far worse.'

Julio was pale and skinny and he wouldn't meet my eye when we were introduced. He motioned for us to come in, all the while looking nervously at the floor. His room was even more horrible than Alonso's. It was lit by a single bulb dangling from the ceiling by a thin cable. The concrete walls were unpainted and, apart from a pile of dirty clothes on the floor, it seemed Julio owned nothing in the world.

Ricardo held out two coins and Julio almost snatched them out of his hands.

'Why did you give him two bolivianos instead of one?' I asked once Julio had left to buy the base.

'You'll see in a minute.'

When Julio returned, he had two packets of cocaine base, known locally as *basé*. He sat down on the bed, placed an entire packet in the pipe and lit it. As he sucked furiously, the veins on his forehead popped and his whole face turned ghostly white. He held the smoke in for so long that I thought he'd stopped breathing. For those few moments, he didn't seem human.

After he'd finally blown out the smoke, Julio stood up suddenly, reached into his pocket and produced a knife. I jumped back instinctively, thinking he was going to attack me, but instead he lifted up his shirt and slashed the knife across his stomach, drawing a perfectly straight line of blood. Just as quickly, he put the bloodied knife back in his pocket and sat down.

Ricardo said something and I watched, still completely horrified, as Julio stood up again and took his shirt off. Blood was trickling down his stomach and I noticed his entire torso and both arms were covered in thin, white scars from similar cuts. I felt sick in the stomach. I was also completely disgusted with Ricardo. The extra boliviano had obviously been to pay for Julio's show.

'He cuts himself to stop the paranoia,' Ricardo explained softly as Julio put his shirt back on and began unfolding the second packet of base. 'The sudden pain jolts him out of it.'

I looked at Ricardo and didn't say a word.

Afterwards, I realised he had shown me these things in order to scare me off taking base. The first time you try it, a packet costing one boliviano – twenty US cents – lasts you a whole day. Eventually, you need that same amount every fifteen minutes. Ricardo's plan worked. In all my time at San Pedro, I never touched the stuff. But I saw many people who did. One of my neighbours, who had been sent to San Pedro for a relatively minor crime, became completely addicted to base. He arrived with money and everything necessary to make his stay comfortable – a big-screen television, stereo, kettle, cooker and refrigerator. His family and friends visited him at least three times a week. But within six months he had quite literally sold everything he owned in order to buy base – including his clothes and even the blankets from his bed. His wife left him. His children stopped visiting. Eventually, someone he owed money repossessed his cell and he had to leave the section and move to a cheaper one.

I didn't see anything more of the inside sections because I cut the tour short, claiming to be hungry.

'But you haven't seen where they manufacture the leather jackets yet,' protested Ricardo.

'Another day, maybe. I'm really hungry, man.' I didn't want to see anything more. I'd made up my mind: I didn't care if I had to pay a million dollars to sleep on Ricardo's floor. I wasn't going to live down there in one of the inside sections. And even if he wouldn't let me stay, I still wouldn't sleep inside. No way. I would rather sleep outside, under that pine tree.

That's not to say that everyone in those sections was a drug addict or a murderer. There were many decent people, often with loving families, who lived there simply because they were poor, but at night these people locked their doors and didn't come out for any reason. Eventually, I made a lot of friends down there, especially in San Martín, and I visited them regularly. But my first impression always stayed with me. Sometimes I couldn't help shivering as I went down the corridor that led from the courtyard to the very inside of the prison.

8
BUYING A CELL OF MY OWN

The British Embassy never did believe me about the room system. No one ever accused me directly of lying, but it was obvious what happened. They must have rung or visited the prison administration and asked whether any of what I had said was true. It was my word against that of the Bolivian police force. I was an international drug trafficker and the embassy probably already had a file on me a mile long, so who do you think they were going to believe?

Ricardo told me not to kick up a fuss; if the embassy asked too many questions, there could be consequences for me in the prison. Besides, I would never convince them. I would only succeed in looking like a worse liar and reduce the chances of the embassy ever helping me in the future. Luckily, Prisoners Abroad, the charity organisation Mr Harris had contacted on my behalf, was far more understanding. The driver from the British Embassy delivered to me in the interview room a big package from Prisoners Abroad. It contained a knife, fork, spoon, plate, bowl, cooker, another blanket – all the things I needed to start a new life in prison – and five hundred dollars in cash to help me buy my first prison cell in San Pedro. I got the driver to ask the guards to escort me back to Ricardo's room. Two days later, he came again, this time with money from the contacts that owed me in London.

As soon as I received my money, I tried to pay Ricardo back, but he would only accept half of what I owed. I wanted to buy a room straight away; however, even though I now had money and knew how the titles system worked and where I wanted to live, I still needed Ricardo's help in conducting the actual negotiations. I didn't know the correct price to pay, and I thought the sellers might try to trick me because I was a foreigner. Ricardo got very excited when I asked for his help. He boasted that he had studied economics at university. He sat me down at his table and gave me a full lecture about the best buying strategy.

'It's just basic supply and demand, Thomas. Buy low, sell high. Simple capitalism,' he declared, leaning back in his chair and lighting up a joint. The way he held that joint between his index finger and his thumb and the way he blew out the smoke, I could have sworn he thought he was some famous economist puffing away on a Cuban cigar. 'Anyone with half a brain can understand it.'

I understood most of his explanation, but Ricardo made it hard by blowing marijuana smoke in my face and using technical words whenever he could. It was all common sense, really, but he made it sound far more complicated.

'Timing is everything in these matters, my friend. You've just got to be smarter than the rest to beat the market.'

I nodded my head, but when he could see that I wanted him to explain further, he took a deep breath and went through the whole thing, step by step.

The room prices went up and down as in any property market, so the important thing was to make the right decision about when to buy in order to get the best deal. Rooms were usually put up for sale when a prisoner knew for sure that he was leaving, although sometimes trades were made as prisoners upgraded or downgraded before their sentences had expired, according to their financial situation. The prisoners called this 'moving house'. For the seller to get the highest price, it was best for him to sell the room a long time before his actual release date because as that date got closer, buyers would know that he was desperate and would sell cheaper. The best thing to do as a buyer was the exact opposite: delay purchase until someone who hadn't managed to sell was about to leave.

'So, to get the best price, I should wait and find someone who is leaving very soon?' I asked.

'If the market permits, yes,' Ricardo agreed, offering me the joint.

I looked at him questioningly and held up my hand to refuse. I needed all my concentration for this one.

'You see, sometimes that option isn't available,' he explained, 'because the prison is totally full. It all comes back to your basic supply and demand.'

He started to explain supply and demand, which I already knew about from the drug market. Ricardo became so enthusiastic at this point that he decided to draw me some graphs. There was no time to waste in finding a pen and paper, so he picked up his kitchen knife and started carving lines into his wooden table. We started with the supply side, being the available accommodation. The prison was in a situation of what Ricardo called 'limited' or 'capped' supply. This was because there was no space left to build any more rooms. Apparently, the prison had been originally built for two hundred and fifty inmates, but at times the population could reach up to fifteen hundred prisoners, plus their families, all crammed into one city block. If they had wanted to, the government probably could have built more rooms on top of the existing ones, but there were no funds available to do so. Besides, who really cared about the conditions of a bunch of prisoners, when most of the country was living in poverty? The politicians kept the money for themselves.

Then Ricardo explained the demand side of things. The demand was determined by people who needed to buy cells and it was rising because the prison population was expanding every day, mainly with people accused of drug-trafficking offences under a law called *la Ley Mil Ocho* – Law 1008 – which was the law I was being charged under. According to Ricardo, the reason for all this overcrowding and for Law 1008 was the US government's 'war on drugs'.

Ricardo was proud of having lived in the United States and of speaking English, because it made him feel superior to the Bolivians. However, at other times, he really hated the Americans. This was one of those times. Bolivia is one of the poorest Latin American countries and the US regularly made kind offers of humanitarian aid to help out the poor, the starving and the homeless. However, this was on the condition that Bolivia agreed to fumigate its coca plantations and go after the people who controlled the drug trade. Of course, the Bolivian politicians were always glad to accept all donations, most of which never made it to their intended destination. They jumped up and down, promising to destroy the crops and hunt down the evil people responsible for drug trafficking, but in reality their efforts were only minimal; coca was the most valuable industry Bolivia had and it was making a lot of people in power very rich.

'They never actually go after the big fish,' said Ricardo. 'They're untouchable. They just lock up the small fry like us to make it look like they're cleaning up the country. There are people in prison for two grams, and others who weren't even caught with anything. Just on suspicion.' He banged his fist on the table to emphasise his point and the wood shavings from his supply and demand graphs jumped out of their grooves. 'So, you see, that's why we Bolivians hate the Americans,' he concluded in his New York accent.

I could see that Ricardo was capable of talking about American politics for hours, but I wanted to get back to the subject of buying my room, so I cut in before he could continue.

'I get it. So, if the prices are always going up, that means I should buy as soon as possible before it gets more expensive. Right?'

'Not necessarily,' Ricardo the politician went back to being Ricardo the wise economist. He stroked his chin and drew back on his 'cigar' as though he had just been asked a very controversial question by a clever journalist and needed time to formulate his response. Of course, I could tell that he had already thought about these things a lot and was simply enjoying the opportunity to show off his knowledge. In fact, he was loving every minute of it and stringing it out for as long as possible. Or maybe he was just getting his revenge because I had interrupted him just as he was getting to an important point about the Americans. He repeated very slowly, 'Not necessarily, my friend.'

Occasionally, room prices did actually go down, he explained. There were two things that could cause this; the first was when more people were leaving prison than were entering. This occurred when a lot of prisoners were pardoned or given early release, which meant there were more vacancies and so the cell market went down. This happened by pure necessity when the prison was full and the administration used any excuse to reduce the number of prisoners. That was easy enough to understand. In fact, I later experienced the biggest example of this first hand when a new law called *Extra Muro* – 'Extra Wall' – was passed, which halved the sentences of most prisoners in the country. This law led to hundreds of prisoners becoming eligible for immediate or early release.

The second reason was what Ricardo called 'market scare'. Frequently, the Bolivian government announced plans to pull down San Pedro prison and transfer all the inmates to a new jail it wanted to build in El Alto. And since it was officially denied that prisoners actually paid for their own cells, no one would be refunded any of their purchase money. The first few times this was announced, the prisoners believed the politicians and panicked. Prices dropped overnight because of what Ricardo called a 'fire sale' – hundreds of inmates put 'En Venta' signs on their doors, trying to get anything they could for their rooms.

'If I'd had money, I could have bought up everything and retired a rich man,' Ricardo sighed. 'I did get a cheap television out of it, though,' he pointed proudly to the cardboard box at the end of his bed where his purchase was sitting. 'Supposedly, no privileges were going to be allowed in the new prison. It's amazing what market hysteria will do to people,' he said, shaking his head at the irrationality of humans.

'So, it was just a rumour, then?' I asked. 'They're not really going to knock it down?'

'Of course they're going to knock it down. Are you stupid? You really don't understand economics, do you?'

Ricardo had to explain yet again. I got the feeling that he was doing all of this on purpose just to make me look like an idiot and himself look smarter, but I let him get away with it because I was captivated by what he was saying. Besides, he was really quite entertaining when he got in these moods and I liked watching him; he really did seem to think that he was giving an important speech at Harvard.

According to Ricardo, it made sense to knock down San Pedro prison, since the inner-city real estate on which the jail was located was worth millions. After that, they would need to build another prison to house all the inmates, which would require the use of public funds. These public funds would obviously be controlled by corrupt politicians. So, of course it was in their interests to knock down the prison. One day they would actually do it, predicted Ricardo. The only problem was getting the funds from the Americans.

Although fascinating, all these explanations left me more confused than when we began. Before, I had known nothing, but now, with the help of economics, I knew even less. To me, every single one of Ricardo's arguments went around in circles. No sooner did I think I understood what he was saying than he would deliberately contradict it. Sometimes prices went up, sometimes they went down.

Sometimes it was best to wait as long as possible, sometimes you should buy straight away. People behaved rationally according to graphs carved on wooden tables, but sometimes they were stupid and sold their televisions very cheaply. You could make money on property, but then the government might take everything away from you. Oh well, I never liked economics, anyway. I think that's why I dropped out of school early and became a drug trafficker.

'So, how do I know if it's the right time to buy, then?' I asked, trying to get back to the original topic, being when I was going to buy a room.

'You don't. *No one* does, really. You can make a guess, but it's impossible to predict a market perfectly. And it's irrelevant, anyway.'

'Why is it irrelevant?'

'Because you've got no choice. You have to buy a room right now or you'll have nowhere to sleep,' he laughed and pointed to the door, grabbing my arm and pushing me towards it as though he were evicting me. 'It gets quite cold out there at night, you know.'

I knew he was only joking, so I laughed too.

'So, that means this whole conversation was also irrelevant?'

'No. Not at all, my friend. You learned something. You're intelligent and I enjoy talking with you,' he complimented me, even though I had hardly said a word and was clearly not as intelligent as he was. Ricardo then put his joint out and concluded his university seminar.

'So, you see, Thomas, San Pedro prison, apart from being a social microcosm, is also a microeconomy that operates under basic capitalist principles. In fact, it's probably more efficient than the whole Bolivian national economy. And more democratic, too, but I'll explain the prison election system to you another day. I'm tired now. You ask a lot of questions, *inglés* – you know that?'

I was glad we stopped there, too; I needed a joint to help my brain recover from Ricardo's economics lecture.

卌\\

The room I liked most was in Pinos on the second storey. It had a window overlooking the courtyard and it was only a minute's walk from Ricardo's apartment. The owner was an old Bolivian prisoner who was shortly due for release. He wanted twenty-five hundred dollars, but Ricardo managed to bargain him down to eighteen hundred dollars, and persuaded him to include his television, refrigerator as well as some furniture into the deal. With the contribution sent by Prisoners Abroad and some money a friend sent to the Embassy for me, I had enough, although on the sale-purchase agreement we wrote down twelve hundred dollars less than the actual price to reduce the transfer fee I had to pay.

9
PREPARING FOR TRIAL

Having money and owning my own room in Pinos made me feel more settled, but it didn't end my problems with the other inmates who were still convinced that I was American. Even for those who finally worked out that I wasn't from the United States, I was still a foreigner, which meant I was a fair target anyway. In my fourth and fifth weeks, I was attacked five times, usually on the way to the bathroom. None of the attacks were as severe as the first two, but this was in Pinos, supposedly the quietest neighbourhood. I can't imagine how I would have survived in the dangerous sections.

Initially, I was afraid and did my best to avoid these conflicts by going out as little as possible. Whenever anyone said anything to me or spat on me, I kept my head down and kept walking. However, I had to go to the bathroom at some point each day and there was often someone waiting. They knew I had just purchased a room, so sometimes they asked me for money. If I refused, they would use that as an excuse to start a fight. At other times, there was no excuse required; they would insult me and spit on me for no reason. Usually, it was only one or two people who actually hit me. The trouble was that there was always a group of them watching and I was scared that they might join in. When I was attacked, I defended myself, but never really fought back, figuring that would only escalate things and I might be stabbed.

I was hoping that this was just part of my initiation to the prison and that they would tire of it after a while, especially if I didn't react. Unfortunately, things didn't work that way and the attacks became more severe; the less I fought back, the bolder they became until it became too much. I couldn't spend the rest of my time locked in my room hiding from the world. I had to fight back.

At first, I never really had time to notice what my attackers looked like. I knew that most of them came from the more dangerous sections, but everything always happened so quickly and they all looked the same to me. However, none of them were very big. Although I had lost a lot of weight while in the FELCN cells, I was still a lot bigger and stronger than most of the other inmates in San Pedro. There was one prisoner I had seen with a scar across his face who was a giant. He must have been almost seven foot tall, but luckily he wasn't involved. Apart from him, I could have fought most of the other inmates if it was one on one, which is what I decided to do: take the fight to them.

I took note of who was the leader. It was the same guy with the mean eyes from the first time I had been attacked in the bathroom. One day I went looking for him in the inside sections. When I saw him coming, I hid around the corner and then attacked him without warning, just like they had done to me. I had to do it quickly so that no one else had time to come to his aid, and I had to do it properly so that he wouldn't come back for more. The first punch broke his nose and knocked him to the ground. He wasn't getting up, but I didn't stop there. I had to put him out of action completely, so I kicked him again and again until one of his gang arrived and tried to pull me off. I went for that one, too, knocking his head against the wall and kneeing him in the groin before giving him the same kicking as the first one.

'Who else? Come on!' I punched the wall.

Two more of the gang had arrived by that stage, but when they saw their friends on the ground and my fierce expression, neither of them wanted to risk it.

I had done the job properly, but for the next few weeks I had to be constantly on the lookout in case they were out for payback. I carried a thick metal bar with me everywhere I went, banging it against the walls every now and then, and I never smiled. People had heard what I'd done and I wanted them to know I was still on edge, and could snap at any moment. To be honest, it was all an act. I was even more afraid than before, although I never showed it. Luckily, it worked and they left me alone. I had finally earned some respect in prison.

卌\\

After buying a room, my next priority was to sort out my legal situation. The lawyers who had visited me at the FELCN interrogation cells had all been confident that they could get me out, provided I had money. I now had that money, as much as they could ask for. I had had my emergency credit card sent over from Europe and, for a small fee, one of Ricardo's trusted friends on the outside would pick it up and get cash advances from the teller machines down on the Prado whenever I called her. I never liked going into debt so I hadn't used it before, but this was definitely an emergency.

Once she knew that I could pay her fees, Constanza Sanchez, one of the lawyers I had met after I was arrested, came to visit me several times a week to discuss my case. I paid her three thousand dollars up front. I knew it was a lot of money but I didn't want to argue, as that might have induced her to work less hard on my case. Besides, at that stage I didn't really care how much it cost me – I just wanted to get out of there.

Over the following weeks, Constanza visited me a few more times and we went over every detail of what had happened at the airport again and again. She then introduced me to another lawyer, who was apparently the best of the best *Mil Ocho* lawyers in town. I then had to explain the whole thing to him, even though Constanza had taken notes. Then she brought in another lawyer, who was also needed for my legal 'team', as she kept calling it. Initially, I was against the idea of having three lawyers and wanted to know why I needed a third if I already had 'the best of the best', but Constanza convinced me. Apart from adding extra knowledge and experience to my defence, the more lawyers I had, the better the impression I would make in court when I appeared before the judge, she said.

Although the colonel had cleverly let me pass through customs at the airport, making my charge 'international trafficking' rather than 'possession', my lawyers told me that my case was strong because I hadn't signed a confession. Between them, they believed that they could create 'reasonable doubt' as to whether the drugs actually belonged to me. This would force the judge to find me *inocente*. The major problem we faced was the delays in the court system, which in some cases meant waits of up to four years before a trial even started. In the meantime, there was no presumption of innocence in Bolivia and no right to apply for bail in drug cases. Luckily, there were ways of fast-tracking the whole procedure by making applications to the court and using my lawyers' contacts. But it would all cost money.

After six weeks in San Pedro, I received even better news – my case mightn't even get to the trial stage. My team of lawyers knew a man who was a friend of the judge that had been assigned to my case, and he was going to see if the judge was prepared to come to an 'out-of-court settlement'.

In a short space of time, everything in my life had turned around completely. Although I obviously wasn't happy about having to wait it out in prison, things could have been a lot worse.

10
LA NOCHE DE SAN JUAN

wanted to celebrate the good news immediately. 'Let's get a bottle of something. My shout,' I suggested to Ricardo.

'But we're already going to Carlos's party.'

'But I don't know him.'

'Doesn't matter. You're invited.'

After what had happened with the standover gang, I was becoming more accepted in the prison and Ricardo had started introducing me to other inmates. Occasionally, they invited me around to their rooms. The rest of the prison was also celebrating that night because it was the twenty-first of June – the longest night of the year and around the same time as *la Noche de San Juan* – a significant date in the Bolivian calendar. I wasn't sure if it was the longest night, but it certainly felt like the coldest, and it took several rums to get warm.

A group of about seven of us, including Ricardo, Carlos, Carlos's wife and some of her girlfriends, were sitting around a table in Carlos's room. Not all the women who came into San Pedro were wives, sisters and girlfriends. Sometimes women accompanied their friends to parties. The girl sitting next to me was beautiful. After a few more rums, I felt confident enough to try out my Spanish, which was improving rapidly by that stage. I couldn't understand every word she said, but if I concentrated, I could follow the general conversation well enough.

Then someone pulled out a small plastic bag of cocaine and handed it around with a key to sniff *puntitos*, which was done by scooping a small amount onto the tip of the key, putting it just below your nose and inhaling. Everyone took two small *puntitos*, one in each nostril.

When the bag came around to me, I said that I was quite happy just drinking. However, they insisted that I try some.

'Come on, Thomas. You've got your first room in San Pedro. You're one of us now. Join the party. For Pinos.' Everyone raised their glasses and toasted the section.

I didn't want to make a big deal out of it, so, instead of arguing, I dipped the key into the bag and pretended to scoop some coke onto its tip, then held the bag in front of my face as I sniffed so that they wouldn't notice that I was pretending. Everyone cheered, except the girl sitting next to me.

'You didn't have any,' she cried, pointing at me. 'There was nothing there.'

'Yes, I did.'

'No, you didn't. I saw you. Cheat!' She was half-joking, but it was also embarrassing because she was showing me up in front of my new friends in the section.

'I did.'

'OK. Do it again, then!' she challenged, grabbing the bag and holding the key under my nose, loaded up with a huge *puntito*.

'But I just did,' I protested, looking to Ricardo for support. Ricardo shrugged his shoulders casually, as if to say, 'I don't care. It's up to you,' but at the same time, 'Why not? You're not going to die or anything.'

'Come on. You need to take your medicine or you'll catch a cold.' The beautiful girl waved the key around in the air and made an aeroplane noise. With all her confidence and joking around, she had everyone laughing and watching to see what I would do. There was no getting out of it. I was trapped.

'OK, then.' I let her put the key right up to my nostril and when she nodded, I sucked in hard through my nose.

'And another one for this side,' she said, administering more medicine to my left nostril. 'And one more for good luck,' she made me take a third dose that was even bigger than the first two. 'That's it. There's a good little boy,' she kissed me on the cheek and the others laughed before returning to their conversations.

I had been trafficking drugs for years, but that was the first time in my life I had ever tried cocaine.

The girl was smiling at me. 'You see,' she said. 'It wasn't that hard now, was it?'

'Mmm.'

'How do you feel? Do you like it?'

Yes, I liked it. I liked the feeling it gave me and I liked the way she was looking at me, but at the time I also thought that what she had done was wrong. No one should put pressure on anyone else to take drugs, I thought, especially if it was their first time. What if they became addicted or something went wrong? But now I don't blame that girl for pushing me to try some, because later I was to do the same thing myself many times with tourists who visited the prison. Maybe what they say about drug-takers is true – that they try to get everyone around them hooked, so they don't feel so bad about it themselves. I'm sure that neither of us had any evil intentions. Maybe it just comes down to this: when you're happy, you want everyone else around you to be happy too.

In any case, I certainly can't say that it was the girl's fault the next time I tried cocaine, or the time after that. It wasn't like someone was pointing a gun at my head. I made the choice. I liked cocaine the first time I tried it. I liked it the second time. I've liked it ever since. At times it's been my saviour. At times it's almost been the death of me. But even when I started doing it too much, I didn't blame anyone for it, not that beautiful girl, not even the drug itself. I sometimes ask myself whether my life would have been better without cocaine. Really, I can't say. It certainly would have been different. But I can tell you this: it certainly wasn't what I thought it would be and it certainly isn't like they say it is.

I was expecting the effect to be instantaneous, but nothing happened for a few minutes; when it *did* kick in, it was nowhere near as strong as I expected. The first thing I noticed was that my front teeth went numb, followed gradually by other parts of my mouth. Next, I realised that I was wide awake, but the effect still wasn't that strong. I felt more confident, but it wasn't at all like being drunk because I was still in control of everything and it didn't affect my coordination. The world didn't look any different; it didn't go blurry and I didn't see things that weren't there. It didn't even change the way that I thought. It was just a good feeling. In fact, I felt better than good – I felt *very* good. No, I felt *fantastic*. For several minutes I couldn't think of anything except how amazingly happy I was feeling. It was like I was flying in my emotions. I can't describe it any other way. I felt that I was somehow more alive than I'd ever been before.

For several minutes I couldn't get beyond that feeling. I had never experienced anything like it. I looked around the room at everyone else, wondering how they could act as if everything was so normal, when it so clearly wasn't.

The girl next to me caught my eye again. She smiled at me and raised her eyebrows, and I smiled back. Then we launched into a long conversation. I had no trouble speaking to her because my thoughts were coming to me more quickly. In fact, my Spanish seemed to have improved and I began talking non-stop. If I didn't know the word for something, it didn't bother me; I could get around it or have a guess based on the word in English. Sometimes I'd get it wrong, but that didn't matter, she could understand me and I could understand her too. I could now do what I wanted and say what I wanted. I was communicating! But most of all, I was just plain happy. I felt connected to the people in the room. Everyone was talking, but even without saying anything, it's like we were all on the same level.

'I told you,' she put her hand on my knee and kissed my cheek again. She knew.

The strongest part of the effect began wearing off after half an hour. I was still high, but I wanted more. I had two more *puntitos* when the bag came around again, which brought me back up, although not like the first time. A third set kept me high, but after that it reached a plateau.

When I did more after that, my leg started shaking and I couldn't stop it. My nose also started sweating and I could feel my heart racing.

'That's just nerves,' Ricardo said to me in English when he saw me observing my knees as if they weren't part of my own body. 'It's perfectly normal. Have some more rum if you feel nervous.'

'No, I feel great. Thanks for this. It's amazing.'

'What did you expect, my friend? That's San Pedro vintage you're trying there.'

'Well, then. I think maybe I should get thrown in prison more often.'

Ricardo laughed. 'But remember it's your first time, *inglés*, so take it easy. You really don't need too much coke if it's pure.'

It was probably good advice, but I didn't follow it. I didn't *want* to take it easy. I wanted more cocaine and more to drink with it. Everyone did. We partied until ten o'clock the next day. The Bolivians had been right: it definitely was the longest night of the year.

11
JACK

The first night I tried coke was also the first night I met Jack the Mexican. This, I later discovered, was no coincidence. Jack had a nose custom-built for cocaine: for sniffing it out, then sniffing it up. As soon as anyone opened a bag of it in the prison, he would magically appear.

On this occasion, he had actually been invited, although he turned up late. The celebrations were already well under way when he sat down beside me. At first, I was a little afraid of him; although he was skinny, he was also very tall – about six foot three – and even sitting down at the table, he towered over me. It was night time, but he was wearing a huge pair of sunglasses so that you couldn't see his eyes and he was talking at me in Spanish at a hundred miles an hour. He kept leaning towards me so suddenly that several times I thought he was going to hit me.

'¿Habla inglés?' I asked very cautiously, when he finally paused for breath.

'Of course. Why didn't you say before?'

But even when he switched to speaking English, I couldn't understand much because his massive nose was blocked and the way he spoke sounded like a trumpet. I still thought he was going to hit me.

Nothing could have been further from the truth. Although Jack looked dangerous when you first met him, he was as soft as they come. People assumed that he was tough because of his height, but deep down, he was extremely shy and anyone could push him around, even tiny guys, and he never fought back. In fact, he was embarrassed about being so tall because it made him stand out and, he thought, made him easier to pick on. Once, when he got sent to the punishment section of the prison, known as La Muralla, Jack was beaten up by a skinny Bolivian prisoner and forced to hand over all his warm clothes. Afterwards he was too embarrassed to ask any of his friends to help get them back.

The talking thing was a front also. If you met Jack when he was partying, you would think he was the funniest guy in the world with loads of self-confidence, because he had hundreds of stories to tell and he only ever stopped talking to smoke his pipe or take cocaine. But when he wasn't on drugs, it was hard to get so much as a word out of him.

Jack took some getting used to, but when you knew him well, he was like a big puppy dog that needed lots of affection; once you had won him over, you could make him run around in circles and chase his tail, or fetch an imaginary stick you hadn't actually thrown. He became one of my best friends in San Pedro, but I was forever playing with him and tricking him into doing things he didn't want to do.

One time, about a year after I arrived at San Pedro, Jack came to my room crying. It was about nine in the morning and I could tell that he was coming down badly.

'Do you mind if I come in? I need to talk to someone.'

'Of course. What's wrong?'

'I'm fucked up, Thomas. That's what wrong. I'm totally screwed in the head.'

Jack wasn't suited to prison life at all; he wasn't tough enough. He came from a wealthy family and I don't think he had worked a day in his life. He certainly never lifted a finger in San Pedro. His cell was always a mess, because there was no one to tidy it for him. He started complaining that no one in the prison liked him. In fact, that no one had ever liked him his whole life. Not even his own father. He began telling me in detail about his family problems, which were mainly to do with his father, a tough businessman who had made it from nothing and was disappointed that his son hadn't turned out the same.

'You're a failure, son. Look at you. You can't even deal drugs properly,' the father had remarked on his first, and only, visit to San Pedro. After that, he pretended he no longer had a son and Jack's mother had to send him money secretly.

'But *I* like you,' I said.

Jack looked up at me suspiciously, 'You do? Really? You're not just saying that because I'm crying?'

'Hey. I didn't even know you were crying,' I lied. 'How can I see anything when you wear those stupid sunglasses all the time.' I pretended to be angry with him and it worked. He took his glasses off slowly and looked at me, embarrassed. It was the first time I had ever seen his eyes. The whites were all bloodshot, but the irises were a beautiful green and his tears made them look translucent.

'Hey. You've got nice eyes.'

'Do you think so?'

'They're not contact lenses, are they?'

'No.' Jack sat up straighter in his chair and lifted his head. 'They're natural.'

'Well, you should take those glasses off more often, then. You might get a girlfriend.'

'You think so?' I could tell that he was already starting to cheer up.

'Sure. All the Bolivian men have brown eyes. You'll look like an exotic foreigner to the women with those green contacts.'

'But they're not contacts. I already told you. You don't listen, Thomas.'

'Prove it. Take them out and show me.'

Jack's hands made a movement towards his eyes and then stopped. 'I can't. How can I if they're real?'

'No. I saw you move. You were about to take them out.'

'I promise you, they're real.'

I nodded. 'Uh huh. Yeah. Real contacts.' Poor Jack. He was like a kid. It was never hard to trick him. Sometimes I felt bad doing it to him – he was vulnerable and it was almost too easy – but it was always very funny, so I couldn't help myself. 'That's OK. Don't be embarrassed. They still look good on you.'

'No. They're my real eyes, Thomas. That's their natural colour, I promise you.' He started getting really frustrated.

'A promise isn't good enough. You expect me to believe that a Mexican can have green eyes? How are you going to prove it?'

Jack thought about this for quite a while. 'I can't. It's impossible.' He looked down sadly. 'The girls will never believe me either. I can't exactly take my eyeballs out.' Then, suddenly, he had an idea. 'Wait! Yes. I can prove it. I've got photos from when I was younger.' And with that, he bounded out of my room to find his photo album.

'That won't prove a thing,' I called after him, just to keep him confused. 'You could easily have had contacts since you were a kid.'

Jack was like that; one minute coming down and crying, the next minute running around completely absorbed in something different. He would probably puzzle over that problem for the rest of the day, but at least he'd forgotten how sad he had been feeling.

Jack's main problem was that he smoked base, which made him paranoid. There was only one other inmate in Alamos who smoked more base than Jack: an inmate who went by the name of Cámara Lenta. I didn't know his proper name, because almost no one in San Pedro was known by his correct name. The foreigners were always referred to by their nationalities; I was always *inglés*, Jack was called *méjico*. The Bolivians usually had nicknames based on the town they came from. This meant you could see someone every day for several years and only realise when he'd left prison that there was little chance you would ever meet him again. What were the chances of tracking down someone named Cochabamba in the city of Cochabamba, population one million?

Cámara Lenta's nickname meant 'slow motion'. He lived on the ground floor in my section, but I only saw him twice during my whole time at San Pedro. The reason for this was that he smoked so much base he had become too afraid to leave his room.

It was rumoured that several ghosts flew about our section at night, although I had never seen any. There was also a surprising correlation between those inmates who claimed to have seen the ghosts and those who smoked loads of base. Because of these ghosts, inmates like Jack and Cámara Lenta rarely emerged from their rooms after dark, except in an absolute emergency, or in Jack's case if there was free coke on offer. Jack had an ensuite bathroom, one of only two in Alamos, so he rarely needed to go out. Cámara Lenta wasn't so fortunate; although he kept buckets in his cell to piss in, he had to leave his room in order to empty them from time to time.

On my way downstairs one evening, I encountered Cámara Lenta several metres from the bathroom door. He was hunched over with his head forward and back arched, carrying his two urine buckets, one in each hand. I assumed that he was resting, since he didn't appear to be moving. I went into the bathroom and came out five minutes later to find him in exactly the same position. He appeared to have progressed only a few steps closer to the bathroom.

I yelled out, 'Hey there! Are you OK? Hey, *hombre.*' There was no reaction. 'Do you need any help?' Still he didn't move. I clapped my hands, thinking he might have been a bit deaf.

Finally, there was a gradual, although delayed, reaction. Very slowly and precisely, Camára Lenta moved his eyes towards me. Then he cautiously twisted his head in my direction. All the while his body remained motionless and his expression remained unchanged. Using a series of eye movements up towards the ceiling, around the corridors and in the direction of the stairs, he indicated that it wasn't safe to talk here, or to make any sudden movement, in case the ghosts saw you. If you wanted to survive in this prison, you had to creep around every-where in slow motion.

12
THE GOVERNOR

My lawyers made contact with the judge. Unfortunately, he had said the case would definitely have to go to trial, but for ten thousand dollars I could be found innocent. I agreed to pay the money, although it would take a few weeks to get that amount together. My lawyers said that would be acceptable and they issued me with another bill. They promised to have me out by Christmas.

With the frequent visits from my lawyers, my new room, my new friends, a new stereo system and these small parties we were having, everyone knew that I now had money. And no one was shy about asking me for a loan. Other inmates asked to borrow ten bolivianos here and there, and the police were always asking for a *colaboración* for their wives, who were sick in hospital, or for their children, who couldn't afford school books. None of the money was ever for them personally. I don't know whether that meant the payments were technically not bribes or whether they thought it made them seem like nicer people. The amounts weren't large, but they asked every time I saw them. I didn't feel that I could refuse them until Ricardo gave me an invaluable piece of advice: 'Don't waste time with these small guys. You've got to control the head and the tail will follow automatically.'

I had to get the boss of the whole prison – the governor – on side. I did that, and more; we actually became good friends. Every now and then he would call me to his office to practise his English. He spoke with a terrible accent but he had mastered one expression, which he repeated to me every time we met: 'Life is expensive.'

I couldn't disagree. Everything cost money and life *was* expensive, especially for those around the governor. Whenever I visited, I would take him money to help out with various expenses: the petrol for his wife's car, the household electricity bill and school uniforms for his children.

The governor required a higher bribe than the other officers, but because it wasn't every day, it was far cheaper in the end. In return, I was given certain privileges: I could do whatever I wanted, and if ever I got in trouble with the lower-ranking police or needed something, I could call the governor in his office or visit him in the administration block on very short notice.

It was during one of these initial visits that the governor suggested I help other inmates to learn English. There was already an education program in place, but it didn't work efficiently because the teachers, who came from outside, went on strike when they weren't paid.

'They are too expensive,' the governor told me confidentially.

That's how I got my very first job at San Pedro. Well, it wasn't a proper job because I didn't get paid, but it was something to occupy my time. It also made me feel good to do something positive for the other inmates. The classes were slow because it was the first time I had ever taught anything and my Spanish was very basic, but I had a lot of fun explaining everything with gestures and by drawing pictures on the blackboard. I also took some Spanish and Chemistry classes, managing to come first in some of the tests.

The close friendship I had with the governor created a lot of jealousy among the other inmates. Anyone who had money could bribe the governor, but not everyone could go and visit him or call him whenever they wanted. I didn't mind the jealousy, though. With such a powerful ally, I was now fully protected; the prisoners steered clear of me and the guards also left me alone. What I never expected was that, many months later, the governor would come to rely on me for more than money and friendship.

卌\\

By the time the following incident occurred, I was well established in the prison, but I still rarely left my cell at night. That was when all the *borrachos* and serious base-smokers really let loose, looking for fights and stirring up trouble.

This particular night I had just finished smoking a joint and was turning the light off to watch television when there was a knock at my door. I was too stoned to answer it, so I turned the sound off using the remote control and kept perfectly still. Whoever it was knocked again.

Everyone in the section knew my rule: I never opened the door unless the visitor announced his name, so I guessed it would probably be Jack, or someone like him who couldn't sleep, trying to trick me into letting him in. But if it was Jack, there was no way I was opening that door because then I might be tempted to take some coke. He always did that to me, right when I wanted to go to bed.

'Just one line, Thomas,' he would insist. 'Then I'll let you rest.' And he never went away until I agreed. But my time in San Pedro prison had taught me that there is no such thing as just one line of cocaine if you can get your hands on more. And the last thing I needed that night was him keeping me up until dawn again.

However, when there was another round of more insistent knocking, I realised it wasn't Jack. It was way too loud. Jack would always knock really fast like there was a major emergency, but also extremely softly because he was paranoid about anyone knowing he was there. Sometimes he knocked so quietly that even I couldn't hear him and then he would get angry when he had to wait for ten paranoid minutes, tapping the door lightly with his fingers, until I realised there was someone there.

But if it wasn't Jack, who was it? Whoever it was knew that I was there and definitely wasn't going away.

'Who is it?' I finally called out from my bed.

'It's me,' replied a female voice.

'And me, too,' came another female voice.

That could only mean trouble. The section gates had been locked, which meant that my visitors had to be wives from the section. The only reason the wives visited other prisoners without their husbands was if they were having problems at home. The fact that there wasn't one but two women at my door meant that it was probably even bigger trouble. I didn't like it at all.

'Who?' I demanded again and got the same response, although this time I thought I heard laughter. It certainly didn't sound like they were upset. 'Yes, but what are your names?'

'Marcela . . .'

'And Maria-Teresa,' they giggled. I didn't know them, and my first thought was that someone was playing a trick on me.

Putting the packet of *ganja* in my pocket, I opened the door to be confronted by two young, attractive Bolivian women I had never seen before. The taller one was wearing red lipstick, a thick pullover of the same colour and chunky, gold-coloured earrings. The shorter one, who wore less makeup, was far prettier. She had on a full-length overcoat and I knew there was something hidden underneath because only one of her hands was showing through the sleeves.

'*Hola, Thomas. ¿Cómo estás?*' they chanted in unison. I could have sworn I didn't know them, but they were acting as though we were old friends. They both kissed me on the cheek and brushed passed me into my room without being asked. They didn't even bother looking around; they just sat down at the table as if they had been there many times before. I looked at them more closely. Maybe I was too stoned, but I was sure I hadn't met them before. I didn't know what to say, though, just in case I had.

'We brought you a little present, didn't we, Maria?' said Marcela, the taller one, producing a bottle of whisky from beneath her overcoat. Maria-Teresa took the bottle and held it up to me and pouted like a little girl.

'Well, aren't you going to get some glasses for us?' she asked, pretending to be upset. I went into the kitchen and did as I was told, all the while trying to work out what was going on.

'We're friends of Colonel Montesinos,' Marcela announced when I came back with two glasses. 'He should be here soon.'

'He sent us around as the advance party,' giggled Maria-Teresa. 'He said you wouldn't mind entertaining us for a while.'

That might explain things. Everyone knew that the governor liked to play around with women. Maybe he needed somewhere private to go where his wife wouldn't find out? That was possible, but I was still suspicious that my friends were playing a joke on me, or setting some kind of trap. And if it was a trap, I wasn't going to fall into it easily.

'Suit yourself,' Marcela snapped when I refused a sip of the whisky she was holding out to me. 'More for me, then!' She drained the glass and her friend giggled again.

Even though it was almost freezing, the girls insisted that they have ice in their whisky, so I went to get some from the freezer, glad of the opportunity to be out of their way. Then there was a firm knock at the door.

'Who is it?' I called out from the kitchen. I had hardly got the question out before Marcela leaned back in her chair and unlatched the door and the governor of the prison, Colonel Montesinos, came into my room. He was wearing his usual shiny black shoes and green uniform, but he was wearing a casual sweater over the top, which made him look a bit younger and not so serious.

I stood to shake his hand and greeted him in the most formal manner, 'How are you, my governor?' We were friends but I always showed him complete respect, calling him by his full title, especially in the presence of other people.

'*Hola, Thomas. Bien,*' he answered casually, greeting each of the girls with a kiss. 'I see you've met the girls. What's the latest news from San Pedro, my friend? You look hungover . . . *mucha fiesta* or what?' he asked, sitting down and pouring himself a whisky in one of the girls' glasses.

The governor seemed perfectly relaxed – like this was a completely normal situation. I was the exact opposite: perfectly nervous. He had visited my room before and we had always been very friendly, but never this late and never this friendly. He was still a colonel in the Bolivian police and the most powerful person in the whole prison and I didn't know what he wanted with me, turning up at my room like that with two beautiful women so late at night. However, I couldn't say anything, especially in front of his guests. I hoped he would explain, but he didn't. Instead, he offered me a glass of whisky.

'No, thank you, my governor.'

'Don't like whisky, hey Thomas? Not even Black Label. Well, I'm sure you're accustomed to finer things. We should obtain something a little stronger perhaps?' He raised his eyebrows at me knowingly and added, 'I want the best stuff you can find.'

At first, I wasn't sure if I had understood him correctly. I looked at him blankly, wondering if he really meant what I thought he meant. Maybe my mind was playing tricks on me because I was stoned. But then he repeated his request and there was no doubt.

'Bring me five grams,' he commanded, pulling out a wad of cash from his top pocket and peeling off a few notes. 'How much will five grams cost?'

Marcela stared at the bundle of cash and whistled, but I stared straight at the governor's face, completely stunned. Suddenly everything seemed surreal; I was stoned, two strange, beautiful Bolivian women were in my prison cell drinking Black Label whisky, and the highest-ranking official in the jail was asking me to buy cocaine for him.

'Well?' he asked, raising his eyebrows again, but I didn't know what to do. I was almost lost for words.

'Five grams of what, my governor?' I managed to stammer, pretending not to know what he was talking about. I honestly wished there was a black hole in the floor next to me. I wanted to step into it and just disappear.

'*Coca*, what else? *Pollo*. Don't play stupid with me,' he said gruffly, fixing me with a heavy stare. He even knew the code name for cocaine.

'But . . . you're not joking with me, my governor, are you?' I asked as politely as possible. I suspected a trap and there was no way I wanted to fall into it, but I didn't want to offend him either. He was the head of the whole prison. 'I honestly don't know about this stuff.'

'Come on, Thomas,' he patted me on the shoulder and smiled. 'The coke here in the prison is better than anywhere else in the whole of Bolivia. And if the governor of the prison can't get some coke, then who can?'

Both the girls burst out laughing and the governor joined in, adding, 'Don't look so confused, my friend. Tell me. How much is a gram these days? Still twenty bolivianos or has the price gone up again because of those bastard *gringos* and their crop fumigation?'

This made them laugh even more. Then I started laughing too, finally realising that it had all been a joke. And once we were all laughing, no one could stop, especially me – I was laughing the loudest of anyone, mainly from relief. In public, the governor pretended to be very strict and I had forgotten that when no one else was there, he always joked around with me. I was so stoned that I had taken him seriously and fallen for it; he had had me completely convinced.

Then the laughter stopped just as quickly as it had begun and everything changed back in an instant. My mind had played another trick on me. The governor became serious again and held out the money to me, demanding that I take it. It was no joke – he really did want me to get him some cocaine. I tried to get out of it again without being rude, but he kept insisting.

'Come on, Thomas, get me five grams. Of course you know where to get it. Come now, we're all friends here.' He pressed a pile of notes into my hand and opened the door, motioning me towards it.

'But, my governor, I don't know where to get any of that stuff. I don't take it and I don't know who does.'

He didn't like me arguing with him in front of his friends. 'Stop playing games and just get it!' he snapped at me suddenly, and I had no choice but to obey. I took one last look at him to make sure he was really serious, then went out of my cell and Marcela closed the door behind me.

Outside, the air was cold and I hadn't had time to put a jacket on, so I was even colder. All of a sudden I was no longer stoned. In fact, I was feeling remarkably sober.

I leaned back against the door, wondering what I should do. I needed to think fast, but I still couldn't believe that any of this was actually happening. The governor wouldn't have been risking his own reputation by being in a prisoner's room with two young women and a bottle of whisky for nothing. Unless it was a very elaborate trap.

Yes! I decided it was a trap. They were taping everything I did in order to set me up and track down the source of cocaine in the section. I wouldn't fall for it though; I would simply say that I couldn't find any. I knocked on the door and the governor opened it immediately.

I felt like I had been outside for a long time, but in reality only a few seconds had passed. The governor was surprised that I had come back so quickly, and empty-handed. When he saw how worried I was, he came outside, leaving the door slightly open, and wanted to know what the problem was. I tried to explain once more that I didn't take drugs and couldn't get anything, but he looked me directly in the eyes and spoke sharply.

'You're not going to embarrass me in front of these girls, are you? I promised them a good time. Don't disappoint me, Thomas,' he commanded, patting me on the shoulder again. Then he gave me a short but strong squeeze on the bicep before going back inside and closing the door again, locking me out of my own room.

The governor was a man who rarely gave orders because he rarely needed to; he was used to having his will obeyed. However, this was an order, and there was no way out of it. Even if it was a trap, I now had to comply. So off I went, with the governor's money in my hand, to buy five grams of cocaine.

As I walked through the section, I heard strange sounds and I stopped every now and then to look behind me and see if anyone was following, but there was no one around. Well, no one that I could see anyway. However, that didn't prevent me from feeling that I was being watched.

Before I bought the stuff from my usual dealer, who we called Comandante, I knocked on three different doors and asked to borrow things from inmates who weren't dealers. That way, if there was anyone following me, they would hopefully get thrown off the scent. And also, if Comandante got busted by the police, I would be able to prove to him that I was trying my best not to cooperate.

I bought the stuff, slipped it into my shirtsleeve, ready to drop it if anyone stopped me, then hurried back to my room. Footsteps echoed in the corridor behind me. I wasn't sure if they were all mine, but I didn't stop or turn around to check. I climbed the wooden ladder to my room and knocked to gain entry.

The governor opened the door once more and when I handed him the package I closed my eyes, expecting to get arrested on the spot but he only inspected it and then handed it back to me.

'So. Is it good quality?' he asked, closing the door.

'I don't know, my governor. I don't take drugs.'

'Oh. So you've never taken cocaine, Thomas?' he asked sarcastically, showing off to the girls. 'What are you in here for? Didn't pay your parking fine?' Maria-Teresa laughed as if this was the funniest thing she had ever heard. Then the governor became serious again. 'Thomas. You make the lines, will you? I'm too lazy.'

Maybe the police wanted to catch me in the act; that way, I couldn't deny it was mine. I pretended I didn't know how to make lines, but Colonel Montesinos looked like he was losing his patience, so I did as I was told, cutting up some coke on the wooden table. However, I only made three lines so that they wouldn't think I had any intention of taking any myself.

'It looks good,' he commented, 'but we can't be giving the *señoritas* just any old rubbish. So, you try it first, Thomas, and let me know if it's good quality.'

When he said that, I was totally convinced that my friend, the governor, was setting me up. If the police caught me in my own room with five grams of cocaine, making lines on the table and actually sniffing it, there was no way I could deny a thing. But I refused to fall into their trap. They couldn't force me to take cocaine and if this conversation was being taped, I wanted my disagreement – and the governor's name – to be on record.

'With all due respect, Colonel Montesinos, you and I are friends and I respect you a lot, but you must look at it from my point of view. I am an inmate here and you are asking me to take drugs in front of you. You are the governor of the whole prison. I could get in a lot of trouble for that. If you are serious, then would you please go first?'

I tried to phrase this as politely as possible, bowing my head as I spoke, so as not to offend him, but it didn't work. The girls stared at me like I was crazy and the governor looked like he was ready to explode; however, not wanting to cause a scene in front of the company, he produced a note from his pocket and rolled it up, then bent forward over the table. Just as he was about to sniff one of the lines he stopped, sat back and said.

'What's this, Thomas? That's not how you make lines. Here, give me the stuff. And why are there only three lines when there are four of us?'

The governor pulled out an American Express card and scraped the cocaine from my table onto a plastic CD cover, then added more from the bag. In a matter of seconds, he had four massive, perfectly parallel lines of cocaine laid out on the smooth surface of the CD case. Not even Jack could have made them better; you had to go to university for that.

The governor bent forward and took one of the lines, half in each nostril, like a true professional, then sat down in the chair for a minute with his head tilted back, as though he was concentrating.

'Not bad. A bit too much acetone, maybe. But not bad, Thomas. *Primera clase*. Well done, my friend.' He handed the note to one of the girls and the CD case went around and finally came to me. As I sniffed back my line, I kept an eye on the door, half-expecting it to be knocked down by a tactical response team and the two girls to pull out undercover police badges. But nothing happened. I finally relaxed and even allowed a little laugh to escape. It had all been in my imagination.

'Thomas, you are acting very strangely tonight. What's wrong, my friend?'

'I'm just tired, I guess,' I said.

The girls tipped back their whiskies and made a few trilling noises as the coke hit home. I sighed. The danger had passed, but it was still going to be a long and interesting night.

131

13
THE INTERNATIONAL UNIVERSITY OF COCAINE

O nce I was friends with the governor, I managed to get the FELCN police to return my possessions. A *taxista* called me to the front gate where several boxes were waiting for me. When I sorted through the boxes, I noticed that most of the valuable items were missing: my money, my best clothes and my gold jewellery, including my good luck ring. Surprisingly, however, they gave me back my industrial hair dryer and steamer, which were worth over a thousand dollars each. They probably didn't know what they were.

My machines were still in pieces from when the colonel's men had dismantled them at the airport. I reassembled them but, unfortunately, I didn't have them for very long. Ricardo had told me about surprise raids the police sometimes conducted, known as *requisas*. He told me to be careful when they searched my room, because they often planted drugs, then asked for a bribe to make them disappear, especially with foreigners and new prisoners. The best way to avoid this was to demand that a witness be present during the search.

The first time the police performed a *requisa* in my room, I didn't have time to call a witness. Immediately, four policemen crowded around my steamer, blocking my view.

'Stand still. Right there!' they ordered me when I tried to get closer to make sure they couldn't plant anything.

I stood by helplessly as, one by one, they inspected inside the head mechanism while the others stood back, nodding and whispering to each other. Any second, I was expecting one of them to produce a bag of cocaine. But they didn't. They continued pointing and whispering to each other as if they had found something suspicious, although they weren't quite sure what. It took me some time to realise that it wasn't anything hidden inside the steamer that they were concerned with, but the steamer itself. They started backing away from it.

'Careful. Don't get too close,' the policeman who had made the original finding warned his friend who was sneaking up for another look.

They backed away towards the kitchenette, leaving me standing in the middle of the room wondering what was going on. They spoke in hushed tones, so I couldn't pick up much. However, I did hear one word repeated several times: *bomba*. I laughed to myself.

'It's not a bomb,' I said loudly, smiling in relief. 'I'll show you.' I bent down, picked up the power cable and went to plug it in at the wall but two of the police crash-tackled me to the ground before I could get there. The lieutenant then jumped on top of me, digging his knee into my neck.

At that exact moment, the major in charge of the prison *requisa* appeared in the doorway. He took one look at me choking on the ground and immediately demanded an explanation. The lieutenant did a re-enactment of what had just happened, completely exaggerating the part where I went to plug in the steamer. He made me look like a suicidal terrorist making a desperate leap with a fuse in my hand, and himself look like an action hero who had stopped me. The major glared at me. He wouldn't go near the machine, but he wouldn't let me get up to tell my side of the story either. Since the policemen were still sitting on top of me, I couldn't show him how the machine worked. I did my best to explain without the use of my hands, but admittedly, I was never good at doing sound effects and my impression of the noise the steamer made did sound rather like a bomb exploding.

My machines were confiscated and the governor couldn't get them back for me. I didn't want to push him. There was still so much more for me to learn about the way things worked and I might need his help in more important matters.

San Pedro wasn't like any other prison – it was like a small city with its own unique set of rules and its own bizarre economy. For a start, you couldn't count on the prison administration for anything, not even to maintain the buildings, so everything that needed to be done or bought was done or bought by the prisoners themselves. And because of this, anyone who wasn't independently wealthy had to have a job.

At the very top of the prison economy were the big businessmen who continued to manage their empires using specially installed fax and phone lines. Among them was San Pedro's most notorious inmate. Barbachoca – 'Red Beard' – had been charged with trafficking 4.2 tonnes of cocaine after his aeroplane, which the newspapers called 'el narco avion', was intercepted in Lima, in Peru.

The prison middle class was made up of those inmates lucky enough to have had a trade or profession on the outside that they could continue to practise on the inside. There were cooks, painters, restaurateurs, carpenters, electricians, cleaners, accountants and doctors. There were *artesanos* who sold their artwork and tiny handicrafts – such as paintings and figurines – to visitors. There was even a lawyer in for fraud, who, although he obviously couldn't accompany them to court, offered cheap legal advice to the inmates. Basically, anything you wanted done or anything you wanted to buy, you could, and if they didn't have it, someone could get it in for you for a small commission. But in fact, many of the services were actually cheaper than on the outside, so sometimes bargain hunters came into the prison to visit imprisoned barbers and dentists who offered cut-price deals to attract trade.

At the very bottom of the economy were those who didn't have a trade or profession, but who performed the countless small jobs around the place that needed to be done. These ranged from being one of the messengers – known as *taxistas* – who informed inmates when they had a visitor waiting at the gate, to people who shined shoes or sold tokens for the phone cabins. These prisoners made next to nothing, but at least they managed to stay alive.

And finally, for those who couldn't find a ticket to survival within the legitimate economy, there was an even bigger black-market economy in which inmates could continue to practise their other trade – being criminals.

〜〜〜

They say that prisons don't actually help to reform prisoners; that, in fact, they make them worse because all the time they are mixing with other convicted felons, which allows them to make new contacts and share knowledge and skills that help them to commit bigger and better crimes once they get out. Well, if prisons are no more than schools for further criminality, then San Pedro prison was the International University of Cocaine, where you could study under some of South America's leading professors: laboratory chemists, expert accountants and worldly businessmen.

And at this particular university, students didn't even have to wait until they graduated and got back out into the wide world in order to start practising their careers. We had all the necessary conditions to work right there on the inside, including investment capital, factories, a captive labour force, transport couriers, telephones and faxes, as well as friendly police who got their cut for looking the other way.

There were all sorts of scams going on inside the prison, but the main business was definitely drugs; that was what most of us had been convicted for and that was the most profitable product to sell. Trading in cocaine was so common that in San Pedro it was simply known as *negocios* – 'business'. Everyone in prison talked about *negocios*, which was natural enough – they all needed money and, for many, that was the only way they knew how to get it.

Reasonable cash could be made by supplying the local demand, including the La Paz market and inside the prison itself, but of course the highest profits were to be made in exportation. And in the case of exporting cocaine, the fact that I was a foreigner worked to my advantage, for a change. Bolivia, being one of the biggest cocaine producers in the world and San Pedro prison being where many of the sellers were concentrated, there was no shortage of people willing and able to export; however, what these people didn't have were buyers at the other end. And that was what I did have. I knew the European market, and my people with ready cash had exactly the opposite problem: they didn't have sellers. Because of this, the other inmates were always making me business proposals that involved using my contacts. At first, I wasn't interested. I knew there was definitely money to be made, which would have been helpful when I got out, but I had recently sent five thousand dollars to the judge and I believed that I would be leaving San Pedro shortly anyway. My lawyers promised me it would be before Christmas. There was no point in taking any stupid risks that might jeopardise my chances.

The fact of being stuck in prison meant that the risks were definitely higher, since I would have no choice other than to rely on outside people whom I hadn't met. It had always been my policy not to work with people I didn't know, and I already knew that you could trust barely anyone in Bolivia – I had learned that the hard way with Colonel Lanza, who I still intended to kill when I got out – but it was even more obvious in prison where people were desperate and would betray you for only a few bolivianos.

First, there was a chance that someone might try to set you up with the police. More likely, though, they would just rip you off. That could be done easily enough – once you have hooked up the buyer and the seller and they have done the exchange, how can you make sure you're going to get your cut? Your business partners could say that the deal didn't go through or that they hadn't received the money, or they could just disappear completely. And what are you going to do about it when you're locked up in prison? We had telephones and we could send the merchandise directly from the prison, but once it left our hands, how could we solve any problems?

Fortunately, Juan Carlos Abregon was one person I could trust.

14

ABREGON: BROTHERS IN CRIME

J uan Carlos Abregon was a smart man. He always had cash and if he
didn't, then he could get his hands on some, if he wanted to. I
don't know how he did it, but he always managed somehow.
Apparently, he had been busted for his part in a drug ring in the city
of Santa Cruz, although they never got him with anything, so maybe
he still had some funds stashed away somewhere. From what people
told me, his fortune had gone up and down over the years. Even when
it went down, like now, when he was in prison, he always came up
with some new plan to get rich and, more often than not, he pulled
it off.

Abregon was also a tough man, you could tell that much straight
away. He wasn't big, but even if you had never met him before, you
could tell that he was tough by his eyes and his silence. Physically,
he was no different from most of the men from Santa Cruz: he was of
medium height with dark skin and a small pot belly from eating so
well. He also had the obligatory moustache that all the men from those
parts had at the time. No one was exactly afraid of him, but he was
given a certain amount of respect for being dangerous, although I
didn't know what he had done to earn his reputation. Occasionally he
got moody and would refuse to speak to anyone. But when that
happened, you just knew to stay out of his way. Mostly, he was friendly
enough; he shook hands and made small talk with people he passed in
the corridors. So, tough and moody, yes. But dangerous, no.

It took a while for us to become friends, or even to meet each other,
for that matter. He didn't associate much with other prisoners, so no
one really knew him too well, which may have been part of the reason
why he had maintained his reputation for being dangerous. Abregon

never had many visitors to his room except for one girl who came to see him a few times a week. She was quite a lot younger than he was, and apart from the fact that her name was Raquel and that she was from Santa Cruz, no one knew anything about her. Whenever she came to see him, the door would remain locked until it was time for visitors to leave, at which point he would walk her to the main gate and wait with her in the queue until she left.

Abregon later told me that Raquel was his wife, although it seemed to me, from the way they acted, that they hadn't known each other for very long, maybe since just before he went to prison, or maybe even while he was inside. He never told me the full story, not even when we became brothers. Anyway, it seemed that Raquel was going to stick by him. Anyone whose wife or girlfriend stands by them and visits them all the time in prison is a lucky man.

When Abregon and I did finally meet, we established a kind of mutual respect immediately. He already knew who I was, because all the foreigners in the prison stood out a mile, and I knew about him by reputation. After a few months we became good friends, and eventually I was one of the very few people he allowed into his room. Even then, we never really discussed personal things too much. Abregon was fairly secretive about his past and we always spoke about things in a general, roundabout kind of way. I liked the way that he talked *negocios*, though; he talked about it a lot, but he never boasted about his direct involvement because he never needed to.

In fact, he never told me anything about himself even when, after several more months of friendship, we made a brotherhood pact: we swore that we would always do whatever we could to look after each other, and whichever one of us got out first couldn't rest until the other one was free.

It was strange to have someone that I could count on as a brother, but who wouldn't tell me anything important about his life. However, that was the way it was with us and the fact that he was so serious and disciplined about it made me even more confident that I could trust him in everything. I knew that he would never get me in trouble if something went wrong with any of our joint *negocios*, which is why I agreed to do that first prison deal.

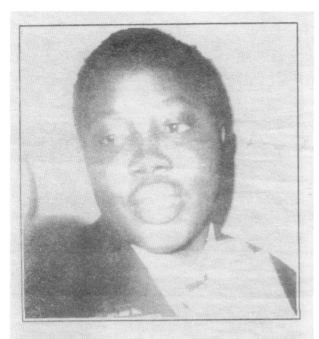

This newspaper article states that FELCN agents, with the help of trained drug detection dogs, intercepted 'Thomas MacFaddon' at El Alto Airport. The headline reads: 'The FELCN detain an Englishman with 850 grams of cocaine'.

La FELCN detuvo a un inglés con 850 gramos de cocaína

El súbdito inglés Thomas Mac Faddon fue capturado ayer en el aeropuerto de El Alto cuando intentaba traficar 850 gramos de cocaína escondida en el fondo de dos maletas, informó el director distrital de la FELCN, Médardo Flores.

Mac Faddon intentaba abordar un vuelo del Lloyd Aéreo Boliviano, pero fue sorprendido por los efectivos de la FELCN con la ayuda de canes especialmente entrenados para detección de drogas.

Flores explicó que el ciudadano inglés tenía visa de turista y que llegó a La Paz el 4 de abril desde Brasil. Ayer pretendió abordar el avión con un itinerario de escala en Santa Cruz de la Sierra, San Pablo, París y finalmente Inglaterra.

En presencia del fiscal de narcóticos se procedió a la apertura de las maletas y en las próximas horas se llevará a cabo la investigación pertinente al caso.

Según el director distrital de la FELCN, el de ayer es el tercer operativo que se realiza en el Aeropuerto Internacional de El Alto y recalcó que los detalles de la investigación se llevarán a cabo en los proximos días.

Por su parte, Mac Fadden dijo que desconocía la procedencia de la droga, que nunca la compró y que no sabe cómo apareció en ambas maletas.

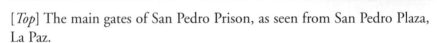

[*Top*] The main gates of San Pedro Prison, as seen from San Pedro Plaza, La Paz.

[*Bottom*] The main gates from inside the prison. Messengers are paid a small amount of money to wait at the gates and fetch inmates when visitors arrive.

[*Top*] A cell door in San Pedro's 'one-star' section.

[*Bottom*] The main prison courtyard – a place for socialising and drying washing.

[*Right*] Some of the wives of San Pedro inmates sell fruit and vegetables in market stalls inside the prison.

NIELS VAN IPEREN

[*Left*] One of the many restaurants owned and run by inmates.

NIELS VAN IPEREN

[*Right*] Playing draughts is a popular pastime in San Pedro.

NIELS VAN IPEREN

TRANSFERIDO A THOMAS McFADDEN

TÍTULO PROPIETARIO
DE CELDA SECCIÓN "ALAMOS"

SECCIÓN "ALAMOS"

CELDA No -104- UBICACIÓN PLANTA BAJA

SE REGISTRA AL NOMBRE DE SR. JULIO ESPINOZA ANTELO

VALOR ESTIPULADO $US. 400.- CARACTERÍSTICAS UN AMBIENTE

MONTO ADJUDICADO POR TRANSFERENCIA $US. 50.-

Registro No 104-05-97 Recibo por Pago de % Transf. No 001881

Fecha de Emisión San Pedro 15 de ABRIL de 1997.

DELEGADO DE SECCIÓN   STRIO. DE HACIENDA   PROPIETARIO

[*Top*] San Pedro prisoners are obliged to purchase their cells. Upon payment, they receive an official Cell Title, which is signed and stamped by the section delegate and treasurer.

[*Bottom*] Thomas in his Alamos 'cell' with a Bolivian inmate.

[*Top*] Cells in some sections of San Pedro have all the luxuries of a modern hotel – a comfortable bed, private bathroom and cable television.

[*Right*] Poorer inmates sleep in cramped dormitories, sometimes sharing a tiny living space with up to four or five other people.

NIELS VAN IPEREN

[*Top*] Children live in San Pedro with their imprisoned fathers. During the day they leave the prison to attend local schools.

[*Bottom*] Thomas with the daughter of an inmate.

[*Top*] Poorer inmates perform section chores such as sweeping and cleaning the bathrooms in return for cheaper rent.

[*Bottom*] An inmate making handicrafts to sell to visitors and tourists.

The Alamos section courtyard, with Barbachoca's two-storey apartment (top left).

[*Top*] Some inmates run small businesses from their cells in order to make a living inside the prison. Thomas supplemented the income from his shop by charging a fee for his prison tours.

[*Right*] Many of the conveniences of the outside world are available in San Pedro. This small business offers photographic services.

One of the crude cocaine manufacturing laboratories, set up in an inmate's cell.

[*Right*] Lucho, Thomas's bodyguard and one of the most feared inmates in San Pedro, shows his softer side.

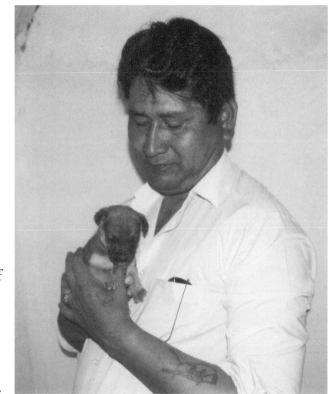

[*Bottom*] Many of San Pedro's inmates keep pets. Some, like 'Crack Cat', become addicted to cocaine smoke.

[*Top*] Inmates pass the time talking and playing games. During the day, San Pedro is a relatively safe place.

[*Bottom*] *La piscina*, the prison 'swimming pool'.

[*Top*] San Pedro inmates are permitted to vote in national elections. Here Thomas appears with a female political candidate who campaigned inside the prison.

[*Bottom*] Cocaine is widely available in San Pedro, though the majority of inmates can't afford it.

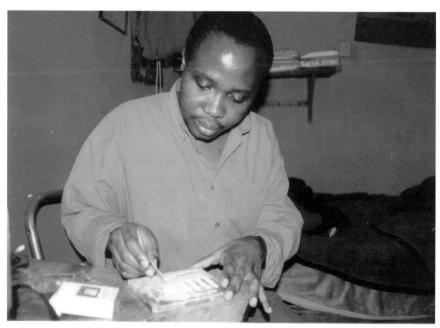

[*Top*] San Pedro became one of the most popular tourist attractions in Bolivia. As well as taking guided tours of the various sections of the prison, visitors could also stay the night.

[*Left*] Thomas and Rusty, his 'international human rights lawyer', before Thomas's court appearance for drug charges.

[*Top*] Rusty and Thomas organising a colouring-in competition with some of the San Pedro children.

[*Bottom*] Thomas and Rusty in Thomas's cell.

Having my credit card and the money sent by my friends in Europe meant that I wasn't forced to get a job in the prison or become involved in *negocios*. However, Abregon's first proposal was too good to refuse – he would put up all the money and organise everything, while I simply had to find a reliable buyer in Europe who could be trusted to pay when the merchandise arrived. We would split the profit fifty-fifty. I could use the money to pay my lawyers, bribe the judges or save it for when I got out.

The deal came off. There were some small hitches and we had to pay a few people more than expected, but the deal went through and Abregon received our sixty thousand dollars. I asked for my share straight away. I paid five thousand dollars to my lawyers, and sent another ten thousand for the judge – making the total five thousand more than he had asked. My lawyers were now one hundred per cent confident I'd get off. It was only a matter of waiting a little while longer. But the trouble was where to keep the rest of the cash in the meantime. At any time the police could raid my room (particularly if anyone found out about the money) or I might be sent to Chonchocoro, the maximum-security prison, before my trial began. Abregon had legal bank accounts outside where he could safeguard the money for me. So, that's what I did with my remaining fifteen thousand. Abregon put some of his in the bank, but no one ever messed with him – not even the police – so he often kept a lot of money in his room for when he needed it on short notice.

Not long after that first deal, Abregon's brother-in-law suggested another scam, which was also very easy money: bringing stolen cars across the border from Chile and rebirthing them. Bolivia was a far poorer country than Chile, so the price you could get for stolen cars was a lot lower, but it was far easier and safer to get rid of them because the controls on secondhand car sales were almost non-existent. With a little help from the police, you could be the legal owner holding all the right papers. And how would anyone from another country ever trace a stolen car in a place like Bolivia?

It sounded too good to be true and I wondered why other people weren't doing it. The answer: *capital.* Abregon explained to me that lots of people knew about it, but not everyone could do it because you needed to put up a significant investment to buy the cars in the first place, which most people didn't have. However, once you had that money, you could make a lot more and then, by reinvesting the profits and doing it on a bigger and bigger scale, even more money could be made. I was reluctant because it required me to hand over ten thousand dollars to Raquel's brother, who I didn't know. I would have only five thousand dollars remaining in the bank, but Abregon convinced me that after two or three times I would have enough money to bribe my way out of prison on the spot and then live like a king on the outside.

15
A NIGHT ON THE TOWN

Once I had established myself, life in prison wasn't too hard. I had my own comfortable cell with a warm bed, kitchen facilities, a stereo system, a mobile phone and a television. I had bought new clothes, was back to full health and never hungry, and the other inmates had stopped attacking me. I also had the protection of the governor, and with all the cocaine parties and my new friends, those first few months passed fairly quickly. I kept my spirits up because I was constantly learning new things and, best of all, I had my freedom to look forward to and hopefully a big chunk of money from the secondhand car deal to go with it.

However, I noticed that things really started to slow down around late October. It had been six months since I had arrived, and obtaining my freedom was taking a lot longer than my lawyers had first promised. I know I shouldn't complain, because prison life was pretty soft. The only obligation was to be out of bed for the morning roll call, known as the *lista*. After that, the guards almost never entered the prison complex, so I could do anything I wanted: I could sleep all day, study Spanish, cook a meal, smoke dope, read, talk with Ricardo, get drunk, watch television or sniff cocaine with Jack.

So, as far as prisons go, San Pedro was a good one. But it was still a prison. I was still stuck there all day, every day; I still had to sleep on the same mattress every night; I still had to wake up every morning surrounded by the same four walls and look up at the same ceiling. And although I was now free to move around the other sections during the day, I didn't feel completely safe doing so. The other prisoners still resented me for being a foreigner, so I kept to myself a lot of the time. When I wasn't taking cocaine with Jack, I spent entire days locked in my room doing almost nothing. It felt like I was slowly going crazy from being in the one place all the time and never meeting anybody new.

The worst days were Thursdays and Sundays, which were visitors' days. You might think that I would have enjoyed the contact with the outside world, but I didn't. There were certainly more people around on those days – families queued up outside the gates from early in the morning and stayed until the last bell, and in between times the place was filled with the colourful dresses and lovely smiles and laughter of wives, girlfriends and children. But all this only made me feel lonelier. I had no family in South America, so no one came to visit me. The few inmates I had made friends with were busy with their own families and didn't want to be disturbed. I needed to do something about it.

One Saturday I was feeling even more restless than usual. It had been months since I had been dancing and talked with pretty girls, so I decided that I would go out and find some action. I took a shower, dressed in a casual shirt with my best suit, which I'd had drycleaned by one of the wives, put on some cologne, and went to speak with the major on duty about taking supervised prison leave for a night on the town. The major said that it would cost me one hundred dollars, plus the cost of my police escort, which I calculated would probably be another thirty dollars. I agreed to the price. I left San Pedro prison that afternoon at three o'clock through the main prison gates, in full view of all the other inmates. I had twelve hours of prison leave before I had to be back in my cell.

My escort was a short, stocky policeman called Jaime. He had strict instructions to keep an eye on me and make sure that I returned to the prison on time. The first thing I wanted to do was eat a nice meal, so I ordered the taxi driver to take us to the most expensive hotel in La Paz. On the way, we stopped at a jewellery store on the Prado so that I could buy a watch to replace the one the FELCN police had stolen from me. When Jaime wasn't looking on the way out, I bought him a cheap watch also and gave it to him as a present in the taxi. Our relationship was off to a good start.

We must have made an odd couple walking past the hotel reception – a Bolivian dressed casually in old jeans and a red T-shirt accompanying a foreigner dressed in a smart suit.

'A table for two, please,' I said to the head waiter as we entered the restaurant. He raised his eyebrows, but said nothing.

Two waiters showed us to a table and pulled out our chairs so that we could sit down. Then another waiter came over and handed us leather-bound menus and explained the specials of the day in great detail. Finally, a fourth waiter brought me the wine list. It felt strange dealing with these situations again and I almost didn't know how to act. At first, I couldn't get used to having such well-mannered people dressed in bow ties treating me with such courtesy. In the San Pedro restaurants, I only ever heard grunts and the sound of my cutlery being thrown down on the table in front of me. I had forgotten how, outside prison, free people will treat you like a king if you pay them enough, and I almost felt guilty about all the fuss the waiters were making over me. In fact, I became paranoid that they were being *too* nice, calling me '*señor*' all the time and bowing every time I said something.

They must know, I thought.

It took me several hours to get rid of the feeling that I had a big sign on my forehead saying 'Prisoner', so that everyone who saw me knew immediately that I was a cocaine trafficker. Of course, there is no way they could actually have known, but I kept looking suspiciously at the waiters to see if they were watching me, just in case. Jaime was also looking around, but with a look of absolute amazement on his face.

He must have been about thirty-five but for some reason was still only a private. I had seen him around the prison gates many times, but he was always fairly quiet and stayed out of everyone's way so I had never had much to do with him. I couldn't work him out but I could tell that he was very serious and responsible, which is probably why the major had chosen him to accompany me.

I doubt that Jaime had ever been to a restaurant of that quality in his whole life; the meal would have cost him a month's salary. He didn't know which spoon to use for the soup, and he slouched in his chair and forgot to use the napkin. I was tempted to correct his manners, but I didn't want to ruin the moment by arguing with the person I would be spending the next twelve hours with. Besides, I didn't want to spoil his fun either – although he was awkward with his table manners, he was obviously enjoying himself a great deal.

'Would you like a beer, *señor*?' asked the waiter. 'Paceña?'

As soon as I thought of Paceña beer, I remembered Colonel Lanza instructing me on how to pour beer in La Paz. And when I thought of the colonel and what he had done to me at the airport, I found myself screwing the napkin tightly around my fingers, cutting off the circulation. I tried not to think about Lanza because it made me so angry. Besides, it wouldn't be too long before I would get my revenge. Instead of a beer, I ordered an imported Chilean red from the wine menu. For the entrée, we had *camarones al ajillo* – prawns in a rich garlic sauce – a luxury in a landlocked country like Bolivia.

By the time the main course arrived, we had already finished the bottle of wine. I was finally beginning to relax and think like a normal person again, but when I got up to go to the toilet, Jaime jerked to attention and asked me where I was going. He insisted on accompanying me to the bathroom.

I guess he's only doing his job, I thought. Nevertheless, having a policeman look over my shoulder when I was standing at the urinal destroyed the illusion of freedom. I decided to look on the bright side, though. At least I'm not handcuffed, I thought, as we returned to our seats.

I ordered another bottle of the same wine to have with our main courses. We toasted to freedom and then set about eating our filet mignons. Jaime was already tipsy and when the waiter went to refill his glass, he covered it with his hand.

'If you can't drink any more, I'll drink the rest myself,' I teased him. He grabbed the bottle from the waiter and poured himself a glass, spilling some on the white tablecloth.

These Bolivians love to get drunk, but they really can't drink much, I thought. Perhaps I could get my escort paralytic and give him the slip?

'Don't be stupid, Thomas,' I told myself. I couldn't possibly. It wasn't worth the risk. My lawyers had already paid the judge and I would be free within a few weeks. They had promised that I would be out by Christmas at the latest. The money I had could last a few months, and if I was allowed out on prison leave occasionally, there was no reason to be stupid and risk getting more charges laid against me, which could mean five more years in prison.

With the next glass, we toasted the Republic of Bolivia and after that, Jaime wasn't following the conversation at all. He stopped eating and his head rolled to the side slightly as though he was about to fall asleep. Every now and then he would sit upright suddenly, raise his glass to Bolivia, take a sip of wine and then drift off again. As I ate my steak, I watched him closely. This time, when thoughts of escaping came to me again, I didn't stop them.

It certainly wouldn't be hard to trick him. He was already drunk. Another half a bottle of wine and he wouldn't know what was happening. But where would I go? I had no passport and knew no one in the city, apart from the prisoners in San Pedro. True, the money I had in my wallet would last several days, if not weeks, in such a cheap country. I could hide in a shabby hotel somewhere and they would never find me. However, if I wanted to move anywhere, I would run into trouble. My photo would be in the paper the next day, so I would never get very far travelling by public transport. It would also be dangerous in a private car, because there are military and police checkpoints on every road and I had no ID to show. I knew people who sold fake Bolivian IDs, but that would take time. And even if I could find a way to travel around safely, which country would I go to and how would I survive there? How could I get back to England without a proper passport? Even if I did get back, who was to say that England wouldn't send me straight back to Bolivia? It probably had an extradition treaty or something similar.

I couldn't do it, I decided. If I was going to make a break, it would have to be planned and timed perfectly, because if the police captured me, they would probably beat me to death. And if the guards didn't kill me, the inmates certainly would, because if anyone escaped while on prison leave, the privilege would be taken away forever. So, it was a stupid idea. I only had to hold out a few more weeks. I took another big sip of wine and tried not to think about the fact that I was still a prisoner. I should just try to enjoy myself.

For dessert I ordered tiramisu and when we had finished that, there was still half a bottle of wine left. Jaime shook his head when I offered him more. Although I was a bit drunk myself, I wasn't going to waste expensive imported wine. Besides, there was plenty of time and I was in no hurry to leave. I carefully filled my glass to two-thirds and took my time enjoying each sip. Then I began to look around the restaurant again, taking in even the smallest details, as I did in airports. I had decided not to escape, but I still wanted to remember the look and location of every single object. There was a chance that it might be some time before I got the opportunity to be in a place like this again, but the memories would last me ages, if I created them properly.

Neither of us said anything for a long time and I was lost in my own thoughts until the drinks waiter came over and poured the remaining wine.

'Anything more?' he asked.

I shook my head, and five minutes later the head waiter presented me with the bill. The hotel guests had begun to drift into the restaurant for dinner and it seemed that they wanted us to leave. I drank the remaining wine, paid the cashier and we made our way shakily out of the restaurant, quite drunk. It was still light outside and far too early to go to a bar, but there was another thing I missed doing in prison: going to the movies.

I was about to get in a taxi, but Jaime told me the cinemas were within walking distance. It was further than he made it sound but I was glad that we went on foot – just being free in the streets was a pleasure I hadn't experienced in a long time. The thing I liked most was that no one really paid me any attention. The 'Prisoner' sign on my forehead had obviously disappeared completely, because most of the people on the street didn't look at me twice. They seemed to be just doing their own thing. It may sound strange, but being completely ignored made me feel more like a normal member of society.

When we reached the cinema strip, I thought the area looked familiar. Then I remembered that I had seen it from Colonel Lanza's four-wheel drive on the way to his house. We were on the main road called the Prado, just up from the large roundabout intersection that marks the Plaza del Estudiante.

I looked at all the posters and decided on an American action film that was about to start. There were two types of tickets you could buy, depending on whether you wanted to sit upstairs or downstairs. I couldn't believe how cheap it was, even for the first-class *galería* tickets, but I understood why when we sat down and the movie started. It was impossible to get comfortable on the hard wooden seats, and the sound was so bad that I could hardly understand what was being said, even though it was supposed to be in English. The Bolivians obviously didn't mind, since they were reading the subtitles.

After a while I managed to get settled and gradually, with the alcohol still in my system, I got sucked into the plot. It wasn't the most amazing movie I have ever seen, but I eventually became so absorbed in it that it didn't matter. For two hours I was so completely taken in that when we came out of the cinema, I hardly recognised where we were. The street had completely changed. Darkness had fallen and the city was starting to come alive.

There were so many more cars, honking and blocking up the roads. There were more people on the sidewalks: groups of young students wandering up and down the Prado and others gathered in small bunches in the strip that divides the traffic. To them, it was probably just an ordinary Saturday night – the girls were dressed up, everyone had started drinking and people were more relaxed – but to me, it was completely magical. It had been so long since I had felt the sense of anticipation that a Saturday night can evoke and a small wave of excitement came over me. I was going out on the town.

I knew exactly which club I wanted to go to, but it didn't start filling up until late. In the meantime, I didn't know the best place to be. It wasn't important, though, as long as I could have a drink and there were people to look at. The taxi driver took us back up towards the prison to a small bar called La Luna. The place was almost empty; the only people there were a few Argentinean *artesanos*, who tried to sell me handmade necklaces and some marijuana. However, the music was good, so I ordered a jug of beer and we sat at the bar. The bargirl kept playing a catchy song by Manu Chau that I had heard on the radio. I liked it because I could now recognise many of the words in Spanish and knew that they were singing something about Bolivia.

'*Boliviano clandestino. Mano negra ilegal.*'

We sat there drinking slowly until it was late enough to catch a taxi to Forum.

卌||

There was a queue outside the gate and when it was our turn to go through, the two muscly bouncers looked Jaime up and down in disgust. It was obvious they didn't like his cheap clothes. Forum was the number-one nightspot for foreigners and wealthy Bolivians. Anyone who was anyone in La Paz went there on Saturday night. Overseas DJs played the latest music, and the drinks were the same price as in Europe and America, if not higher. A nice cocktail could cost the same as the average weekly wage in Bolivia. Still, the women there were beautiful and all the clients had been to the United States and spoke English, so I was determined to get in.

I pleaded with the slightly friendlier-looking bouncer, telling him that I was a foreigner visiting Bolivia on business. I only had one weekend and had heard that this club was the best in the country. He shook his head. Then I asked him whether they accepted credit cards and let it slip that Jaime was actually my police bodyguard. Jaime played his part perfectly, too: he nodded that it was true and nervously flashed his police ID, all the while looking around to assess the security risk and consulting his new watch. Suddenly, the bouncer seemed more interested and started speaking quickly in Spanish. I was just about to ask him to repeat what he had said when I realised that he had an earphone and was talking into a small microphone pinned to his shirt. When he got a reply, his attitude changed completely.

'*Siga señor, por favor.*' He motioned for us go in and patted me on the back as I passed through. We didn't even have to pay.

At the end of the entrance passage, we came to two large, wooden doors, which were opened for us by an attendant. Almost immediately I was deafened by the electronic music and had to blink because of all the flashing lights overhead. Inside, the club was amazing. We were in a huge, open room that was split into two levels; the ground level had two bars with the dance floor in the centre and the upstairs section had a balcony that looked down over the dance floor. Both levels were packed with partygoers. Some danced salsa, while others jumped around to the European music. The clients in the exclusive upstairs section held on to the railing as they danced and watched everyone below. Around the dance floor small groups sat at tiny, black tables drinking rounds from bottles of imported alcohol, and along the outer walls there were more people seated in small booths.

I stood there taking all this in until a waiter offered to lead us to a table, where he asked us what we would like to drink. I ordered two Heinekens and had to pay up front. He came back almost immediately with the beers and the change, which I said he could keep. I always give the best tip of the evening on the first round to get better service. I looked around the club again. The atmosphere was alive but the place was almost too full and, to be honest, I felt a little anxious at first. The lights and the music and the bare skin all seemed to dissolve into my mind. Pretty girls looked me up and down. Some of them smiled. I tried to smile back without giving too much away, but it had been a while since I had played these games and I couldn't relax properly. I drank beer after beer and then switched to stronger drinks.

Surprisingly, Jaime was almost keeping up with me one for one. Given the price of the drinks, I knew that my money wouldn't last very long, so I went to the bathroom to have a line of the stuff I had brought from San Pedro. This time, my escort didn't follow me. Over the course of the afternoon, we seemed to have established a friendship, or perhaps he was just too drunk to care. I was drunk too, so the effect of the coke was even stronger than usual. I immediately felt in control. In fact, as I strode out of the bathroom, I was no longer an officially imprisoned man. I was wide awake and ready to meet the world.

A pretty girl dancing with her friend caught my eye. She was too beautiful for me, but I was high and feeling extremely confident so I called her over to where we were sitting. She whispered something to the friend, who shook her head and kept dancing, and the girl came on her own. Man, she was pretty, but she wasn't Bolivian. That much was obvious. I was talking a lot and asking a lot of questions and we hit it off straight away. Her name was Yasheeda and it turned out that she was from Israel. She was in La Paz for a week travelling with a group of friends after completing her national military service. Within a few minutes she asked me if I knew where we could get some cocaine. She had heard that Bolivia had the best in the world but didn't know where to get it. Her guidebook warned that it was too dangerous to buy it off the street, since the dealers often work with the police. 'Wait here, then, I'll see what I can do.' I went to the bar, bought her a drink and when I came back, I handed her the small envelope under the table. 'Wow! Thanks. That was quick! You're amazing! I'll be back in a minute.'

When Yasheeda returned from the bathroom, she was smiling. 'That stuff is strong!' she whispered, hugging me and slipping the package into my hand. 'Do you want another drink?' I asked. 'No way. I can't sit still. I have to move.' She grabbed my hand and we went out onto the dance floor together. I danced around her, and the shimmering lights above flowed into my eyes and I was drunk with life and with being alive and having blood in my veins and a beautiful girl in front of me. Man, she was pretty. And she seemed to like me, too.

16
YASHEEDA

Yasheeda had a magnificent air of untouchability, as if she knew that everyone in the room wanted her but no one could have her. But I had to try. It was now or never. I moved in to dance closer to her and touch her body. She let me hold her closely every now and then, but whenever we were too close she looked away over my shoulder so there was no chance to kiss her.

Maybe I have the wrong impression, I thought. Maybe she's just a friendly sort of girl. Or maybe she just wanted some coke.

I had to find out, though, so I pulled her in close and kissed her on the cheek. She laughed and broke away from me, twisting around the dance floor. She was still smiling at me, so when she came close again I kissed her lightly on the lips but this time she stopped dancing and went back to the table without saying a word.

At first I thought I had offended her but she waved to me to come over and I sat down next to her. 'Do you want another line?' I put my hand on her knee.

'You're not trying to seduce me, are you? It won't work,' she said provocatively.

'Not at all. I thought *you* were trying to seduce *me*. Would you like another line?' I asked again. She liked this play; the only way to approach confident girls is with confidence.

'I don't know if I should. I don't want to do anything I might regret,' she said, grabbing my hand again and dragging me towards the bathrooms.

'I promise you, you won't regret a thing,' I whispered in her ear.

I had forgotten the excitement of these chases; saying one thing and meaning another; with everything working on touch and smell and some innate sense; the knowledge that every move is critical but not wanting to think about it too much – in case you got it wrong; the sense that there was nothing more important in the world than this moment and being able to touch this other person. This girl who was striding in front of me to the bathroom like a proud and playful kitten.

We both went into the men's toilets and quickly shut the cubicle door. There were four guys in the bathroom, but they didn't say anything. They hardly even looked up – this sort of thing was normal in South American nightclubs. Occasionally, the police did raids on places, but usually there was a tip-off beforehand so that the management could clear the bathrooms. I made two lines of unequal size and quickly sniffed the smaller one. I handed Yasheeda the rolled-up note, hoping she hadn't seen what I had done. There was hardly enough space for two people standing in the cubicle and it was almost impossible for our bodies not to be touching. As she leaned forward to take her line, I rested my hand on the exposed part of her back and shoulders and stroked her skin gently. When she stood back up, with the note still in hand, her face had changed.

Something about the excitement of the confined space, the danger of the situation and maybe the drug had transformed her expression so that I couldn't tell what she was thinking. I never expected that she would, at that moment, come for me, pressing herself against me and seeking out my mouth with hers. I leaned back against the cubicle wall as the cocaine rush shot through the floating drunkenness and I felt like I was somewhere out of my body watching the whole situation as she kissed me. Then someone banged on the door, telling us to hurry up.

We returned to the bar and Yasheeda went straight over to her friend, who had stopped dancing and was now sitting at a table on her own, looking extremely bored.

'This is Sharon.' Yasheeda introduced us and we shook hands, but it seemed the friend was angry and wanted to leave. It was already past three o'clock, so Jaime and I should have been leaving too, but I didn't care. I would deal with the major later. I felt really close to Yasheeda and wanted to be with her, but the night looked like it would come to a sudden end unless I could entertain her friend somehow.

I went to the bar where Jaime was slumped over on a stool and bought Sharon a cocktail. I was down to my last bolivianos, but hopefully it would keep her happy and give me more time with Yasheeda. I also dragged Jaime back to the table, hoping that he could keep her friend occupied. There was little chance of that, though, since Sharon spoke only the most basic Spanish and my escort was so drunk that he could hardly focus. He needed to wake up, so I offered him the envelope of coke but he suddenly became nervous and refused to take it. '*No consumo. Nunca consumo.*'

I knew this was all an act, though – hardly anyone in Bolivia ever admits to taking drugs, but a lot of people do it behind closed doors. How could you *not* take cocaine in a country where a gram is cheaper than a beer? Jaime eventually accepted the packet, saying it wasn't for him but for a friend he knew who took it, and went off to the bathroom. After that, he became more talkative and Yasheeda's friend played along politely, even though she was clearly bored by the standard list of questions he asked: 'Where are you from? You are very beautiful. Do you have a boyfriend?' She was rolling her eyes but he continued, oblivious. 'You are very pretty. What language do you speak in your country? Do you like La Paz?'

The nightclub was closing at four o'clock and I knew I had to go back to prison. There was nothing I could do about it, so I kissed Yasheeda again, though not as wildly as before. We stared into each other's eyes and I was so riveted by her that I only wished I could go somewhere private to spend more time with her.

'Where do you live?' she asked me. The question took me aback. I didn't want to lie, but I didn't have the energy to explain the whole situation to her.

'A place called San Pedro. Have you heard of it?'

'Oh, yes,' she said excitedly. 'I walked past there today. It's a really nice suburb. I'd love to see your house. Is it near San Pedro Plaza? That plaza is really pretty.'

Over the past twelve hours I had begun to believe I was a free man, and now the injustice of having to return to a prison cell irked me all the more.

'Yeah, right on the plaza,' I responded, trying not to show how sad I felt. 'You should come around and visit some time. I'll give you my mobile number if you like.' However, Yasheeda wasn't going to give up. I could tell that she was drunk and high as she leaned in close and whispered in my ear, 'So . . . who do you live with? Do you live on your own?'

'Yes. Sort of,' I smiled nervously, trying to avoid the question. I could tell that it was about to get difficult.

'What does "sort of" mean? Do you live with this Bolivian guy here or another friend, or do you live on your own?' Then her expression changed and she suddenly became suspicious. 'You don't have a wife, do you?'

'No. I'm not married,' I took a deep breath and decided to tell her the truth. 'Actually, I live in San Pedro prison.'

'What? I don't understand. You work there and that's where you sleep?' She had stopped being suspicious and now looked confused.

'No. I'm a prisoner there.'

'Very funny. No, seriously, where do you live?'

'I'm a prisoner in San Pedro. I live and sleep in the prison. Seriously,' I told her, trying my hardest to make it not sound like a joke, but she didn't believe me. She got really angry and shook her head at me, as if the whole time I had been deceiving her.

'You don't have to lie to me. I know you've got a girlfriend. I knew there was something strange about you. Getting me drunk and feeding me up on coke. I've met guys like you. Your girlfriend probably thinks you're an angel, right?' she said, leaping up from the table and taking a step away from me in disgust. Her friend also stood up, pleased that they were finally leaving.

'No. No. No. You've got it all wrong. Please listen. You have to listen to me. Please! I swear to you on my life that I'm a prisoner in San Pedro jail. This guy here is my escort for the night. I'm out on leave, but I have to go back now. You have to trust me,' I pleaded, taking a step forward and trying to put my arms around her, but she pushed me off.

'Get away from me!' she yelled, and the people sitting at the next table looked up. 'Leave me alone, will you?' She looked like she was about to cry but I kept trying to convince her in a soothing tone.

'I know it sounds unbelievable. I don't blame you. But it's true, I promise you. Yasheeda. Honestly. I paid to go out for the night. If you don't believe me, ask him!' I said, pointing at Jaime.

'Don't lie to me! I'm not a little girl.'

'I'm not lying, I promise you it's the truth. Ask him.' Yasheeda looked at Jaime who couldn't understand what was going on but knew there was some kind of argument. But then she shook her head again and took another step backwards. 'Why would I ask him? He'll only lie as well. He's your friend.'

'He is a policeman. He can show you his identity card, if you want.'

'Well, what did you do, then, if you are in prison? Kill someone?'

'No. Drugs.'

This seemed to make sense to her and I could see that she was no longer so sure that I was lying.

'I'm sorry. I just don't know what to believe. This coke is so strong. I don't know what I'm thinking. I don't even know you. I have to go now. I think it's best if I just go.'

'Well, if you don't believe me, why don't you come with me?' I said.

It was a big risk. The major would already need extra payment because we were late and it would be hard to convince him to let her in. However, it might just work and even if it didn't, at least she would see that I wasn't lying. Maybe she would come and see me on visitors' day.

'Come with you? What, to the prison, you mean?'

'Yes. My curfew was half an hour ago. I have to go back now.'

'You want me to come and see if you actually go into the prison? What's the point of that?' She was softening and I had my arms around her once more. 'No. I want you to come into the prison with me. To stay the night.' I kissed her. I felt her body relax. She was thinking about it. She said something to her friend, Sharon, in Hebrew and they had a short argument. Sharon was even more annoyed than before, but finally they agreed to something.

'OK, then. Let's go,' she announced and the two girls walked quickly towards the entrance to get their jackets, with Jaime and me trailing behind. I hailed a taxi and opened the back door for the girls. Jaime put his arm around Sharon to help her into the taxi but she broke away and got into a different taxi and drove off without saying goodbye to anyone. Yasheeda shrugged and we got into the back seat together, with Jaime sitting in the front. We kissed most of the way back to the plaza. The driver and Jaime kept their eyes straight ahead and said nothing until we pulled up outside San Pedro prison.

'*Muy bien, señor.*'

'Well, here we are. This is the prison,' I whispered to Yasheeda.

It was past four in the morning, so the plaza was completely empty and the metal gates of the jail were shut tight. Everything was completely quiet until we started banging and yelling to wake up the night watchman.

'Open up, please. Open the door! Are you there?' Eventually he stirred and went to fetch the major, who was the only one with keys. The major arrived and looked through the gap between the gates. He was clearly not pleased about being woken up.

'*Buenos días, mi mayor. ¿Cómo está?*' I whispered politely, trying to sound sober. There was a long pause, during which I assumed he was looking for the right key. But the gate didn't open.

'Are you there, major?'

'*Sí,*' he sounded tired and angry.

'I'm sorry, my major. Can I come in, please?' But he was obviously in no hurry to open the gates. He didn't answer.

'Major?' There was a long pause before he said anything. 'What time is it, *inglés?*'

'I'm sorry. I don't have a watch,' I said, slipping off my earlier purchase and hiding it in my pocket. Jaime did the same.

'Late.'

'I'm sorry. Can I come in, please?' It seemed ridiculous that I was pleading to be let back into prison, but that was what I was doing. In fact, I was even going to have to pay to be locked up again. 'Can we talk?' I asked, showing him my remaining money through the gap. I kept it scrunched up so he couldn't see the exact amount. I knew it wouldn't be enough, but I could promise to give him more later.

Finally, the heavy gates creaked open and I went through. Yasheeda waited outside and Jaime followed behind me, clearly drunk. The major must have been able to smell the alcohol on us, but he said nothing as he locked the gates behind us.

'My major, a favour, please,' I slipped the remaining notes into his top pocket so he wouldn't be able to count it until I was out of sight. 'My girlfriend has arrived from Israel. I haven't seen her for a year and I want to spend more time with her.'

'And?' Although there wasn't much light, I could see the major raise his eyebrows. 'Don't worry, my major. I will fix things with you later. We are friends. You have a wife. You understand,' I placed my hand on his shoulder and squeezed firmly. 'Please, I need your *colaboración.*'

The major said nothing for some time while he considered my offer. I had learned with the higher-ranking police that the length of the silence was usually proportional to the amount of bribe they required. This was a particularly long pause and I calculated it was going to cost me at least fifty bolivianos. But it would be worthwhile, if it worked.

'OK. *Más tarde*, then,' he finally agreed, unlocking the gates again.

'It's OK. You can come inside now,' I called to Yasheeda, who was standing just outside on the footpath, wrapped tightly against the cold in her thick jacket. By then, the cocaine and cocktails had started to wear off and she was faced with the prospect of voluntarily entering a third-world prison at four in the morning, accompanied by a drug trafficker whom she had only just met while he was on prison leave in a nightclub. Not surprisingly, she was a little hesitant.

'Is it safe?'

'I promise I will look after you if you come in. No one will touch you. But you don't have to come in, if you don't want to. There's no pressure. You can get a taxi back to the hostel and we can talk tomorrow, if you want.'

Yasheeda looked at me and then at the major. The major nodded to her. She hesitated for another moment, then made her mind up.

'It's already tomorrow,' she declared, passing through the gates. 'So, let's talk.'

卌ⅱ

It had been an exhilarating day and when we reached my door, I was very happy and completely exhausted. I wanted to go to bed, but Yasheeda got really excited as soon as I turned on the light in my room. She couldn't believe what she saw. 'This is actually your prison cell? But you've got absolutely everything here. Is this some kind of joke? It's not really a prison, is it?' she exclaimed, rushing back and forth from the kitchen into my bedroom, touching everything in sight and making a lot of noise. 'You've even got a fridge! And a television!'

'Cable.'

'This is a joke! There's no way this is a prison. It's impossible. It's more like a hotel. You know, it's actually better than the place where we're staying.'

I made her a cup of tea and we smoked a joint to relax.

'Just let me know if you're tired,' I said, hoping she would want to go to bed straight away.

'I am a bit, but have you got any of that coke left? That stuff really makes you want more, doesn't it?'

'OK, but let me make another joint first.'

We smoked that and I asked her again if she was tired, but it didn't work. She wanted to keep talking.

'You promised we could stay up and talk. Come on! Just for a little bit.'

That night we didn't do anything other than talk. I made four more lines, lit a candle, turned the light off and we stayed there, sitting next to each other at my little table, chatting about absolutely everything. Yasheeda and I had so much in common it was ridiculous. We had exactly the same taste in music and movies. We even liked the same food.

'When's your birthday?' she suddenly asked.

'Twentieth of November.'

'I knew it!'

'Knew what?'

'That you were a Scorpio.'

'How is that?'

'Just the way you are. You are *such* a Scorpio. It's so obvious.'

'Do you think? I don't really believe in astrology.'

'Well, you should. Not the horoscopes about romance and money they print every week in magazines – that's all rubbish. I mean the proper books on astrology. You can learn a lot about people.'

We talked and argued like that for hours until I heard the bell for morning *lista*. But I didn't go. I couldn't; there was no way I could face daylight in my state. I would have to fix the major up later.

We finished the rest of the coke and kept talking until the candle finally burned out. It must have been bright outside, but the one window in my cell had wooden shutters so everything went pitch-black.

'I think that's a sign,' she laughed.

'What a crazy night. What time is it?' I lit a match and read the time from the clock on the wall. 'Ten o'clock. Are you tired?'

'Yes and no. It's funny, I know I should be, but I don't feel tired at all,' she leaned against me.

'Why? Are you tired?'

'I think so.' I took her hand and led her over to my single bed and we got under the covers. My heart was beating heavily and my mind was still humming from the coke, but I fell into a kind of half-sleep, listening to her breathing beside me.

卌II

I woke up to find a beautiful woman sleeping in my bed. It was early afternoon but the room was totally dark, so I lit the candle on my bedside table and began to study her face as she slept. I couldn't make out all of her features properly, but I could tell that she was beautiful. She had the softest olive skin, dark hair and lovely long eyelashes. I propped myself up on one elbow to look at her from a different angle, but when she felt me moving, she began to stir. I heard her murmur something and then she hugged up to me closer, kissing me on the chest, even though she wasn't awake yet. I found, as I got to know her better, that Yasheeda was a naturally affectionate person; she was always touching me and even when she was asleep, she always held me tightly, as if by instinct, so that I couldn't leave her. I also discovered that she was a very determined person – when she had made a decision, she launched herself into it and never looked back. She was probably also a little crazy, though. There aren't many girls in the world who would have done what she had just done. I managed to get out of bed without waking her and made scrambled eggs and tea for breakfast. Just as I was ready to bring it over, she opened her eyes.

'Mmmm. Smells nice. I'm starving. What time is it?' I turned on the light and pointed to the clock. She swore in Hebrew.

'I have to go. Right now,' she said, grabbing the plate I was offering her and swallowing everything down in big mouthfuls. 'Sharon will be so worried about me. She's going to kill me.'

'Give her a call, then.'

'Can you phone from inside the prison?'

'Right here from this bed, if you want.' I took my mobile phone from the charger, switched it on and handed it to her. 'I can bring you a telephone directory from the office downstairs if you don't know the number.'

'The office?'

'Yeah, the section has an office where the delegate and secretary work. They have a phone and a computer down there for the business of the section.'

'Wow. This place is completely *loco*!'

'You're the one who's crazy,' I said playfully, taking the empty plate from her and kissing her.

'Why am I crazy?'

'Wanting to stay here with me in prison.'

'Well, you're crazy too, then. And it's your fault I'm in prison,' she kissed me on the lips, pulled me back into the bed and climbed on top of me.

'I think so. Crazy can be a good thing, you know. You have to be a bit crazy to survive in here.'

Yasheeda called El Lobo hostel where she was staying and told her friend Sharon that she was OK and would be back tomorrow. After that we only left the room twice: to go to the toilet and to fix things up with the major.

17
A VOLUNTARY INMATE

The next morning, Yasheeda called Sharon at the hostel again, saying that she was going to stay with me another night. This time, Sharon was even more worried. She thought that maybe I had kidnapped Yasheeda and was holding her hostage. I didn't understand the whole conversation, because most of it was in Hebrew, but Yasheeda switched into English a few times for my benefit.

'Look, I'm fine. Honestly. It's perfectly safe. There are women and children here . . . I can leave whenever I want . . . No, but I don't want to leave right now . . . I know, I know . . . but we can do the Salar of Uyuni tour in a few days . . . Seriously, I'm fine . . .'

I could hear Sharon yelling on the other end of the telephone. I couldn't really blame her; she was only acting as a good friend should and it must have been hard to believe that Yasheeda was perfectly happy and safe in prison with me.

'Why don't you go outside today and show her that you're fine,' I said. 'You can come back later. Or invite her to come in and see for herself.'

She did both. She went back to El Lobo and returned in the afternoon with Sharon and a bag of supplies, including fresh clothes. When the pair arrived at the gate, they sent a *taxista* to call me. Officially, we were only allowed visits from family and friends on Thursdays and Sundays between 9 am and 5 pm. Unofficially, you could receive visitors whenever you wanted, provided you paid. Even on non-visiting days, there was always a constant flow of people through the main gate: lawyers coming to see their clients, wives and girlfriends bringing food, and the San Pedro children travelling to and from school. All visitors had to leave their *carnet* – the national ID card – at the gate, and the head *taxista* made a note of their names and who they were visiting and they had to pay before leaving. The cost was only seven bolivianos, but with visitors for over a thousand inmates, the money from the gate added up to big business for the police.

At that stage, foreigner visitors without this national ID were rarely allowed to enter the prison. I explained to the lieutenant that my wife needed to come back in and her friend also wanted to visit me. They had come all the way from Israel. I was expecting him to argue, but luckily the Israeli girls' dark features meant they didn't stand out too much from the other wives and girlfriends. The lieutenant agreed to let them in, provided we went straight to my room and stayed there. We came to an arrangement that Yasheeda would pay twenty-five bolivianos to spend another night and her friend would pay the standard seven bolivianos to enter.

Sharon was still very suspicious of me, even though I tried my hardest to be polite and charming. I can usually make people laugh with some of my stories, but she didn't want to listen to me at all. I bought her a soft drink and tried to start up a conversation about where she had been travelling, but nothing seemed to work. I have never had so much trouble getting along with anyone in my whole life. Her face had that same sour expression as on the other night at Forum, so I made myself busy in the kitchen while the girls talked in Hebrew. They started having another argument. I wondered how the two of them had ever become friends. Yasheeda was so open and warm in everything she did, but her friend was the complete opposite – angry and cold, and she hardly ever said a word.

Yasheeda later explained that Sharon was angry with her for disrupting their travel plans. They had originally planned to catch a bus south with some other Israeli friends to see Potosí, the highest town in the world. The main attraction there is the ancient mines where workers still slave under the same conditions they suffered hundreds of years ago – breaking the hard rock using hammers and chisels with nothing more than a candle on their helmets for light, then carrying the sacks of broken rocks on their backs up to the surface through the dangerous mine shafts that are filled with toxic gases.

Afterwards, the group had planned to make a tour of the Salar of Uyuni, which is a salt lake that evaporated completely, leaving thousands of square miles of salt crystal. Although I had never been there,

I had seen photos of this incredible place. It is flat and white as far as the eye can see and many people have become lost out there, because there are no roads and it is completely empty except for the pure white of hard-packed salt.

Yasheeda didn't want to leave right then; she wanted to spend a few more days in La Paz. The Potosí mines and the salt plains of Uyuni would still be there next month, but it wasn't every day you could live in a prison. It was the experience of a lifetime. Sharon started yelling, saying that she and the others weren't prepared to wait. She left the prison, even angrier than when she had arrived. We waved goodbye to her from inside the gates, but she didn't look back. I felt a little sorry for her, but I was also glad that Yasheeda was going to stay. I was really starting to like her – a lot. Besides, they could meet up in a week or so and go travelling together again then.

Yasheeda stayed that night and the next, and then all the following week. Sometimes she left during the day to check her email and visit friends staying at El Lobo, but she would always return with provisions and small gifts for me. After ten days, she was friends with all the guards and had moved her belongings out of the hostel and into my room. We started living together in prison, sharing my single bed and eventually negotiated a weekly rate with the major, which worked out to be only slightly more expensive than the hostel she had been staying in.

Yasheeda's friends came back from the Salar of Uyuni tour two weeks after she had moved in with me. Their next adventure was going to be a downhill bike ride to a town called Coroico. Yasheeda had to go with them because they had planned this trip together back in Israel and she felt she couldn't let them down. She kept apologising and saying that she wanted to stay with me, but I could tell that, deep down, she was quite excited about going. I didn't want her to leave, but I also knew that I had no right to ask her to stay. She was young and beautiful and free, and she was in Bolivia for a holiday, not to live in prison. ·

'OK, then. Goodbye. Have fun,' I tried not to sound sad.

'Don't say that, Tommy.'

'Don't say what?'

'Goodbye. Never say "goodbye", Tommy. I don't believe in goodbyes. Goodbye is too permanent. You should always say "*Hasta luego*", like the Bolivians do. That way you will always meet up again sometime. Even if it's a long time in the future, you'll always meet again. One day, at least.'

'OK, then. *Hasta luego.*'

Yasheeda was away for exactly six-and-a-half days that first trip. I almost went out of my mind worrying about her. The bike ride was only supposed to take half a day, then the group had planned to spend the night in a hotel, wander around the town in the morning and come back to La Paz the following afternoon. However, she didn't arrive at the prison and she didn't call my mobile phone. I left it on the whole time and I must have checked the dial tone a hundred times to make sure the phone was working.

The road down to Coroico was officially the most dangerous road in the world; it twisted and turned along sheer cliff faces that dropped thousands of feet into the valleys below. In most parts, the dirt track was barely wide enough for one vehicle, but since it was the only road linking the town to La Paz, vehicles travelled in both directions. There was a fatal accident every single week. In fact, deaths on the road were so common that the media often didn't bother reporting them.

Nevertheless, I watched the news closely for accidents. On the fourth morning, I found a small article saying that a minibus had gone over the edge in the fog, killing eight people. The paper didn't mention if there were any foreigners involved, or even which direction the minibus was travelling. I rang the newspaper and television stations to try to find out. No one knew anything.

Eventually, Yasheeda turned up at the prison, tanned and smiling, like nothing had happened. I was so happy to see her and so relieved that she was alive, but I was angry with her. I was also angry with myself for letting myself think about her so much.

'Did you miss me?' she asked.

'A little bit,' I answered, not wanting to let on just how much she had put me through.

'Ohhh.' She appeared to be disappointed. 'Only a little bit?'

'No. A lot. I missed you a lot.'

'That's better,' she said, hugging me. 'We were having such a good time. You should be grateful I came back at all! The others are still down there. I came back especially for you.'

I doubted that was true. I didn't believe it until the next day.

18
HAPPY BIRTHDAY

When I came back from the bathroom the following morning, I got the shock of my life. At first, I thought I had walked into the wrong cell by mistake. There were about ten people, sitting around a table, wearing those party hats that are made of coloured tissue paper. They all looked up at me when they heard the door open.

'I'm so sorry. *Perdón*,' I mumbled, backing out into the corridor.

'*¡FELIZ CUMPLEAÑOS!*' they shouted at the tops of their voices.

It was only then that I recognised Jack, sitting there with his dark sunglasses on. And there was Carlos, with his wife next to him. And Ricardo. And most incredibly, up the far end of the table, sat Sylvia Venables, my 'angel' from the Anglican Church. She smiled at me and blew on her plastic party whistle, the type with paper that unravels when you blow into it.

Without warning, Yasheeda sprang out from behind the door. 'Surprise!' she yelled, kissing me on the lips and pushing me into a chair. 'You get to sit here at the head of the table, since you're the guest of honour.'

On the table in front of me sat a massive birthday cake. It was my birthday! I had completely forgotten about it. My birthday had always been important to me on the outside, but the thought of celebrating it in prison that year had made me deliberately wipe it from memory. However, Yasheeda hadn't forgotten. I couldn't remember when I had told her.

'I'm sorry, Tommy,' she apologised, lighting the candles. 'I didn't know how many candles to buy. How old are you?'

I still hadn't said a word. I was too stunned. I just sat there, looking around me.

In the time it had taken for me to walk down the stairs, take a shower and then return to my room, Yasheeda had completely transformed the entire space. She had put all my clothes away, made my bed, cleaned and tidied everything and moved all my furniture around to new positions. The bed was now up against the opposite wall, the table was in the centre of the room, the posters had been swapped over, and there were streamers and decorations dangling from the roof. It was no wonder I hadn't recognised my own room.

On top of that, she had managed to have all my friends arrive without me so much as suspecting. She could hardly speak Spanish, so I don't know how she had organised for the guests to be there exactly on time, or how she had known where to contact Sylvia. But she had.

'So. Do you like it?' Yasheeda asked, pointing at the new furniture arrangement. However, I still couldn't answer. I was speechless. Luckily, Ricardo came to my rescue.

'Well. Come on, Thomas. What do you think of your new décor?' he demanded, doing his gay interior designer act again.

Everyone laughed, but my eyes filled with tears. I didn't know what to say. No one had ever done anything like this for me before. Whenever I'd had a party on the outside, I'd had to buy the cake, invite the guests and do all the organising. But here I was, in a prison on the other side of the world where I barely knew anyone, the least likely place for anyone to celebrate my birthday, and Yasheeda had done all this for me.

'Happy birthday, Tommy,' she said when she had finished lighting all the candles, kissing me again.

'But . . . but how did you know?' I finally managed to stammer. No one in the prison knew.

'Oh, come on! Where's your memory gone, Mr Scorpio?' she teased. Then I remembered the conversation we had had about star signs on the night we'd met. 'That's right. Now you remember?' she said, seeing the recognition register in my eyes.

'Now, blow out the candles and make a wish,' urged Sylvia. 'And don't tell anyone, or it won't come true.'

I did as I was told and made a wish. Then they made me cut the cake. When the knife came out with crumbs on it, I had to kiss the prettiest girl in the room. I stood up and went around to give Sylvia a big kiss. Her pale cheeks turned bright red. The other guests thought this was hilarious.

'Stop it, Thomas,' she protested. 'Get your hands off me. I'm a religious woman and I'm old enough to be your mother. I don't dare to think what you may have wished for when you cut that cake.' Sylvia had a wicked sense of humour for someone who was the wife of an Anglican bishop.

We were all in high spirits after that, laughing and making jokes, but no one was higher than Jack, who I suspect was having an extra party of his own on the side. When I took the dirty plates back into the kitchen, he followed me. I could tell that he wanted to say something, but he was too nervous.

'Thomas. I . . . I just wanted to tell you that . . . well . . . you know what I wanted to tell you,' he said, reaching into the secret pocket sewn into the lining of his jeans. 'I got you a little present.'

'Not here, Jack!' I warned him, as he started opening up the small packet of cocaine.

'No one will see us,' he whispered. 'Just a quick little *puntito*. It's good stuff.'

'Not while everyone's still here. Try and be a bit considerate, Jack.'

Jack looked down, completely ashamed. 'No. You're completely right, Thomas. It's very rude of me. I'm sorry. It was very selfish of me.'

'That's OK. You don't have to apologise. I was mainly thinking of Sylvia.'

With that, Jack pricked up his ears. 'I didn't know Sylvia did coke!' he exclaimed. 'There's probably enough for her, too. But only her. There's not enough for everyone. So, we'll have to do it carefully. Don't tell Ricardo. You give Sylvia the signal and I'll –'

'Jack!' I interrupted him.

'Oh. I'm sorry. OK. Yes, you're completely right. Sorry. I thought you meant . . .'

༅༅༅

The party itself was a quiet affair. Because of Sylvia, we didn't buy any alcohol. She was now like a mother to me, so I didn't want her to think that I drank or did drugs in prison. Besides, we managed to have a lot of fun without drinking.

The guests departed just before lunchtime, and then everything went back to being really quiet. Jack stayed behind for a few minutes, wanting to do some coke, but I was already happy and didn't want to risk ruining it. He told me I was an ungrateful friend and took back the present he'd given me. He even did a few lines in front of me to show me what I was missing out on. Eventually, he took the hint and left also, leaving Yasheeda and me alone in the room at last. We lay down on my bed.

'I'm sorry I couldn't afford to get you a proper present, Tommy,' she said. 'I'm running out of money. I don't know how I'm going to afford Peru. But did you like your party?'

I nodded and looked around the room again, noting with approval all the changes she had made. With only a minimum of effort, Yasheeda had succeeded in making the whole place feel new. Once more, I didn't trust myself to speak. It was the best present anyone had ever given me.

卌〢

Yasheeda didn't need much sleep. From the moment she first opened her eyes in the morning, she was wide awake and full of energy. I, on the other hand, was always sleepy. Even when I didn't drink or take coke, I liked to sleep in. The morning after my birthday was no exception. We had gone to bed early, but I was still tired and wanted to catch up on some rest. However, she wouldn't let me.

'Tommy. Are you awake?' she asked, leaning across my body in order to light the candle. I never let her turn the lights on or open the window until I was ready.

'Mmmmm. I wasn't. But I am now.'

'Well. Come on then. Tell me!'

'Tell you what?' I was still half asleep.

'What you wished for.' It was way too early to play her guessing games, but that was another of her tricks; she would sometimes wake me up by asking me lots of questions that I had to think about.

'What I wished for when?'

'When you blew out the candles.' She was always doing that. Her mind went all over the place and often she'd come out with something that she was thinking about, assuming that I would automatically know what it was. Or she would suddenly decide to continue on from the middle of a conversation we'd had hours, or even days, before, but hadn't mentioned since.

'I can't tell you. Remember? Or it won't come true.' She had succeeded – I was awake now.

'That's OK. You don't have to tell me, Tommy. I already know any-way.' Now that she had my eyes open, Yasheeda clambered on top of me, kissing my ears playfully.

'All right. What was it, then?'

'To get out of prison.'

'No. Wrong.'

'Yes. Right. Don't lie to me, mister.' She slapped me lightly across the face, pretending to be angry. 'What else could you possibly want more?'

'No. Wrong.' I grabbed her wrist to stop her hitting me again and rubbed my cheek where she had slapped me, pretending it was sore.

'Yes! Right. Of course, I'm right. I know you, Tommy. That's what you would have wished for. And I can tell when you're lying, too,' she reprimanded me, shaking her finger in my face. 'So, don't even try it.'

Yasheeda could often guess what I was thinking, but on that occasion she was wrong. However, I couldn't tell her the truth. My wish hadn't been to be released from prison – I had wished for the first thing that had come into my mind and it was something I wanted even more than being allowed to go free. I had wished that she would stay with me forever. I didn't care where we were. Even if it meant being in prison, I just wanted her to be there next to me.

I couldn't say anything, though; in three days, she was leaving for Peru with Sharon. Seeing Machu Picchu and doing the Inca trail had been the whole reason behind them choosing South America. They'd had the trip planned for months and she couldn't break her promise.

'How long will you be gone?'

'I don't know, exactly. Maybe a month or two,' she answered, cautiously. Then, sensing my reaction, she added, 'But don't worry. I'll come back for you, Tommy.'

'Do you promise?'

'Of course, I promise. I came back last time, didn't I?'

19
CHRISTMAS IN PRISON

After Yasheeda left, I tried my hardest not to think about her, but it was impossible. Although we had only been together for five weeks, it felt like a lot longer because we had spent almost every minute of every day together and I was already used to having her around. I took the batteries out of my clock because I found that watching the hours go by made things go slower. Besides, what was the point of keeping track of time in prison? Without her, the only thing I had to do each day was report for the morning *lista*, and for that they always sounded a bell.

Basically, my life went back to being exactly the same as it was before we had met, only now it was worse because I had had a taste of what it was like to be happy again. I got back into my old routine, spending the days in my room and keeping myself as busy as possible with all the things I could do to take up time. But even without the ticking clock to remind me, each day passed very slowly.

After roll call, I slept for as long as possible and then took a long time over my grooming – showering, shaving, doing my hair and rubbing skin cream into my face. Next, I would clean the room for at least an hour. It was never really dirty because I never did anything that made any mess, so after a while I usually became bored. If I smoked a joint beforehand it made things a lot more fun because I would forget where I had put things and would have to spend ages trying to find them again. After cleaning and smoking, I always had a big appetite, especially if I hadn't eaten breakfast. I still loved preparing and cooking food, but it wasn't as enjoyable cooking a meal for only one person and sitting alone to eat it.

One thing I really liked to do was watch my favourite Latin talk show, *Laura*. The program was the same every single day, but it always made me laugh and I never missed it. Laura is a nice little middle-aged woman who invites couples to appear on national TV in front of a live audience and then asks them if they love each other.

'Yes, truly. Forever. Until I die,' they always answer. 'I couldn't be with anyone else. Never. Not even if you paid me.'

Laura then points to a big television screen that shows video footage of the man being unfaithful, and all hell breaks loose. The girlfriend starts screaming and attacking her boyfriend, but they calm her down and the boyfriend apologises for what he has done.

'That was a mistake,' he says. 'I'm so sorry. You're the only one. It was only the once with that girl. It didn't mean anything. I love you so much.'

Then Laura raises her eyebrows as if to say, 'Really? Is that so?' and again points to the big screen, which shows video footage of the man being unfaithful again, this time with another woman. The girlfriend starts going really crazy, breaking furniture in the process. Eventually, the security guards have to escort her off stage, while the audience cheers her and boos the boyfriend. Meanwhile, Laura gets the third tape cued up, just in case.

In the afternoons I read until my eyes hurt and then tried to watch the evening news, just as I used to do with Ricardo.

But things had changed. I hardly saw Ricardo these days, and I now found the news too depressing. There were never any happy stories. It was always about government corruption or murder, or something else bad that had happened in the world. The main news headlines at that time were about a gang of rapists that had finally been captured, and a government official, Gabriel Sanchez, who managed to run off with forty million dollars from a government workers' pension fund. They arrested him but let him go on bail and he fled the country, causing a scandal. When I couldn't handle watching television, I smoked dope and listened to Bob Marley on my tape player instead.

I had always liked Bob Marley's music, even before I went to prison. I had memories of hearing some of the classic songs on the radio from when I was a young boy, even before I knew that Bob Marley was the singer. Now that I was in San Pedro, I began to listen to the lyrics properly and I liked him even more. His music is really simple but powerful, and it gave me a lot of hope in my difficult times. Whenever

I felt bad, I would smoke a joint and put on a cassette of his and he would chill me down a lot. Listening to Bob made me realise that I wasn't the only one who had faced tough things in life. It helped, but it didn't make me stop thinking about Yasheeda.

The time of day I missed her most was in the evening, when the prison went quiet for a few hours while everyone was cooking. That was when we used to have our best conversations. I also missed her during the nights. It took longer to get warm when I went to bed. It also took ages to get to sleep, even if I smoked a lot of dope. One night I had a terrible dream that she hadn't gone to Machu Picchu at all; she had flown back to Israel and was seeing her ex-boyfriend again. I knew it was a silly dream but I couldn't get back to sleep. I lay there wondering if she was thinking about me. I doubted it. She was probably having the time of her life.

〰️ ||||||

Apart from a visit from two of my lawyers, I spent Christmas completely alone that year. Sylvia had other commitments with the church, but I was still half-expecting her to drop by or at least phone. Yasheeda was off who knows where, having a good time. She was the best thing that had happened to me, but now I wasn't even sure if she would keep her promise and come back to see me.

It was the worst Christmas I've ever had in my entire life. Constanza Sanchez had only come back once after she had organised the rest of my 'legal team'. I never saw her again. My two remaining lawyers had promised to have me out by Christmas and since I had sent money to the judge, I had started selling my things in anticipation of my release. But it hadn't happened.

'Merry Christmas,' my lawyers said when I opened the door. They both hugged me.

They had bought me a fruitcake. I should have been grateful that they had at least thought of me, but seeing the cake actually made me angry and I wanted to throw it back in their faces. I didn't want cake, I wanted answers. I wasn't paying them to make me a courtesy visit at Christmas or to buy me cakes; I wanted them to get me out of prison.

They didn't have any updates on my situation. They couldn't tell me when I would be out. In fact, they had no answers at all; everything was up to the judge, and he hadn't communicated with them for weeks.

'Why can't you call him, then?' I demanded.

Apparently, it was best not to pressure him. He had received the money, so all we could do now was wait. My lawyers started cutting up the fruitcake. However, I was so distressed that I couldn't eat. They ate it in front of me.

Fruitcake was the only Christmas present I got that year. It was the world's most expensive fruitcake. All up, it had cost me over twenty-five thousand dollars and I didn't even eat a single slice myself. It cost even more if I included the three thousand dollars I had lost with Constanza Sanchez. Maybe I was naïve to give them all that money, but they gave me a receipt for every payment and I had to trust them – they were my lawyers.

They kept promising to get me released, but they were the same promises they had made six months before, and nothing ever changed, not even the promises. They used exactly the same words as before. They didn't even have enough respect for me to change their lies: they needed some more money to pay for photocopying, a filing fee, a witness who was going to be my character reference, administration charges, someone they knew who might be able to take a message to the judge, or a specialist lawyer who was going to make a technical submission. Everything required money.

They weren't lying when they said that. I had already established that that much was true after eight months in the Bolivian prison system. However, I now understood how much things were really worth. Nothing cost anywhere near what they were asking. I was being taken for a ride because I was a foreigner. But what could I do? I could fire them on the spot, but that would mean losing all the money I had already paid and starting afresh with new lawyers who might be worse. Without their help, I couldn't see any way out. So, although I knew they were ripping me off, I felt I had nowhere else to turn. I began to regret not having escaped when I had the opportunity.

After my lawyers left, I got a bottle of rum and started drinking it on my own. I drank it too quickly and after half a bottle, I felt like vomiting, so I bought a small envelope of cocaine to sober me up before finishing the rest. In the section courtyard below, the celebrations were just getting under way, so I bought another bottle. Christmas wasn't traditionally a big part of the Bolivian calendar, although it was catching on. For the children it was all about the presents and this new character they were beginning to believe in, called Santa Claus. For the inmates, it was another excuse to get drunk. After spending some time with their families in the morning, that was exactly what they did.

The next day the party was still going, so I bought another bottle of rum and another few packs of cocaine and continued partying on my own. Christmas dragged on until it turned into New Year's Eve and then it all stopped suddenly and the prison returned to normal. Not for me, though. I carried on drinking in my room and thinking about Yasheeda and worrying about whether I would ever get out of there.

20
LOS VIOLADORES

L ater that week, I was resting on my bed listening to Bob Marley when I heard loud chanting coming from outside. It was the kind of noise made by a football crowd. At first I ignored it, thinking it was a drunken neighbour watching a game on television at full volume. But as the noise grew louder, I could tell that the voices were real. Even then I assumed that it was just a group of angry protestors passing by in the street outside the prison. However, the sound didn't fade away; it got stronger and, judging by the volume, it seemed to be coming from somewhere inside the prison. I got up and opened my door to investigate.

From my doorway, the noise was even louder. Although I couldn't see them, or catch what they were saying, there must have been hundreds of men shouting the same two words, over and over. The sound was definitely coming from another section in the jail, but even in Pinos, a general panic had broken out. Our normally tranquil section courtyard was in absolute chaos, with inmates running about in confusion, shouting urgently. My neighbours also started coming out of their rooms to see what the fuss was and as soon as they heard the chanting, they slammed their doors behind them and ran downstairs. Something was definitely going on. I didn't know what, but it was big – that was for sure.

'What's happening? Where are you going?' I tried asking, but no one had time to answer. They were all too busy running down the stairs and out of the section towards the uproar. I eventually managed to slow someone down enough to get a response, but the only word I could actually make out as he slipped past me was '*violadores*'. Unfortunately, I didn't know what it meant and by then, there was almost no one left in the section to explain it to me. They had all disappeared. It must have been a mass breakout, and I was about to miss out. In fact, I might already be too late!

I jumped into my trainers and grabbed all the money I could find. I would have liked to have taken more stuff, but there wasn't time to look for anything else. Besides, anything I had to carry would only slow me down. I hadn't even done up my shoelaces before I was running so fast towards the main courtyard that I almost tripped over. As I approached the section gateway, the noise became deafening and I could finally make out what they were shouting: '*¡Tráiganlos! ¡Tráiganlos!*' I didn't understand what that meant either, and I still didn't know what was going on.

When I arrived at the courtyard I had to stop suddenly. There were so many people that you could hardly move. Apart from when we had to line up together and sing the Bolivian national anthem, I had never seen so many inmates in the one place. I stood there, out of breath, looking around wildly for a hole in the wall or an open gate, while the crowd surged around, shouting and yelling and punching their fists in the air.

'*¡Tráiganlos! ¡Tráiganlos!*' they chanted, but I couldn't see where they were escaping from.

A big roar then went up from the crowd and it surged towards the narrow corridor that led down to the inside sections. Ahead, I saw that a man had been lifted above the heads of the crowd and was being carried down the passageway. Most of the prisoners started heading that way, so I joined them and, being taller and stronger than most of them, managed to push my way through faster. I accidentally knocked a few people over in my haste. I didn't know exactly where we were going or what we were doing, but I wasn't going to miss out.

When we reached the main section of Cancha, everyone stopped running and I noticed that another man had been hoisted above the crowd. The pair were looking around worriedly, wanting to get down, but I assumed that was because they were afraid of being dropped.

Still the crowd was shouting, '*¡Tráiganlos! ¡Tráiganlos!*' but now that we weren't moving, I concluded it wasn't a breakout. I didn't know what to think, really, but it was obvious that no one was escaping. Maybe they had won a football match, or it was some type of protest and these men were the leaders.

The main action was concentrated around where the swimming pool was located. I thought perhaps they were going to be thrown into the water as part of the celebration and I wanted to get a closer look, so I started pushing towards the pool. The crowd swayed back and forth violently and I really had to use my strength to get through. Then there was a huge splash and a warlike roar went up from the spectators. I still couldn't see what was going on, but if it was a celebration, it was a very angry one. There was another splash as the second man went in, and this time everyone cheered. No one wanted to let me forward but I was determined to see, so I continued to struggle. The closer to the pool I got, the more aggressive the crowd became.

When it seemed I could get no closer to the pool, I recognised the giant inmate with the scarred face towering next to me and asked him what was happening.

'What is it? Who are they?' I shouted above the intense clamour of the crowd.

'*Los violadores. Se van a morir.*' He pointed to a third man who had just been brought into the section and was being carried towards the pool. There was that word I didn't understand again – *violadores*. I understood the second part, though: 'They are going to die.'

'What does "*violador*" mean?' I tugged at his sleeve and when I heard the word '*violación*', I finally understood. These men were the gang rapists I had seen arrested on television before Christmas.

Somehow I made it to the very front, staying about half a metre from the edge of the pool for safety since the people behind me were still pushing and fighting to move forward. From there, I could see exactly what was happening.

There were now two men in the water and I got there just as one of them was struggling to get out via the steps that ran down the side of the pool. I don't know what they had done to him beforehand, but he was bleeding from cuts and wounds and looked like he was thoroughly exhausted. However, the crowd wouldn't let him out. As soon as he made it to the final step, one of the spectators barged him with a shoulder and he went back in, hitting his head on the concrete edge as he fell. Everyone laughed and another cheer went up from the crowd. At first, I thought they were just going to teach him a lesson, but then things got more serious.

When he tried to get out the second time, someone attempted to loop a length of electrical cable around his neck. He managed to free himself using his hands and jumped back in the water, but then the crowd began throwing things at him – rocks and debris, or anything they could get their hands on – and kicking him whenever he came near the edge. This went on for quite some time. Bit by bit, they were drowning him. I stood glued to the spot, fascinated.

The second rapist was having even more trouble. He was also being beaten and bombarded with chunks of brick, but it was worse for him because he couldn't swim; he was splashing about everywhere and wasting most of his energy simply trying to stay afloat. He kept going under and swallowing mouthfuls of water and I think after a short time he realised that if he didn't get out of the pool soon, he would drown.

When he came up for air the next time, he looked around frantically for a way out. Seeing that the stairs were guarded, he put his hands over the cement edge to pull himself up, but one of the inmates stamped on them, hard, and he cried out. Then he tried again on the other side of the pool, but this time two inmates trod on his fingers and ground them into the concrete. He struggled to pull his hands free but with the full weight of a man crushing down on each hand, he couldn't. Then another prisoner from the crowd stepped forward and booted him hard in the face and he fell back, almost unconscious, held above the water only because his fingers were still trapped.

When the men lifted their feet, the rapist's hands fell away and he slipped under the surface for quite some time. Part of me wanted to help him, but there was no way I could fight against so many people. It would have been too dangerous to attempt to drag him out with a thousand angry prisoners behind me who wanted him dead. Besides, a strange part of me wanted to see what would happen. I continued watching with a sick curiosity.

He was still alive, although only just. He made it up for air, coughing, and managed to recover enough breath to start splashing around again. Not for long, though. The third rapist was now thrown on top of him, and that man's hipbone connected directly with his head. Everyone roared with laughter. After that, he didn't surface again.

While all this was happening, the first rapist had still been trying to get out. One of the prisoners had fetched a plank of wood and the next time the rapist came near the steps, he smashed it over his head and he also began to lose consciousness. Meanwhile, another prisoner had got hold of a live electrical cable and was dipping two wires into the water, trying to electrocute him. At that point, he looked like he was about to give in – one more hit would have finished him – but that was when all attention turned to the third rapist, who had just been thrown in.

The third rapist went straight for the steps, but the crowd punched him and kicked him and the blows sent him tumbling back into the pool. When he surfaced and tried to lift himself over the edge, the spectator with the thick cable whipped him across the face and his whole cheek opened up. He managed to avoid the man with the wooden plank and tried again and again to scramble out, but each time he got to the edge, he was kicked in the head and pushed back in.

Eventually, he found his way to the stairs again and this time forced his way up, taking all the blows with a new-found strength. Even when the plank of wood was cracked across his face, he didn't stop. I thought he was going to make it, but then I saw a hand shoot out of the crowd and strike him just below the ribs. It wasn't a very hard blow but I could tell immediately that something was wrong. He froze on the top step and looked down to where he had been hit. Then he clutched his stomach and it began to bleed. He'd been stabbed.

Because he hesitated, the next punch hit him properly and its impact caused him to overbalance. Someone spat on him, and another kick sent him tumbling into the water. Even though he was bleeding heavily, he kept trying to get out but every time he approached the edge, a cheer went up from the crowd as the man with the plank of wood forced him to retreat. I could tell that he was getting tired. Eventually, he stayed in the very middle, just out of reach of the prisoner with the plank of wood. The water began turning a nasty brown colour and, next to him, the body of the second rapist floated to the surface.

With the crowd's attention fixed on attacking this third rapist, the first man had managed to climb out of the pool without being noticed. He was lying half-drowned, only two feet from where I was standing, dripping water and blood and panting desperately to recover his breath. I thought he had had enough punishment and they would just leave him alone, but now that the third rapist was out of reach in the middle of the pool, the inmates turned their focus back on him.

Someone kicked him in the neck. Then another prisoner started stomping on his head. Another one actually jumped on his head with both feet and I heard the most horrible sound as his skull split. I hadn't done anything about them attacking the rapists before, but seeing this was too much for me.

'Stop it!' I shouted in English and a few people looked at me, wondering what I was saying. I was so distressed I couldn't remember any Spanish. 'You're killing him!'

At that point I think I must have started going into a kind of shock because of what I was seeing, because my memory of what happened after that is a bit confused. Certain things are very clear, but there are gaps where I don't remember properly. And everything happened so quickly that it's difficult to remember the exact order.

'*¡Basta!*' I think I yelled again, more forcefully, remembering the Spanish. This time they understood. I could see their angry faces telling me not to get involved, but I moved forward to stop them because I couldn't bear what I was seeing. It was too horrible. I just wanted it to stop. Then the crowd started to turn against me. One of the men made a movement to hit me, and when I put my hands up to defend myself someone grabbed me around the neck from behind and pulled me backwards.

It was a thick, strong arm that held me but I managed to free myself by lifting my feet off the ground and using my falling weight to slip from under his grip. Clenching my fists, I turned to defend myself against the attacker. It was the big man with the scar. He must have been twice my size and there was no way I could win against him, so I tried to step sideways but someone pushed me in the back and he grabbed me again, spinning me around effortlessly and getting me in another hold from behind.

I had never felt anyone so strong in my life, and all I could do to avoid being thrown in the water myself was to use my legs. I got a good foothold on the ground and jumped backwards with all my force, trying to push us both back away from the pool or to knock us over so as to make it more difficult for them to get me in the pool.

It didn't work, though. The man with the scar was so big and heavy and his feet were so firmly planted on the ground that nothing happened. I tried to push us back again and again, but we weren't going anywhere. Instead, he tightened his grip and lifted me up so that only my toes were touching the concrete. In that position, all I could do was wriggle helplessly and kick out at anyone around me. The crowd moved out of the way, leaving an almost clear passage to the water. There was only one thing on the ground between myself and the pool and it was the most horrifying thing I have ever seen in my life. I only saw it for a few moments before I was lifted completely off the ground, but I will never, *ever*, forget it.

I thought that I was about to be thrown into the pool, but the opposite occurred. Still gripping me strongly under the arms, the big man with the scar pulled me away from the pool, half-dragging, half-lifting me through the angry mob until we were in the open. He didn't harm me at all, and once we were outside the crowd and away from danger, he let me stand up properly.

'*Tranquilo, hombre*,' he said in my ear, trying to calm me down. When I finally realised he wasn't trying to hurt me, I stopped struggling and he loosened his grip slightly.

'*Tranquilo. ¿Sí?*' he repeated, letting me go completely. When I turned and looked at him, he gave me a warning look, said something about not interfering, then went back into the crowd, leaving me standing on my own.

I was now safe from attack, but I was so shocked by what I had seen that I started shaking uncontrollably. I ran for my life, back up through the passage that led to the main courtyard, which was completely empty. There were lots of policemen gathered at the gates, staring towards where the cheering and shouting was coming from.

I ran back into Pinos and through the empty section courtyard with my footsteps echoing off the walls. It seemed that no one was there, but out of the corner of my eye I saw a door move slightly and instinctively turned my head. I couldn't see properly because the opening was narrow, but there was a woman who was nursing a baby peering out, watching me. I think my shoelaces must still have been undone, or maybe it was because my muscles were so weak that they couldn't support my weight. I tripped and fell on the concrete. When I tried to get to my feet, I fell back down. Then, what I had seen at the pool came back to me and I started vomiting.

The rapist's skull had been cracked and the top of his head was completely open, so I could see right inside. A section of his skull was still attached and it looked like a lid with all the brains spilling out over it onto the concrete. There was also a lot of blood; a thick, dark pool of it had formed around his head. He was probably dead by then, but the inmates just kept jumping up and down on top of him and there was a horrible crunching sound as his skull fractured into small pieces. Brains kept coming out as his head was squashed flat. Everything was a big, sticky mess of different colours with clumps of hair mixed in. The blood itself was a really dark red colour, but there were also grey and blue parts of brain that looked like raw meat. I think I even saw something that was green.

I remember that one of the prisoners had stopped then and stood back from the body. I thought he must have finally finished, but it was just to wipe his shoes on the concrete because they were all bloody and there were stringy pieces of brain and bits of hair stuck to them. Then he went back and kept treading on the mangled face. Behind him, the water had turned a horrible, murky brown colour and the crowd had started attacking the third rapist again. He was too exhausted to escape and was just trying to keep out of their reach in the middle of the pool, using the face-down body of the second rapist to stay afloat.

That was all I saw, because the man with the scar started pulling me away, but it was too much for me. I had never before seen anyone killed. I had never even seen a dead body. And to see someone killed like that, right in front of me, was the most horrible experience. No one deserves to die like that. I don't care *what* they have done.

I vomited again. I thought the woman with the baby would come out to help me, but when I looked up at her, the door clicked shut. I looked around, thinking that someone else might be able to help me, but everything was shut up. There wasn't a single soul in the section; they were all down by *la piscina* or behind their doors, so I had to make it up to my room on my own.

As soon as I opened the door, I vomited on the carpet. I hadn't even felt it coming. After a few more times, there was no food left in my stomach, but the muscles inside my body kept contracting as if there was. I leaned forward, supporting myself over the table with a stream of thick saliva hanging from the corner of my mouth, until the contractions subsided. Then I sat down on a chair, feeling weak, and wiped my mouth clean using my T-shirt. It was only then that I noticed the Bob Marley tape was still playing. My stereo was set on continuous play and Bob hadn't stopped singing about peace or hope for humanity.

21
SLEEPING PILLS

When I first arrived at San Pedro, I didn't feel safe leaving my room; now, nine months later, I didn't even want to. Even if I *had* wanted to, I *couldn't* have, because I didn't have the energy. For two days I hardly ate, and after that I couldn't get my appetite back. The sight of meat made me sick and I stopped eating it altogether. Even if it was cooked, I still saw that man's brains spilling out onto my plate.

I couldn't do anything. I was depressed. On the rare occasions when I was hungry, I ate. I drank when I was thirsty and went to the toilet when my body told me to. That was all. The only thing I actually *wanted* to do was sleep. And much of the time I couldn't even do that.

That was the period when I started taking sleeping pills. I was having real trouble sleeping, so I went to see the doctor for a prescription. He didn't ask any questions. Why would he, I suppose? On the scale of drug problems in San Pedro prison, sleeping pills didn't even rate.

Once I started taking pills, I did even less. I only saw light once a day. With less food in my body, I didn't need to go to the bathroom as much. When I needed to urinate, I did so in a bucket that I emptied whenever it became full. And when I got sick of emptying it all the time, I bought another bucket.

I couldn't think properly. Even my mind had slowed down. The only reason I ever had to get out of bed was for the *lista*, and if that hadn't been compulsory, I wouldn't have gone. Getting up was a lot more of a struggle with the sleeping pills in my system, but somehow I still managed to set my alarm clock and make it down to the court-yard every morning. If ever I didn't wake up, my neighbour Gonzalez would bang on my door and force me to get up, or they'd send for Ricardo, who had a spare key to my room.

After falling out of bed and stumbling down the stairs, it was easy to pass the actual roll call. All you had to do was wait, hidden among the other prisoners, listen for your name and then call out '*¡Presente!*' before heading back to your room. The guards sometimes looked at me suspiciously because I could hardly keep my eyes open. Once or twice they checked my breath for alcohol, but nothing ever happened. They all knew that the governor was my friend.

After *lista*, I would take another sleeping pill. And when I woke up, I would take another one. With the pills, sometimes I could sleep for sixteen hours straight, although at other times I hardly slept for days and nights on end, even if I took three or four. It was dark in my room and I began to lose track of time. Eventually, my whole body clock became completely disoriented. Sometimes I would look at the clock, just out of habit, but after reading it I wouldn't have known whether it was three o'clock in the afternoon or three o'clock in the morning.

I began ordering more and more pills from the doctor to help me get back into a normal sleeping routine. There was no limit to the number of boxes he could order from the prison clinic, and they were very cheap because the pills were copies manufactured in the factories in El Alto. When I needed stronger dosages, one of the inmates knew of a *farmacia* on the outside that didn't ask for prescriptions. These pills were more expensive and I had to pay someone else a *propina* to get them, but it was worth it because I didn't need to take so many doses in one go.

I don't recall much of what happened during those few weeks, but it wasn't much, I know that. When I wasn't asleep, I often got drunk on my own. One afternoon, I woke up and felt that my lips were caked with dry blood. When I looked in the mirror, I had cuts and bruises all over my face. I didn't know if I had been in a fight or if I had simply fallen over. I never found out. I was too embarrassed to ask anyone.

The few times that my head was clear, I remember the main feeling I had was simply that I wanted to die. I thought about death a lot, but I was afraid to kill myself. I was a coward. Every time I thought of suicide, the image of that rapist's head being stomped on came into my mind. So, I started fantasising about a little red button in the middle of my wooden table that I could press to end my life in an instant, without pain. I could press it and just disappear.

One thing I noticed about sleeping pills is that they rob you of your dreams. I think I stopped having dreams completely, or maybe I just couldn't remember them. Whenever I tried to get off the pills, I had the most horrible nightmares, usually about Yasheeda, and I always remembered the exact details. The one that recurred most strongly involved her ex-boyfriend. I had seen his photo when it fell out of her diary one morning, so I knew what he looked like. He was tall and strong and, in my nightmares, he was always nice to me.

The worst nightmare occurred on the night that the police informed me I was due to go to court the following day for the beginning of my trial. In the nightmare, Yasheeda's ex-boyfriend sat me down and explained that she had made a big mistake because she had been confused at the time she met me.

'She's with *me* now,' he said. 'I just wanted you to know it was nothing you did wrong. Don't feel bad.' He was really apologetic. And then they kissed in front of me and it was like I wasn't even there.

22
MY TRIAL BEGINS

On the day that my trial was scheduled to begin, I lay in bed all morning, watching *Laura* on TV. But not even that could make me happy. I didn't bother turning on the light, and I couldn't bring myself to get up and eat breakfast or lunch. My stomach was in knots.

Finally, I rose and began preparing for my court appearance. I took special care to look well dressed. I was ready when the announcement about my court appearance came over the tinny prison loudspeaker system.

'Thomas McFadden to the *puerta principal.*'

I left my room and walked quickly towards the main courtyard.

'Well, well, well. If it isn't San Pedro's international loverboy,' said a familiar voice as I passed through the Pinos gateway. I turned around and gave a cry of surprise. It was Ricardo. In my misery, I had completely forgotten about him.

'Hey, man!'

'Why do you look so surprised to see me, *Inglaterra*? Don't you recognise me?' He had obviously heard my name called and had been waiting for me.

'Hey, man! Ricardo.'

'Yes, I'm Ricardo,' he said, taking my hand and shaking it as we walked along.

'Pleased to meet you again. I'm glad you remembered my name at least.' I'd also forgotten how funny he was.

'Hey, man! Where have you been?' I asked.

'What do you mean, where have I been? Where do you think I've been? Did you think I sold my house and moved suburbs or something?'

Ricardo accompanied me to the main gates where I lined up with the other inmates on the transport list. The police marked our names off, and we then filed out into the street and onto the green police bus to be driven across town to the court.

'Good luck, *inglés*!' he called to me before they closed the doors.

There were about ten of us on the bus, with two guards. They didn't bother handcuffing us. San Pedro was for minimum-security prisoners, and the only time we would be out in the open was when we were getting on and off the bus, when there were plenty of police around. (Later on, they did handcuff us, but that was only after an accomplice had handed one of the inmates a gun in the courthouse and he'd shot three policemen before escaping on foot.)

卌ll

When we arrived at the court building, I saw my lawyers waiting for me at the entrance. They welcomed me with smiles and handshakes and then introduced me to a female colleague, who kissed me on the cheek.

'Hello, Thomas,' she said. 'How was your ride?'

The policeman assigned to guard me stood aside, waiting to take me to the holding cells.

'Don't worry, Thomas. Leave everything to us,' my lawyers assured me. 'We'll see you in there.'

I had been in those same court holding cells on my way to the prison from the FELCN eleven months previously. I wasn't in the same cell as then, but it was almost identical – plain walls, no furniture, one small window high up, and an observation hatch in the door for the guards to look through. It didn't seem as horrible as I remembered. I had been through a lot since then.

To me, eleven months was a very long time to have to wait for my first court appearance. However, by Bolivian standards, it was considered speedy. My lawyers said this was a good sign: it meant the money we had sent to the judge was working. There were inmates who had been in San Pedro for six years without a trial, they said. But I didn't know whether to believe my lawyers, since originally they had said that my case wouldn't need to go to trial at all.

The courtroom was very simple, like an old-fashioned classroom. There was nothing modern, such as cameras or microphones. All the furniture was wooden. The prosecutor, known as the *fiscal*, sat on one side of the room and the judge's desk was up the front, in front of a Bolivian flag hanging on the wall. Everyone else, including my lawyers and I, sat in the middle of the room on uncomfortable chairs that made a terrible noise when you moved them. For my first appearance, there weren't enough chairs, so the police had to go out and borrow some from other courtrooms.

When I first saw the judge coming in, I was hopeful.

'Please stand,' called one of the court officials. Everyone bowed as the judge took his seat. He had a nice face. It looked like the face of someone who had children. I know that doesn't sound important, but when it's your trial, the judge's face is something you notice.

The proceedings began very slowly. Everything that was said had to be typed using an old-fashioned typewriter. The typist was fast, but it was impossible for him to keep up with everyone, especially when they all talked at once. Often he had to interrupt in order to get people to repeat what they had just said. On top of that, whenever anyone spoke, they had to wait for my interpreter to make the translation into English.

I watched the judge closely. I found it hard to believe that this man had received fifteen thousand dollars from my lawyers and was now sitting there, pretending he hadn't. At first, this made me feel confident; I thought he was a good actor. However, he kept his performance up for so long that I began to doubt whether he was corrupt at all.

In the whole time I was there, the judge looked at me only once, when the prosecutor said my name and pointed to me. When the judge's eyes met mine, his expression was completely blank and there was no hint of softness in his face. I began to wonder whether the two bribes had reached him. By the end of the afternoon, I was convinced that they hadn't.

No significant developments occurred during that first hearing. I had been hoping that the judge would dismiss the charges immediately, but it had become obvious that this was not his intention. Reaching a finding of *inocente* was going to take longer than expected. My second court appearance was scheduled for three weeks later.

'How did it go?' asked Ricardo, when I arrived back at San Pedro. He had been waiting for me at the gates.

'I don't know. It's hard to say.'

'Apparently he's a good judge,' Ricardo said, rubbing his fingers together. 'Very fair. So, you're lucky, *inglés*. You might be out of here before you know it.'

'How long, do you think?'

'What are you asking *me* for? I'm not a lawyer.'

'Come on! Let's go and have a chat in my room,' I suggested, not wanting to think about it anymore.

'Ahhh, so you want your old friend back. Didn't have time for me when the girly was around, hey?' said Ricardo. 'But now she's gone . . .'

'I'll cook you something.'

'I'd love to, Thomas, but I can't. I'm sorry, I'm busy.' He tapped his watch. 'Gotta fly. I've got a hot date tonight. You know how it is.'

'Come on! We'll smoke some *ganja*. I'll pay.'

'You'll pay, hey? So, she's rich too and giving you money!' He put his arm around me and we walked up the stairs towards my room. 'You must be San Pedro's only toyboy.'

Ricardo kept making jokes about what a bad friend I was, but I could tell that he was actually a little hurt that I had forgotten him when Yasheeda was around. I knew that he wouldn't stay mad at me for long, though, and after the first joint he stopped teasing me. Just like old times, we were stoned and watching the ATB news, when Ricardo suddenly jumped out of his chair. 'Look! There's that politician. They caught him again!' It was Gabriel Sanchez, the director of the workers' pension fund who had stolen forty million dollars. The reporter said that there had been an anonymous tip-off that he was hiding out in Mar de Plata in Argentina. They brought him in by plane under armed guard. The picture showed him at El Alto Airport, handcuffed and surrounded by police, about to be transported somewhere. But you could hardly recognise him because he'd had plastic surgery.

Hundreds of the workers who had been cheated out of their retirement money were protesting with their families. Some of the women were crying. The police had formed a ring around Sanchez, but they weren't trying very hard to protect him. Sanchez didn't try to shield himself, either. In the short time it took to bundle him into a vehicle, the protesters spat on him and threw things at him and one guy got past the guards and landed a big punch. The angry mob continued to kick and bang the car until it sped off. The reporter then started interviewing some of the people in the crowd.

'Can you believe that guy?' yelled Ricardo, pointing at the television and banging his fist on the table. 'When he goes to prison, he's not going to last the first night. They'll kill him. Just like they did those rapists.'

'He's not going to prison, man. He's got money. It's all a show trial. Money buys you a lot of friends.'

'But he *has* to go to prison,' argued Ricardo. 'He's already escaped once, so now the whole country is watching. There will be riots if he doesn't go to prison, at least for a little while until things calm down.'

I disagreed. 'No way, man. Where's the forty million dollars he stole? They haven't found any of it. I say that while he's still got the money, he can pay his way out.'

'I still say he's going to prison.'

'How much will we bet, then?' I asked, holding out my hand.

'Forty million.'

'OK.' We shook hands.

'Wait!' I said, not letting his hand go. 'Dollars or bolivianos?'

'Hey, *inglés*. You know this is a Bolivian jail,' Ricardo laughed. 'Everything is in dollars, remember?'

23
THOMAS THE TOUR GUIDE

I was in a good mood the next morning when two *taxistas* called to me from the courtyard below, saying that someone was waiting in the interview room to see me. My heart leapt, hoping it was Yasheeda.

'Who is it?' I opened my door and yelled down.

'I don't know. About five or six foreigners.'

At first I felt disappointed, and then confused. I didn't know that many people in the whole of La Paz. There must have been some kind of mistake, but I went to the gate just to be sure. And there, behind the bars in the interview room was Yasheeda with her friend Sharon and two other Israeli girls. It had been months since she had left, but she acted as if it was just the day before.

'I thought you might be lonely, so I brought you some visitors,' she said. 'There are two guys waiting outside. Can we come in?'

I hesitated. It would be difficult to get six visitors in at one time. Especially since they didn't have Bolivian IDs.

'Well! Aren't you going to get us in, Tommy?' asked Yasheeda. 'All my friends want to meet you.'

'Wait! Let me check first.'

I left the interview room and hurried around to the main entrance. I didn't know what lie I could tell the police to get all of the Israelis in, but since they had made the effort to visit me, I at least owed it to them to try. At a minimum, I needed to get Yasheeda in. I didn't know why she hadn't contacted me, but I had already forgiven her. Luckily, the lieutenant on duty that day was my friend. He was standing by the metal gates with his set of keys, controlling the flow of people.

'*Mi teniente*, a small consultation please.' I said, holding up my thumb and index finger with a small gap between them, which was the Bolivian way of asking for a quick chat. He leaned towards the bars and said, '*Dígame*' – 'Tell me.'

I told him that some people had come from the other side of the world especially to visit me. 'Can you help me? I don't have any family here,' I pleaded.

'Do they have their *carnets*? If they don't have a *carnet*, they aren't allowed in the prison,' he stated. I already knew that was the rule, but I kept arguing.

'But my lieutenant, that doesn't seem fair. I am a foreigner, so all my family are foreigners! That means my family can't visit me.'

'So, these people are your family?'

'No, but all my friends are foreigners, too. Please, maybe I can help you also,' I hinted. His expression began to change. 'Where are they from, your friends? From your home town?'

All the guards knew me as '*inglés*' and I thought about saying my visitors were from England too, but they definitely looked Israeli.

'They are from Israel. I used to live in Israel where I met my Israeli girlfriend. You know my *chica*.' I had seen the lieutenant admiring Yasheeda whenever she was leaving, so with my hands I made an outline in the air of a full-figured woman, exaggerating the size of her breasts and buttocks. The lieutenant and his men all started laughing.

'Ahhh. *¡Su chica!*'

I had them now. 'Can you help me?' I winked at him. 'I can introduce you to her pretty *amigas!*' I traced another curvaceous woman in the air, this time pulling her towards me and grunting when I got to the hips. They laughed even louder.

'*¡Qué bueno! Gringas.* Just a moment.' He went off to discuss it with the major. Things were looking good.

That was the first of many lies I told to the police in order to gain admission for foreign tourists to San Pedro prison. Yasheeda had always been friendly with the major, which probably helped with getting her friends in that time. However, later on, when travellers I had never seen before began turning up and asking to be let in to see me, it became more and more difficult to come up with new excuses. My family tree became more and more complicated as distant cousins, nieces and half-brothers with passports from Egypt, Iceland and Japan came to visit me. The guards must have joked among themselves about some of the stories I told them. In the end, I doubt that they believed a word I said. At the peak of my career as tour guide, two or three girls I had never laid eyes on would turn up each day claiming to be my wife. However, provided I made the police laugh and there was money in it for them, they seemed to play along with most of my lies.

The lieutenant came back from the major's office with good news. 'He says it's OK, but they have to pay. And keep them away from the main gate in case the *gobernador* sees them.'

'Yes, of course. Of course, they will pay. *No hay problema.*'

'Ten bolivianos each person,' he whispered through the gate so that only I could hear. 'Straight up to your room.'

'Yes. Of course,' I agreed willingly. I didn't think Yasheeda's friends would mind. Three bolivianos more than local visitors paid wasn't much extra, even for travellers on a backpacking budget.

I ran back to the interview room and told Yasheeda to call the boys in and come around to the main gate, where the lieutenant took their passports, making a big show of checking that the photos matched the person. Then he handed the key to his junior and nodded at the gate. The junior policeman opened the padlock, the tourists passed through, and then he locked it behind them and handed the key back to the lieutenant.

'*Gracias, mi teniente,*' I said, but the lieutenant didn't look up. He was too busy studying his tiny notepad, doing the figures. Normally, all the money from the main gate was divided between the police on duty, according to their rank, but I noticed that this time he hadn't made an official record of the tourists entering. Today would be a good day for the lieutenant; the sixty bolivianos from the Israelis would be shared between him and the major only.

When Yasheeda came through the gates, I wanted to hug her, but there wasn't time. I hadn't had any trouble from the other inmates for months, but I was still careful not to do anything that might cause a stir in the prison. Unfortunately, this was exactly what was happening. The inmates weren't used to seeing foreigners and there were now six visitors standing in front of me inside the main gates who were clearly not Bolivian. People stopped what they were doing to stare. I was worried that something might happen to one of the Israelis. I had to get them away from the main gate and out of sight before they attracted any more attention.

'OK, everyone. Follow me, please.' I tried not to sound anxious as I led the group in single file across the main courtyard. Yasheeda's friends looked around nervously, staying as close to one another as possible. 'And make sure you hold on to your wallets!' I called back to them as we started through the gates into Pinos, with all eyes still fixed on our little group. We made it up the stairs, into my room and I shut the door behind me, leaning against the wall and panting from the rapid climb, but relieved that nothing had happened.

Even though I now felt safe, it still wasn't the right time to say anything to Yasheeda. I wanted to ask her why she'd taken so long, and why she hadn't called, but I couldn't say anything in front of the others. I had to wait until we were alone. Instead I motioned for everyone to sit down. Later, I bought more chairs for my small wooden table, but at that time I wasn't used to receiving visitors and there weren't enough seats to go around. Yasheeda and Sharon sat on my bed and the others sat at the table. I remained standing. It was only then that I had time to take a proper look at my visitors.

They were all tanned and healthy-looking after their hike along the Inca trail to the famous ruins of Machu Picchu and had clearly been shopping at the local markets because they were wearing traditional Bolivian clothing. I looked more closely at their faces. Not one of them was flushed from the climb to my room, but I could tell that they were quite shaken by the experience of entering a real prison and being stared at by hundreds of strange-looking South American prisoners. They all gazed back at me, waiting for me to speak.

I knew I had to say something, but I didn't know what. I couldn't understand why anyone on an overseas holiday would want to go to a jail to visit a drug trafficker they didn't know. It seemed such a strange thing to do. I guess it was just as strange for them; I was probably the first real criminal in a real prison they had ever met and, for all they knew, I might have been dangerous and violent.

'So . . . Welcome to San Pedro prison . . .' I stuttered. 'I'm Thomas the tour guide.' They all laughed.

I didn't mean for it to sound funny, and I don't really think they thought it was, but it broke the tension. Afterwards, that line became the standard opening for all my tours. *Thomas the tour guide*. It was a good way to overcome people's fears on entering the prison. As time went by, I became better and better at understanding how other people felt in awkward situations, and eventually I could make tourists feel safe almost as soon as I met them at the entrance.

Thomas the tour guide. Actually, I kind of liked the sound of it. Each time I repeated it over the next few years, I thought back to that very first tour, sitting in my room with my first group of tourists.

'Well, here we are. This is my prison cell. Welcome!' I plugged the kettle in and asked who wanted tea or coffee. They seemed to be relaxing, but it was still difficult to know what they wanted to hear. Luckily, before another uncomfortable silence fell, Yasheeda suggested that I tell her friends about the night I came to San Pedro.

I started telling them about my time in the FELCN and about how the police had virtually starved me there. Then I told them about arriving at San Pedro by taxi and being asked to pay the entrance fee. And about how I had slept in the abandoned building, almost freezing to death there, because I didn't have enough money to buy a cell. No one said anything but they all looked shocked.

I continued talking, gradually feeling more confident as the story progressed. I explained how the prisoners had to pay to belong to a section and then pay a transfer fee in order to get the legal title to a cell. I explained how everyone had to have a job in order to survive. I told them about the restaurants, and about the guards and the corruption. I also explained about how many of the inmates were addicted to smoking base. I could sense the Israelis were starting to believe me. Under the table, Yasheeda gave my hand a squeeze of encouragement. I saw from her friends' faces that they were now totally involved in my experiences. Yasheeda winked at me. As her friends became more comfortable, they began firing questions at me: Where are you from? How long have you been here? What's it like living here? What did you do? Are you innocent? Is it dangerous? Is this your first time in prison? Did you get caught with drugs? What's the food like? Is there a school inside the prison for the children? Where is your family? When do you get out? Isn't it against human rights to make you pay for a cell?

I did my best to answer all their questions, although I avoided the ones about what I had done. I didn't want people I had never met before knowing details about what I was charged with, especially since I was in the middle of my trial.

'Well, can we see the rest of the prison now?' one of the guys asked.

'Yeah, let's go and have a look around,' suggested his friend. 'I want to see those restaurants. I've never eaten prison food.'

The Israelis were no longer frightened. Even though I didn't like the idea, they insisted that I show them around the other sections. I didn't want to ignore the lieutenant's order about staying in my room, but neither did I want to disappoint my guests. As a compromise, we went downstairs and ate a meal of fried chicken and rice in Pinos. I hoped the inmates wouldn't cause any trouble. In fact, they were quite friendly. A small group came over and began asking the Israelis questions about where they were from, what they thought of Bolivia and what they thought of San Pedro prison. The Israelis answered all their questions happily and even began to joke around with them. After we had finished eating, the bravest of the group asked, 'And these inmates that smoke cocaine – can we see that now?'

'No,' I replied. 'That section is dangerous, man. We can go there another day. It's not a good idea.'

We ended up back in my room, sitting around my table again. After talking with the other prisoners, they were even more excited than before. They had many more questions to ask. They also wanted to know more about the prison, so I started telling them about the prison elections and the rules we had in each section. They sat there completely captivated until a *taxista* knocked on my door to tell me that the lieutenant wanted the tourists to leave. They didn't want to go and I didn't want them to go, but I had to stay on the lieutenant's good side.

We said our first goodbyes in my room and they offered me small amounts of money. I refused them, but they insisted and left some notes on the table saying. 'Don't worry, you need it more than we do.'

'OK. Thanks very much.'

I accompanied my new friends to the gate, where the girls kissed me goodbye – except Yasheeda, who was staying behind. When I went to shake hands with the guy who had asked most of the questions, he gave me a hug. I was surprised and very moved. We had only met each other a few hours before, but in that short time there had been a strong connection.

'You know what? You should become a proper tour guide,' he suggested. 'You're an amazing person. I know about ten people who would come right now, if I told them.'

The others joined in enthusiastically, 'Yeah, that would be cool.'

'We're going to send our friends to visit you. They'll love it.'

'And you could charge them all an extra five bolivianos. No one would mind. This place is worth paying for. I've never seen anything like it.'

Everybody needed a job in San Pedro. Quite by accident, I had stumbled upon mine. I was to be the prison's tour guide. The guards would make their share of profit from the tourists and I could make enough money to get by. I wouldn't have to clean shoes, run errands, sell drugs, wash clothes, lend money or stand over people. Everyone would be happy, especially me.

卌Ⅱ

Although the Israelis didn't get to see much of the prison, that was my first official prison 'tour'. I was grateful to that group of backpackers for helping me to find a way to spend my time in San Pedro and distract me from my trial. I felt inspired by the encouragement they had given me, but when I got back to my cell a strange thing happened: I started to cry. It was partly from happiness – I was so happy that people had come to visit me – but at the same time I felt very sad, because I wished that they didn't have to leave. Or, better still, I wanted to go with them. But I couldn't.

For a few hours, people I didn't know had made me forget my problems and feel like a normal person. They treated me like a real friend, not just someone they had to get along with because we lived in the same prison block. I had forgotten what it was like to be around nice people who don't want something from you and whom you can really trust. They had listened to what I said and had wanted to know everything about me. Now that they were gone, I was on my own again.

I wasn't completely alone, of course. Yasheeda was still with me and she was wonderful – she never got in bad moods, not even in the mornings, and she never said anything nasty about anyone. But it wasn't the same as having whole groups of wonderful people to keep me company. I really missed just sitting at a table with friends and letting the conversation go everywhere and anywhere. I knew Yasheeda and I needed to talk about our relationship, but I decided to put off the conversation until another day. Right then, I didn't trust myself to speak.

'Are you OK?' she asked. I didn't want her to see my tears, so I lay

196

on my bed and buried my face in the pillow. Yasheeda sat on the bed and put her arms around me.

'Yes, I'm fine. I'm just tired, I guess,' I lied. How could I explain to her that I felt so alone, even with her there?

'Are you sure?'

'I'm not used to so many visitors, that's all.'

'OK, then. I'm just going to the bathroom. I'll be back in a minute.'

As soon as the door shut behind her, I began to sob. I couldn't help it. And once I started, I couldn't stop. Since Yasheeda had gone off to Peru, I had survived San Pedro by closing myself down into a little ball, but when the Israelis came to visit, they opened me up again and made me think about things that I hadn't allowed myself to think about for months. What it might be like to have a normal social life. To get in a taxi and go anywhere in the city I wanted, whenever I wanted. To have friends around for dinner. To run across a road. To go to the cinema. To have money in my pocket all the time. To stop off at a coffee shop just because I wanted to. To buy an ice-cream from a proper ice-cream shop. To arrange to meet friends on a street corner at a certain time. To wait at a pedestrian crossing. To drive a car and get stuck at traffic lights during peak hour. Oh God, I was crying because I even missed traffic lights!

When I heard Yasheeda climbing the noisy, wooden ladder that led up to my room, I quickly wiped my eyes. I tried to concentrate on the good time I had just had with her and her friends in order to make my sad thoughts disappear. As Yasheeda climbed into bed next to me, I felt safe again, but I knew that one day she would leave me too. I rolled over and pretended to be asleep and she didn't notice my puffy eyes or my unhappiness.

24
SENTENCING

For my second court appearance the bus didn't arrive, so the police handcuffed the prisoners together in pairs, assigned each pair a guard, and we had to make our own way to court. There was an odd number of prisoners, so I was handcuffed to my escort instead of a prisoner.

'Can't we catch a taxi?' I asked him jokingly.

'Of course. If you pay,' he answered.

We took a taxi, as I was worried that we might be late if we walked.

My guard was from Santa Cruz. During the taxi ride, we joked about which city had the best-looking girls and the best-tasting beer.

'The Paceñas are too cold,' he told me.

'The beers or the women?' I asked, remembering that they shared the same name.

'Both,' he answered and we fell about laughing in the back seat. The taxi driver who was listening in on our conversation and watching us in the rearview mirror started laughing so much that he forgot to watch the road and almost crashed into the car in front. 'I think it's the altitude,' he said, slamming on the brakes.

My escort's name was Fernando. By the time we arrived at the court building, he and I were best friends. We arrived half an hour before the other prisoners, but rather than sending me to the holding cells, he let me sit outside the courtroom.

'Are you thirsty?' I asked him.

'*Claro*. I'm always thirsty.' Fernando laughed. 'Will you shout me a beer?'

'Maybe afterwards.' I didn't think drinking before my trial was a good idea so I sent him downstairs to buy some cigarettes and a Coca-Cola for each of us instead. He handcuffed me to the chair. As I waited, I began to notice some very strange things about the way the court system worked in Bolivia. For a start, absolutely everyone in the building knew each other – the judges, the police, the prosecutors, the defence solicitors and the administration staff. And they all seemed to be friends. Inside the courtroom, they kept a straight face, but as soon as they were outside, they shook hands and made jokes with one another and visited each other's offices, which were all on the same floor. It didn't seem like a place where people's futures hung in the balance.

As it turned out, all my worrying about arriving at court on time was unnecessary. My trial was postponed until the following week because one of the prosecution's documents hadn't been officially stamped. This was the first of many, many delays and postponements in my trial.

'Are you still thirsty?' I asked my escort on the way back to prison, directing the taxi driver to pull over at a nice restaurant down on the Prado.

'Always.'

'Shall we stop and have a Paceña?'

'The beer or the woman?' he asked, then we said at exactly the same time, 'Both!' before bursting into laughter. If I ever needed to escape, Fernando was my man.

卌||

Towards the end of my trial, I sensed that things definitely weren't going my way. Colonel Lanza didn't testify himself, but the prosecutor called policeman after policeman to give evidence that they had seen me arrested at the airport. With the exception of one man, I didn't remember seeing them there. Besides, none of the questions was about whether the merchandise actually belonged to me, but the prosecutor used the same trick with each witness to make me look more and more guilty.

'And can you identify the man you saw that day?' he would ask them.

'Yes,' they would respond solemnly, pointing at me. 'That man there.'

The policeman I did recognise was one of the two who had searched through my possessions at the FELCN offices, putting aside all my clothes that he liked. When he pointed me out as the owner of the suitcases that contained the merchandise, he held his hand up and extended his finger a second longer than the others had, which was how I noticed it: he was wearing my gold ring.

'That's my ring!' I shouted in English, forgetting that I wasn't supposed to speak out of turn. My lawyer nudged me and shook his head for me to be quiet.

'The defendant will remain silent,' the judge reminded my lawyer. He never addressed me directly.

'But he's wearing my ring!' I shouted again. The judge became irritated that I hadn't obeyed him. He glared at me and his face started to turn red. However, I was one hundred per cent certain that it was my ring. I'd had it for years and it was unmistakable.

'*Tranquilo*,' said my lawyer, trying to calm me down. Even the translator, who wasn't supposed to speak to me, tried to persuade me to keep quiet. But I wouldn't let the matter drop. I thought that if I could prove that the police were corrupt and had stolen my property, it would help my defence that they had set me up. I kept complaining and eventually I jumped out of my chair and made a lunge for the policeman. Two guards rushed forward and pushed me back into my seat, then stood there guarding me, waiting for the judge to say something.

At that point, the judge couldn't ignore me any longer. He was forced to interrupt the proceedings and ask the translator to explain what was happening. When the translation was made, a murmur went throughout the courtroom and everyone looked straight at the policeman. He was smart; he didn't try to hide his hand – that would only have made him look guilty. Instead, he frowned innocently and shook his head at me like I was sadly mistaken or crazy.

The judge asked the policeman if the ring was his. He answered that of course it was and that he had bought it in a jewellery store several years before. It was made of gold and had cost him several hundred dollars.

'He's lying. It's mine,' I jumped in, even before the interpreter made the translation. 'I can tell you what picture is on it. Ask him!' I pointed at the policeman and the two guards got ready in case I tried to stand up again. 'I bet he doesn't even know.'

The judge asked the policeman to remove the ring and hand it to the clerk of the court, who handed it on to the judge for inspection.

This time, the policeman was stupid; in his attempt to appear innocent, he didn't look at the ring as he took it off. When the judge asked him to describe the ring, he couldn't.

'I can't remember precisely,' he said confidently, as though it was an unimportant detail and that his forgetfulness didn't prove a thing.

'It's a portrait of the Queen of England,' I announced triumphantly once everyone had had time to assess the policeman's answer and it was clear that he had nothing more to add. 'You can't buy that ring in Bolivia.'

The spectators in the courtroom stirred when the translator repeated what I had said. The judge handed the ring to his assistant for his confirmation, and the prosecutor stepped forward to examine it also. The spectators remained quiet, waiting for them to decide. None of the three said anything aloud, but it was obvious that they agreed I was right.

'The defendant will have an opportunity to give evidence later, if he so chooses,' the judge informed the court, sitting back in his chair and placing the ring in his pocket. He was eager to move on.

'But that's my ring. He stole my ring,' I said weakly, not wanting to let the issue die. However, by then the prosecutor had resumed his position behind his desk and he immediately continued his examination of the police witness.

'And you say that there was a controlled substance in the defendant's suitcase?' he asked in a loud voice that drowned out my protests. I wanted to say more, but my lawyer didn't agree.

'Keep quiet, Thomas,' he advised me in English out of the corner of his mouth, still facing the front. 'You have more at stake here than a gold ring.'

꜀꜀꜀꜀

My team of lawyers remained confident that I would be let off, but I was no longer so sure. After what had happened with my ring, I was worried that the judge was no longer on my side, if he ever had been. On one of the final court dates before the verdict was to be handed down, Fernando was in charge of escorting me back to San Pedro. When there was a slight delay in taking the prisoners down to the transport bus, I saw my opportunity.

'Just a *momentito*, please,' I begged him, slipping away and down the corridor. 'I just need to see someone.'

'But . . .' he stammered, making to follow me. However, when he saw that the corridor led to a dead end, he let me go ahead.

The judge's door was slightly ajar and I could see him working away at his desk. On that occasion, my hands were cuffed in front of my body, so I knocked with both hands and went in before he even had time to respond. I closed the door behind me.

'With your permission,' I said, facing the judge and bowing in exactly the same way as I had seen everyone else do whenever they entered or left the courtroom.

The judge looked up from the document he was studying and adjusted his glasses. He was surprised to see me, but he didn't say anything. I bowed again and cautiously approached his desk.

'*Señor juez*, I am a foreigner. I am very sorry. I have a family in England with two daughters. Please, pardon me,' I stammered in my broken Spanish, producing an envelope from my suit coat. The judge put his hand up to stop me, but I slipped it under a book that was on his desk. In the envelope was five thousand dollars that I had taken out of Abregon's bank account. It was the remainder of my money. The judge looked from me to the book, then back to me, with his hand frozen in the air. Still, he didn't say anything. I bowed once more and left quietly, leaving the door open exactly the same amount as when I'd entered. Fernando was waiting outside the door, looking nervously up and down the corridor. I had taken too long and he was worried about getting into trouble.

'*Vamos*,' he commanded, taking me by the elbow. 'The transport is waiting.'

꙰ ꙰

The money I gave the judge didn't help much. He gave me six years and eight months at the sentencing hearing. My lawyers had told me that I would get off completely, but they were happy with the result.

'It could have been a lot more,' they congratulated me, shaking both my hands because they were cuffed. 'Of course, we will have it reduced on appeal. The judges need to show they are tough at first instance on foreigners. And no one ever serves the full sentence, anyway.'

I was still in shock. I had tried to convince myself to expect the worst in order to prepare for it, but deep down, I wasn't really prepared. I certainly wasn't in any mood to listen to any legal explanations; I just wanted to know the facts.

'So, how long will I be in prison?'

'I think maybe four years, maximum five. It's a good result.'

25
TROUBLED TIMES

The night I got my sentence, I got drunk. Really drunk. And I got high, but it didn't seem to work like it usually did. Maybe the stuff was cut with something, or maybe I just wasn't feeling anything. When I arrived back from court, I bought two packs of cocaine on the way up to my room. Yasheeda was lying on our bed, watching TV. She had been waiting all afternoon for me to return, but I wished she hadn't. I wanted to be alone.

'How did it go?' she asked as soon as I came in. In the transport bus on the way back to San Pedro I had decided not to say anything about what had happened. I would tell her at a better time.

'The same as last time,' I answered, sitting down to make a few lines on a CD cover. 'Postponed again.' Deep down, however, I was afraid of telling her. It had been six months since we had met, but I thought that if I told her, she would leave me.

Although I had been a prisoner all the time I had known Yasheeda, it had never felt that way. We had been able to do most things that normal couples do. We had lived together, we'd had friends around for dinner parties, we had eaten in restaurants. I had even been able to go out of the prison occasionally to spend time with her on the outside. One time, I had a guard escorting me who trusted me a lot and he left us alone together in a hotel room while he waited downstairs in reception.

One night before I was sentenced, Yasheeda and I had talked about our future together. We were both drunk, but she said that she would wait. 'I want to be the first person to hug you when you're a free man,' she said. 'I'll be waiting at the gates when you get out.' At the time, we didn't know how long that would be, but Yasheeda said it didn't matter; she would wait for me. If it took longer than expected and she couldn't stay in Bolivia, then she would fly over from wherever she was.

Now that I had been sentenced, I was worried that everything would change. For a start, I could no longer pay to go out of the prison because the police considered me a higher escape risk. Also, I had spent my last five thousand dollars on bribing the judge. And any money I did get, I would need to save for my appeal.

Yasheeda had never cared about whether I was rich or not, but being completely poor meant that we wouldn't be able to live like we used to. And the thing that would change most would be me. The whole time I had known her I'd been expecting to get out at any moment, so I had always felt like a free man. But now I wasn't.

I couldn't tell her. I did a line and held the CD case out to her.

'Mmm. Not tonight,' she said, looking at the coke out of the corner of her eye and waving it away. 'I'm tired, honey. Let's just relax and watch some TV.'

'There's nothing on. Come on. Just a little one. It's no fun doing it on my own.'

She looked at the coke again and hesitated. 'No, Tommy. What for? It's a Tuesday night. Let's do something else. We could borrow your friend's video player, like you promised.'

'Fine, then.' I did Yasheeda's line for her. She shook her head and sighed loudly so that I would notice, then went back to watching television.

'What's that supposed to mean?' I could tell that she wanted to start an argument.

'You know exactly what,' she said, trying to change the channel with the remote control, but the batteries were flat.

'What, then? Come on. Tell me.'

Yasheeda sat up in bed and leaned forward to get the remote closer to the TV. She held the button down, waving the control in front of the screen, still refusing to look at me. She always did that when we argued. Finally, she answered.

'Tommy, I love you without the drugs. That's not what I'm here for.'

I wanted to say to her, 'That's good coming from you,' but I held back. We had met in a nightclub taking cocaine. She did it every single time I did. In fact, I had never seen her refuse before. Not once. Instead, I said, 'But we always do it together.'

'Yes, but I don't do it every day and I never do it on my own. Cocaine is fun, Tommy, but I just think it's not good for you to do it while you're in prison.'

'Well, I'm stuck here now. I haven't got any other fucking option, have I?' I yelled, banging my fist on the table so hard that the coke went everywhere. 'I'm sorry that I can't go out dancing and sightseeing like all your other boyfriends.'

'Yes, you do,' she said, throwing the remote control on to the blanket and getting up from the bed. 'You do have an option, Tommy.' I could see tears starting to form in her eyes. 'You could not do it at all.'

'Where are you going?' I demanded, scraping the pile of coke back onto the CD case.

'Out,' she said, glaring at me in a way that dared me to say something or try to stop her. I turned my back on her and started chopping up another line with the same defiance, daring her to say something more.

'You don't need it, Tommy. You think you do, but you don't,' she whispered softly, closing the door behind her and pushing it from the outside to make sure it had shut properly.

It was dark, but I wasn't going to chase after her. That was exactly what she wanted. Visiting hours were over and the gates were locked, so I knew that she would have to come back eventually. Half an hour went by, then another half-hour. I changed my mind and went out looking for her. However, she had left the prison on her own. Apparently, she had banged on the main gates and yelled until the guards came and let her out. The lieutenant told me she was crying.

'What did you do to her, *inglés?*' he asked me through the bars. 'She's a very pretty girl.'

'I didn't hit her,' I snapped at him, and suddenly kicked at the gate without knowing why, so that he jumped back in surprise. If it had been any other officer, I might have been in trouble, but that guy was my friend and he was also fond of Yasheeda.

'All right. *Tranquilo.*' The lieutenant shook his head and looked at me strangely. 'I didn't say you did.'

卌‖

Two days after our fight, Yasheeda went on another trip, this time to Rurrenabaque to do a tour of the Amazon jungle. After that, she was due to head home to Israel. Even though we had fought, I missed her a lot more than I imagined. She was the first thing on my mind when I woke up and the last thing I thought about before I fell asleep. During the day, I also had plenty of time to think about her. I was expecting a call from her any time and I must have checked that my phone was working at least ten times a day.

To pass the time, I began cleaning my room again; once in the morning, again after lunch and a final time before it got dark, even though it was already spotless. I must have folded my clothes a million times, and the plates and cutlery were always sparkling clean. I wanted everything to be absolutely perfect in case Yasheeda came back to surprise me. It would be just like her to turn up without warning. I waited and waited to hear from her, but she broke her promise. She didn't call or write to me – not even once.

Whenever I could get hold of him, I sent Alejandro to check my email account for news from her. Alejandro was the son of one of the inmates, Emilio, who was in for trafficking. I don't know how old the boy was, but he was only small and he didn't speak much. At first he seemed shy, but you could tell that he was a tough little kid underneath, just like his father, which is exactly what his mother wanted to avoid. She had left Emilio when he was sentenced and taken their child and gone to live with another man in a small apartment. She had never visited her husband in jail and refused to let their son visit him either, but Alejandro used to sneak out from school and come to San Pedro. Whenever he came to the prison, his father sent him outside on errands in order to make a bit of extra money. With such a small and innocent face, he was the perfect mule; the guards let him in and out whenever he wanted and never searched him.

There probably weren't any Internet cafes in the jungle towns where Yasheeda was, but I kept sending Alejandro to check my email anyway. If he didn't visit, I would ring him at home. Whenever his mother answered, she told me he wasn't there. I knew that wasn't true; when he wasn't at school, she never let him leave the house. At first, I thought she was the one lying to me, but I later learned that it was Alejandro who was pretending he wasn't there. He must have felt bad every time he had to tell me that Yasheeda hadn't written.

I started getting depressed. During the first week, I was worried that something bad had happened to her. I checked the newspapers every day for accidents involving foreigners, like I had the first time she went away. After ten days I knew there had been no accident – she was having a great time and had forgotten all about me. By then, I had forgotten about our argument, but she obviously hadn't. She might have already returned from the jungle and left the country, or maybe she had met someone else.

Each time I heard a *taxista* call my name, I prayed it was her and was always disappointed when it was another group of Israeli back-packers from El Lobo wanting to visit me. I was glad to have people to keep me company, but I still missed Yasheeda. Sometimes I couldn't put my full energy into telling my visitors my stories and, although they found the prison interesting, I got the impression that they had heard incredible things about me and were a bit disappointed when they met me in person.

A few times, I felt so depressed that I asked the *taxistas* to apologise and say that I was too sick to receive any visitors. I started having nightmares in which I could see Yasheeda kissing someone else, although I couldn't see his face. I tried not to be jealous, but I wanted to kill him, whoever he was. After these dreams, I even began to hate her.

26
HASTA LUEGO

When Yasheeda had been around, I had never had trouble getting to sleep. But after the argument we'd had, I was convinced that she was never coming back. I was looking at another four or five years in prison on my own. My insomnia returned and, with it, the little red button reappeared in the middle of my table. I increased the number of sleeping pills I was taking.

During the day I was overcome by drowsiness. I wanted to die. I went back on the higher-dosage pills and one evening, when Ricardo didn't come around to watch the news, I decided it was time to stop thinking about it. Before I went to bed, I swallowed an entire box of pills. I didn't feel anything for a long time. I watched television and I don't remember falling asleep.

In the morning I woke up with blurry thoughts and the feeling of having been cheated. My neighbour was pounding on my door, because I hadn't appeared for *lista*.

'Hurry up!' he called. 'The major will send you to La Muralla.'

I fell out of bed and went downstairs in my pyjamas, holding on to the railing.

'*Presente*,' I answered when the major called my name. No one noticed anything different about me except for my neighbour, who saw that I wasn't walking straight. He laughed and asked me if I was drunk.

'I've got a cold,' I told him.

卌〢

Three weeks after Yasheeda had left, a *taxista* called up to me that I had a visitor waiting at the gate.

'Who is it?' I yelled through the closed door, assuming it was another tourist and not really caring if the *taxista* heard me or not.

'Tho-mas Mc-Fa-dden,' came the call again, closer this time. I opened the door. It was a *taxista* called Freddy. He had climbed the two flights of stairs and was now looking up at me from the bottom of my wooden ladder and waving for me to come down.

'Who is it?' I asked him again.

'Your *chica*. Your girlfriend.' My heart started racing. I had to be careful not to get too excited, though; the *taxistas* always said that any girl who came to visit was my girlfriend.

'What does she look like?'

'Your *chica*! The beautiful one! Hurry up! She's waiting.'

It *had* to be her! But I wanted to be certain, so I asked again. 'What does she look like, Freddy?'

'How many *novias* do you have, *inglés*?' he teased me, showing his toothless smile and holding out his hand for a coin.

'Freddy, I'm serious. What does she look like?'

'You don't even know what your own girlfriend looks like! Lend me a boliviano, Thomas. Please! I haven't eaten. I'm hungry.'

I reached into my pocket, threw him a silver coin and received my answer immediately.

'Long black hair. Good body. It's her. The one you have been waiting for. Your *israelita*. The one from before. *¡Apúrate!* Everybody is trying to steal her from you!'

I was so excited that I slammed the wooden door behind me without thinking and leapt down the stairs, two at a time, almost falling over at the bottom. Freddy chased after me, begging for more coins, but I was going too fast for him to keep up. I rounded the second corner without looking and crashed into Ricardo, who was on his way up to visit me. I didn't have time to stop and explain. Halfway down the next set of stairs I began to worry about whether I looked OK. But it was too late for that now. I had to get to the gate in case the guards turned Yasheeda away. Behind me, I could hear Ricardo calling something after me, but I was already too far away to hear what it was.

Yasheeda!

There she was, more beautiful than I remembered. One of the guards was trying to make her leave. I went straight up to the bars, ignoring the head *taxista*'s warning to keep my distance.

'Yasheeda!' I called out, but I must have yelled louder than intended. Everyone stopped what they were doing and stared at me. Yasheeda looked up and when she saw me, she smiled.

'Just wait there! I'll get you in. Don't leave!' However, the lieutenant shook his head when I asked him.

'No *turistas* allowed in. Governor's orders.' Apparently there were television crews outside the main gates. The lieutenant turned away and headed towards the office.

'But she's not a tourist,' I protested, rattling the gates in frustration. 'She's my wife! You know her. She's been here before.'

'*No importa*. No visitors today,' he called back over his shoulder. At the last moment he softened. 'You can have an interview, but nothing more.'

I told Yasheeda to quickly go to the women's interview room and I raced around to meet her.

Up close, Yasheeda looked even prettier. Her face was glowing and healthy and she had put on a little weight, which made every part of her body stand out and her skin stretch tighter over her muscles. Her long hair was tied back so that I could see every feature of her face clearly, from her dark, sparkling eyes to her tiny ears that stuck out a bit. We stood there, just staring at each other, not knowing what to say. She spoke first, sounding slightly awkward.

'Hi! How are you?'

'Fine. And how about you?' I replied. I hated those types of conversations. There were so many things I wanted to say to her, and so many questions I wanted to ask, that it was hard to know where to start. 'How was your trip?'

'Good! We had so much fun,' she answered, forcing a smile. Again, I sensed something strange in the way she was acting. I began to worry that she had bad news to tell me.

'So, how was the jungle?'

'Excellent. Really good. Thanks, Thomas.' She *never* called me Thomas. It was always Tommy.

'Oh, that's good. You had a good time, then. I'm glad.'

'Yeah. It was good,' she repeated calmly, nodding her head as though she were somewhere else, far, far away.

'And your friends?'

'They're good, too,' she nodded again, and looked down.

'Good. That's nice.'

There was a long pause. I thought of asking her if something was wrong, but I didn't want to push her. When she looked up, she noticed the dark circles under my eyes.

'You look tired,' she said.

'Yeah. A bit.' I still felt sleepy from the pills. She looked down once more.

When she looked up again, our eyes met for a moment and she smiled, properly this time. I could feel her coming back to me. I had to say something before she looked away.

'I thought you weren't going to come.' I started to stutter. 'I thought ... when you didn't send any emails ... I thought maybe you left without ... I thought that –' She interrupted me.

'No. I would never ... I mean, there was a landslide on the road back to Coroico. We had to wait three days for them to repair it. And I had no way of calling you. At first we were going to get the plane, but all the tickets were sold out so we had to get the bus.'

'Oh. So nothing bad happened, then?' I asked, finally coming out with it.

'No. Of course, nothing bad happened. Don't be silly, Tommy! Why would you think that? I'm here, aren't I?' When she said that, all the stupid doubts and fears went away and in their place I felt a rush of happiness and relief. I gripped the metal poles with both hands and leaned forward to kiss her.

'Hey. You look beautiful! I really missed you, you know?'

It was the wrong thing to say. Yasheeda stood back and folded her arms and immediately a deep panic went through my insides. All of my fears came back, only twice as strong. Something had definitely happened. I was absolutely sure of it now. I stared at her, waiting for her to speak, but she said nothing.

'Yasheeda. What's the matter? Is something wrong?'

'No, nothing. Why?' she answered quietly.

'Are you sure? You know you can tell me,' I whispered back.

'No, nothing. I promise.'

Yasheeda kept insisting that nothing was wrong, but I could sense that there was. We stared at each other a while longer, then she looked down and I knew that I was losing her again. I waited and she finally looked like she was about to say something, but then a guard came over to tell us that our interview time was up.

'Five minutes more, my brother,' I begged, flashing him some coins I had ready. I'm sure he would have accepted them, but Yasheeda seemed to want to leave.

'I'd probably better go,' she said. 'I don't want to get you in trouble with the police or anything.'

'OK, then. You can come back tomorrow. I mean, if you want to, that is. We can talk. I'll arrange permission for you to get in. I can ring the governor tonight to make sure.'

'I'll try my best, Thomas. But I'd better go now.'

She came up to me at the bars to say goodbye. I moved forward and closed my eyes, hoping our lips would meet, but she kissed me just to the side of my mouth and when I opened my eyes again she had her back to me and was squeezing her way past the Bolivian wives who were blocking the corridor. At the last moment, she turned and mouthed the words 'Hasta luego.' Then she was gone.

27
SAN PEDRO PRISON TOURS

After Yasheeda left, I was in a state of shock for several weeks. I was too numb even to think about killing myself. I didn't need to kill myself, anyway; I already felt like I was dead inside. The only things that made me aware that I was alive during that time were regular visits from Sylvia, who continued to keep a watchful eye over me, and Ricardo's friendship.

The Chilean car deal went wrong, so Abregon and I lost our money. After a month I was forced to sell my room in Pinos and move into Alamos in order to pay my lawyers' fees. Transferring my possessions into a new place helped me to face up to the fact that this was going to be my home for the next five years. I began the appeal process immediately because the sentence had to be certified by a superior court – if an appeal wasn't lodged, they assumed you were guilty and could increase your sentence.

Gradually, I started to come out of my depression. As I did so, I discovered that although Yasheeda was gone, she had left behind a gift for me: the tourists. At first, my only visitors were a handful of Israelis who had heard about me through Yasheeda and her friends. However, La Paz is a small city with only a few hotels and bars catering to foreign tourists, so word spread quickly.

The San Pedro prison tours began slowly, but it wasn't long before they really started to take off. My second and third years in San Pedro were the busiest and happiest of my whole life. Tourists began arriving at the gates in larger and larger groups, sometimes up to ten or fifteen at a time. When they came, the *taxistas* would send for me. I would explain to the tourists through the bars that they had to leave their passports with the lieutenant and then he would let them into the main courtyard. Once they were inside, I would introduce myself properly before taking them straight to my room where I would offer to make them a cup of tea or coffee. When everyone felt comfortable, I would give them some background information on the prison. Then I would show them around the various sections, except for the five-and-a-half-star section of Posta, which you needed permission to enter.

Everything was quite peaceful in San Pedro during the day and there really wasn't all that much to see. What the tourists enjoyed most of all was the thrill of actually being inside a prison, as well as hearing about how the San Pedro system worked. As I took my visitors around each part of the prison, I told them about my own experiences. I showed them the prison church, the abandoned building where I had slept the first night, as well as *la piscina* – 'the pool' – and explained a little about the property system, the prison economy and the prison hierarchy. They were always fascinated by the luxurious cells they saw and by the fact that there were young children about as well as cats and dogs.

The tour itself ran for less than an hour. What happened afterwards depended on what the tourists wanted. Sometimes we ate a meal at one of the restaurants, which the tourists often claimed served better food than the ones outside. Then, if there wasn't another group waiting for me, we would go back to my room for a chat. When it came time to leave I would accompany them to the gate to make sure that they got their passports back and made it safely out of the prison.

†††\\

Running the tours was quite easy money and a lot of fun. Within a few months, I had worked out which parts of the prison and which stories the tourists found most interesting. I established a kind of routine in the way I did things, but I never got bored because no two groups were ever the same and I never got tired of seeing people's reactions to how crazy San Pedro was. However, being a tour guide wasn't all smooth sailing. There were a lot of people I needed to keep happy, which involved a lot of juggling.

First, the police wanted their cut. In the beginning, they were content to receive ten bolivianos per tourist, which was three bolivianos more than the standard entry price paid by the locals. However, they worked out very quickly that the foreigners would be willing to pay more. I had no choice but to agree to whatever terms the guards set, because without their cooperation there would have been no prison tours in the first place.

Eventually we struck a deal that I would increase the tour price and they would receive half the takings. However, the real cost of bribing the police was much more than that. I paid the fifty per cent directly to the major on duty after the tours, but on top of that I had to keep the low-ranking guards happy by buying them food and soft drinks and handing out small *propinas*, as well as paying larger sums to any new officers who arrived at the prison.

For policemen, working at San Pedro was one of the most profitable postings you could get in the whole country. In fact, many of the officers actually paid to be transferred there. The cops had their hands in absolutely everything and with so much money involved, a lot of power struggles and politics went on behind the scenes. As a result, the prison administration was constantly being reshuffled and, unfortunately for me, every change of personnel meant starting again from scratch with the bribes. Just when I had started to get a good relationship going with one of the majors or captains, he'd be replaced by a new man, who would pretend not to be corrupt in order to get bigger bribes. At any one time there was a governor, three majors, four captains and about five lieutenants. The staff turnover was so high that it was impossible to remember all of their names, so I took to calling each policeman by his rank. The privates I just called '*amigo*'.

The cost of a tour was twenty-five bolivianos, about five US dollars, although gradually this price went up as police cracked down and made it tougher for foreigners to visit. Sometimes tourists would claim that they didn't have enough money to pay the full amount. Many of them were used to the Bolivians trying to rip them off and had the mentality that you were expected to bargain for everything. They assumed that I was no different, since I was a prisoner. But what they didn't understand was that I had to pay the police no matter what; the head *taxista* counted heads as each person came in and every single one of them had to be accounted for. If I ever claimed that a tourist hadn't paid, the police might think that I was trying to cheat them, which would make it harder for me to get the next group in.

The other big expense was keeping the inmates happy. When I first started running the tours, I was scared that something might happen to one of the tourists, so I stuck to the main courtyards and didn't stay too long in the dangerous sections. The tourists were always polite and respectful, but their presence created resentment among the inmates; many felt that they were being made into exhibits, and others were jealous because I was a foreigner who got more visitors than they, as locals, did. However, the main source of jealousy was money.

The gangs that controlled the economy of the prison liked to run everything themselves, so they tried to set up rival tour operations in order to run me out of business, using as guides a few cheaply paid Bolivian prisoners who could speak a little English. They enlisted the help of the *taxistas* to call for these guides, and keep me away, whenever foreigners turned up at the main gates. However, even when they did succeed in tricking tourists into coming inside, their tours were nowhere near as popular as mine. The word at the hostels was that you had to ask for me by name.

The same thing happened when the gangs got some of the English-speaking foreign prisoners involved; people still demanded that I be the one who took them around.

'Thomas is sick,' the *taxistas* would say, or, 'Thomas isn't doing the tours anymore. Freddy is.'

But the tourists insisted. 'We only want to see Thomas. Otherwise, we're not coming in.'

So, eventually, my competitors realised that I had to be part of the business and they decided to get involved by force.

The tall man with the scar across his face who had saved me at *la piscina* came to my door, flanked by his two henchmen. I knew by then that his name was Lucho, which is the nickname in Bolivia for Luis. His other nickname was Burro – 'donkey' – owing to his strength and inability to feel pain. He was the biggest man in the prison and the most feared. On the outside, he had killed people; on the inside, he worked together with his gang to control the most dangerous sections in the prison and also as a standover man for anyone who paid him. Funnily enough, everyone in the prison liked Lucho. He was always very polite and nice in the way he did his job. He could probably afford to be, since no one ever argued.

'*Tomás*, we need to have a small word with you,' he said quietly, his huge frame filling my doorway. I invited them in and they seated themselves at my table. There was no aggression at all. They had simply come as friends to offer me some advice. There were rumours that many of the inmates were annoyed about the tourists visiting the prison. Some of the gangs were planning to rob them and create problems for me inside the prison. I had to be careful: if any foreigner was ever attacked, that would mean the end of the tours immediately. Lucho had a generous proposition for me.

'*Mi amigo*, I want to help you with the tours,' he said, linking his index fingers together in a symbol of unity. His companions nodded. 'I think we will work well together. Like brothers.'

As with the police, I had no choice but to agree. Lucho and I became what was known in San Pedro as *socios* – partners. For a share of the tour profits, he and his two men, Victor Cartagena and Lucho Vaca, would accompany the tour groups as official bodyguards, while I showed them around the various sections. Although this meant less money for me, it did solve two problems in one go: it kept the tourists protected as they moved about the prison, and it kept me protected from the other gangs.

One of the gang leaders was only a boy, although a very dangerous boy. His real name was David Cordero; however, he was known to everyone simply as Fantasma – meaning 'ghost' – because he believed in spirits and read books about black magic. He was only nineteen years old when he arrived at San Pedro. Legally, he shouldn't have been in an adult prison because he was under twenty-one, but no one did anything about it. In Bolivia, there were inmates as young as fourteen.

Fantasma was Bolivian but he had spent many years in the United States on a green card, so he spoke English with a strong American accent. He acted a lot tougher than his age because he had hung out with street gangs in New York, where he had become known as 'The Latin King'. Fierce tattoos now covered his hands, and he wore American-style gang clothing and listened to rap music. Despite his tough act, I did my best to make friends with Fantasma when he first moved into Alamos. At that stage, I didn't know his background and I thought I might be able to save him from being attacked, like I had been. However, I soon worked out that Fantasma didn't need any looking after.

Within a month of entering San Pedro, he had stabbed an inmate in a fight. He was immediately sent to La Muralla, the prison's punishment section. When he got out, he stabbed another inmate in the leg and was sent back to the isolation cells. I wasn't sure if all this was an act to gain respect in prison, but I didn't want to find out either. I was certain that he would eventually end up going too far and be transferred him to Chonchocoro, the harsh, maximum-security prison Ricardo had mentioned in my first week. But in the meantime, I wanted to stay on his good side.

After that second incident, Fantasma continued to establish himself as someone who was prepared to go to any length to win a fight. The other inmates already steered well clear of him because of the crime he had originally been charged with. Gradually, as I learned more about what that crime was, I began to cool down our friendship.

Fantasma was in San Pedro for killing his best friend. When he had come back from America, bringing with him the latest rap music and dress code from the New York gangs, he became a local hero and formed his own gang known as 'The Latin Kings'. He fell out with his best friend and one night, when a group of them were drunk and high at a party, they started to fight. Fantasma pulled out a sawn-off shotgun. The friend took a step back, but Fantasma fired a round into his chest. The friend fell to his knees and begged forgiveness, but Fantasma reloaded, lifted the barrel, pointed it directly at his friend's face and pulled the trigger.

When I found out what he had done, I didn't say anything because I didn't want Fantasma to think that I was turning my back on him or that I was scared of him. To be honest, he had never shown me his violent tendencies. In fact, one day he had started crying after he'd had a few drinks in my room. He told me a bit about his tough childhood. When he was younger, he had been sent to live with an uncle who had punched him in the head and chained him under a cold shower or locked him in a closet if he misbehaved. I didn't know whether to believe Fantasma or not, but something had to explain how a boy of nineteen could calmly blow his best friend away in front of several witnesses.

卌‖

During the first year and a half that the prison tours ran, all of my visitors were backpackers aged in their twenties who were looking for adventure. Although the jail wasn't as dangerous as people might have expected, these were the only foreigners who were brave enough to risk it. With the bodyguards protecting them, there was really no need to be afraid. In all of my time as a guide, not one tourist was ever hurt in San Pedro. In fact, once visitors got over their initial fear of coming through the gate, most were amazed at how safe and relaxed the atmosphere was inside. In broad daylight there was little chance that any of the inmates would be stupid enough to try anything; apart from the payback they could expect from my bodyguards, the police would have severely punished anyone who attacked a tourist.

Eventually, the inmates welcomed tourists because they brought cash into the prison economy. I tried to spread business around so that everyone benefited. The *taxistas* made very easy money – normally, they charged half a boliviano per callout, but I let them charge double that, and to each tourist in the group; the restaurant and shop owners sold extra food; poorer inmates were often able to sell their artwork and souvenirs, such as key rings or small figurines; and even the beggars managed to scrounge a few small coins. During that initial period, at least, most of my visitors were attracted by the unique opportunity of seeing what life was like inside a Bolivian prison. But there was also another major attraction for the backpackers: taking cocaine.

With the police only ever entering the prison to carry out the *lista*, it was actually safer to do drugs inside the prison than outside. Ricardo used to joke about this all the time: 'What are they going to do if they catch you with coke in here? Send you to prison?' It was also safe for tourists to take cocaine in the prison. The guards knew exactly what went on in my room, but providing I was discreet and paid them their cut, they never bothered me.

Many tourists simply wanted to sniff one or two lines before they went out the gates, just to know what pure Bolivian cocaine was like. For others, it was the first time they had ever done it. And if you were going to try cocaine at all, why not in San Pedro? The cocaine was made in our laboratories, so it was cheap, and you knew it wasn't cut with anything nasty.

The trouble was, once we had started sniffing, it was hard to stop. My visitors always wanted to buy one more packet, especially when they became entranced by my stories about the jail. We would do more lines and then buy some cans of beer, and when it came time for them to leave, they wouldn't want to go. They wanted to hear more. Luckily, there was a solution: tourists could also sometimes stay the night in San Pedro.

It depended on which officer was on duty and how strictly the guards were cracking down, at the time. If something had ever happened to one of the tourists, the major would have lost his job. But for a few extra dollars, he usually considered that to be a worthwhile risk. He always asked that I keep visitors in my room to prevent them being seen by too many people and to minimise the risk of any incidents. This limited what we could do, but it didn't stop us from enjoying ourselves. For most tourists, it was the excitement of being able to spend the night in a third-world prison that mattered. That's one experience that very few people in the world get to have. It's something they would remember and tell people about for the rest of their lives. Besides, at the going price, with all the modern conveniences, including a private room with comfortable mattress, television, electricity, running water, cooking, washing and laundry facilities, and a wide selection of quality restaurants, San Pedro prison was one of the better-value accommodations for backpackers in La Paz. And with no police around and a constant supply of cheap, pure cocaine, it was one of the best places to party in South America.

Usually, I would cook a meal and get the spare mattresses and sheets ready for when we wanted to sleep. Then we would buy some more beers or a bottle of rum and more packets of cocaine, and maybe some marijuana to bring us down at the end of the night. But always, there was cocaine. Outside, people normally take cocaine when they're at a club, drinking and dancing. That wasn't an option in jail, so the main thing we did on cocaine in San Pedro was talk. We talked a lot. Once I'd had a few lines, the stories I had stored up from seven years of international drug trafficking would flow and the tourists would sit listening, spellbound.

I also enjoyed hearing my visitors' stories about their travels. There wasn't enough space in my room for more than five people to sleep, so if a whole group wanted to stay, we would have to stay up until morning, doing coke, drinking and talking.

One night, five or six backpackers were sitting around my table at three in the morning, completely drunk and high on coke. They were from various countries and no one could stop talking, least of all Jay, an American, who had studied anthropology at university. He was explaining something about the Incan empire, which I was finding interesting, but everyone else had become bored.

Paul, an Australian, interrupted Jay. 'So, where exactly are you from again?'

'It's hard to say, really,' sighed Jay. 'I've been travelling for some time now. I don't feel like I belong to any one place in the world. I'm really from nowhere and everywhere at the same time, if you know what I mean.'

'How long have you actually been on the road?' asked Giles, a long-haired backpacker from the UK.

'Oh, approximately thirty-four days,' replied Jay, nodding his head proudly.

Paul raised his eyebrows. 'A month, you mean?'

'Well, it's not really a question of chronological time,' said Jay, sounding defensive. 'I don't measure things in that way. I've done more than ten countries during that time and it's impossible to measure any cultural experience in terms of number of days. It's more of a personal growth thing . . .' His voice trailed off as though he were allowing the thought to linger for dramatic effect. As an afterthought, he added, 'Besides, thirty-four days is more than a month, isn't it?'

'How can you "do" ten countries in thirty-four days?' said Giles, using his fingers to indicate the inverted commas around the word 'do'.

Before Jay could answer, Liz, a South African girl, diplomatically changed the subject. I got the impression that there was something going on between her and Jay.

'Cheers, everyone!' She raised her glass and we were obliged to reach for our own. 'And what about you?' she asked Paul. 'How long have you been travelling?'

'Oh, I left Melbourne, let's see . . . I think it was March, April . . . a bit over four years ago. I worked in London, 'did' Europe . . .' he said, making the same inverted-commas gesture as Giles had. Giles laughed so suddenly, he almost choked on his drink. '. . . travelled through the Middle East and Africa, then flew to Mexico, down through Central America, Colombia, Ecuador, Peru, and now I'm here in Bolivia. Pretty much the standard story.'

'Standard story! That's totally awesome,' said Jay, who had completely missed the joke on him, even though Giles was still in a coughing fit. 'You must speak good Spanish, then.'

'Not a fucking word, mate! *Cerveza, por favor*. That's all you need, really. I can get by. Just flash these South Americans some cash and they usually understand, hey!'

'So, you haven't seen your family for four years?' said Liz.

'Nup. I don't reckon I've even spoken to them for about two years.'

'Why not?'

'Well, it's so fucking expensive to call home from these countries, isn't it? Three minutes on the phone costs more than my daily budget.'

'What about collect call?' Jay asked.

'Collect what?'

'Reverse charges,' Liz translated.

'Oh, no, my old man ain't gonna pay. No way. I reckon he'd hang up on the operator.'

I suddenly had an idea. There was a Chilean guy in my section who rented out his mobile phone to make cheap international phone calls. You paid a set fee and you could make as many calls as you wanted to anywhere in the world in a half-hour period.

'How cheap?' asked Paul.

'Very cheap. Five dollars for half an hour,' I replied.

'That's impossible. There's no way.'

'I'm not joking, man. Seriously, you just pay the guy the money, he brings you the phone and you have it for half an hour. You can call as many times as you like to anywhere in the world.'

'How come it's so cheap?'

'I don't know exactly. The Chileans are smart, man. They are a lot more intelligent than the Bolivians in prison. I think it's because there's not much oxygen up here, so the Bolivian brains don't develop properly. This guy rewires the phone and breaks into the telephone network and he gets free calls. Every few days they cut him off. But then he does it again. What are they going to do if they catch him doing it – put him in jail?' I laughed, stealing Ricardo's joke, and everyone thought I was funny.

'But there's no risk for me? They're not going to trace the call or anything?' Paul asked.

'Hey, man, this is Bolivia.'

'Sweet as! I just have to remember my home phone number now. Bring it on!'

'OK. You wait here and I'll go get the phone. Have another line, man! It will help you talk.'

卌||

The phone was one of those old, chunky models with a wire aerial that you had to extend.

'OK. You have half an hour starting from now,' I said, handing it to Paul, who eyed the cracked display panel suspiciously.

He dialled the number and put the phone to his ear.

'Is it ringing?' asked Jay.

'Yeah, seems to be working. It's dialling at least. What? . . . Hello Mum . . . yeah, Mum, it's me . . . I'm calling from Bolivia . . . *Bolivia*, Mum. It's in South America . . . yeah, I'm fine. I'm calling from prison . . . the prison . . .' The others in the room started giggling. 'Yes, I'm in jail, Mum . . . Mum! . . . Can you hear me? Fuck! It cut out. Fuck!'

Everyone stopped laughing. No one said a word. We were all imagining what Paul's poor mother must have been thinking on the other side of the world, having not heard from her son in over two years, only to receive a call from him on a bad connection telling her that he was in prison in South America.

'Quick. Press redial!' said Liz.

'Where's redial? *You* do it!' he shouted, thrusting the phone at her.

'Here, have another line,' I said. 'It'll make you chill down.'

'I thought you said it makes you *talk*?' Giles queried sarcastically.

'It's ringing!' yelled Liz, and handed the phone back to Paul.

Paul tried to explain to his mother what was happening. 'Yeah, Mum. It's me again . . . I'm fine . . . the phone just cut out . . . Yes, I'm in jail, but I'm not in any trouble. It's not an ordinary jail . . .'

Paul was now raising his voice because of the bad connection, 'Mum . . . listen to me! No, I haven't been taking drugs . . .' As Paul tried to calm his mother, Giles offered him the CD case, where a line of cocaine was set up. Paul shook his head and waved it away angrily. 'I'm telling the truth, Mum . . . I'm not making it up . . . yes, I know that cocaine is evil, Mum . . . I know you're not stupid, Mum . . . I've never touched it . . .' He rolled his eyes. 'Mum, why won't you just listen to me?'

At that point he changed his mind and motioned to Giles for the CD case. Holding the telephone between his ear and his shoulder, he rolled up a Bolivian banknote, covered the mouthpiece and quietly sniffed a little line. He had a lot of explaining to do. And cocaine really helps you to explain things. You can explain a lot on cocaine.

28
THOMAS THE SHOPKEEPER

The tours didn't run every day but overall, things were going really well. Business tended to come in waves – some months there would be a mad rush, while other months were completely flat, owing to the transport strikes and road blocks that interrupted tourism. After one of these slumps, it would take a while for the word to spread around the backpacker hostels again. Sometimes, the guards got tough and wouldn't let anyone in. There might be a high-ranking official or politician hanging around, or there may have been a report in the media about corruption in the prison. Or they just might have wanted to remind me who was in charge – I might have been the one running the tours and taking the money, but they held the keys to the gate.

However, even with these interruptions, I could rely on a certain income every month and managed to save up some money. I didn't want to leave the cash just sitting there in my room, so I decided to invest it: I bought another prison cell. Prices were low during that period and I was counting on the value going up by the time I got out so that I would have some money to live on for a while on the outside. Unfortunately, as Ricardo pointed out, when prices are low it's because there's not much demand; so, no one wanted to rent it from me. In the meantime, I had a better idea: I would start my own shop. Aside from the extra income it would generate, it would give me something to do during the quiet times. When things got too busy, there were plenty of people who would work in the shop for a few coins.

Running my own *tienda* was a lot of fun. The business side of things was simple enough to handle. I had to remember to put my supply orders in before anything ran out and be careful not to buy too much of products that went off, such as milk and cheese. I also learned some basic bookkeeping skills, writing down every transaction and counting my stock and cash each morning to make sure I hadn't made any mistakes and that nothing had been stolen by my employees. So that part, at least, wasn't too difficult.

The main skill you needed was in dealing with the customers. Owning a shop in prison wasn't like owning one on the outside. In the outside world, provided your prices are fair, a customer will come to your grocery store for two main reasons – if it has an adequate selection and is close to wherever the customer is. In the prison, however, all the shops had the same suppliers and the same prices, and every shop was close by, so the one thing that made a difference was how you treated people.

Bolivians are strange in the way they do business. I'd found that out very early on when Ricardo used to send me to the shops. I was still learning to speak the language back then. A lot of words are similar in Spanish and English, so I learned quickly, but I often had trouble with pronunciation. Many times I came back empty-handed or with the wrong item. Ricardo would always laugh and give me a lecture.

'Chilli is *ají*. I repeated it to you twice,' he said one time, pointing to the floor, meaning that I should go back downstairs. He held out the joint he was smoking so that I could have a quick puff before I went back to the shop.

'But that's what I said – *aji*. He's run out,' I said, reaching for the joint. It was my third trip and I was sick of climbing the ladder.

'No. No. No,' said Ricardo, suddenly deciding not to give me the joint after all, because it would ruin my concentration. 'Listen. Not *aji* – it's *ají*. Ah-heeee. The accent is on the second syllable. If you get it wrong, they won't understand you.'

'*Ají*,' I said, testing my pronunciation.

'*Correcto*.' Ricardo gave me a small round of applause, then handed me the joint as a reward.

'This language is ridiculous.' I inhaled the smoke deep into my lungs and held it there.

'No, it's not. Not to them, it's not,' he said, stamping his foot and laughing at me. 'Now go! You're ruining my cuisine.'

My pronunciation improved, but I suspected that the shopkeepers sometimes deliberately chose not to understand me. One time I was absolutely certain of it: Ricardo had sent me to buy some meat – *carne* – from a guy called Simón all the way around in Cancha, and I had come back empty-handed. Three times.

'Did you pronounce *carne* correctly?' Ricardo asked impatiently, putting his hands on his hips when I came back shaking my head.

'Of course, I pronounced it correctly. I'm not stupid, you know. *Carne. Carne. Carne.* See!'

'Were you nice to him? I keep telling you that you have to be nice to these people.' He had told me hundreds of times that learning the words and their pronunciation was only the first step. You also had to learn the culture and how to speak to the people.

'Of course, I was nice to him!' I yelled back. I was beginning to suspect that Ricardo was in on the joke too. 'I'm always nice.'

'*Tranquilo, inglés.* Just tell me, what did you say exactly? Maybe you offended him in some way.'

'I didn't offend him. He doesn't have any *carne*, that's all.'

'Of course, he's got *carne*. He's a butcher. I saw him today and he told me he'd just bought a new lot. That's why I specifically told you to go to him.'

'Well, he's the best butcher in the world because he's sold it all.' There was no way I was going back to visit Simón a fourth time. If he didn't have any, he didn't have any. But Ricardo insisted.

'I saw him less than an hour ago, Thomas. Now just tell me what you said.'

Ricardo made me feel like a child sometimes. I sighed heavily and recounted my conversation with Simón the butcher.

'OK. I went down there and I said, "*Buenas noches, Simón. ¿Cómo está?*" ' I pronounced his name right, then I asked him for two pounds of *carne*. I said *por favor* and I called him *usted* to be polite, just like you told me. But he still said he had nothing.'

Ricardo made a clicking sound with his tongue like I had committed a glaring error.

'Well, *of course* he wouldn't sell you any.'

'Why? What did I do wrong this time?'

'You can't just walk straight up to him and ask him for meat without talking to him first.'

'I did talk to him.'

'Not properly. You don't know these people, Thomas. If you don't talk to them first or if they don't like you, they won't sell you a single thing.'

'So, you're saying that even if he *has* meat, he won't sell it to me?' I said sarcastically.

'That's right,' Ricardo replied, as though he was making a point that was very obvious.

'That's ridiculous! He's running a business. If he has something and I want to buy it and I have the money, then why won't he sell it to me? Who cares if he doesn't like me, he can still take my money. Doesn't he need money?'

'Thomas, you're not in Europe anymore. This is a different culture. Of course, he needs money, but you have to talk with the people. They are a proud people, especially the Aymarans.'

'So what? They still need money. If they don't want money, then they're stupid.'

'They are not stupid at all. Don't ever call them stupid! They just think differently. You have to show them respect, and you have to make them laugh.'

I tried to understand this, but it was illogical. Maybe the Bolivians weren't stupid, but they were definitely a bit crazy.

'So, what should I have said to him, then?'

'You have to talk to him. You have to call him *Simoncito*. They like it when you put '*ito*' on the end of every word. *Momentito, bolivianito, pequeñito*. Especially with their names. It's not Carlos, Juan or Tomás. It's Carlitos, Juanito and Tomacito. It shows you're friends with someone.'

'Then what after that?'

'Just talk about whatever you feel like until they laugh. But remember, it's not for the money. You are asking them a favour as a friend and they are giving you something as a present.'

'But how can it be a present if I have to pay for it?'

'You aren't paying, Thomas. They give you a present, and you give them the money as a present in return.'

By the time I had my own shop, I had mastered the art of dealing with Bolivians. But the only downside with having to be nice all the time was that everyone wanted credit. Allowing convicted criminals to run a tab at your corner shop is a very risky business at the best of times, but it's even riskier when those convicted criminals are still in jail. No one in San Pedro would have qualified for a bank loan – there were many dishonest people who would take advantage whenever they could, and the honest ones weren't much better. But it was hard to refuse people and stay on their good side as well. If I offended someone, they might ruin my reputation and never pay me back. And what could I do then? I couldn't send my bodyguards around just because someone owed me for cigarettes and milk from a few months back. It would have been better if all the shopkeepers had joined together and not given credit to anyone, but that wasn't how things were done. Besides, most of the inmates did pay eventually. And when they got money, they remembered who had looked after them and who had cut them off.

However, that didn't make it any easier at the time. I tried to stay well stocked because of the frequent worker strikes and protests in the country that made supplies unreliable, but on several occasions I had no cash because I was owed hundreds of bolivianos.

'*Mañana, mañana,*' they promised, even when I knew they had the money in their pockets. And in Bolivia, *mañana* never seemed to come.

美ΙΙ

The period of time I spent working in my shop was when I really got to know the people well and became properly established and respected in San Pedro. When there were no tourists around, I didn't have much to do and all day to do it in, so I would spend hours on end talking and laughing with the other inmates who came to my store. Often, people would visit me and we would talk for so long that they would forget what they had come for and leave empty-handed. Other times, they didn't come to buy anything at all, just to talk.

Apart from being nice to customers, you had to be careful running any business in prison. There weren't any standover men demanding protection money from you, but there were certain powerful people who you knew you had to look after. The Velascos were two of them.

Jose Luis Velasco and Jorge Velasco were father and son. On the outside, the Velasco family had had money. They had been into all sorts of illegal businesses until they got busted and sent to San Pedro prison, where they were also well connected. The father and son were now living together in the same cell, while the family worked on getting them out.

Shortly after I started my *tienda*, the son got married in the prison to a woman named Angela. By coincidence, I already knew her; we had met several times in Sweden through our business connections. It was quite a shock to see someone in a Bolivian jail that I had met on the other side of the world in more glamorous surroundings, but it wasn't really all that surprising given the circles we both moved in. The visitors who attended the wedding were very well dressed and they all brought presents. I was invited along and I donated ten cases of soft drink for the celebrations after the ceremony.

The Velascos were also two of my most regular customers at the shop. They never liked to pay for things up front; they preferred to buy everything on credit and then settle their bill at the end of the month, like rich people on the outside did. They always paid, but very often they were late. I never said anything, however – these sort of people could be good friends if you kept them on side, but powerful enemies if you didn't.

I had one other regular customer who was even more powerful than the Velascos, although you wouldn't have known it by the way he looked or acted. Barbachoca dressed casually and, apart from his distinctive red beard, he looked like a regular inmate. However, he wasn't a regular inmate at all, he was big. Mr Big. Nobody saw him much, because he rarely left his apartment. But even the czars of the drug-dealing world have to eat sometime, which is the reason I eventually met him.

Barbachoca had been caught attempting to transport a large quantity of cocaine from Bolivia to the United States in his own airplane. How much is a 'large' quantity? Four thousand one hundred and eighty kilograms. That's almost 4.2 tonnes – 4.2 million grams – of pure cocaine, enough to get all the party people in the whole world high for one hell of a New Year's Eve party. And if you sold it on the street at one hundred dollars a gram, that's $420 million dollars worth of merchandise, even more when it was mixed.

Barbachoca's plane had been intercepted by the authorities in Peru, en route to Mexico. Normally, big fish like him are too well protected to get busted themselves, but this was an operation run by the un-corruptible DEA, so he couldn't get out of it. In fact, it was the biggest drug bust in Bolivia's history. Once the media got hold of the story and dubbed the case '*narco avion*', there was so much publicity that not even the Bolivian judges could have saved him. They did their best, though. The judges gave him only thirteen years. That didn't make sense. I knew people in San Pedro who had been given the maximum twenty-five years for less than a hundred grams. But there was a public outcry over the sentence and the prosecutor appealed. He eventually secured a longer sentence. So Barbachoca appealed against the appeal.

In the meantime, the US government was trying to extradite him and send him to a proper jail for the rest of his life, but Barbachoca had no plans to move anywhere. In fact, he was quite determined to stay in San Pedro, where the conditions were a lot better than elsewhere in Bolivia. The only problem was that the cells in Alamos were too small. Luckily, he had enough money to call in some contract builders to put up an extension on top of his room. Once his two-storey apartment was fully furnished, he was content to live there quietly until he could find a way out of prison.

Barbachoca kept to himself; he wanted to maintain a low profile in the hope that the publicity surrounding his case would eventually die off. And the other inmates respected that. They had to. That kind of wealth commanded respect, so people kept their distance. I had never talked to him myself, until he came to my shop to buy supplies.

'Hi, Thomas. Do you have ketchup, please?' was the first thing he ever said to me. He spoke perfect English with a strong American accent. When I handed him the bottle, my hands were shaking. I checked the label to make sure it didn't have chilli in it and counted his change twice. You don't want to make mistakes around people like that.

There was no need to have worried. You might expect people who get to the very top of the drug-dealing world to be violent and ruthless mafia types, but Barbachoca wasn't. He was smart. He was educated. He was polite. And as far as I knew, he had never threatened or said so much as an angry word to anyone. Basically, he was a really friendly guy.

Gradually, we became friends and he started to invite me up to his apartment whenever he had a small *fiesta*. I always liked to bring a bottle of something because I didn't want him to think that I was trying to take advantage of his wealth. Besides, Barbachoca supposedly had no money. He told me the cops had confiscated everything. I never believed him, though; he must have had some stashed away somewhere. You can't buy 4.2 tonnes of cocaine and be stupid enough to leave all your money lying under your mattress for the police to find it.

When we used to drink together, Barbachoca was always relaxed, but I wasn't. His parties were very civilised, so I tried not to get too drunk or to sniff too much coke. Barbachoca was extremely disciplined; he never lost control and he liked everyone to leave before midnight so that he could get a good night's sleep. I tried to leave before that time so that he wouldn't have to ask me to. He also had an ensuite on the second floor of his apartment, but I always went downstairs to the public toilets out of respect. I didn't want to stink his bathroom out. What if the toilet hadn't flushed properly? How would you explain that to a guy who owned his own aeroplane with four million grams of cocaine in it?

29
MIKE

The tours and my new *tienda* continued to do well. When I got out of prison, I wanted to have some money saved up so that I wouldn't have to go back to trafficking, but I knew if I had the cash in my hands, I would spend it on partying with the tourists. I decided that it would be safer to have everything tied up in assets, so I began to look around for other ways to invest my money. Eventually, I chose to buy another prison cell, on the ground floor in Alamos. Because of its four-star rating, the prices in Alamos rarely went down, so it was a good investment. However, rather than renting it out, I converted it into a restaurant.

Setting up a restaurant was a lot cheaper than setting up a shop because I didn't have to invest money to purchase stock, apart from the food for the day. I didn't need to provide tables or chairs either, because the section already had them. We had signed a deal with the Bolivian distributors of Coca-Cola – we would sell only their soft drinks and, in return, they loaned us tables, chairs and umbrellas, as well as providing cash that was to be used for improving the inmates' living conditions. I only needed a cooker, some plates and some plastic knives and forks, which I already owned. The restaurant soon started to do well, and it was obvious that I would need some help, which is how I became close friends with Mike.

Mike was one of the biggest personalities in the prison. When I met him, he was fifty years old and had grey hair that ran down past his waist. He tied it in a ponytail, which made him look like an old hippy. Two years later, after the night he went crazy, he shaved off all his hair in order to start his life over again. When people kept commenting on how young he looked, he decided to lower his age to forty and keep his hair that way.

Mike was one of the few English-speaking foreigners in San Pedro. He came from Canada, but he spoke German, Russian, Spanish and Arabic as well. But you never knew whether he was telling the truth or not, because Mike was also a compulsive liar. Before prison, he'd had the most exciting life of anyone I've ever known. He had dined at the Bolivian president's home. He had been an international spy and a hired assassin. He used to deal cocaine to Hollywood movie stars. He'd been on first-name terms with the Colombian drug lord Pablo Escobar. He had taught mathematics at a Canadian university before the physics department headhunted him to work on their black hole research team. He had a law degree. He knew how to assemble bombs. His ex-girlfriend was a famous model.

Most compulsive liars become very boring after a while. They repeat the same lies over and over until you can recount their stories better than they can. And you also start to notice inconsistencies in their stories. But Mike had an excellent memory, which made it very hard to disprove anything he said. He remembered every little lie he ever told and they never contradicted each other. In fact, he even started weaving them together.

'I thought you had a wife and kid then?' I'd jump in, trying to catch him out. But I never could. He was too quick for me.

'Yes. That's how I met Pablo Escobar in the first place. He was a friend of my wife's sister. They met in Panama when she was a diamond trader. Remember, I told you about the diamonds?' Mike was good. In fact, he was very good.

Mike was also a coke junkie. He had been caught with fifty grams of cocaine when the police carried out a dawn raid on his house in the south of La Paz. It wasn't even a proper raid; they just walked through the door, which was left open, and crept into his room on tippy toes, trying to stop their boots from squeaking so as not to wake him. The drugs were on the bedside table and Mike was half-asleep next to them. From the moment the police first interrogated him until his sentencing hearing, Mike's defence didn't change: he claimed the fifty grams were for personal use. The judge didn't believe him, but if you had known Mike, you would have known that that amount wouldn't have lasted him a month.

Mike said he was clean now, but I never believed him. Everything went at full speed when he was around. I had real trouble keeping up with him. He couldn't sit still for one minute; he spoke at a million miles an hour; and he worked flat out all day in my restaurant, even when there were no customers.

'These Bolivians are lazy,' he would say. 'I can't stand it. They do nothing all day except eat and complain. Look at them. They're fat.'

Not everyone in San Pedro got along with Mike, because he was so highly strung. His personality also made it tough to work with him in the restaurant, especially since the kitchen area was small and crowded. However, once you knew how to handle him, Mike was quite a good employee. For a start, he was an excellent chef: he could produce a delicious meal using a few simple ingredients, and he always seemed to know how much salt to add or how many more minutes the fries needed cooking. He hated it if he thought I was interferring.

'You've hidden the salt again, McFadden. I can't work under these conditions,' he said one time when I moved some things during the morning preparation.

'I'm only trying to help.'

'Well, you're *not* helping. You're slowing me down,' he complained, throwing a tea towel over his shoulder and then flapping his arms like a distressed bird.

Mike was very polite and professional in the way he dealt with customers. He was meticulously clean; he tucked his ponytail into the back of his jeans so that it wouldn't get in the way, and he always wore an apron while he cooked. And like all good chefs, he couldn't stand anyone being near him when he was cooking.

'I can't have this stress hanging over me all the time, McFadden. When I was working on Fifth Avenue in New York, they gave me complete creative control.'

Mike also had eyes in the back of his head. He could be crouched down, getting something out of the refrigerator, but he would still know exactly where I was and what I was doing. I would sneak over to eat a french fry when he wasn't looking, but he always caught me.

'That's it, McFadden. Get out of my kitchen. Out!' He'd stamp his foot and then point to the door in the same way as Ricardo did, except that Mike was serious. 'I've warned you before about touching my french fries.'

'*Your* french fries?' I'd laugh, wondering how he always got me. '*I* paid for them.'

But Mike had an answer for everything: 'Well, they're my fries while I'm cooking them. Now get out!'

Then I'd politely remind him that I was the owner of the restaurant and he was my employee.

'OK, then, McFadden. You just sit there and keep out of the way. I'll call you when I need you to serve up.'

I was supposed to be the boss, but somehow I ended up as waiter and drinks boy. I didn't mind, though; Mike made me laugh. While Mike cooked, I sat in the corner and cut the onions or peeled potatoes and listened to him go on and on. He would talk the whole time and do at least four things at once, without ever losing his concentration. I never got bored listening to him, either. He fascinated me, even when I knew that he was lying. He had an entire imaginary world that he had created for himself and sometimes he lived in it, or reminisced about it, and he always added new details and elaborated his stories until they almost got to the point of being ridiculous, but not quite.

'And I said to Pablo, I said, "Pablo, don't be fucking with me. This is Canadian Mike you're talking to here." And you know what? He listened. Pablo actually listened, for a change. He never listened to anybody else, but he used to listen to me. You know why? I've got a theory I developed from when I was a psychologist in Montreal: I think it was because Pablo wasn't used to anyone standing up to him. In fact, I'm convinced of it. He'd been surrounded by yes men his whole life, when all along he was just waiting for somebody to say no. And you want to know something else about Pablo? Listen to this . . .'

Mike was funny. He didn't know it himself, but Mike was very funny. He took himself way too seriously, which is what made him so funny. His funniest obsession by far was hygiene. One time I bought a bucket and some special soap for rinsing his hands, but he said you could only use the water once before it got infected with bacteria. Between orders, he would run to the bathroom to wash his hands and change the water. He always came back even more energetic than before. That guy could sniff a lot. And he had been doing it for so long that it was his normal state of mind, so you hardly noticed. He never admitted to it and even if you had caught him in the act, he would have denied it, because Mike had convinced himself that he wasn't doing coke anymore.

30

NIGHT SHIFT IN THE COCAINE LABORATORIES

It was also during my period as a shopkeeper and restaurateur that I made friends with the bigger dealers and finally got to see the cocaine laboratories. The first time I saw them operating, I was so fascinated that they offered me a job working there. It didn't pay well, but I learned a lot and it kept me out of trouble at night.

I was amazed at how easy it was to make cocaine. Very few people were needed and the equipment used was nothing fancy or scientific: a few buckets, hoses, pieces of cloth, strainers, several lamps and some flat trays for drying the crystals. In fact, the hardest part seemed to be getting hold of the chemicals, which were expensive and hard to find since they had been made illegal as part of the United States' 'war on drugs'. But once you had those, the process was surprisingly simple.

The coke came into the prison in the form of *pasta básica*, a thick, off-white–coloured paste extracted from coca leaves by soaking them in kerosene or gasoline and then adding alcohol, followed by sodium bicarbonate. This process was always carried out where the coca was grown, mainly in Bolivia's Chapare region. Most of the *pasta* was then sold and transported to the labs in Peru and Colombia, but a small amount managed to find its way into San Pedro prison. It was usually smuggled through the main gate by the inmates' wives. Among the hundreds of boxes and sacks of food that arrived to supply the prisoners' daily needs, it wasn't difficult to hide a few kilos in bags of sugar or rice, or hollowed-out fruit. The liquid chemicals were more difficult to get in, but the searches were never thorough, especially if the guards had been bribed in advance. Besides, if anyone was caught, the penalty was simply a bigger bribe.

The laboratories were run out of inmates' rooms at night. The bigger ones could produce several kilos a night, but there were also smaller operators who ran cruder laboratories using makeshift equipment and substitute chemicals, although the quality was never as high.

The whole process, from *pasta básica* to the white cocaine crystals that you sniff, could take several nights' work if it was done carefully, or one night if they were in a rush. The *pasta básica* was first treated with water and sulphuric acid, then stirred to separate out the cocaine solution, before being siphoned off using a hose. Once that concentrated paste had been filtered and dried, you had cocaine base – *basé* – which was sold to the inmates to be smoked. Or if you added more chemicals, such as hydrogen chloride, ether or acetone, you could then filter it through strainers and pieces of cloth to refine it further and get a better product. The resulting substance would be left to crystallise properly, leaving you with pure cocaine crystals. This final drying process took many hours, which was why they did everything at night, when the other inmates were asleep and there was no chance of the police coming into the prison. The paste was usually dried under lamps or heated to make it crystallise faster.

The chemist – known as the *cocinero* – supervised each of these steps, but went to sleep in between times. Nevertheless, someone had to be awake the whole time in order to keep an eye on how things were going. My job was to stir the mixture regularly, making sure that it was consistent and dried evenly and that the right temperature was maintained. If any of it settled on the bottom of the tray, it could burn and ruin the whole batch. A single mistake would cost thousands of dollars, so I had to set the alarm clock and wake the *cocinero* up every hour to check, or whenever something looked like it was going wrong.

The actual steps involved in making cocaine seemed simple when you watched someone who knew what he was doing. But there was a lot of skill and experience involved for the *cocinero* to get the exact chemical balance, knowing how long to allow for each stage, and when to add more of a chemical. The top *cocineros* earned good money, but the actual laboratory workers, like myself, were never paid much, and only when the money from a sale came through. Or you could take the salary option I did, which was to be paid in cocaine. At the end of a night, you might be given ten or twenty grams, depending on how much had been produced and how generous the bosses were feeling.

Inside the prison, that quantity wasn't worth much, but if you knew how to get it out of the prison, there was definitely some money to be made.

The final product went out of San Pedro the same way it came in – through the main gates. Sometimes, school children were used as the mules, since they were less likely to be searched properly. Or more innovative techniques might be used, such as the one I later invented, which was virtually undetectable.

31
THE VELASCOS

Because I was running the tour business, a restaurant and my own shop, the other inmates seemed to think that I was made of money. In fact, I wasn't; buying supplies for the shop and paying off the guards used up most of my cash flow. That was the only money I had left since I'd called on every contact around the world that owed me money to help me fund my court appeal, which had been unsuccessful. The appeal judges had confirmed my original sentence. I had only one appeal avenue left: the Supreme Court in Sucre, the nation's capital. Those judges were going to be expensive but the inmates were always begging me to lend them something. And very often, it was hard to refuse. Especially if they were good friends, like the Velascos.

The Velascos were into all sorts of money-making scams in the prison. One of them was receiving and distributing counterfeit banknotes, which was big business in Bolivia. Fake bills were circulating in every part of the economy. You had to look out for them at the markets, in shops, and especially with the moneychangers along the Prado. I even heard that employees in the banks were in on it. Some of the cash teller machines dispensed the occasional fake 100-boliviano bill, especially on weekends, and then the banks refused to accept responsibility when they reopened for business on Monday.

Fakes were so common that it was standard practice for anyone receiving cash to check it thoroughly. Mostly, the copies were easy to distinguish, if you knew what to look for – the feel of the paper or the colour – but the quality was getting better and there were always people who got fooled or forgot to check, especially tourists. I never heard of a traveller making it through the country without getting stung at least once.

Obviously, the inmates in San Pedro knew to be wary. There were even rumours of a counterfeiting press inside the prison. I doubt that this was true, but it made everyone more suspicious. There was a shortage of coins in Bolivia, which meant that people were always running about looking for someone to break up larger bills. But many of the shopkeepers refused to change them because they were worried about fakes.

Although it was impossible to get fakes past the suspicious eyes of the inmates, San Pedro was still the ideal distribution centre. Trading in counterfeits seemed to go hand in hand with all the other types of illegal activity already going on, and there was always someone down on their luck who was willing to have a go at passing off a few fakes. Inmates would send their friends and wives out with loads of notes, either to sell them on or to try their luck themselves. They were hard to get rid of, but it was worth a shot – if you pulled it off, it was money for free.

It worked well enough for the Velascos until Angela, the son's new wife, got busted by the lieutenant. One visitors' day, he pulled her aside for a search at the gate on the way out and went straight for her wallet, which was filled with fakes. She was then held in the prison office for questioning. The lieutenant needed fifteen hundred dollars to make the problem disappear.

'You have to help my son, Thomas,' Jose Luis begged me. 'Please. For the family.'

'Hey man, I've got nothing.'

No one ever said 'no' directly when asked to lend money. That would have been considered rude. You simply had to say you didn't have anything, even if you did. The trouble was that when you genuinely had nothing, no one ever believed you.

'I would if I could, believe me. But I have no money. Honestly. Everyone owes me from the shop.' And on this occasion, I wasn't lying. Apart from two hundred dollars that I needed myself, I had nothing.

'But we'll pay you interest. However much you want. You just say the amount.'

'But I don't have money. *Nada.* I'm sorry. I can't help. Honestly.'

I wanted to help Angela, but I wasn't prepared to mortgage my properties in order to do so; they were everything I owned in the world. It was clear, however, that Jose Luis still didn't believe me. He didn't say as much, because it was part of the same prison etiquette that the person asking for the loan couldn't directly accuse you of lying when you said you had nothing. He would just continue on as if you hadn't said anything in the first place.

'You've known Angela for years,' Jose Luis persisted. 'We've asked everyone. You're our last hope.'

Then the son, Jorge, knocked at my door. He was on the point of tears and it took him a while to compose himself. He had been negotiating with the lieutenant and believed that he would now accept one thousand dollars. Then he started crying. I pulled out a chair and guided him gently towards it.

Jorge sat with his head bowed, staring down at my table and crying quietly. The tears ran down the bridge of his nose and clung to its tip until the next one came along, making the two combined drops too heavy, and they would fall into a small pool directly beneath his nose. Having a grown man cry like that in my room made me feel ashamed for not helping.

While Jorge sat weeping, his father continued to beg. The whole family would be in prison. What hope would any of them have, then? He assured me that they did have the money, just not on them. They had made phone calls and it would be brought later that day, but the lieutenant needed it right now or Angela would be charged. And if I didn't believe that their relatives had money, then Angela knew hundreds of people in Sweden who could wire it over. One thousand dollars meant nothing in Sweden. Three days. Maximum four. Still, I resisted.

Finally, Jorge raised his head as if to speak. He had stopped crying, but his eyes were red and there was still a silvery trail over his nose where the tears had run. He looked straight at me.

'Thomas, you have to help her. Angela . . . she's pregnant.'

I stared at him.

'My God! Why didn't you say anything?' Jose Luis said.

'We wanted it to be a surprise.'

'Yes, what a surprise!' his father said sarcastically. 'My grandchild being born in prison.' He looked down, shaking his head slowly, and fell silent. He looked like he was ready to cry too.

That changed things for me. I had seen enough children growing up in prison to know what it does to them. 'There might be a possibility,' I said. 'Wait here!'

I went to see Abregon, but he didn't like the idea much. He was a businessman and he looked at the situation like a businessman would.

'I don't even know these people and, really Thomas, I would prefer not to get involved. Anyway, how well do you know them yourself? I've never heard you mention them before.'

'They're customers of mine. I've known them a few months. They'll pay whatever interest you ask.'

'It's still not smart to get involved in other people's problems. You never know what might happen in the future. The police could ask for more money, or these Velascos might say we're involved somehow. Anything could happen. This is prison. You have to be careful. Don't let your emotions cloud your judgment, my brother. At the end of the day, they are still people wanting money from you.'

I knew that he was right, but the thought of Angela in Obrajes, the women's jail, with a newborn baby made me sad. I persisted until, finally, Abregon gave in.

'OK Thomas. I'll lend the money, but it's up to you to get it back. They're *your* friends. I'm doing it for *you*, not for them. OK?'

Between the two of us, we lent them the money. I put in my two hundred and Abregon put in the remaining eight. The Velascos signed a contract with witnesses but it was unsecured because Jose Luis said he couldn't find the title to their cell. I suspect that it was already mortgaged, but the important thing was that Angela was released.

Three days later, the Velascos had not repaid the money. A fortnight later, I asked them again – they still wouldn't pay up. I yelled at them to at least pay Abregon back. The money I had loaned them wasn't overly important to me, because the tour business kept me afloat, but I felt responsible for Abregon's money and hassled them every time I saw them.

32

'ONE OF THE WORLD'S MOST BIZARRE TOURIST ATTRACTIONS'

Many of the tourists who visited San Pedro were so fascinated by the prison and my stories that they came back to see me several times. I estimated that every tourist who visited me told at least five other travellers, and at least that number of people again when they got home. Tourists started coming in larger and larger groups and many of them had to be turned away at the gates.

During my second and third years in San Pedro, it seemed that the prison cocaine parties would never end. I had quickly gained a reputation for showing people a good time, so when backpackers arrived saying they had heard about me and wanted to try some coke, I never felt that I could refuse them. The trouble for me was that one group would arrive and want to party hard for a whole night, but while they spent the next day recovering, I had to get up and run another tour and party all night again with the next group.

Luckily, not everyone wanted to try cocaine. Once the word had spread that the prison wasn't dangerous for tourists, it was no longer only young backpackers who visited San Pedro. People of all ages and from all walks of life began to visit me and the tours became more respectable. So much so, that *Lonely Planet* listed the prison as one of the 'things to do' in the La Paz section of its South American guidebook, describing it as 'one of the world's most bizarre tourist attractions'.

With all the publicity, I sometimes worried that the tours might be getting too big and would cause me problems, but they never did. What went on inside San Pedro was no secret to the people of La Paz. The prison was like a sad joke that had been repeated to them over and over again. They had been hearing about it for decades, and an endless stream of articles continued to pour out of newspapers and television about it. The drug police were filmed delivering suspicious-looking bags to the prison gates after midnight. Countless prisoners were said to have died under suspicious circumstances or from lack of medical attention. Wealthy inmates, who were supposed to be in their prison cells, were photographed at shopping malls with their girlfriends. The prisoners regularly organised hunger strikes to protest against court delays and judicial corruption; when the police accused the protesters of eating, many of them sewed up their mouths to prove that wasn't the case. A racket of bringing prostitutes into the prison was uncovered – there were even allegations of inmates prostituting their teenage daughters.

The corruption in the Bolivian prison system went all the way to the top. One of the friends I made in San Pedro knew more about the high-level corruption than most of us. He was a Brazilian inmate named Samir Mustafá Ali, and he was probably Bolivia's best car thief. Samir could break into a vehicle and hotwire the ignition in less than sixty seconds. He was a little crazy, but we immediately became friends. Samir had been in and out of jail since he was a boy. Every time he got drunk, he used to tell me stories about the time he was in prison in Santa Cruz and how several high-ranking officers used to take him out of his cell at night to steal cars. They did the same in San Pedro. They would have him back in his cell before morning *lista* and pay him a few hundred dollars each time to keep quiet.

The stories that came out about the maximum-security prison, Chonchocoro, were worse. During one surprise raid police found hundreds of litres of *chicha* (an alcohol the inmates manufactured themselves by fermenting corn), several kilos of cocaine, four handguns and two dead bodies. Inmates were regularly tortured to death by the police if they threatened to expose the police corruption. Among all this, the availability of drugs was barely an issue.

'San Pedro Prison: *Cocaína* for 3 bolivianos. *Basé* for 1.5 bolivianos,' read the headlines, and hardly anyone battered an eyelid.

Occasionally, these exposés caused a brief scandal. There were often crackdowns and promises by the politicians and police to fix up the prison system. However, one corrupt administration was always replaced by another, so nothing ever changed. And to the people of Bolivia, who had been living in poverty and political turmoil for centuries, it all seemed inevitable. For them, things would always stay the same and a few tourists getting high in the prison wasn't anything amazing.

Every now and then, the guards would warn us that they were about to conduct a *requisa*. If there wasn't enough time to hide your stuff properly, or if you were afraid that they might bring dogs, there was an arrangement that all contraband would be dumped in the bathrooms. The guards could then collect all the drugs, alcohol and illegal weapons on a table and show the media how they were cleaning up the prison, but none of us would get busted because they couldn't prove who everything belonged to. That way, everyone was happy.

After a *requisa*, prices went up because the prison was supposedly in 'drought'. In the meantime, all the confiscated contraband was placed in a small room in the punishment section called the *depósito* for safe-keeping, away from the main prison population. That place was like a small fortress; it had thick walls, no windows and a metal door with two padlocks. No one would dream of breaking into it – the guards would've killed you. Besides, we never needed to break in because the droughts never lasted too long, just until the guards sold our stuff back to us.

卌ll

As far as the tours went, the police caused me very little hassle. I was more concerned about the gangs, especially the one controlled by Fantasma. Eventually, he had told me himself about how he'd blown away his friend at a party. It was one evening when we were doing coke together in his room. There was a knife on the table and he became very agitated.

'You know, that guy was my best friend.' He looked over at the knife again. 'Just like you are now, Thomas. And he pissed me off, so I killed him.'

When he mentioned helping out with the tours, I invited him to join my business.

Fantasma was dangerous. Before I met him in Alamos, he had been kicked out of Posta for having cocaine and fourteen bottles of whisky in his room. Eventually, he got kicked out of Alamos, also. The inmates complained because he did coke at night and walked around talking to himself. He said he was communicating with the devil.

Then he killed a black cat by twisting its neck, because the devil had told him to. He had to move to Pinos, but then he was kicked out of there and eventually ended up in Prefectura.

After he killed the cat, I didn't visit Fantasma for quite some time. We were still on reasonable terms, but I only saw him when he wanted to help with the tours. Then, one afternoon, he unexpectedly showed up at my room.

'Thomas! Open up!' he yelled, banging on my door urgently. I pretended not to be there.

'Now! Thomas, open it! It's me.' As soon as I unlatched the door, he thrust something wrapped in a T-shirt into my hands.

'Quick! Take this,' he said, looking around to make sure no one had seen him give it to me. 'I'll be back for it soon.'

I didn't see him again for two days, but when he finally reappeared to collect his package, I was relieved. Inside the T-shirt was a gun. He was more relaxed this time and wanted me to hold it, so that I would know how powerful it made you feel to have a gun in your hand.

'No way, man,' I said, making my fingers into the figure of a pistol and touching them against his temple. 'I might get carried away and shoot you.' But really, I wasn't stupid enough to put my fingerprints on any gun owned by Fantasma.

'*No hay problema*, homey.' He gave me a friendly punch in the chest that knocked the wind out of me. From that day on, I stayed on Fantasma's good side. He was no longer *acting* tough, he *was* tough. And since he now wanted to run the tours himself, I had to come to an agreement with him.

Of course, I still had my bodyguards, although they sometimes gave me problems, especially Lucho. During one of the gang wars he had been stabbed five times in the stomach with a huge knife. Before passing out from loss of blood, he managed to strangle his two attackers almost to death. When he returned from hospital, Lucho had become a legend, and with all the money he was making he became lazy and often refused to work. Other times he was too drunk or hungover to help with the tours. He was also jealous of the friends I made and all the girls who came to see me. Eventually, I told him he couldn't be part of the business anymore. That very afternoon, Lucho was waiting for me in the stairwell with two other inmates as I went down to the bathroom.

'We need to talk, *Tomás*,' he said, pulling his jacket aside slightly to reveal a machete hidden underneath. The other two had hunting knives tucked into their pants.

'OK, then. Fine,' I said, turning my back on Lucho to show him I wasn't afraid. 'Follow me.'

I led them up to my room and invited all three to sit down, which caused them great embarrassment because they had to take their knives out of their pants and didn't know where to put them.

'That's OK,' I said. 'Just put them on the table there.'

'Now *Tomás*,' Lucho began, slapping his palm down hard on the table and looking at me fiercely. 'You listen to me.'

'Wait!' I interrupted him, and walked casually into the kitchen. 'Who wants tea or coffee first?'

When I came back and sat down, Lucho had lost a lot of his confidence. They insisted that I give him his job back. I apologised for what I had said earlier in the day.

'Lucho. I like working with you. We're *socios* and we're *amigos*. But just remember that I am the one paying you,' I said, picking up one of the hunting knives from the table. Lucho made a sudden dive for his machete, which was leaning against the wall, but I dipped the tip of the knife into the sugar bowl and used it to stir my tea. The other two laughed and even Lucho shook his head and managed a smile.

33
WORD SPREADS

Two things kept me in power as San Pedro's main tour guide. First, my bodyguards couldn't cut me out of the business because they couldn't speak English. Second, I wasn't greedy, like the gangs who tried to promote their own tour guides. Whenever backpackers came into the prison, I did my best to show them a good time. I spent a lot of the money I earned from the tours buying the tourists food or beers or cocaine. I had learned my lesson from being too greedy with drug trafficking, and I also felt that the tourists were doing *me* a favour by visiting me in the first place. I also looked after all the guards very well, especially the officers and the governor. The other tour guides, like Fantasma, were greedy though; they wanted to increase the tour price and sometimes they tried to avoid paying the guards their fair share. The end result was that the tourists always asked for me and the police also preferred to work with me. I couldn't ignore the threats from the gangs, so eventually we came to a compromise: we would share the tour business, week by week.

The only other thing I had to worry about was coming to the attention of the United States' DEA, which had undercover agents in all the South American countries as part of its 'war on drugs'. I was worried that it might try to bust me for dealing inside the prison.

I liked most of the Americans I met. Of all the nationalities, they were usually the nicest and therefore the easiest to shock. None of my American visitors could believe that a place like San Pedro actually existed and I got an extra kick out of telling them about what went on in there.

'But this *must* be illegal!' they would exclaim. 'I can't believe they don't do something about it. This is worse than *Midnight Express*. Someone should complain.'

I liked shocking them when I could, but unfortunately I usually had to avoid taking Americans on the prison tours. Apart from my own fear of the DEA, the other inmates hated *gringos* and if I had welcomed too many American visitors, they might have suspected that I was working secretly with the US authorities.

For this reason, I wouldn't have received Mark Johnson. He fitted the undercover stereotype perfectly: a serious American man of about twenty-seven, well built, blond hair gelled back, white T-shirt and blue jeans – except for the fact that he got in past the guards without calling me. He spoke almost perfect Spanish and I could tell by his hurried manner that he hadn't come for a tour.

'Are you Thomas McFadden?' he asked, as soon as I opened my door.

I nodded. 'Have a seat, man. Would you like some tea or coffee?'

'No. That's fine. I've just eaten,' he replied. He had a strange way of talking and it was obvious he wanted to ask me something.

'OK, then. Let's chat, or do you want to do a tour?'

'How long have you been doing the tours?' he asked immediately.

'Two years almost, off and on. Sometimes the tourists can't get inside because the guards won't let them. And sometimes I get tired of doing them.'

'Why? Because you do drugs with them?'

'No, because you know, it takes a lot of energy dealing with people. I like to show them a good time, and if I can't put in all my energy, I prefer not do it at all. You understand?'

'I'm informed that the tour price is fifty bolivianos. How much of that goes to the guards and how much to you?'

'Hey man, slow down. A lot of questions.' It wasn't that I minded answering questions – all the tourists were always curious – but this boy had just charged straight in there.

'Sorry, I should ask you how you are feeling. How are you today?' He was certainly strange, this one.

'Good, I'm fine. Thanks. A bit tired, man, a lot of tourists are coming through.'

'How many do you think?'

'Ufff – I don't count. I think sometimes up to fifty, maybe even seventy a day.'

The American pulled out a pen and small notepad. 'Between fifty and seventy, you say,' and he noted it down on his pad.

'You're writing a travel diary?'

'Actually, no. I'm a freelance journalist working with the *Bolivian Times*. Mark Johnson. Pleased to meet you,' he stood up, extending his hand to greet me and at the same time asked, 'How do you spell "McFadden"?'

I didn't answer because I was thinking about what I should do. I had never met someone who did things in such a strange order. He had been in my room almost five minutes and only then had he decided to shake hands. And he hadn't even warned me that he was a journalist, but there he was, still writing down everything I said without my permission.

'Sorry. I guess we should start at the beginning. What did you do to get in here? Oh, by the way, I can pay you for the interview, if you want. How much do you need?'

'No, it's fine.' This guy just didn't get it. I still hadn't even agreed to an interview.

'OK, then,' he continued, seeming pleased about not having to pay me. 'Are you in here for drugs?'

Another direct question from Mark Johnson, freelance journalist from the *Bolivian Times*. I didn't want to be rude and tell him to leave, but there was no way I was going to give him any information. How can you trust someone you have just met with information that they might publish about you the next day? Besides, I wasn't going to admit something in a newspaper that might affect my Supreme Court appeal. So, I decided to lie. If this guy wanted a story out of me, he could have one, but it wouldn't be the real one.

'No, not drugs. And I think you've spelled that wrong. My name, I mean,' I pointed to where he had written my name on his notepad. 'It's not Thomas, it's Tomo – T-o-m-o. And my surname is spelled M-a-c-f-a-r-g-y-e-n, although you pronounce the "g" like a "d". It's Jamaican. I'm from Jamaica.' He wrote that down, too.

'Oh, thanks,' he said, crossing out the correct spelling and replacing it with the bogus one I'd given him. 'May I ask you for what crime you are in here?'

'Yes, you may. Terrorism,' I informed him, sitting back in my chair and folding my arms. I was trying not to laugh, but he caught me about to smile so I tried to make it look like I was very proud of being a terrorist.

'Terrorism?' he looked surprised.

'Yes. Terrorism.' He wrote the word down in his notepad, with a question mark after it.

'What exactly did you do?'

'Well, I didn't really do anything. I mean, I hadn't done anything yet when they caught me. It was more about what we were *going* to do.'

'Can I ask what?'

'Sure man, but be careful what you write. I'm trusting you with this information.'

'Of course. There's no need to worry about that at all. I always protect my sources.'

I was beginning to enjoy this interview. He was solemnly writing down almost everything I said as though it were gospel. It would have been the scoop of his short career, except that none of it was true.

'OK. They got us with some explosives. We were in the street –'

'OK, slow down there please, Mr . . .' He looked down at his notepad. 'Macfargyen. Who is "we" and what sort of explosives?'

'With some friends. We had dynamite. The cops got us with sticks of dynamite. Although *I* didn't have any on me.'

'How much was there?'

'Oh, a lot, man. Enough.'

'Where did you get the dynamite from?'

'Hey man, I'm not going to tell you that. I have to protect *my* sources, too. I'm not going to put my cause in trouble. What kind of journalist are you? Do you want this interview or what?'

Someone should have been filming me. I was playing the part to perfection.

'Sorry. You're right. Would it be all right if I asked you what you were going to do with the dynamite?'

'Hey man. That's a stupid question. What else can you do with dynamite? Are you stupid, or what?'

'Sorry, you're right. What I meant to ask was what was your target, your mission objective, if you like?'

This guy was also really getting into the interview; he had even started using terrorist terminology.

'Our mission objective, if you like, although that is more a term that Hollywood invented rather than one we freedom fighters use, was the destruction of a few central locations in La Paz.'

'Can I ask which ones?'

'No, you can't.'

'I'm sorry. So sorry. We'll move on . . . How long have you been in San Pedro?' He was lapping it up now, apologising frequently so that he could get more information out of me.

'I've been here ten years. Long time.'

'You must have been young when you first arrived?'

'Too young. And they tortured me . . . with spoons.'

'With *spoons*? How?'

'Yes, with spoons. What do you mean *how*? They hit me with spoons, all over my body.'

My story became more and more ridiculous as the interview progressed, but to stop myself from laughing I only had to look at Mark Johnson's sober expression as he conscientiously transcribed every word I said.

I followed the newspapers for two weeks and finally his article appeared. It was an exposé on San Pedro, but unfortunately not all the details I had given him were included, and most unfortunately, there was nothing about the previously unheard-of Bolivian form of spoon torture. Nevertheless, it did say something about one inmate called Jamaican Tomo being an 'unscrupulous terrorist', and when I showed it to Ricardo, neither of us could stop laughing.

卌\\

Apart from pushy journalists, I received a lot of other weird visitors from all over the world. There was the Dutch backpacker with blond dreadlocks who would set up his tent in parks and main plazas and wash in public fountains until the police told him to move on. It wasn't that he didn't have money, he just didn't like hotels.

'Why pay money to stay on a mattress with fleas when I have a very good air mattress?' he asked me.

There was the couple that was travelling the entire South American continent on bicycles because they said cars and buses were unnatural and caused pollution. They were nice, but they were also against deodorant and smelled a bit. There was a Japanese guy who not only couldn't speak Spanish but couldn't speak any English either. I wondered how he got around Bolivia at all, because with me, he just kept bowing and smiling all the time. He drank about fifteen cups of tea. When I came back from buying him more tea bags, he had left without saying goodbye.

There was also the former corporate high-flyer who now liked to climb really high peaks, where he would spend the night on his own, without telling anyone. For altitudes above five thousand metres, he had two high-tech thermal sleeping bags which fastened up so tightly that he only had a tiny mouth hole to breathe through. 'Once, it was so cold that I had to close it right up and breathe through a straw to avoid getting frostbite on my lips,' he told me.

Why do people do these things to themselves? I wondered. Don't they have families? Doesn't anyone care about them?

The strangest thing about all these strange people was that they thought I was strange too, and that we had some sort of connection, like I was one of them. I didn't know whether I should have been flattered or upset by that. Things could be tough in the prison and I had probably suffered as much as they had, but I certainly hadn't done so by choice.

The most unexpected visitor was Fat Joe, although when I first met him I didn't know how bizarre the purpose of his visit would turn out to be.

34
'FATHER THOMAS'

Fat Joe was really fat. I don't know how much he weighed, but it was a lot. He had trouble moving about and had to sort of turn sideways to get in my door. The very first time he came to visit, he broke my chair when he sat down. I'd had it since the very beginning and I was a bit sad to see it go like that.

'I'm so sorry. I'll pay for the damage,' he insisted. 'Or I'll buy you a new one.'

'That's OK. It was already broken,' I lied. It was a perfectly good chair, but I guess it just couldn't take Fat Joe.

'We're off to a bad start, aren't we? It's probably best if I sit here on the bed.' He started manoeuvring sideways but before he could get there, I intercepted him with my reinforced stainless-steel chair.

'No, no, no! Here – this one's stronger.' I liked my bed and didn't want him breaking any of those springs. They're very hard to replace. Besides, I had the mattress just right, with the groove in the centre how I liked it, and I didn't need him ruining it. 'And it's not already broken, like the other one was,' I added, to save his feelings.

Fat Joe's real name was just Joe, but in my mind I always called him Fat Joe. It just seemed to suit him better. Several times I think I almost said it aloud because he always arrived completely unannounced and I was often so stoned that I couldn't distinguish between the voice in my head and my real voice. He probably wouldn't have minded me thinking of him as Fat Joe, though; he had a good sense of humour and made jokes about himself all the time. Deep down, he must have been pretty unhappy about being so big, but he made such an effort to be jolly all the time that I came to admire him.

Fat Joe was American. And while I usually didn't accept Americans on the prison tour, he got himself through the gates on his own and turned up on my doorstep, just as Mark Johnson had.

'You must be Thomas!' he shook my hand warmly. 'I'm Joe. I've heard a lot about you.' I couldn't just turn him away.

'Joe. Hi. Come inside.' I was used to people visiting me through recommendations, although I avoided asking who had recommended me. With so many visitors coming through my door, it was impossible to remember some guy called Alex or John I had met eighteen months before.

Fat Joe was really friendly and, although he had broken my favourite chair, I liked him a great deal. He asked a lot of questions, mainly about what conditions were like in the prison, whether I was happy, and so on. He was absolutely amazed that we had to pay for everything ourselves and wanted to know how prisoners without money survived and if there were any organisations that supported them.

'No. Just their families,' I told him. 'And the other inmates some-times. If they're lucky.'

When he was leaving that first time, he gave me fifty dollars to cover the damage to my chair. Chairs certainly didn't cost that much, but I didn't argue because I saw how much money he had in his wallet.

卌||

A couple of days later, Fat Joe arrived unannounced a second time.

'You came back!' I said, offering him the steel chair straight away before he got the chance to line up any more of my furniture.

I still wasn't keen on taking him on a tour around the prison, but it seemed that he didn't want to, anyway. He had just come to talk to me again. We chatted about the same things as before and this time he placed a hundred dollars on my dresser as he was leaving. I liked it when people left me something to help out, but a hundred dollars was a lot of money, so I was a bit suspicious of what strings might be attached.

'No. There's no charge,' I told him. 'You already paid more than the cost of a tour last time. This time you're my visitor, so you just pay seven bolivianos to the man at the gate.'

'I know, but it's a present for you, Thomas. You need it. Don't be ashamed if a man offers you something from the goodness of his heart.'

'I can't take it. It's too much.'

'It's OK. We want you to have it.'

I accepted the money, but it was strange that he had said 'we'. Fat Joe was a big man and ate for two people, but as far as I knew, there was only one of him.

On his fifth visit, Fat Joe finally revealed the real purpose behind these trips to the prison.

'Are you a religious person, Thomas?' he asked casually, but I immediately saw where the question was leading.

'Not very. But I'm a Christian, I guess.'

It had happened to me countless times during my time in San Pedro: someone would arrive and befriend you, then try to convert you to their religion when you were at your most vulnerable. The only thing I didn't know was which particular church Fat Joe belonged to. Most of Bolivia was Catholic, and we had a beautiful church in the prison with a statue of Santa Guadalupe, but we also had priests from the Evangelical Church, the Seventh Day Adventists and even a few Jehovah's Witnesses.

'Thomas, do you have many dark moments here in prison?' Joe asked next.

I was a bit stoned and didn't want to get involved in a heavy discussion about religion. But I didn't want to be rude, so I decided to make light of the situation before he could get started properly.

'Yeah, I do. All the prisoners do,' I bowed my head sadly. 'Especially at night. They cut the electricity all the time.' But the look Fat Joe gave me made me feel guilty.

'In all seriousness, Thomas, do you ever pray?'

'Sometimes. When I'm down and I need hope. But at the moment I'm OK, really.' I tried to slide out of it again, but he kept repeating my name and asking me questions that I had to answer 'yes' to.

'Thomas, do you ever feel that you are alone in the world? That there's no one to turn to?'

I nodded. Of course I did.

'Well, you're not. God is with you. Do you believe in God, Thomas?'

'Sort of. Well, not really. I believe in God, but it's more my own version of God.'

Fat Joe exhaled loudly and placed his hands on the table, palms facing upwards and I knew something big was coming.

'Thomas, I am a Mormon,' he declared.

The way he said it was like a confession and the words were just left there, dangling in the air, like he had informed me he was a homosexual or had cancer. He looked at me very earnestly, but I didn't know how I was supposed to react.

'Really?' I nodded my head. 'That's nice.'

It was a stupid thing to say, but I couldn't think of anything else. To be honest, I had a bad impression of Mormons. Even though I didn't really know much about them, people always talked about them in a negative way, like they do about bible bashers and all those religions that take your money. Fat Joe was the first Mormon I'd met in person and I really liked him. If the rest were like him, then I figured the Mormons couldn't be too bad and I should at least hear him out.

'Thomas, if I gave you some of our literature, would you be prepared to read it? Don't worry. I'm not going to push anything on you. It's up to you.'

'Sure. Why not?'

He tried to leave another fifty-dollar note that time, but I refused. I intended to read the material he had given me, but I wasn't going to do it because he was paying me to. Besides, if I accepted the money, it would only make it harder to say no when he came again.

卅〢

The next time Fat Joe visited, things got even more serious than I expected.

'Have you read the material I gave you?' he wanted to know.

'Some of it. But I've been very busy,' I lied. I hadn't read much of it at all. Since his most recent visit, there had been several parties with the tourists and I always found it very difficult to concentrate on reading when I was high on cocaine. Especially the Mormon bible.

I don't think he believed me – what could keep me so busy when I was stuck in prison? – but he nodded kindly. 'Yes, I understand. And what did you think of what you read?'

'Interesting . . . umm . . . I'm not sure about it, though.' I told him I wasn't ready to commit. Actually, I wanted to say 'no' outright, but it was so difficult because Fat Joe was such a nice man and I felt like it would break his heart if he had to condemn me to burn in Mormon hell for refusing to believe in his religion. It got worse, though. Not only did he want to convert me to Mormonism, he also wanted me to help find other people who were 'in need', as he put it.

'We are looking for someone to help other people to understand. That person is you, Thomas. God has chosen you. The word is only just arriving in Bolivia, and we want to give everyone the opportunity to share in our beliefs.'

Fat Joe explained his master plan: he wanted to open a chapter of the Mormon Church inside the prison itself and he wanted me to be the head of it. They would cover all the expenses and send me the materials and money required to set everything up. He needed a decision soon because he was heading back to the United States in a few days. It was a grave responsibility; if I said no now, I would be denying other people the opportunity of being saved.

'I don't think I know enough to teach other people,' I said, hesitantly. 'There's no way I could read your whole bible in such a short time. And to be honest, I'm really not sure about it myself . . . I just . . . I'd feel guilty accepting if I didn't truly . . .'

'That's OK. You don't have to believe in everything one hundred per cent right now. As long as you have an open mind and you think there's a chance to learn about our ways. In the meantime, you can still give other people hope. There's nothing hypocritical about that. You're a good person, Thomas. Anyone can see that. People listen to you.'

When he put it that way, I didn't see anything wrong with agreeing to being a Mormon, at least for the time being. I didn't have to commit myself completely, but everybody would benefit: the Mormons would get their church, other people would have the chance of being saved and I could make some money on the side.

'OK, then.'

'That's fantastic,' Fat Joe shook my hand. 'Welcome to the church, Thomas.'

'Thank you.'

And that's how I became Bolivia's first ever Mormon priest in prison. Father Thomas. It had a nice ring to it. Even nicer than Thomas the tour guide.

彬彬

I kept my word to the Mormons. Well, sort of. The money arrived first, then a week later a whole bundle of bibles and promotional material came by courier. I bought a cheap room in one of the other sections and converted it into a kind of church. I didn't really know what a Mormon church should look like, but I laid out lots of candles, bought some cheap furniture, set the bibles out and sent Joe a photo to show that I was as good as my word. The leftover money I kept for myself.

Quite frankly, Father Thomas was a complete failure. No one ever set foot in my Mormon church apart from me, and I never managed to convert anyone to the religion. Not a single person. I handed out free cups of hot chocolate, but everyone just drank them then left. Even those inmates who weren't strict Catholics were strongly against Mormonism.

'That's a *gringo* religion. They just want to take all your money,' they warned me.

'That's not true at all,' I argued back. 'I don't have any money for them to take.'

But even when I explained that it was the other way around and that they were paying *me* and maybe others could get some commission too, it was impossible to persuade anyone to so much as consider becoming a Mormon. No one was interested at all. I felt bad, so when Fat Joe and his colleagues rang for progress reports every few weeks, I lied to them about how things were going. I told them that my following was growing rapidly and they should send me more money.

If they ever made the trip back down to San Pedro to check up on my religious leadership, I had paid about ten of my friends to go along with the story that they were devout Mormons who came to my little church regularly. And the other fifty followers I had converted? Well, they'd finished their sentences and been released, hadn't they? They were now out in the wide world converting other people who were in need.

35
MIKE GOES CRAZY

Throughout all this, the parties with the tourists continued. We partied a lot. Sometimes, I even got sick of partying. I developed major problems with my sinuses. My nose was permanently running and often it bled when I blew it. I had great difficulty getting to sleep. I got severe headaches that lasted for days on end. Apart from these symptoms, I thought that sniffing cocaine was relatively harmless until I watched Mike the chef completely lose it.

He was drunk and high that night, but since he had a perfect memory, he remembered our conversation word for word. We laughed about it afterwards, but at the time it was scary. It happened shortly after Ana, Mike's Bolivian girlfriend, had broken up with him. They had been together before he was sent to prison, but had separated over some small incident. When Ana began to visit him in San Pedro, the relationship started up again. They had only been back together for two months, however, before Mike got himself so twisted up with jealousy, imagining what she did on the outside, that he destroyed the relationship. Every time she came to visit him, he would abuse her in public: 'You're late, you fucking *prostituta*. Who have you been with this time?'

On one occasion, Jack and I pulled Mike aside after Ana had left in tears. 'Hey Mike, chill down,' we told him. 'You can't treat her like that, man. She'll leave you.'

'I don't care. She's a *puta*.'

But Jack stood up to him. 'You're a prisoner, Mike,' he said. 'She's beautiful. What she is doing in here with you, I will never know.'

Mike glared at him. I think Jack wanted Ana for himself, because whenever she was around he took his sunglasses off and moved his head around to different angles so that the light would catch his green contacts.

'That girl loves you. You're just paranoid, Mike,' I told him, but he insisted he wasn't.

'She's fucking with someone else. I know she is. I can smell it on her.'

It turned out I was right – he *was* paranoid, but I didn't find out the full extent of his paranoia until the night he actually went crazy.

༄༅༎

Eventually, Ana got sick of the way Mike treated her and said she would never come back to see him. She left her answering machine on and didn't return his calls. Mike's relatives had given him some money to buy a better room. Instead of upgrading, he sold his existing room in San Martín and then went on a three-day binge with the proceeds.

At four in the morning on the third night, he came knocking at my door. I didn't want to let him in because having visitors after one in the morning was against the section rules and could cause big trouble with the delegate. However, Mike said that he needed to talk to me urgently. It hadn't even occurred to me to wonder how he'd got from San Martín into Alamos when the section gates were locked.

'What's wrong? What happened to you?' I asked as soon as I opened the door. His clothes were covered in dirt, especially his knees, and his hands were cut.

'That roof needs cleaning. Fucking lazy Bolivian police never clean it,' he snarled, striding into my room. 'Too busy stealing our money and snorting our drugs. Now, where is she?' he demanded, his eyes darting everywhere.

'Where's who?' I laughed, knowing exactly who he meant, but thinking he was joking.

'You've taken her. I know you've got her in here. I heard her voice when I was standing outside.' Mike pointed at me threateningly between the eyes. His finger was shaking. 'What have you done with her, McFadden?'

When I saw the look on Mike's face, I stopped playing games. Every muscle in his neck was tensed and the veins in his forehead were throbbing. His eyes were big and wild, and he was sweating heavily.

'She's not here, Mike. Why would she be in here, Mike?' I said quietly so as not to agitate him. I also kept repeating his name softly, which usually calms people down.

Reasoning with him only made him angrier. He started searching everywhere for his girlfriend. There were only two small rooms in my apartment – nowhere you could hide a person – but Mike ran from the kitchen back into my bedroom, then back again, thinking I was changing her hiding spot. He looked under the bed, behind the curtains and even between the mattresses. It was the first time I'd seen Mike so confused and it scared me. He was delusional.

'Calm down, Mike . . . Mike, you're being silly. How could she be under the carpet, Mike?' But even when he was crazy, Mike was still totally switched on. On the next trip back from the kitchen, he was clutching my new kitchen knife.

'Fuck you, McFadden. And stop saying my name, will you? I've studied psychology too and this is not a hijack situation. It's kidnapping and you're the fucking kidnapper,' he held the knife up under my chin. 'Now, what have you done with her?'

I stopped arguing and helped him search for Ana. All the time, Mike kept the knife pointing at me in case I tried to escape. Eventually, I got him to leave by playing along with the delusion: 'Maybe she's back in your room. Maybe she wanted to surprise you.'

Mike looked at me and then left in a hurry, taking my knife with him. I locked the door behind him and leaned against it.

It wasn't long before Mike realised that he no longer had a room to go back to, because he had sold it. He came straight back across the roof, thinking that I'd tricked him because I really had stolen his girl-friend. This time, the delegate heard him coming and was already outside when Mike landed on the Alamos roof.

'Get down,' hissed the delegate, trying to keep his voice low so as not to wake anyone. There was a strange rule in our section that prohibited anyone except the delegate from climbing on the roof after 9 pm. 'Now,' he insisted. 'Or I'll call the police.' But Mike refused to obey and the delegate was forced to send for the major.

Mike was lucky that the major who was on duty that night was reasonable. Otherwise, the police might have shot him for attempting to escape. The major also tried to persuade Mike to climb down, but he wouldn't come. So, the major decided to go up after him.

The chase that followed was like a stunt scene in an action movie. The major went around to San Martín with his men to intercept Mike, but then Mike jumped across the roof to Alamos. Then, when the major came back around to our side, Mike leapt back again. Every time he cleared the two-metre gap between the sections, he would make a loud yelping sound, like a wounded animal. He made so much noise, what with his yelling and crashing about on the metal roof, that the inmates from both sections woke up and came out to see what was the matter. Jack appeared by my side in his pink pyjamas and fluffy rabbit slippers.

'Look at that piece of *mierda*. He's overdosed,' he said, blowing his nose and rubbing his eyes under his sunglasses. 'What time is it, anyway?'

None of the police was brave enough to get up there and bring Mike down. Some parts of the roof were rusted and if you slipped and fell, the drop was three storeys. But Mike was so high that the danger didn't worry him. He made the jump successfully every time, screaming out something crazy that no one could understand. And once he realised there was an audience, he even started to jump back and forth just to show off, bowing dramatically after each successful leap. A few of the inmates applauded until the major started getting mad. The policeman tried everything to get Mike off the roof, but Mike wouldn't listen. He said that if anyone came up, they would have to fight him man to man. I didn't tell the major that Mike also had my knife in his back pocket, in case I got into trouble too.

Eventually, the major posted two guards in San Martín and two in Alamos to prevent Mike from crossing any other roofs and escaping. The guards had to wait there all night and all the following morning until Mike climbed down on his own. They locked him in La Muralla for four days. When he got out, he wanted to come and stay with me, but I said he couldn't. I didn't tell him that I was afraid he might go crazy again. He went back to the punishment section for somewhere to sleep until his relatives sent him more money to buy a room. After that incident, he shaved his head, told everyone he was ten years younger and decided to quit using cocaine.

36
PRISONERS' DAY

After Mike went crazy, I decided to slow down on the cocaine. The amount I was doing was way too much for my system. But although I promised myself many times to stop, I kept taking it; we may have been locked in prison, but there was always something to celebrate.

In addition to the weddings, birthdays and baptisms inside the jail, the prisoners celebrated all the traditional festivals and holidays on the outside: Christmas, Easter, *la Noche de San Juan*, *la Entrada de Gran Poder*, Bolivia's Independence Day, Peru's Independence Day, Ecuador's Independence Day. In fact, any country's Independence Day or anyone's ex-girlfriend's birthday that we could remember. And if there was ever a dispute as to the correct date, we would have two parties – just to be sure that we hadn't miscelebrated.

Basically, the inmates used any excuse to throw a party, but one day stood out as being particularly special, Prisoners' Day, because it was *our* day. On the twenty-fourth of September every year, people on the outside were supposed to spare a thought for us – all the unfortunate inmates incarcerated around the nation. Even if they didn't think of us, it was certainly *our* biggest party of the year.

That was the day we prisoners were allowed to really let loose. The sections hired bands and we danced and drank all day, all night and all the next day. You could do anything you wanted and the police wouldn't bust you. Besides, they were usually too drunk themselves. One year, the major on duty even sent me a few grams of coke. And because you could do anything, there was no limit to the number of tourists I could have to spend the night.

The biggest-ever Prisoners' Day celebration occurred during my third year, which was also when the tours were at their peak. I started inviting people I met on the tours in the weeks beforehand. Others, I invited from the tours on the actual day. Over the course of the afternoon, the small crowd in my room grew bigger and bigger. When we did a headcount at four in the afternoon, the total number of tourists came to forty-five. About half of them stayed the night. We tried to do another headcount at two in the morning, but no one would sit still. Everyone was moving around, talking and dancing. There was cocaine everywhere. It was absolutely out of control.

There wasn't enough space in my room for everyone to be in there at once, so they took it in shifts. There was a constant line of traffic going up and down my wooden staircase as the tourists came in to charge up on cocaine before returning to the main party in the courtyard, where the band was playing. But some of them got stuck talking and forgot to leave, so every now and then I had to drag people out of there to make space for new arrivals.

I eventually gave up on making the lines of coke for everyone myself. It was too slow; no sooner had I finished making ten lines than I'd have to make another ten. If things had stayed like that, I would have had no chance to go downstairs and socialise myself.

'Here, man. You seem to know what you are doing,' I said, dropping ten grams onto a CD case and putting a guy from New Zealand in charge of it. His eyes were already popping out of his head and his hands were shaking, but he was proud that I had chosen him over the other tourists and set about carefully carving up the crystals. He seemed to like his new job and settled in for the night. The fact that he would be in the same spot making lines of coke the entire time didn't worry him in the slightest, and it didn't stop him from talking, which he did a lot of.

When I came back upstairs for my next line, the conversation in the room had stopped completely. I assumed they'd had too much coke and I tried to liven them up.

'Who wants to come downstairs and meet some of my Bolivian friends?'

But no one would look me in the eye. Everyone looked very guilty, none more so than the New Zealander, who was kneeling on the ground holding two credit cards in his hands. Something bad had happened.

'I'm really sorry, mate. It was my fault. I admit it. I'll pay for it all.' He looked down at the carpet in front of him where the CD with all the coke had fallen and started trying to scoop it up using the cards. 'I think we can save most of it, but there are bits of dirt and carpet in it. Just tell me how much I owe you.'

'We'll all chip in,' added a British girl. 'Won't we?'

The others nodded, but I could see them trying to calculate how many days' travelling budget ten grams of coke would cost them. They would all have to cut their holidays short.

'Stop it! What are you doing, you idiot?' I shook my head and took a step towards the New Zealander. He coiled back, worried perhaps that I was about to hit him. 'Here. Give me those.' I pointed at the credit cards and he handed them to me, thinking there might be some special way of recovering spilt cocaine that he didn't know about. Then, I grabbed hold of my broom and swept the coke out the door.

'It's only coke. It's not like you spilled beer or anything,' I said.

He looked at me in complete shock. The others didn't know how to react either; they thought I'd gone crazy.

'But as punishment, you have to make ten more lines. And make them quickly.' I handed the cards back to him, along with ten more grams and a different CD cover to work with. 'You've lost us a lot of valuable time.'

I probably could have saved most of the coke, like he had suggested, but this was during the time I was working in the cocaine laboratories at night, so I had fifty more grams of it sitting in my cupboard that hadn't cost me a cent. Besides, I did it for a laugh. I knew that everyone in that room would be telling the story everywhere they went for the rest of their lives.

The poor New Zealander was so relieved that he would have been happy to stay there until sunrise, serving cocaine to everyone, but by then the party was in full swing and he couldn't keep up with the demand. Instead of having just him on line-making duty, I handed out my entire CD collection so that people could do it themselves. However, there weren't enough CD cases to go around and some people had to resort to cassette cases, which weren't anywhere near as good.

Eventually, my room got so full that people were spilling out onto the landing or sitting on the staircase, chopping up coke and drinking whatever they could get their hands on. No one was interested now in dancing or meeting any of the Bolivians. They just wanted to talk.

I couldn't even get into my own room and in the end I gave up and let them do what they wanted. With not even enough room to stand up, it would have been impossible to find space for people to sleep. Luckily, no one was interested in sleeping. They were way too high.

The party kept getting bigger and bigger. People who had never met before decided they would go travelling together, starting the following day. Others, who had nothing in common whatsoever, decided they were best friends and would visit each other on the other side of the world. A few small romances between the backpackers also sprang up over the course of the evening. I even caught one of the Canadian tourists, a blond guy who was really shy and couldn't have been more than twenty, deeply involved in a conversation with one of the Bolivian wives, who must have been about fifty and had no teeth. She was feeding him *chicha* and they were flirting outrageously. He hadn't spoken a word of Spanish when he came in, but he was now jabbering away at a million miles an hour, and she was enraptured by what he was saying.

'I thought you couldn't speak Spanish,' I interrupted him.

'I couldn't. But I'm fluent now. It just came to me all at once.'

'Be careful,' I warned him. Her husband had fallen asleep drunk, but I was worried that he might wake up and wonder where his wife was, or that the inmates might talk.

'It's OK. She's teaching me to speak Quechua, too.'

Later I caught the two of them dancing together. He was enjoying himself, but I didn't want him to get too carried away.

'I thought you said you couldn't dance?' I called to him as I went past.

'I couldn't. But I'm a very fast learner. This stuff is excellent.'

The party kicked on until seven the next morning. The New Zealander was still sitting in the same position on my bed, chopping up lines, even though everyone had stopped taking them. I wanted to keep going also, but once it was daylight, many of the tourists suddenly remembered that they were in a prison and became paranoid. Some panicked and wanted to leave immediately, but the major, who had just come on duty, made them wait until after nine o'clock and then exit in small groups so that it wouldn't be so obvious. It was clear that none of them had slept, and twenty-two drunk, coked-up foreigners pouring out of a Bolivian prison during peak-hour traffic looking like they had been to a nightclub might lose him his job.

I took the tourists to the gates in groups and said goodbye. 'Thanks, Thomas. This is the best night of my life,' declared my new New Zealander friend, even though the sun was shining and the music had stopped. He had done so much coke that the party was still going on in his head. One of the girls who was in a similar state gave the major a big hug when she got through the gate, and all his men laughed.

I was extremely tired, but with all the drugs still in my bloodstream, it was several joints and many hours before I finally managed to get some sleep. The day after that, the truce with the police ended and they went back to busting us as per usual. It was one hell of a party, though, and I had a two-day *chicha* hangover to prove it.

37
THE AUSTRALIAN'S WALLET

It may sound strange, but I had never had friends like the tourists I met while in prison. I had always had friends on the outside who were ready to party whenever I turned up with a few kilos of cocaine in my suitcase. But where had they been when I needed them? Who had sent me money when they had heard that I was stuck in a Bolivian jail? Who had bothered to find out where I was?

Doing time is a real test of friendship. None of my old friends passed that test. Maybe none of them had even noticed that I was missing. To me, that made it even more special that people I had never met before came to visit me and did stick by me.

Most of the travellers who had visited me were just passing through La Paz and couldn't visit more than once or twice. However, many of them stayed in contact by letters and email. I glued the postcards they sent me from all over the world onto my wall. I received mail from the United States, Australia, Canada, Germany, England, Israel, Turkey and Japan. Whenever I felt sad, I would read what the tourists had written to me, and I would soon feel better again.

Even though I only met many of these people once, I knew that they were real friends. You know how? I had nothing to give them. I couldn't give them money, I couldn't give them status, I couldn't take them to fancy places and buy drinks for them. All I had were my stories and who I was, and that was enough for them to want to stay in contact. For the first time in my life, that was enough.

However, many of the tourists did a lot more than just remain in contact – they came back to see me a third or fourth time. Some even postponed their travel plans in order to stay with me. In fact, one group of backpackers actually seemed to get stuck in La Paz, coming into the prison to do coke with me every day for weeks on end, until their money ran out.

In my first year as a tour guide, which was my second year in prison, there were Yasheeda and her friends from Israel. But in the following years there were others, too, who hung around for months and months, sleeping in the prison and going in and out whenever they pleased. Till and Caroline, a hippie couple from Wales, were my absolute favourites, although they didn't take cocaine because they said it had too many synthetic chemicals. They came to South America to go trekking. On their way, they collected all types of herbs and natural hallucinogens, such as the ayahuasca plant. On one trip, they hiked out into the Chilean desert in order to harvest the San Pedro cactus, which a shaman uses for spiritual healing during special ceremonies that last up to twelve hours. Till and Caroline probably could have paid for some that had been pre-prepared to save themselves the hassle, but they said it was better energy if you brewed it yourself. In between these hikes, they always came back to see me. During my time in San Pedro, those two flew back to South America three times and must have visited me on at least a hundred occasions. I lost count of how many nights they stayed and how many postcards they sent me when they were out of the country.

There was no way I could repay any of these people for what they gave me when I was in San Pedro. There was only one time when I got the chance to show someone how much it meant.

卌‖

The tour business wasn't always booming; it went up and down according to the seasons. I also discovered that the restaurant business was dependent on the outside economy. When times were tough, the inmates would cook for themselves in order to save money and my income would drop to almost zero.

Jerome was one of the tourists who came to see me many times during my more difficult times. He was a tall, blond Australian and he didn't come for the cocaine. In fact, he was strongly against drugs. He came back because he was amazed by the way the prisoners and their families lived and survived, and he wanted to see more. He also felt sorry for me.

When I first met Jerome, he knew that I was desperate for any help that I could get. At the end of his visit, he left me his sunglasses and promised to bring food for me and presents for the San Pedro children the following day. He turned up a week later.

'Hey, man. I thought you had left the country,' I said, when I saw him coming through the gates the second time. He had a big smile because the guards had recognised him and let him in without paying.

'Yeah, mate. I'm a bit late, eh?' he said from the corner of his mouth, pointing to his watch. 'Sorry 'bout that. Got caught in traffic.' He winked at me and I couldn't help smiling. Jerome kept a straight face the whole time I knew him, so I often couldn't tell if he was joking until he winked.

'Thanks for coming, man,' I said, shaking his hand and then giving him a hug. 'It means a lot to me, you know.'

'Yeah. Look, mate. We're in a male prison. There are people watching us. You been on that charlie again, haven't ya?' He shook his head at me and clicked loudly with his tongue. 'It'll rot your brain, Thomas.'

'No! I've just woken up,' I said, defending myself. But as always, Jerome was only joking.

'OK, OK. I believe you. Now, don't go getting all emotional on me again, but I brought you a few presents. These,' he held up a big bag full of fruit, 'and these'. He jerked his head back towards the gate and winked again. Waiting on the other side were four blond Norwegian girls. Jerome had met them at his hostel and persuaded them to come along. 'Looks like you could use a bit of both,' he said, reaching down to pick out a bunch of bananas that was falling out of the bag. 'I told dem dat you was Jamaican, man. Is dat OK, man?' he said, trying to copy the way I spoke and tapping the largest banana in the bunch with his index finger.

The Norwegians were too afraid to come through the gates. The lieutenant didn't help matters by telling them that tourists were banned from entering. It took me a few minutes to convince the lieutenant to let them in and then a few minutes more to convince the girls that it was safe to leave their passports with him.

'So, welcome to San Pedro prison,' I said, when they were finally inside. 'I'm Thomas the tour guide.' But my usual joke didn't work; the four girls looked at me nervously, shifting awkwardly on the spot. I tried a different approach. 'We had a lot of fun last week, didn't we

Jerome?' But when I turned to Jerome for support, his face had gone completely pale and he was staring at the ground.

'What's wrong, man?' I asked, thinking he was about to be sick.

'My wallet. They've taken my wallet,' he said quietly, shuffling his feet in case he was standing on top of it.

'Who has? Are you sure? Check your pockets.'

'I have. Three times.'

'Who took it?'

'I don't know. I didn't see. It happened just a second ago when you were getting the girls in. They were all knocking against me. It was in this pocket right here.' He pointed to his grey cargo pants, the same type that all the tourists were wearing at the time. The zipper on one of the pockets was undone.

The wallet was definitely gone. It was the first time anyone had been robbed in all my time as a tour guide. I looked around at the inmates in the courtyard, trying to spot a guilty face. It could have been any one of them.

'Do you think there's any chance?' asked Jerome, seeing that I was looking around.

'I don't know. I'll do my best.' I was searching for two or three known pickpockets who had targeted Bolivian visitors before. I saw one of them, Camacho, sitting on the garden's edge deeply involved in a conversation. He must have sensed me staring at him, but he didn't look up.

'They can keep the money,' said Jerome. 'I don't care about the money. I just need my credit cards back. I'm stuffed without them.'

'How much money did you have?' I asked, still watching Camacho. 'And what colour is the wallet?'

'It's green. There were exactly one thousand bolivianos in it. I withdrew it this morning from the ATM.'

One thousand bolivianos! I had expected him to say fifty or maybe one hundred. San Pedro was safe, but it was still a prison. Jerome already felt stupid enough so I didn't say anything. Instead, I waved to my bodyguards, who were standing by, waiting to start the tour.

'Lucho. Cartagena. Come with me.' We left Jerome and the girls with the head *taxista*, and marched straight over to Camacho to demand the wallet back.

'Thomas, my brother,' he said, looking up innocently. 'What's with you?' He was a good actor, but there was something in the way he moved his eyes that told me he was lying.

'You've got three seconds,' I growled, putting my hands on his shoulder so that he couldn't get up. Lucho and Cartagena moved in closer to block the guards' view. The inmate Camacho had been talking with stood up and left.

'What are you talking about?' Camacho protested weakly.

'I think you and I need to have a little chat,' I said, nodding for my men to take him to my room. 'In private.'

Lucho took one elbow and Cartagena took the other. They led Camacho through the courtyard and up to my room. Camacho knew better than to make a scene. Once we reached my room, he realised that he was completely on his own. He kept his cool, though. After we searched his pockets and found nothing, I began to doubt whether he had done it. I might have been wrong, but I couldn't afford to show any weakness, especially not in front of my men. I punched him in the stomach and he cried out, struggling to get free of Lucho and Cartagena.

'You're making a big mistake, *inglés*,' he said.

I hit him again.

'You'll pay for this, you black cunt.'

I punched him in the stomach again.

When he recovered his breath, he spat on me and swore loudly.

'Listen!' I cupped my hand to my ear. 'No one can hear you up here.' Then I slapped it across his face. We placed him on the metal chair and strapped him to it with electrical tape. Camacho still refused to confess.

'You can't kill me,' he said, gritting his teeth. 'People know where I am. You're going to pay for this, black cunt.'

Camacho was tough. Even with his mouth taped up, he managed to scare Lucho and Cartagena with his eyes. He looked at them as if to say, 'And that goes for you two as well.' It worked. Lucho and Cartagena called me into the kitchen where he couldn't hear us.

'You'd better be sure about this, Thomas,' said Cartagena. Falsely accusing someone was an extremely serious offence in San Pedro.

'The *gringo* said the money doesn't matter,' I explained to them. 'He just wants his credit cards back.'

'How much?' asked Lucho. I told him the amount and he nodded thoughtfully. I could see him trying to divide one thousand by three evenly. However, Cartagena wasn't convinced, even with the money.

'Fine,' I said, shrugging my shoulders. 'We'll let him go, then. But as soon as the guards hear about this, no more tourists will be allowed in.' I paused to let this information sink in. 'And when other tourists hear that San Pedro is dangerous, they won't want to come in anyway. It's simple. No wallet means no more tours. No more tours means no more money.'

After that, I stood back and let my bodyguards do the work. They pounded Camacho until he nodded his head frantically to tell us he wanted to give in. Lucho ripped the tape from around his mouth, taking hundreds of hairs with it.

'OK, OK. I'll show you where it is,' he said, spitting blood onto his chin. Just as he confessed, there was a knock at the door. Cartagena and Lucho covered Camacho's mouth again and dragged him into the kitchen.

'Who is it?' I asked, trying to sound relaxed.

It was only Jerome. I had told him I'd be five minutes, but he had become impatient and brought the girls to my room. I let them in.

'Hey, man. Good news,' I said to Jerome as he came in. 'We're going to get your wallet back.' Jerome didn't say anything. He stopped in the middle of the room and the Norwegian girl following him knocked into his back.

'Oh, my God!' she exclaimed, when she saw what Jerome was looking at. 'Quick. This man is hurt.' She rushed forward to attend to Camacho.

One of the other Norwegians turned to me and said coldly, 'Do you have any ice, please?'

I pointed to the refrigerator. Jerome looked at me and shook his head, pretending he was disappointed with me for the benefit of the girls.

'Hey, man. This is a prison, understand?' I said, not wanting to look bad myself. 'I thought you said you needed your credit cards back.'

'I did, Thomas. But I didn't say you had to torture someone to get them.' I smiled and waited for Jerome to wink, but he didn't. He shook his head again. 'You just don't get it, do you, Thomas?'

While the Norwegians made a fuss over Camacho, Lucho and Cartagena cut the electrical tape from around his arms and legs. We left Lucho with Jerome and the girls in my room and went to collect the wallet from Camacho's friend in Prefectura. Camacho complained the whole way, calling me a *gringo* lover and a traitor. He said I wasn't a tour guide but a zookeeper.

When we reached his section, he insisted that Cartagena wait at the entrance because there were lookouts. Three of us entering together would look suspicious. Before we reached his friend's room where the wallet was being kept, Camacho made me an offer: 'Let's split the money, fifty–fifty. I won't say anything to Lucho or Cartagena. Tell them the money wasn't there.' I didn't answer him. I tightened my grip on his elbow and we kept walking.

On the way back, Cartagena made me the same offer. 'Is it all there?' he asked. 'Let me count it.'

I nodded and held up the wallet, then put it back in my pocket. I had already counted it. Ten notes of one hundred bolivianos with the ATM receipt still wrapped around them.

'Well?'

'Well, what?' I snapped back at him. When he realised what I was thinking, he started to protest.

'You're not going to . . .?' But he couldn't finish his question. And he knew the answer by my silence.

'But why?' was all he could say as he chased after me up the stairs, putting his hand on my shoulder to slow me down. The money that Jerome and his girlfriends spent in one night out drinking could feed an entire family in San Pedro for a month. I could have used the money myself. I tried to think of how I could answer him, but all I could hear were Jerome's words and sarcastic voice playing over and over in my mind: 'You just don't get it, do you, Thomas?'

I almost gave in. Then I saw a little girl sitting by herself on the steps carefully peeling the skin from a piece of fruit. I looked at Cartagena.

'I don't know. He brought me some bananas, man,' I said. 'They looked like nice bananas.'

38
PRISON ELECTIONS

At the time, it was very difficult to give Jerome back his wallet with all that money in it. A few years earlier, I wouldn't have thought twice about keeping a wallet I found in the street. In prison, it was even harder. Not only because of the other inmates pressuring me, but because I had very little money myself to survive on. But afterwards, I felt really proud of myself.

I can't claim to have been an honest person my whole life. I had done many things that were against the law. I was a drug trafficker. I did it for the money and because I was addicted to the excitement. If I said now that I was sorry and that I realised it was wrong, I'd be lying. But being friends with the tourists showed me that there were more important things than being rich and having adventures. I realised that the most important thing anyone has is their freedom, but it wasn't going to jail that taught me that lesson. It was the people I met in there. They made me want to be honest. I didn't even care anymore about getting my revenge on Colonel Lanza. I just wanted to finish my prison term and lead a normal life once I got out. It was going to be hard, but I was determined to try.

The money I returned to Jerome came back to me in other ways. He told everyone he met outside about what had happened. Many people couldn't believe that San Pedro prison was a safe place to visit and that some of the prisoners were honest – they wanted to see it for themselves. After that, more and more tourists came in to see me and with each person that paid to come through the gates, more money was injected into the prison economy, and my influence with the police and other inmates increased. In those days I could get away with anything. I was still friends with the governor. I had regular dealings with the guards at the gate. I bought merchandise from all the drug dealers. And because I moved about the prison so often with the tourists, every inmate knew who I was.

In the quiet times when no tourists were around, prison life was quite boring, so I made an effort to be friendly with everyone. Sometimes that was hard, because you can't force yourself always to be in a good mood. However, I at least said hello to everyone I passed on my way around the various sections.

One thing I learned from coming into contact with so many people each day was how to make people smile just by always being happy myself, or ready with a quick comment. Despite their poverty, the Bolivians are basically a very happy people, and they like it when you make them laugh. I'd say to the inmates, 'When are you going to introduce me to your sister? You promised.' Once they laughed, it was hard for anyone to get angry with me.

The other thing was to make each person feel important. Many of the inmates were curious about foreigners, and some secretly looked up to them, so they loved it when I introduced them as someone special, especially to the girls.

'This is Chapako,' I'd say. 'He's the champion striker in the Prefectura football team, aren't you?' Chapako would laugh, and then I would take it a step further by making the others around him laugh: 'He used to play for the Bolivian national team, but then he got too fat. That's why they put him in prison.' Once you made people laugh, you could get away with anything.

My influence extended all the way around the prison, but it was especially strong in Alamos, where I lived. One day, Julián and Uruguayo, two of the inmates from the section who were respected by everyone, approached me.

'We need your help,' they said.

They had a proposition: they wanted me to help them get voted in during the next prison elections.

'You know the people, Thomas. We need you to get them on our side.'

༒

Annual election time in the prison was fun, especially when a candidate was trying to get re-elected. This meant there were several campaigning celebrations in the lead-up to the actual voting, paid for out of the section funds. Unfortunately, these re-election campaigns only happened every second period, since there was a rule that people could stay in power for a maximum of two political terms.

The two most important positions to be voted for were the delegate and treasurer of each section. The delegate was the prisoners' representative to the authorities and he also had power over everyone in the section, including the ability to send inmates to the isolation cells. The treasurer controlled the section's finances and made the spending decisions. Anyone who had been a resident in the section for more than six months could run for election. The only requirements were that you had no outstanding debts and that you owned an unmortgaged cell; otherwise, you had to put down a bond of four hundred US dollars, as insurance against embezzling the funds.

Candidates campaigned in pairs for these two major postings, but they also had a political team behind them that helped get them into office, which is where I fitted in. Julián wanted me to talk to the people and convince them that he would be the best delegate ever. Once in power, the delegate decided on the minor positions and together they formed the section *directiva*. Other positions included the discipline secretary, who was in charge of maintaining order and good conduct, the secretary of culture and education, who looked after the library books, and the sports secretary, who ran our football team and tried to get corporate sponsorship for the annual inter-section football cup. The easiest job by far was the health secretary, who was supposed to be in charge of medical supplies. There never were any, so he did nothing.

During election week, all the voting inmates from the section, known as the General Assembly, would gather in the courtyard and listen to speeches by the various candidates on how they planned to improve our living conditions. Sometimes, they paid people in the crowd to cheer or boo during the speeches. Meanwhile, supporters handed out flyers and cups of *chicha* and beer, and tried to persuade you to vote for their team. If you were like me, and never made up your mind until the last moment, you could get a lot of free stuff.

The actual vote was done by secret ballot in the section courtyard. You wrote the names of the delegate you wanted on a piece of paper, folded it over and inserted it into a box. Next to the box stood the three members of the electoral committee, who were appointed by the voters to ensure that the elections were conducted fairly. On the day, they made sure that the ballot box was empty to start with and that no one voted twice or tried to slip in two pieces of paper. The votes were then read out, one by one, and tallied on a chalk board. I usually tried to disguise my handwriting on my voting slip. That way, no one ever knew which candidates I'd actually voted for and I could get more free stuff at the next election.

As each vote was read out, a cheer or boo went up from the crowd, depending on which candidate the vote was for.

'¡*Viva Juan Ricardo!*' or '¡*Arriba Jorge Mendez!*' they would shout, then everyone would touch plastic cups and take a sip of their drinks. The losing side would stamp their feet in disappointment: 'Down with corruption.'

By the end, everyone was completely drunk, except for the electoral committee, who banned themselves from drinking. They weren't allowed to cheer, either, in case it made them look biased. Afterwards, there was always music and dancing, and more celebrating and commiserating.

The first time I witnessed one of these elections, I couldn't believe it. When Ricardo saw the look on my face, he put his arm around my shoulder and said, 'This is nothing, my friend. Voting when you are drunk is a tradition in South America. You know, in some countries, they have to make alcohol illegal for a week before elections in order to stop politicians from bribing voters.'

The annual elections for section delegate and treasurer weren't the only political campaigns conducted in San Pedro. Bolivian inmates were also entitled to vote in national elections, so many politicians came into the prison to win votes before the presidential elections. Most of them told us that we weren't bad people; the real criminals were walking free on the outside. Others said that they would repeal the *gringo* drug laws under which most of us had been charged.

'Bolivia doesn't have a drug problem. The United States does. They're the ones demanding cocaine. Why should you people be suffering in prison for something that is their problem?'

All the politicians promised to improve our living conditions if we voted for them, but nothing ever changed. For this reason, we took the internal prison elections far more seriously than the national elections. It wasn't compulsory to vote, but everyone did. The delegate had a lot of power, both in representing our interests to the prison authorities, and in keeping peace and order in the section. If we chose a bad team, our lives could be miserable for a whole year. And if we chose a dishonest team, the section might go broke.

At the end of their term in office, the delegate and treasurer had to present the members with the financial accounting records, including a balance sheet and profit-and-loss statement. There were also supposed to be audits of the accounts conducted every two months, but they never happened. In the meantime, the delegate and secretary had complete control over all the section's money. They could do whatever they liked with it, and some of them did, which is why I agreed to support Julián.

'OK. I'll help, then,' I said. Normally, I didn't like to get too involved in prison politics, but I did it because Julián was my friend and I was sure he would never steal from anyone. He got elected easily. There was a big party that I don't remember much of. I just recall waking up with a lot of confetti in my bed.

I was happy for Julián and knew that he would do a good job as delegate. I didn't want a position in his *directiva*, but I knew that he might be of help sometime down the track. If I ever got in trouble, he would back me up. That time came a lot sooner than I expected.

卅‖

If the good times had continued, I would have been happy to serve out the remainder of my sentence in San Pedro without complaint. The inmates were my friends. The police were my friends. The tourists kept me company. I was high all the time. I had influence within the prison, and I was making enough money to survive. I thought that nothing could touch me and that things would stay like that until I was released.

Then, in the space of two weeks, my whole world was turned completely upside down. Everything went wrong. I watched helplessly as all the things that were important in my life came tumbling down around me: the friendships I had made in prison, my tour business, and even my hopes of obtaining my freedom soon. What happened during that period was the beginning of a passage of events that would see me betrayed by people I had trusted, witness the deaths of two of my best friends, and put me through the worst hell I had ever known. And at the end of it all, I would be facing an extra ten to fifteen years in prison.

39
HIDDEN ENEMIES

The first blow came one morning after *lista*. Abregon came rushing up behind me as I was returning to my room. He was flushed and out of breath. He didn't even have time to say hello.

'Thomas, they're transferring me to Chonchocoro,' he panted.

'What?' I looked at him in amazement. Abregon nodded that I'd heard correctly. I hardly knew what to say. It was everyone's worst nightmare to be sent to maximum security. The conditions up there were horrible. It was even colder at night because of the 4000-metre altitude; the cells were small and bare; the guards were tough; and the prisoners were even tougher. Compared with Chonchocoro, San Pedro was a holiday resort. 'But what for?' I asked.

'They won't say.'

'But they have to tell you the reason. They need an order from the judge, don't they? Just wait. I'll ring the governor.'

'It's too late for that. They're taking me now.'

'When?'

'Right now.' At that moment, we heard Abregon's name being called from down in the courtyard. I looked over the balcony and saw the lieutenant and two guards striding purposefully towards the stairs.

'Here. Take my spare key,' Abregon said urgently, struggling to twist a silver key off his key ring. He held it out to me, his hands shaking slightly. 'You remember where everything is hidden?'

I nodded. The second floorboard back from the wall, directly beneath his chest of drawers, was loose. He placed the key in my palm, but when I went to take my hand away, he wouldn't let it go. His fingers wrapped tighter around my hand, with his thumb pressing down on the key. 'I'm trusting you, my brother.' He squeezed even harder. 'You understand?'

'Why? How much is in there?'

'Twenty thousand,' he whispered, releasing his grip just as the lieutenant and his men rounded the first flight of stairs.

'Why don't you take something with you now?' I asked quickly, slipping the key into my pocket before the police could see it.

'Too dangerous. They'll search me as soon as I get there. The cops wouldn't leave me with a fucking boliviano. I'll send Raquel to pick up some *plata*.'

The guards had reached the top of the stairs by then and were coming towards us.

'*Vamos*,' ordered the lieutenant, nodding to his men to take Abregon.

'I trust you like a brother, Thomas,' he said again, looking me hard in the eyes. I winked at him to say that I wouldn't let him down, then they took him away.

Taking hold of one arm each, the two guards guided him down the stairs with the lieutenant leading the way. Abregon looked back over his shoulder at me and managed to get one arm free.

'I'll call you,' he mouthed, holding his free hand up to his ear like a telephone.

He did call eventually. But this was the last time I ever saw him alive.

卌||

I found out through some contacts in the prison administration that Abregon had been reclassified as a high-risk inmate. The reason: planning to escape. They could give me no further details, other than to say that someone had tipped the guards off about his intentions to escape. Abregon was known to have money and a lot of influence inside the prison, so the police believed it might be true.

It was clear that someone was plotting against Abregon, but we didn't know who and there was nothing more I could do to help him until he phoned. Once he had some money with him, I was confident that Abregon could fix the problem. He probably could have bribed his way out before he was transferred, but he never got the chance. It had all happened too quickly.

I told our friends to keep their phones switched on and waited for Abregon's call. He didn't ring me, but after five days his wife, Raquel, arrived to collect the money.

'How much does he want?' I asked her.

'All of it.'

'Everything?' I asked in surprise.

She shrugged casually. 'That's what he said.'

It didn't sound smart to take all the money in one go like that. But it was Abregon's money and I presumed he knew what he was doing. I gave her the twenty thousand and made her sign a letter and count the money in front of Julián, our new section delegate.

Abregon's call came two days later. I woke to someone banging on my door in the middle of the night and I opened it, still half asleep. It was Orlando. He was wearing only his pyjamas and he was wet from running barefoot through the rain to bring me his phone. He was too out of breath to say who it was, but I guessed straight away.

'Is it him?' I asked, taking the phone. Orlando nodded then stood shivering in the cold while I took the call.

'¿Aló?'

'Thomas, you have to listen to me,' I recognised Abregon's voice, but the line was terrible.

'Speak up, brother – I can hardly hear you!' I yelled into the phone, but Orlando motioned for me to keep my voice down.

'Listen to me, Thomas. I can't talk long. I'm on someone else's phone.'

'OK,' I whispered loudly, holding the mouthpiece right up against my lips. Orlando nodded that that was better.

'Thomas, I need money. I need you to get my money to me. I think I can get transferred back to San Pedro, but I'm going to need money. I'll send Raquel around to pick it up. Get it ready for her, OK?'

'Yes, I know. She already came.'

'What?'

I was suddenly wide awake. 'She was here two days ago. I gave her everything.'

'When?'

'Two days ago. On visitors' day.' I wasn't sure if it was the bad connection or if Abregon had fallen silent on the other end. 'Are you there? Hello . . . Abregon? Can you hear me?' The line was still crackling so I moved around, changing the angle of the phone to get better reception. 'Abregon?' Finally, he answered.

'What the fuck did you do that for?' he asked angrily.

'I didn't want to without speaking to you first, but she said it was for you, so I gave it to her. Julián was there, if you don't believe me. I made her count the money in front of him and sign for it.'

'OK, OK. I need to think.' He sounded panicky. 'Have you seen her since?'

'No. But she said she was going straight up to visit you. Didn't she come?'

'That bitch hasn't visited me once.'

'I'm sorry, brother. She said you had asked for it. She's your wife – what was I supposed to do? I had no way of calling you up there.'

I had difficulty hearing his response, but I thought he said, 'She's not my wife.'

'Pardon?' I moved the phone around again.

'Doesn't matter. Anyway, listen, Thomas. Try to find her. Ring my house. Ring everyone you can. I'll try to find her too, but in the meantime, I need you to send me money with one of the wives you can trust. Right now. Anything. I'm desperate here, brother. I've got nothing.'

'I'll try, but I've got nothing either.'

'Well, then get the fucking money back that you made me lend to the Velascos. Do whatever you have to.'

The line then cut out. I didn't know whether he had to hang up or if we just lost the connection, but I had no way of calling him back. I forced Orlando to wait for ten minutes longer in case Abregon tried to phone again, and during that time I started to think about how it was all my fault for having given the money to his wife. The only thing I could do to make it up to him was to get the money back from the Velascos.

I couldn't get back to sleep at all that night. Thinking about Abregon suffering in Chonchocoro made every one of my muscles tense up. All the Velascos had to do was what was right in the first place: pay back the money. I'd sent them several messages since Abregon had been transferred, but they never answered. Abregon had saved the son's wife from going to jail, but now that he was in trouble himself, they refused to help. They were too cheap to admit the debt and too cowardly to face us. By morning, I was ready to kill them.

After *lista* I got even more wound up. Although I hadn't eaten breakfast, I did a line of coke and sent for Lucho. While I waited for him, the effects came on. I paced the room back and forth. I could feel my heart rate going up. I began having violent flashes of what I was going to do as soon as I saw them and found myself throwing punches into the air and thumping my fist down on the table every time I went past it. Lucho knocked. I did another line before opening the door, then we went hunting for the Velascos immediately. Lucho already knew the story and didn't ask any questions. He wasn't there for his speaking ability and, besides, the time for talking was over.

The first thing we did was check their room. We listened at the door for a few minutes before knocking, but they either weren't in or they had been warned and were keeping very quiet. After that, we had no real plan; we simply walked around the prison, looking for them. I asked anyone we saw who might know them. I wasn't even polite about it.

'Where are the Velascos?' I demanded, skipping the niceties.

No one liked to get involved in these disputes so they all gave the same answer: 'Don't know' or 'Try their room in San Martín. They should be there.'

'Tell them we're looking for them,' I called over my shoulder as we walked off without saying goodbye or thank you.

We hunted for about thirty minutes but couldn't find them anywhere. Lucho wanted to keep looking, but by then the cocaine had worn off, and with no alcohol in my system I was left feeling a bit shaky and weak, so I decided to go back to my room and try again in the afternoon. I did some more coke. When later I still couldn't find them, I knew for certain that the Velascos were deliberately avoiding me. But they couldn't hide forever.

卌〢

Later that week, Lucho came to warn me. 'You're messing with the wrong people, *inglés*.' He only ever called me *inglés* when he wanted me to listen carefully.

'What exactly do you mean by that?'

'They've got people everywhere in here. And family connections on the outside. Jorge's uncle is a colonel in the army.'

'But it's only what is right. Everyone knows they owe the money. Abregon is desperate.'

Lucho shook his head. 'You're heading for trouble, *inglés*. That money's never coming back. If Abregon needs *plata*, then get it from somewhere else.'

Lucho always knew what was going on in the inside sections, but I ignored his advice. I was angry. It had been six months since the Velascos were supposed to have repaid the debt. I knew they didn't have much money anymore, but they could have paid it off a bit at a time. Any amount would have helped Abregon. Without money, you could die in Chonchocoro. I kept on doing coke and looking for them on my own.

Two days later, as I was heading into San Martín to visit Lucho, I saw the Velascos up ahead, coming towards me in the corridor. They were talking together and hadn't noticed me yet. I would have preferred to have someone with me, but I knew that this might be the only opportunity I got and even though I was on my own, I couldn't let them get away. I pulled the collar on my jacket up to hide my face and kept my head bowed until the last possible moment. As soon as I drew next to them, I threw my hands at their throats and pushed them both against the wall, hard.

'Where's the money, you bastards? Abregon's in Chonchocoro. We need the money.'

They were both taken completely by surprise and the blow to their throats had them gasping for air, so at first they couldn't even respond. But when Jose Luis recovered his breath, he started to fight back immediately. It wasn't hard for him to break out of my grip because I was concentrating my strength on strangling the son, Jorge, who was the bigger of the two. All hell broke loose. Jose Luis kicked me and tried to get me in a headlock and prise my hands off Jorge.

A crowd gathered around us instantly and began cheering. It was already two against one, so I was lucky that no one else came in on their side. When Jorge was about to pass out, I threw him to the ground and turned to fight his father, but he thumped me in the head. I was dazed and the only thing I could do was knock him against the wall and charge at him. We locked up in a desperate struggle and then Jorge managed to get back to his feet and the three of us grappled, with knees coming from all directions and fists flying everywhere.

The whole fight lasted less than two minutes before someone hissed that the police were coming and the spectators pulled us apart.

'You're dead – both of you! You can't hide forever. I'm going to get you!' I yelled at the Velascos as they scuttled back down to their room.

The other prisoners urged me to keep quiet so that the police wouldn't know who had been fighting.

After the fight, I went back to my room to calm down. I couldn't get any rest because people kept knocking on my door, wanting to hear what had happened. It seemed that everyone throughout the whole prison was talking about the fight, and I was worried the guards would hear that I was involved. At the time, they were really cracking down and you could be sent to Chonchocoro on the slightest pretext. What use would I be to Abregon if I was stuck there in maximum security with him?

Then, a strange thing happened: the Velascos sent word via one of the *taxistas* that they wanted peace. They had the money ready and I should come and get it from their room. I smelled a trap immediately. For a start, how did they have money now if they hadn't had any before? And if they did have money, why had they suddenly decided to pay it to me, rather than keep it for themselves? No one had won the fight, so it wasn't like they were afraid of me.

At the same time, I couldn't ignore the message, because they might blame me later for not going when they'd said they had the money. I sent a guy we called El General, who worked for me in my shop, with a note authorising the Velascos to pay him. El General came back empty-handed, saying that the Velascos didn't want any possibility of confusion – they would only give the money to me directly. This convinced me that it was a trap. However, I couldn't let them think that I was afraid. If I didn't go then, that would mean they had won and there would never be any chance of getting the money for Abregon. So, I had to go. But there was no way I was going on my own.

I asked Julián, my section delegate, to come with me. No one answered when we knocked on the Velascos' door the first time. We knocked again and this time a voice from inside told us to wait a moment. Julián suggested that we stand back from the door, just in case. As we waited against the railing a few doors down, I looked around and noticed that all the inmates were leaving. Within half a minute, the balcony was completely empty and everything had gone dead quiet. I could almost see what was about to happen next before it actually did.

Suddenly, there was a rush of footsteps as police sprinted up the stairs and swooped on us from both directions. They ignored Julián and came straight for me.

'Don't move! Stay right where you are.'

I did as I was told and stayed calm. I had suspected that something like this might happen, which was why I had brought Julián along as a witness.

Two of the police held me while the others knocked on the Velascos' door. At first they wouldn't come out, but when the police threatened to kick it in, they opened up. The police told Julián to stand back and me to accompany them inside to witness them searching the room, but I refused.

'What for? It's not my room. I'm from a different section.'

'What are you doing here, then?'

'Nothing. I'm here with my delegate,' I said pointing to Julián. The police hadn't reckoned on him being there and were a bit confused as to what to do. They told Julián to leave, but he said he had to stay as a witness.

'What are you doing out of your section?' they asked me again.

I repeated my answer of before. I didn't want to mention that I was about to visit the Velascos or that they owed me money. It was best not to give the police any information to go on, even if it was completely legitimate and explained everything, because they would find some way of twisting your words.

Julián was ordered to leave and, despite my protests, the police made me follow them into the room. Jose Luis and Jorge Velasco were inside with a third inmate I didn't know. None of them would meet my eye. We all watched as the cops turned things over and pulled their possessions apart.

'What's this?' asked one of the policemen, who was standing at the bookshelf unravelling a poster that he had slid out of a cylindrical container. Inside was a long, thin plastic bag containing cocaine. All the police looked at me.

'It's not mine. This isn't my room.' I pointed at the Velascos. 'Ask them!'

The police took us all outside to question us separately. They had nothing on me but that didn't stop them from trying to get a bribe. They assumed that, because of the tours and because I was a foreigner, I was a millionaire. They wanted two thousand dollars. Normally,

I would have given them something, nothing like that amount, but just something to avoid problems. This time, however, I had nothing to give.

'I have never been inside this room. The door was shut and when you came I was outside, several metres away, where you found me. It's *their* room.' I pointed to the Velascos again. 'Ask *them*.'

The guards had no case against me and they knew it. They could have changed the facts, except that I had a reliable witness with me to say that the door was shut and I had never been inside. They reduced their offer.

'OK. One thousand dollars, then.'

Still I refused, so they searched my pockets thoroughly. When they found nothing, they insisted on searching my room. I gave them the key on the condition that my delegate be present so that they couldn't plant anything. They didn't find anything there either and although they weren't happy about it, they had to let me go.

When the guards left my room, I was shaking. I sat down to think about what had just happened. Something big was going on. First Abregon being transferred, then this. The whole thing was so obviously a set-up. The police had intended to catch me in the room and say the drugs were mine, but they were stupid and had come too soon. Also, they hadn't counted on me bringing Julián along. I suspected that the Velascos were behind the whole episode and when they weren't charged either, I was sure of it. How could the police find over a hundred grams of cocaine in someone's room and not charge anyone?

That should have been the end of the incident. However, eight days later, someone informed the media about what had happened. There was a television report that several inmates had been caught with two hundred grams of cocaine inside San Pedro, but that no charges had been laid.

The cops came and got me straight after *lista*, just like they had with Abregon.

'Where are you taking me?' I demanded. I already knew what it was about.

'The punishment section.' My heart sank. There was to be an investigation. The culprits had to be found.

'Chonchocoro?'

'No.' The lieutenant shook his head. 'Not yet, anyway.'
'Where then?'
'You're in luck. They're sending you to La Grulla.'

40
SOLITARY CONFINEMENT

La Grulla was the new solitary confinement section to replace La Muralla, although there was nothing new about it. And there was nothing lucky at all about being sent there, either. That place was hell on earth. It was like they had run out of funds halfway through building it. The walls were dirty and unpainted. The taps didn't work. The toilets were permanently blocked. There were light sockets, but no globes. There were beds, but no mattresses or blankets.

My new life was made up of four elements: coldness, darkness, silence and boredom. The daily routine is simple enough to describe: twenty hours in the cell and four hours out. Inside, the cell was small and cold and dark. The walls and floor were made of cement and there were no windows and no light, other than the small amount that came under the door or through the small observation hatch in the door, which I could prop open when the guards weren't around. The bed was just a few planks of wood that I inserted into holes in the wall at night and dismantled during the day to make more space.

There were six of us in the cell block together – Characoto, Chapako, Ramero, Chino, Samir (my Brazilian car-thief friend) and me – and the guards let us out together for two hours in the morning and two hours in the afternoon, although we were banned from talking at all times. When out of the cell, I had to watch my back. Those guys were tough. La Grulla was supposed to be where they sent people as punishment for specific misdemeanours. In practice, however, they used it to house the hard and violent cases that they couldn't control and didn't know what to do with. It was the last step before Chonchocoro. Most of them didn't care about anything, not even themselves.

Ramero was in for punching a guard in the face. Chino spent most of his time in solitary for fighting. Characoto and Chapako were in there for stabbing an inmate to death with a screwdriver. Those two had nothing left to lose; they were already in prison for thirty years for another murder and they probably wouldn't live that long anyway. Besides, if they got a second conviction of thirty years for the stabbing, there was a loophole in the law that would allow them to serve it concurrently with the first sentence, so it made no difference to when they would get out. And Samir? I don't know what he was in for this time, but it was usually something to do with drugs or fighting. The only reason they didn't send him to Chonchocoro was because he was always threatening to expose the police involved in the car-theft ring.

During those four hours we could go to the toilet, have a cold shower, move around in the small exercise pen or eat some food, if there was any. The meal system in La Grulla was the same as in the rest of the prison – a bucket of watered-down soup was sent out from the prison kitchen twice a day to all the sections. That was all you got and if you didn't like it, you had to feed yourself. In La Grulla, there was a small kitchen area next to the bathrooms with running water and a cooker, but it was of no use to us since we couldn't get to the shops. Sometimes the guards forgot to send us our soup and we went hungry unless the inmates from the neighbouring section of Posta sent us their leftovers, which was never enough for six men to survive on anyway.

The conditions in solitary got to me quickly. I was constantly hungry and lost a lot of weight. After one week, I had diarrhoea and a chest infection. A few days later, I started pissing blood because I had a urinary tract infection. But there was something worse than the physical conditions and the sickness: the mental torture that went along with it.

卌ll

The guards in La Grulla were bastards. Real bastards. And they wanted to make an example of us because we were the first group to go through, so that everyone would hear about it and be afraid of being sent there. They did a good job of it, too. They called us dogs. They hit us like dogs. And after a while, we started to believe that we *were* dogs.

The guards were our masters. We were dependent on them for everything: food, water, toilet breaks, even company. They made us beg for everything. If you misbehaved, you would be locked in your cell without food or water. After several days of severe thirst and starvation, there is nothing that even the toughest man in the world won't do for something to eat, no matter how degrading. When Samir was being punished one time, the guards made him lick their boots while they pissed on him. Afterwards, they threw him scraps of food on the dirty floor and he thanked them for it.

Our communication with the rest of the world was cut off completely. We weren't allowed visitors, we weren't allowed phone calls, we couldn't send a message to anyone in the main prison or even call for a doctor if we were sick. Communication with each other was forbidden. And communication with the guards was limited to nodding and shaking our heads. We weren't even allowed to look at them. When they yelled at us, we had to keep our heads bowed. If they asked you a question and you answered it, they would strike you with a wooden baton for speaking. But if you *didn't* answer, you would be beaten for insolence.

There was no point in fighting back. The guards could do whatever they wanted and no one would ever know, because La Grulla was separated from the main prison. One of the other tricks they used to control us was punishing everyone when one person disobeyed the rules, which built up tension among the prisoners and stopped us from uniting against them. Usually, the punishment involved depriving us of yard time or food, or both. When that happened, I wouldn't see another human being or eat a thing for days on end. The only noises I would hear were the ones I made myself – my footsteps pacing up and down the cell, or my own voice when I talked or hummed to myself. We had buckets for shitting in, but I kept mine filled with drinking water for emergencies. Instead, I shat in the corner of my cell on a piece of newspaper and wrapped it up tightly to stop the smell getting out. It never worked, though. On top of all this, I was constantly worried about my future.

I replayed the events in the Velascos' room over and over in my mind, until I thought I was going crazy. The police had no evidence against me, and in any normal country I wouldn't have been concerned. But things were different in Bolivia. They could easily change a few details in order to make me look guilty. Ricardo's joke was no longer funny. 'What could they do to you if they catch you with drugs in prison?' he always asked. There was an answer: 'Keep you in there a lot longer.'

On the scale of cocaine offences, two hundred grams wasn't much. But the amount wasn't that important. Dealing in jail carried a heavy sentence no matter what, since it was a second offence. I didn't know what the exact penalty was, but I guessed the judges could add anything between five and fifteen years to my sentence if the case went to court. And the worst thing about it was that I was actually innocent this time. I have heard that for some people, knowing that they are innocent is the only thing that keeps them going while in prison. For me, it was the opposite; it made it worse. It made me realise that being innocent or guilty wasn't relevant. They could do what they wanted with you, and you were completely powerless to stop them.

I hadn't forgotten Abregon, either. What he was going through in Chonchocoro must have been far worse. I had no way of helping him from where I was. There was now no chance of getting any money to him; I couldn't operate my shop or restaurant; I couldn't run the tour business; I couldn't even sell any of my possessions or mortgage my room. And worse still, I didn't have any way of telling him what had happened to me. For all he knew, I might have been part of the plot to send him to maximum security in order to steal his money.

I often thought of Yasheeda. I had a lot of time to think about our relationship. I kept remembering one crazy night in particular, when we were both drunk and high, and we both said some crazy things to each other. We decided that we were going to get a little house together somewhere. It didn't matter where. Maybe we would have to rent at first, but we would both work hard in order to save up. I was going to quit trafficking. I didn't care what I had to do to get by. Maybe we could stay in Bolivia where everything was cheaper and I could teach English. I would clean toilets if I had to. Anything to be with her. We made love all that night and smoked marijuana and laughed in between times. I think I even proposed to her.

We never mentioned that conversation again, but I remembered it and I'm sure that she did too. We were crazy that night, and the things we said to each other were crazy, but they were true at the time. Part of me still wanted them to be true. But they couldn't be. Not if I was locked up in prison. I wondered which country Yasheeda was in now and what she was doing. I realised how stupid I had been, driving her away like I did. If she had been in La Paz still, I knew that she would have saved me. Or even if she had known where I was, I felt that would have somehow made me stronger. She could have thought about me from the other side of the world. But there was no way that she could have known. No one on the outside knew where I was. I could have died and no one would have known.

Night-time was the most painful. The nights were cold, colder than I had ever imagined. It was difficult sleeping on hard wooden planks, but there was no choice – the concrete floor was colder. Without blankets, I couldn't stop shivering and thinking about all these problems. I knew there was nothing I could do while I was locked up, so I tried not to think about them. But it was impossible. I couldn't get away from my own thoughts, not for one minute. Being stuck in solitary confinement was like being a prisoner in your own head. In the dead cold of night, I became convinced that I was going to die before morning. I knew that I had to get out of there. I would go crazy otherwise.

𝍷𝍷𝍷𝍷𝍷

Julián eventually managed to get past the La Grulla guards, claiming that he had an obligation as delegate to check on the prisoners' welfare. I was so relieved when he arrived. He was my main hope of getting out of there and of proving my innocence.

'How are you holding up, Thomas?' he asked, lifting the flap and poking his arm through the observation hatch to shake my hand and slip me a stack of coins he had taped together for bribing the guards with.

'I'm OK, but how's Abregon? Does he know I'm in here?'

'He hasn't called.' Julián paused and added slowly, 'Someone spotted his woman in Cochabamba.' According to Julián, there were rumours going around that Raquel was dressing nicely and spending up big. It was what I had suspected, but that didn't make it any easier when I heard.

'Can't you send him something?'

'We're trying our hardest.'

'Julián, I need you to get me out of here. I need to speak to the governor.'

Julián persuaded the guards to let me call the administration office.

But the governor wasn't there, not that time or the next, or the time after that; he was always in a meeting or away from his desk. I knew that Julián couldn't keep coming every day just to help me make phone calls, so on the fourth occasion I told the governor's secretary to give him a message that I was going to ring the media. The governor took my call immediately.

'Governor, I'm innocent. Can't you help me get out? I had nothing to do with this,' I said, getting straight to the point. He did too.

'I know, Thomas. I believe you. But it's out of my hands. There has to be an investigation.'

'When?'

'I don't know.'

'But I'm *innocent*.'

The governor kept repeating that he had nothing to do with this type of disciplinary matter and that he couldn't interfere. I offered him money to get me out, but he claimed it was impossible. Too many people knew. Finally, I said I would call my embassy and the television stations unless I was given a chance to clear my name. He didn't like me threatening him like that, but I was desperate and it was the only weapon I had left.

'I can't get you out,' said the governor angrily, 'but I'll see what I can do about speeding up the investigation.' Then he hung up on me.

Two days later, I was summonsed to the administration block to appear before a meeting of the prison discipline committee. This was a panel of prison officials they put together to investigate and judge internal disciplinary matters. On it sat the governor, the prison psychologist, the major, some administration staff and the prisoners' delegate. The meeting was relaxed, and assuming that I had the governor and Julián on my side, I was confident that things would go my way.

I was allowed to give evidence and to put my case to the committee. I explained that I hadn't been inside the Velascos' room at all, and that the police had found no money or drugs on me, and nothing in my room. When the committee asked what I had been doing there, I explained how the Velascos owed me money and how we had had a fight over the debt. I said that I had sent my shop employee, El General, to pick up the money before going myself.

'So, you see, it doesn't make sense for me to be doing a drug deal with them an hour after fighting with them,' I argued, looking into the eyes of the committee members, one by one. Some of them nodded slightly. I was convincing them. That was the atmosphere in the room. I could feel it.

I was also allowed to call witnesses and to tender evidence. El General came and backed up my account about being owed money and of how I had sent him to collect it. He handed over the authorisation note I had written him, as well as the loan contract with the Velascos. But my best witness by far was Julián, who had actually been there when the police arrived. And since he was also a member of the committee, no one doubted that he was telling the truth.

In fact, no one contradicted any of my arguments. I was certain that they were going to let me go on the spot, but the governor stood up and said that the committee needed to finish its investigation before it could arrive at a decision. Until it had done so, the prisoner was to remain in solitary confinement. He nodded coldly to the guards to escort me back to La Grulla.

'But, governor. What more do you need to investigate?' I yelled at him, as they led me to the door. When we were in public situations, the governor and I pretended that we didn't know each other. But by that point, I was too angry to stop myself. 'I'm innocent and you know it. You said so yourself!'

𝍩𝍩॥

After my outburst at the discipline committee meeting, the governor came to see me personally in my solitary confinement cell. He apologised for not being able to help me. I offered him money once more, but he refused it.

'I'm innocent. You *know* I'm innocent.'

'I said I believed you, Thomas. But the media are all over us.'

'Well then, they should get a chance to hear my version.' I no longer trusted the discipline committee's internal investigation. Once people knew the facts, there was no way I could be implicated. And the more people who knew, the better.

'That wouldn't help you or anyone else, Thomas,' the governor warned, adjusting the stars on his shoulders. 'The best thing you can do is to keep quiet. Keep your mouth shut and I promise to get you out of here as soon as things calm down.'

He offered me a deal. The minimum stretch in solitary was ninety days, but he could get me out a lot sooner, with no charges laid, provided I kept quiet. After I got out, he would destroy the file so that there would be no mark on my prison record. In the meantime, he would do whatever he could to make my stay more comfortable. He didn't mention what would happen if I refused his offer, but I knew that he could make things worse for me if he wanted to. I agreed reluctantly and he whistled for the guard to let him out. I still wasn't happy about it, so after he had shut the door I called to him through the flap: 'They found the drugs in the Velascos' room and I'm the one in punishment for it. That's not logical.'

My complaint was effective, but not in the way I had intended. Rather than letting me out, there were two new additions to La Grulla's population that afternoon: Jose Luis and Jorge Velasco. There were eight cells in the block, all in a row. The Velascos were placed together in the very end cell because the seventh cell was being used as the *depósito*, for storing contraband seized in the police raids. As soon as I saw them being led in, I wanted to kill them, but with the guards always watching us during yard time, I never got the chance. I might have got two punches in before the guards jumped on me and transferred me to Chonchocoro. Their time would come though, soon enough.

卌||

Life was still horrible in solitary confinement, but it was made more bearable once the governor had had a few words with the guards. I was permitted to bring some possessions across from my room. I took everything I could carry: a mattress, blankets, light globes, as much money as I could beg from my neighbours, and warm clothing for the other inmates, except the Velascos. On a subsequent trip, I even managed to sneak in a small heater and my television. Samir cut the cables and hooked them up to the wires that ran across the roof.

Little by little, our privileges were extended. The guards began leaving us to our own devices during yard time, letting us talk quietly among ourselves. Some of them started speaking to us, and the cleverer ones would do us small favours, such as taking notes to our friends and bringing us money. Sometimes we were allowed extra yard time. They occasionally let visitors in to see us and, most importantly, I got one guard, Mario, to bring us food. He was reluctant at first, but once we became friends, he would do anything I asked.

Mario was a new recruit who had been transferred to San Pedro directly from the military training academy. He was still filled with ideas about honesty, integrity and serving the Bolivian Republic. He was nineteen years old, but he looked younger because his face was covered with severe acne. The other guards called him Pizza Boy behind his back. For the first few weeks, he did everything by the book. He was always shining his boots, and his green trousers had sharp creases down the front. And he wouldn't talk to me at all, because the guards were under strict instructions not to speak to prisoners.

Finally, I got a response from him, by commenting on how shiny his boots were.

'The secret is cotton,' he answered. 'You have to finish the job with cotton. Not many people know that.' I offered him a few coins to bring me some food, but he refused them outright. 'Put that away, please. I don't accept bribes.'

'It's not a bribe,' I said. 'It's for your lunch.' That usually eased their conscience, but it didn't work on Pizza Boy.

'I'm not hungry, thank you,' he snapped back, then marched off with his head held high.

I tried everything, but the only things Mario was interested in were his shoes and his girlfriend. Our conversations always started in the same way: 'How's your *chica*?' or 'Those shoes are even shinier than yesterday.'

He would respond angrily, 'She's not my *chica*, she's my *fiancée*,' or 'They're not shoes, they're boots. There's a difference, you know.'

Bit by bit, I learned how to get through to him. He was disappointed that the Bolivian government could only afford to give each man one uniform, which made it nearly impossible to have it washed, dried and ironed before work each day. He also confided in me his ambition to make sergeant one day, or maybe even an officer, in order to get enough money to marry his sweetheart.

Even though our conversations became longer, Pizza Boy continued to refuse my *propinas*. Luckily, however, he was a fast learner. Lucky for him, since honest cops were transferred to remote postings as soon as they were found out. Lucky for me, because I was always starving in

La Grulla. Gradually, I got him to accept small amounts of money. I would say that I wanted to buy him some special boot polish, or help him save for an extra uniform, and since I couldn't get to a shop, he would have to make the purchase himself. Provided the money was for work and not for him, it was OK. Then, as the amounts increased, I began to put doubts in his mind about his girlfriend.

'You'll need to start saving right away if you're going to get married,' I declared. 'Or she might leave you.'

'She would never do that. She's not like that.'

'Show me that photo again, then.' Pizza Boy pulled the picture out of his wallet for the tenth time and held it up proudly by the corner. The girlfriend was ugly, but he never let me touch her photo in case I got fingerprints on it. 'She's a very special-looking woman. A woman like that needs a man to care for her. And if you can't do it, there are a thousand men out there with money who will. How are you going to look after her on your salary?'

That made Pizza Boy very worried. The pay for a private was less than one hundred dollars per month. We got started on a wedding fund immediately. I would send him out into the main prison to buy proper food from the restaurants and bring it back to me in solitary confinement. I called this 'cell delivery service'. With the tips I had to pay him, it was an expensive way to eat, but it was worth it. If I'd had more money, I would have sent Pizza Boy outside the prison to pick me up a takeaway ham and pineapple, extra-thick crust.

〄〣

There was only one occasion that I ate better food than what Mario brought me. Towards the end of yard time one afternoon, two guards we had never seen before came into the section carrying a collapsible table. Nothing interesting ever happened in solitary, so we all stopped what we were doing and stared. They left the table lying against the wall and we watched them leave, then come back again five minutes later, this time carrying a huge barrel of steaming soup and a tray filled with fried chicken pieces covered in mushroom sauce. The delicious smell of the food filled our small exercise area.

Then they set up the table and started setting the places with knives, forks and paper napkins. It seemed there was to be some kind of party. But what a strange place to have it! And who was it for? It certainly wasn't for us. They wouldn't waste such good food on the inmates in solitary confinement. Besides, they never let us use metal cutlery, in case we sharpened it into weapons.

'What's happening?' I asked the others.

'It's a new torture they've invented especially for us,' said Chino, who was always making jokes. 'Watch. They're going to eat it in front of us.'

Everyone was curious, but no one spoke for a while. We continued staring at them as they set up for the party. When they were done, someone finally called out.

'Who's all that for?'

'For you lot,' replied the guards. 'Go and bring out the chairs, then you can all have some.'

Ignoring the order to get chairs, the eight of us scrambled towards the table. The others ate standing up, greedily stuffing food into their mouths while I observed them. I was afraid that the food was poisoned, or laced with tranquilliser, and I wanted to wait and see if any of them became sick. They were eating so quickly that there would be none left so I drank a whole bowl of soup in one go, then grabbed two chicken legs in my effort to catch up.

'*Tranquilo,*' said the guard, patting me on the shoulder. 'There is plenty more where that came from.'

After eating, we were told to wash our clothes and clean the cell block thoroughly, and if we did a good job we would be given extra yard time. Something strange was going on, but no one argued; anything was better than being locked back in those dungeons, even cleaning. There was only one broom, but I took my time sweeping out my cell while the others waited their turn. I would make a pile of dust, then accidentally knock it everywhere in order to take longer. Then I washed my clothes very slowly and took them out to dry in the exercise yard, piece by piece.

On my way back in to pick up more clothes, I saw Chino leaning against the door to my cell. He was waiting for me and he looked nervous. Without saying anything, he looked up and down the corridor and then nodded his head towards my cell. He obviously had something important to tell me.

'Quick,' he said, shutting the door behind us so that it didn't click loudly and stood with his back against it.

'Why? What's up, man?' I asked, after he had checked the corridor again through the observation hatch. 'Why are you so nervous?'

'Listen, Thomas,' he whispered. 'I've got a message for you from a powerful friend. But you didn't hear it from me, OK?' I nodded. 'The brother of Jose Luis Velasco works for the FELCN.' I waited for him to say more, but that was all he had to say.

'And what?' I asked.

'I can't say anything more. That's all I was told to say. Your friend just said to be careful about what you say about those two.' Chino checked the corridor again and then slipped out of my cell. I didn't know what to make of it. I wasn't sure if the powerful friend was the governor and he was trying to warn me of something, or if the Velascos had put Chino up to it to scare me.

I went out into the corridor again, but Chino was already gone. I continued with my washing. By the time I was on my last sock, the others had finished cleaning their cells and were back outside. They were sitting on the wooden benches, leaning against the wall, with the afternoon sun streaming down on their faces. The guards were nowhere to be seen. I sat down next to Chino and lit a cigarette. I thought he might tell me something more, but from the way he was acting, we hadn't had the conversation.

It was a beautiful afternoon in the Andean mountain range. We looked upwards, staring into the cloudless sky, trying to spot birds. In La Paz, bird spotting always helped to pass the time, because hardly any lived at that altitude, apart from pigeons. Anyway, none that I had seen from jail. I smoked cigarette after cigarette and squinted into the blueness until my eyes began to itch and my eyesight went blurry. I wasn't used to that amount of daylight so I closed my eyes until the vision blotches went away. I stayed throughout the afternoon in that position: propped against the wall, eyelids shut, the warmth of the sun on my face, thinking about nothing. An hour later, the guards still hadn't returned us to our cells.

'What's going on?' I finally called across to Chapako, who had been in and out of the previous punishment section more than any of the others.

'I'd say we're getting a visit from *derechos humanos*,' he yelled back. The others nodded knowingly and chuckled among themselves, but I didn't understand. My Spanish was good by then, but in all my years in prison I had never heard that expression used once.

'What are *derechos humanos*?' I asked Chino quietly, a little embarrassed not to have understood the joke.

'I don't know how to explain to you, my brother,' he responded loudly, so that everyone could hear. He looked up into the sky for inspiration and said philosophically, 'They don't exist. That's it. *Derechos humanos* are something that don't really exist.' This made the others smirk again.

'What? Like an illusion?' I asked, and the others laughed louder than the first time.

'Something like that,' he responded, smiling wryly at me. I was still confused but no one would explain. Then the others joined in teasing me.

'What are you saying, *inglés*?' Chapako asked in mock seriousness. 'You don't know what *derechos humanos* are?'

'What's so funny about that?' I answered, trying to go along with the teasing. 'So what? I don't know what they are.'

'Neither do we, *inglés*,' Ramero responded and this sent the others into bigger fits of laughter. 'We can't tell you because we've never heard of them either.' This made them hysterical. They kept playing with me like that until, eventually, I caught on.

Human rights. They were coming to visit.

Everyone remained in a good mood sitting along the wall, leaning against the warm bricks, which had heated up over the course of the afternoon. I was beginning to really enjoy this human rights caper. I concentrated hard on absorbing the sun into my body. I only wished that I could be like a lizard and store some of the warmth to stop me from shivering at night. Sometimes it felt like my body wanted to just give up and stop heating itself. But at that moment at least, I was happy, with a full, warm belly.

'What's the time?' I asked Ramero, who was the only one in La Grulla who hadn't sold his watch to the guards yet.

'Four o'clock.' The guards still hadn't come.

No one said anything for several minutes more. I was quite content just resting there, until Jorge Velasco came over and crouched down beside me and ruined it. A shiver of pure hatred ran down my back and my muscles tensed so suddenly that I almost bit through my tongue. Chino gave me a threatening look, warning me not to spoil it for everyone.

Surprisingly, the feeling lasted only a short time. I calmed myself down. I still wanted to punch him, but for the first time in weeks, I could control it. It was true that he had made a lot of mistakes; but now that he was in punishment also, I wasn't so sure that he was the one who had set me up.

I looked at him and he tried to smile at me. I didn't smile back. I could tell that he was about to say something, but when he saw the expression on my face, he thought better of it. I looked up again. It was at that moment that I saw a La Paz bird darting across the sky, my first one since arriving at La Grulla. I turned back to Jorge to check whether he had seen it also and he smiled at me again. Everyone had seen it and was smiling, even Samir. It was the first time I had seen him smile since we had been in solitary. Samir was crazy, but he never smiled.

41
SAMIR

Samir continued smiling at me strangely, and then he stood up and came over too. Jorge Velasco moved over to make space. The other inmates usually avoided Samir because he could go from being very serious to completely out of control in the click of a finger. But of all the inmates in La Grulla, Samir was my best friend. The others didn't know him like I did. Samir and I had spent a lot of time together and he had told me a lot of things about his childhood and his experiences in prison. He had grown up on the streets stealing cars and had spent more of his life inside prison than outside. Jail no longer worried him and solitary confinement was like his second home.

'Nice day, hey?' I prompted him. The Brazilian poked out his thick, bottom lip to show that he agreed, more or less. Even though he was smiling, that day appeared to be one of his silent ones.

Sometimes I worried about what would become of him. I like to think that everyone has a chance to change, but it seemed that Samir was born to a life of crime. I tried to encourage him to use all his crazy energy to do positive things, but it was often hard to talk with him seriously. These days, all he wanted to do was party. I guessed that he would keep pushing the limits further and further until one day he ran into a wall. And there was nothing that I, nor the best psychiatrist in the world, could do about it. It didn't matter, though; Samir was mad and dangerous, but he was my friend.

'What more could you ask for on a day like this?' I tried again, poking him in the ribs to liven him up. Samir's grin broadened, showing his teeth, which were all out of alignment and one of which was black.

He responded with a single word – 'Beer' – although he used the

Portuguese '*cerveja*' instead of the Spanish '*cerveza*'. He often did that, especially when he was drunk, so I had trouble understanding him.

Samir wasn't talkative that afternoon, but he did have that look in his eye that meant he was up to something. I eventually got him to tell me what it was: he was going to escape.

'When?'

'I don't know,' he shrugged his shoulders. 'Soon.'

'But how?'

'Easy.' He pointed upwards with his index finder and then back down, whistling the sound of something falling. He was planning on climbing over the wall, or through the wall, or something of the sort.

'Are you *loco*?'

It was pure madness and I tried to tell him so. San Pedro was like a castle. It had been built over a century before with walls that must have been at least fifteen metres high. Even if someone managed to get up to the top, he would die or break his legs from the fall to the pavement below. Digging under the wall was impossible since the ground was solid cement, and digging through it was also out of the question since there were actually two walls, an inner and an outer, and each was several metres thick.

Although he couldn't tell me how, Samir insisted that he would escape and I knew that he was crazy enough to try. I couldn't prevent him from attempting to carry out his ridiculous plan, but it was worse than that: he wanted me to break out with him! There was no way I was going.

'Forget it, Samir.'

'You're a fucking coward, *inglés*,' he said angrily, spitting on the concrete just in front of my feet. 'You know that? A coward.'

Samir persisted, but I kept refusing until he got sick of asking. I didn't care if I was a coward; I wasn't going over that wall, and certainly not with a crazy Brazilian as my escape partner. It was suicide. Finally, he abused me in Portuguese and stormed back inside, banging his fists on each of the cell doors as he went along the corridor. Which was probably when he had the idea about having a *fiesta*.

Samir was back in the yard almost immediately, all excited about something. He had obviously forgiven me.

'Thomas. My brother, I need you to get us something good,' he whispered, moving his hand closer to his face and flicking his wrist slightly towards his nose. I shook my head.

'I can't.' I hadn't touched cocaine since being set up and I had no desire to. I was too scared.

'You *can't* or you don't *want* to?' He placed his hand firmly on my shoulder.

'I can't,' I lied, not wanting to give him an opening. There *was* a way, but he didn't need to know that.

'Yes, you can. If anyone can, *you* can. You know all the guards.'

'I can't.'

'Come on! We're having a party tonight.' Samir's eyes sparkled and his face got that mischievous look again.

'What party?' The others turned towards us and started listening to our conversation.

'The human rights party.'

I laughed. 'But you haven't got any alcohol. How can you have a *fiesta* without alcohol?'

Samir smiled broadly for the second time that day. 'OK, then, *inglés*. I'll get the drinks, if you supply the dessert. What do you say?' He winked at me and held out his hand.

It seemed a safe enough bet. There was no way that anyone could get alcohol past the guards, not even me. Maybe you could persuade one of them to sneak a few grams of coke in, but not alcohol; even a single can of beer would be difficult to hide. And enough for eight of us? Impossible.

'Whatever, Samir.' We shook hands.

What I hadn't reckoned on, however, was that there was already alcohol in La Grulla. A whole mountain of it, in fact. The seventh cell.

卌\\

Everyone was in on the plan. Even so, I don't know how the Brazilian picked the padlocks. There were two of them and they were the expensive type, made of thick, heavy-duty steel. But he did. He was back in the yard inside of sixty seconds: about the same time it took him to hotwire a car. Two of the others distracted the guards while the rest of us transferred as much alcohol as we wanted into our rooms. It was going to be a big party.

It was then time to keep my end of the bargain. I sent Pizza Boy to get some toilet paper from the shops. I gave him directions on how to find Orlando's *tienda* in Alamos and exact instructions on which brand to get.

'It has to be *Nacional*. And pink. I don't want any other colour. Understand?'

I handed him five bolivianos. He looked at me strangely, wondering why he had to go all that way when there were shops that were closer and cheaper.

'And why do you want to buy *Nacional*? You could buy twice as many if you bought another brand.'

'My arse is very precious, Mario. It "demands the best",' I said, paraphrasing an advertisement I had seen on TV and he laughed. 'And the change is yours.'

This time, he understood perfectly. He went off to Pinos to buy a twin pack of pink *Nacional* toilet paper, which was my code with Orlando for ten grams of cocaine.

When Pizza Boy returned, he was acting strangely. He had the toilet rolls, but he didn't hand them to me straight away. Instead, he walked through the yard and into the cell block, clicking his fingers for me to follow him. I found him leaning casually against the wall, throwing the toilet rolls up into the air and then catching them, waiting for me. One of the rolls was bulging slightly, but I hoped that he hadn't noticed.

Pizza Boy stopped his little game and held out the package. But when I went to take it, he snatched it back, holding it just out of my reach. I looked at him questioningly.

'And my share?' he said, remaining straight-faced.

'You've still got the change, haven't you?'

'But what about the rest?'

'What do you mean? What rest?'

'You don't have to lie to me, Thomas,' he said, bending the packet in the middle to reveal the small cut where Orlando had inserted the bag of cocaine. 'Just give me what's fair.' I had to give him another ten bolivianos.

That Pizza Boy was a fast learner. I had trained him too well. He was heading for promotion; he would definitely make sergeant one day, maybe even governor. And his wedding fund was coming along nicely, too.

卌‖

It was only early, but the party got under way immediately. We went into the common room and took it in turns to stand at the end of the corridor, keeping watch for the guards. It had been weeks since anyone had touched alcohol, so we were drunk very quickly, but the coke sobered us up instantly. It made my mouth go numb for the first time in months. After such a long break, it felt the same as it had the very first time I tried it. I felt fantastic. I even found myself talking to Jorge Velasco and not hating him at all. And once we were high on cocaine, we could keep drinking as much as we liked.

Gradually, the lookout became bored. When it was Chino's turn, he kept returning to check on how we were doing, staying longer and longer each time to join in on the conversation. Finally, the post was abandoned entirely when Samir refused to do his shift.

Just as our party was getting into full swing, the delegation from the Bolivian Human Rights Assembly arrived. Chino, who was seated next to me with his back to the wall, was in the middle of telling a joke about the president's wife, when the others looked up suddenly. We didn't need to turn around to know that someone important was standing behind us; we could tell just by their expressions.

Chino was clever. He pretended that his sudden pause was deliberate, and carried on telling his joke as if nothing had happened, slowly moving the bottle of rum under the table. Following his lead, I slipped the bag of cocaine into my underpants. However, the others were stupid; they scrambled madly to hide all the beer cans.

The human rights visit was only short. They inspected the bathroom area, tested the water, checked the conditions in a few of the cells, and looked in the exercise yard. The head of the delegation then told the guards to leave the room while he interviewed us privately. He wrote down our responses on his notepad.

'Do they give you enough food?' he asked, looking over to the cooker where we had put some rice on to boil, to make it look like we were preparing to eat. None of us seemed concerned that the water had evaporated and the rice was burning. We obviously weren't starving. We nodded our heads.

'How often do the guards let you out?' All the time. All day sometimes. Chapako was sunburned.

'Do you have any specific complaints?' he asked, concluding his investigation. None whatsoever. In fact, we were all really enjoying solitary confinement.

He must have noticed that something was going on. We were far too happy for prisoners who had spent several weeks locked in solitary confinement. He didn't say anything, but I wondered what he was going to write in his report. Whatever he wrote wouldn't have made any difference to us anyway; the president of the Bolivian Human Rights Assembly was later taken off a minibus by police in full view of the public, arrested and beaten. The front page of the newspaper showed him sitting in his hospital bed recovering. He knew the names of the police who had beaten him, but the high-ranking officers who had ordered the beating were never charged. If he couldn't protect his own human rights, what chance was there of him protecting ours?

After the human rights delegation left, the guards locked us back in our cells and left for the night. Each of us still had a private stash of alcohol, so we kept drinking. I still had the cocaine in my underwear. After a while, the others started coming down.

'Thomas, can I have some more?' Samir called out.

His cell was next to mine, so I split the remaining stuff into two bags and then made what the Bolivians called a *pista*, by tying a shoe to the end of a bed sheet and swinging it back and forth out my observation hatch, like a pendulum. Samir couldn't catch the end. We tried several times, and I even stood on a pile of clothes to get my arm further out, but it still didn't reach. Or maybe Samir was too drunk. Then he mumbled something I didn't understand properly.

'What did you say?' I asked, but he seemed to say the same thing again: 'Just a moment. I'll come out and get it.'

I leaned my head against the top of the hatch, trying to see what he was doing. Suddenly, there were two eyes in front of me, less than two inches from my face. I got the shock of my life and jumped back, thinking it was the guards. My stomach sank – I was busted. I was holding a beer in one hand and a bag of cocaine in the other, with no time to hide either. However, it wasn't the guards; it was Samir. He had somehow broken out of his cell.

'Quick, Thomas,' he whispered urgently. 'Give me the coke.' I handed him the bag without thinking. I didn't even have time to ask him how he had escaped before he had sniffed some and was off, banging on doors and offering everyone cocaine.

'Do you want one?' he asked me, coming back to my door and tipping some coke onto the skin between his thumb and index finger and holding his hand up to me, Brazilian-style.

'No. What if the guards come, Samir?' He was making too much noise. 'Are you crazy?'

'Yes.' He sniffed it himself before disappearing again.

Samir spent the next few hours out of his cell, running riot in the solitary confinement section. At first, the others thought it was funny, but then they started to worry. There would be hell to pay if the guards found that we had stolen and drunk their alcohol. Samir became worse. He yelled. He spilled beer everywhere. He banged on our doors to offer us more cocaine. He threw pots and pans against the walls in the kitchen and smashed whatever he could find. Then he broke into the seventh cell again to steal more rum.

We pleaded and pleaded with him to get back in his cell. But he wouldn't go. There was no way of telling Samir what to do when he was drunk. It just made him more determined to do the opposite. I hid the empty beer cans, pushed the remaining bag of cocaine through a tiny crack in the roof and pretended to be asleep like the others. No one could possibly have slept, though; apart from all the cocaine we had taken, everyone was worried about the guards.

卌||

As soon as the sergeant opened our doors in the morning, we ran straight for the bathroom to dispose of the empty cans. In the toilet block, there was a concrete slab you could lift up with a shaft underneath leading down to the sewerage pipe. There was already a pile of cans at the bottom that we'd deposited after the human rights party, but the drain stank so much there was little chance of anyone wanting to search there.

'What a night!' said Chino, sighing with relief. We had got away with it. Everyone looked at each other and smiled. Everyone, that is, except one person.

'Where is he?' Chapako asked suddenly. We all knew who he meant. We had been so worried about getting busted ourselves that we had forgotten about Samir.

'Quick! Let's find him before the police do.'

We raced out and looked in the exercise yard and in all the shower stalls, but there was no sign of him. They even boosted Ramero up to have a look on the bathroom roof, but he shook his head. 'Check under the benches,' suggested Chino.

'We already did.'

'Shit. He's escaped! Let's clean our cells and fix up these beer cans. Drop some toilet paper over the top of them.' Once the guards found that Samir had escaped, they would do a full-scale search.

The sergeant on duty didn't suspect anything at first. He was an old guy who talked about his family a lot and he was always nice to us. He was also easy to trick. When Samir didn't answer his name at the *lista*, we shrugged our shoulders and then followed the sergeant to Samir's cell, pretending to be just as surprised as he was. None of us had bothered to check in Samir's cell because we had seen that his door had been padlocked from the outside when we got up and the sergeant had needed to unlock it.

In fact, Samir hadn't escaped at all. The sergeant swung the door back and there he was, lying fast asleep on his bed, fully clothed with his mouth wide open. The room smelled of beer and vomit. It was only then that I saw how Samir had gotten out: the bottom corner of the metal door had been prised back and he had slid his way underneath, through the small gap. He must have given up on the idea of escaping and then crawled back in there before morning. I nudged Chino behind the sergeant's back and pointed to the door, but he nodded that he had already seen it. He was more concerned about the empty beer cans that were all over the floor.

'What's happened here?' demanded the sergeant, shaking Samir. 'Why won't he wake up?' He still hadn't spotted the door or the beer cans, but it wouldn't be long before he did.

'He's sick. Can't you see he's sick?' Chino answered, pointing to the dried vomit on Samir's chin and clothing, turning it to our advantage. 'We called out all night, but no one came.'

'But I wasn't on duty last night,' said the old sergeant defensively.

While Chino continued to distract him, the rest of us blocked his view of the beer cans by fussing over Samir. 'Someone should get a doctor.'

'Listen. I don't think he's breathing properly,' I said, giving the sergeant five bolivianos. 'Please. Can you go? The other guards won't listen to us. It could be serious.'

The sergeant left and came back with the major. By the time they arrived, the beer cans had disappeared and all traces of vomit had been wiped away. But the major was suspicious. The first thing he noticed was the door, which we hadn't been able to bend back into shape.

'How did this happen?' he demanded, studying our reactions carefully.

'I've only just started my shift and that was how I found him,' the sergeant responded, thinking that the major was referring to Samir.

'It was already like that from before,' said Chino. The major was no fool, so there was no point in pretending that we hadn't seen the door. He then moved forward to check Samir. The first thing he did was to touch Samir's shirt, which was wet where we had wiped it. Then he smelled his breath.

The major paused for a moment, considering what to do.

'This prisoner is sick,' he announced, standing up to his full height. 'Call for a doctor.'

'I already have, major,' said the sergeant, cowering.

'Well, then, what are all these prisoners doing in here? Get them out of my sight.' When the sergeant had his back turned, the major pointed to Chino and Chapako and said, 'You and you, fix this other problem here.' He meant the door.

Samir had got away with it. Luckily, that major was one of the men he stole cars for. The next time, however, Samir wasn't so lucky.

42
TORMENTA

Samir was sick all morning, but by the afternoon he was well enough to make it out into the exercise yard. As before, we were sitting together on the benches against the wall, although this time feeling tired and hungover rather than happy. The sunlight was as bright as it had been the previous day, but the air had turned cold and dark storm clouds were beginning to form on the horizon. The first thing on Samir's mind was organising another party.

'Thomas, we need more cocaine,' he stated loudly, not even using code. I shook my head and told him that I was too sick. They could get someone else to do it. 'But you have to,' he insisted. 'We're having a celebration.'

'I can't get any.'

'You're a liar, Thomas. And I know there's some left. Anyway, you've got no choice,' he said over his shoulder as he walked back into the cell block. 'You have to join me.'

'Why is that?' I called after him.

'Because it's my farewell party.'

As the guards were locking us back in our cells, there was a distant rumbling of thunder from the direction of the mountains and I heard the first drops of rain falling on the metal roof. I lay down on my bed, relieved that I could get some more sleep. Immediately, I noticed there was something hard underneath the mattress. I lifted it up to reveal ten cans of beer. Samir!

I ran to the door and looked through the flap, hoping that one of the others might still be out of his cell and could help me get rid of them. The corridor was empty. Everyone had been locked up.

'Samir!' I called. I heard laughter. 'You bastard.'

The others were at their doors too, wondering what was going on. They had discovered similar presents hidden in their cells. The loud hissing of a beer can being opened and shaken everywhere could be heard.

'Cheers, my friends,' laughed Samir, spraying beer out into the corridor. 'Let's celebrate. It's my last night in prison.' He clinked his can against the metal door.

There was more thunder, this time very loud and very close. The type of thunder that cracks all around you and then comes up through the floor and shakes the whole building. The storm had begun in earnest. It was the perfect night for an escape.

After the next thunderclap, it began raining properly. La Paz was built in a valley with its main road running over the top of a river. For most of the year, the river was dry. However, when there was a *tormenta* – a big storm – it could last for days and water in the streets sometimes built up to flood levels, washing away everything in its path, including people and cars. It seemed that this was going to be one of those storms. The flashes of lightning outside were so bright that they lit up the corridor inside our cell block. Water began pouring in streams from the roof, filling the exercise yard and sending a small trickle into the building.

And as the rain poured down, we began to party again. We *had* to party. We couldn't call the guards claiming that we all desperately needed to use the toilet. Besides, it would have been impossible for even one of us to hide ten full beer cans under his clothing. Our only hope of not getting caught was to empty the cans, crush them and pray that we could get them past the guards again in the morning. We couldn't tip the beer into our urine buckets because they would smell of beer. So, there was no other choice: we had to drink the evidence.

None of us were in the same room, except for the Velascos. We had a series of individual parties going on, with each person standing at his door, drinking on his own, and yelling into the darkness in order to be heard above the howling wind and the sound of the rain pounding on the metal roof. It was a crazy night from the very beginning, but it got crazier with the storm. And Samir got crazier with it.

Samir was like a caged animal, strong and proud and full of energy.

He didn't really understand things. He didn't know why he was locked up or what he had to do to get out of it, or even where he would go if he did. But he wouldn't sit still and wait for them to open the cage – he wanted to get away from the thunder. Every time it cracked around us, he went into long periods of silence, pacing up and down. These were followed by fits of screaming, when he kicked and punched at the door.

As the night wore on, Samir became louder and louder. It wasn't long before he was drunk and yelling abuse through his window. And as he became noisier, the rest of us quietened down, worried that the guards would hear something. They hadn't come for their midnight patrol yet.

'Thomas, I need cocaine!' Samir screamed. I pretended not to hear him, but he knew I was listening. 'Throw it to me or I'm coming to get it!'

The major should have made Samir change cells that morning. His cell door had already been bent back once, so it was even easier for him to get out the second time. In a few seconds flat, he was at my door, pounding on it.

'I haven't got any,' I told him. 'Go back to your cell. They'll kill you.' The guards were due any minute. If they found Samir out of his cell, we would all be busted for sure. I knew that Chapako, who was in the cell closest to the guard post, was listening out for them, but there was no way that he would hear them coming with the wind howling so loudly through the cell block.

'Come on, brother,' Samir pleaded. 'Look, I brought you some more beers. We'll swap. Just a little bit.'

'I don't want any more beer,' I said, grabbing hold of my window flap in case he tried to force them on me. I didn't give him any cocaine either, because it would have made him worse. Samir didn't give up. There was absolutely nothing I could do to make him go back to his cell. He was drunk and would have stayed there all night, arguing with me, so eventually, I closed the door flap and lay back down on my bed, hoping that if I ignored him, he would go away.

He didn't, though. He stood at my door yelling at me to give him the cocaine. It was hard to know whether to stay quiet or try to reason with him, because the longer I didn't answer him, the more violent he became. He began smashing my door with his fists, again and again, chanting like a child at the top of his voice, '*Cocaína, cocaína. Yo quiero cocaína.*'

Then suddenly, his tantrum stopped. I sat up in bed and listened intently. All I could hear was the sound of the storm raging outside. There was also a leak somewhere in my roof that was dripping water onto the floor. I hoped that Samir had gone away, but I doubted it. He was up to something.

I went to my door to have a look. The corridor was empty, but I knew Samir – he didn't give up like that. Suddenly, I heard a scraping sound and looked down. Samir's fingers were poking under the door, trying to get a grip around it.

'What are you doing?'

'You're my brother, Thomas. You're coming with me,' he declared, his voice straining as he tried to bend the door back.

'No. It's too dangerous.' I struggled to slide his fingers off, but they were locked on. 'Quick, Samir,' I hissed. 'The guards are coming.' But it didn't work.

'I don't care about the guards!' he yelled back. 'We're leaving.'

Finally, I managed to unhook his fingers, but then they reappeared further along the door. I prised them off again and then blocked the gap with my feet. That didn't stop him, however, because I could only cover part of it.

We struggled like that for a few minutes; me pushing his fingers off, then him sneaking them under again. It would have been comical, if it wasn't so serious, two grown men on either side of a locked door, finger wrestling through the gap underneath. But the guards could come at any moment, and when they found Samir trying to rip my door open, not only would they find the beers, but we would also both be busted for trying to escape.

'Aaargh!' Samir cried out, as I trod down on his fingers and kept my weight on them.

'Do you promise to stop?' I hissed through the flap.

'Get off me. Aaargh!'

'Promise?'

'OK, OK, I promise.' But as soon as I released him, Samir flew into a rage again, and started kicking my door, over and over. The metal reinforcements held strong, but the sound reverberated down the corridor. The guards must have been able to hear it, even above the noise of the storm. He kicked harder and harder until the door was dented and the whole frame shook, sprinkling concrete dust over me and onto the floor.

'*¡Samir, basta!* I'll give you the coke. You can have it all.' He stopped kicking. 'Here, take these,' I said, holding the empty cans wrapped in a plain T-shirt up to the flap. 'Get rid of them and I'll give you the stuff.'

'Give it to me first!' he shouted, banging his fist against the metal again. More chunks of concrete fell on my head. I thought I heard a door opening and closing out in the exercise yard, but I kept my nerve.

'No. Throw these out first. Then I'll give you all the stuff,' I said, squeezing the bundle through the flap. Samir took it and then put his hand through for the coke. I gave him the whole lot.

'Are you sure you don't want to come with me?' he asked, changing back to his normal tone of voice.

'I can't.'

'English coward,' he muttered, then turned and walked down the cell block, banging at each door and trying to persuade its occupant to escape with him. The others pretended to be asleep.

'You're all cowards!' he yelled at the top of his lungs, before heading off to escape.

Even though the storm was in full force, I could hear Samir throwing things around in the kitchen again. He was smashing bottles and singing something at the top of his voice in Portuguese that sounded like a national anthem. Then I heard him jumping about on the bathroom roof. There was nothing more that I could do. I cleaned up the mess around my door, drank some water and chewed my last piece of gum. Then I lay in bed, wondering when the guards were going to come and what they would do when they found Samir trying to climb the wall.

I kept listening, but I didn't hear anything more after that – only the rain pelting down against the metal roof and the doors rattling as the wind sent blasts of cold air along the corridor. I figured that Samir had given up and crawled back into his cell. But he hadn't. He was still out there, trying to escape. The only thing that saved him from getting caught straight away was the weather. It was so cold and wet that night, that the guards decided not to leave their station for their regular patrol. The exercise yard they had to cross was ankle-deep in water. They didn't come to check on us until morning, but when they did come, we knew about it.

I was awoken by a heavy blow to the chest. The storm had almost completely died out, but I hadn't even heard them come in.

'Get up!'

A guard struck me again with a wooden baton. I put my arms up instinctively to protect my face and the stick cracked loudly across my forearms.

'Get up. Against the wall! Now!'

I did exactly as I was told as fast as I could. There were two guards, and one of them sounded familiar, but I hadn't had time to look at their faces.

'Face the wall!'

I clasped my hands behind my head and pressed my forehead against the bricks. That way, if they struck me from behind, my nose wouldn't break.

'Now, don't move.'

I heard one of the guards leave, while the other one began sifting through my possessions, turning my clothes inside out and then throwing them across the room. It was obvious that they had discovered that the seventh cell had been broken into. In the corridor, I could hear the other inmates being searched and then herded out of their cells and into the exercise yard.

'Out. Get out! Outside! Now!'

The guard in my cell stopped his search and stood to attention when a man wearing heavy boots came to the door. 'Nothing on this one, major,' he reported.

'Are you sure?' The voice belonged to a different major from the previous day, the one they called the 'Devil Major'. He was the cruellest of the officers at San Pedro. He had cold green eyes and he never smiled. Whenever he walked past, prisoners became nervous, even if they weren't doing anything wrong.

'Nothing. I searched everything twice.'

The Devil Major stepped slowly into the room. I could feel him right behind me and hear his breathing. I braced myself for another blow, but it didn't come.

'*Inglés*, tell me what happened here last night.'

'I don't know, major. I promise.'

'Who was involved in the escape?'

'I was asleep, major.'

He asked a few more questions. Each time, I kept my answers short and polite, not wanting to give him any excuse to hit me.

'Turn around, *inglés*,' he ordered. Then, to the guard, 'Smell his breath.'

The guard stepped right up to my face and commanded, 'Breathe out.' He shook his head. 'Nothing, major.' He sounded disappointed. When he stepped back, I finally saw who it was. I knew that his voice was familiar. It was Pizza Boy.

I was ordered to stay standing against the wall and they locked the door behind me when they left. Once the others were accounted for in the courtyard line-up, they were returned to their cells. No one was fed or let out for two days. Nothing more happened to me, except that they took away my television. The others were beaten for drinking, Samir to within an inch of his life for trying to escape as well.

卌||

The first thing the guards had noticed in the morning were piles of sand and rock in the bathroom area. Initially, they probably thought the damage was caused by the storm, but when they saw that Samir's door was bent open, they raised the alarm, thinking there had been a breakout. That was when the guards raced in and started beating us.

But Samir hadn't escaped. This time he had fashioned the planks of wood from his bed into a ladder, but still couldn't make it over the wall, not even placing his ladder on the bathroom roof. Instead, he began burrowing through the wall, using only a knife and spoon he had stolen from the human rights lunch. There were two walls. Somehow, he had made a small hole through the first wall, only to find that the gap between them was filled with sand, which started pouring out all over him and all over the roof. The hole got bigger and the sand didn't stop flowing out. With all the weight piling up, the roof collapsed, crashing into the bathroom below and sending sand and debris flying everywhere. Samir made it back to his cell, where the guards found him in the morning, unconscious, with sand all through his hair and clothes.

Since he was already in trouble for attempting to escape, Samir tried to take all the blame for the stolen contraband, saying that it was his birthday and he had convinced the others they had permission to cele-brate with him. The major didn't believe his story, but he punished him as if he did.

Throughout the day, the police took it in shifts to beat Samir. Between turns, they let him rest, but then another group would come in and start. The first few times, Samir fought back, kicking and punching at anyone who came near him. I heard several cries from the police as he lashed out, all the time abusing and threatening them.

'You bastards! I'll call human rights.'

The police laughed and kicked him harder. 'They've already come.'

Reinforcements arrived. Between them, they managed to pin him down properly and handcuff one of his hands to a water pipe that ran through the cell.

'*¡Hijos de putas!* I'm going to write a letter to parliament telling them everything about the cars!'

With only one free hand, he was an easy target for the group of police. However, even with severe concussion, he didn't give up. He still had the use of his legs and scored a few more kicks on them until the Devil Major returned with a plank of wood and smashed Samir's teeth in. After that, the only screams came from Samir.

Samir was tough and had a lot of determination, but the major was tough and had a plank of wood. He was going to teach him a lesson. Over a period of hours, they wore him down. Eventually, they broke him. And then, once he was broken, they kept going. His howls spread out into the punishment complex, piercing through the walls of La Grulla into the main prison sections. I blocked my ears, but I still heard his cries of agony. I have never heard such wrenching, blood-curdling screams in all my life. Slowly, very slowly, they were killing him. It was unbearable.

'Enough! Please. No more!' We pleaded, but they kept hitting him, each time until Samir was unconscious. Then they would revive him by spraying a fire extinguisher in his face. Eventually, he stopped screaming and began sobbing.

'You want to cry, then?' screamed the major.

He threw a canister of tear gas into Samir's room, closed the door and left. The canister was designed for use against street rioters. Indoors, the gas dispersed very slowly. When it reached my cell, I could hardly breathe. My lungs felt like they were on fire. I had to rinse my eyes and keep them closed for more than ten minutes to stop them from exploding. It must have been much worse for Samir. After the tear gas, we heard nothing more from him.

'Samir! Talk to us! Are you alive? Just make a noise.' We took it in turns to call out to him for more than half an hour, trying to get a response. Finally, we heard him moaning.

'Samir! Are you OK?' I yelled through my hatch. He didn't answer, so I called again. Eventually, he managed a proper reply: 'Thomas, they didn't find the coke. We've still got the coke!'

43
A SPECIAL VISITOR

S amir took several days to recover from his beating. When he did, he was sentenced to another ninety days, and conditions in La Grulla went back to the way they had been when I first arrived there. All privileges were withdrawn: they took away my heater and all our blankets; they fed us on soup twice a day; they removed the light bulbs from their sockets; and yard time never lasted a minute longer than four hours. Things probably would have stayed that way, if it hadn't been for the arrival of a very special visitor.

The politician, Gabriel Sanchez, arrived, escorted by two policemen. He was wearing a suit and tie and walking ahead of his escorts, who were wheeling two large suitcases. As he walked down the corridor, the other inmates rattled their doors and hissed at him. He ignored them, but he looked tense.

'You're dead, Mr Politician,' Chapako whispered, spitting on the back of his suit. His police escorts didn't say anything.

Sanchez had been sent to La Grulla for his own protection. It wasn't difficult to have someone killed in a Bolivian prison – families of murder or rape victims did it all the time. Some of the poorer inmates would do anything for money, but in the case of a politician who had stolen forty million dollars from the Bolivian people and spent it on plastic surgery and a beach house in Miami, they would have performed the service for free. The only other place the politician might have been safe was in Posta, with all the other millionaires. But even there, someone probably could have got to him.

'Wait 'til tonight, *cabrón*!' yelled Chino. 'You'd better have your money ready or we're going to cut you up alive.'

Sanchez was placed in the seventh cell. By then, the guards had moved the remaining contraband elsewhere. As they closed the door behind him, Samir shouted, '*Señor político*, we're going to give you a new face that your plastic surgeon won't be able to fix!' On their way back down the corridor, the guards were smiling to themselves. I didn't think the politician would last long.

His first night was hell. The others stood at their doors explaining to him in great detail what they were going to do when they got hold of him.

'No one's going to save you in here. The police are on our side. They'll give us the key to your cell and they won't find you until the next morning.'

Samir was the loudest, although you couldn't hear him properly because at night the guards kept him handcuffed to the water pipe at the back of his cell so that he wouldn't escape. 'You're ours now. You're going to die very slowly, *cabrón*. Eight hours is a long time to bleed.'

Sanchez didn't say a thing all night. However, when I saw how tired his face was the following day, I knew he'd been awake and had heard every word. He was smart, though; when it was morning yard time, he refused to come out. Instead, he bribed the guards to bring his soup to his window. Chino rattled his door and laughed at him.

'You have to come out sometime, *bastardo*. Politicians have to shit too, you know. And your shit stinks worse than ours, so you can't do it in your cell.'

In the afternoon, Gabriel Sanchez did come out to take his yard time, but it was after the rest of us had been locked up again. He had the entire exercise yard to himself. And since he wasn't in La Grulla as punishment, the same restrictions didn't apply to him. He was given as much yard time as he wanted and got to decide when he should go back to his cell. He sat in the sun, smoking cigarettes, listening to his CD Walkman and reading the newspaper, while the other inmates stood at their doors, going out of their heads in frustration.

Over the next few days, their anger grew. They threw burning toilet paper and cups of urine through his window, but the politician simply stayed at the back of his cell. Samir tried to pick the new padlocks. Sanchez was smarter than Samir, though; he had made a phone call to the governor and had the door reinforced and extra locks installed on the inside. They tried everything to get to him, but no one could even get close.

During this entire time, I didn't say anything to Sanchez. I didn't attempt to stop the others from taunting him – that would have been suicide – but I didn't join in, either. After a while, the politician noticed this. Sometimes, when we were filing past his cell on our way to the *lista*, he would be standing at his window and he would try to catch my eye. I smiled at him once or twice when the others weren't looking.

Sanchez had a lot of visitors – his lawyers, rich friends and some family members. They brought him the daily newspaper and books, and home-cooked meals. Sometimes, he would call the guards and send me his leftovers. I always shared these with the other inmates. Then, on top of my normal yard time, Sanchez started to invite me to join him when he had his.

The others called me a traitor, but when I got Sanchez to persuade the guards to give them extra yard time also, they began to see that having a politician as your friend could be more beneficial than trying to kill him.

卌︱︱

Gabriel Sanchez's brother was in prison also. He lived in Posta and the family was given permission to get together for Christmas. Owing to the dangers involved in entering the main prison population, the politician applied to have his 'bodyguard' accompany him. That bodyguard was me, and it was the best Christmas I ever had in San Pedro.

In Posta, the rules were already relaxed because the inmates were rich, but at Christmastime, you wouldn't have even known it was a prison. There were streamers and party hats and people drinking and tables set up outside in the sun. They treated me like one of the family. They even wrapped me up a present – a bottle of Black Label scotch whisky.

To be honest, I wasn't much of a bodyguard. After a few glasses of whisky, I couldn't have protected anyone. To keep me alert, the politician's brother gave me a few *puntitos*. It was the purest coke I'd ever had in San Pedro. It seems that the people in Posta had very good connections. Officially, we were permitted to stay only until 6 pm on Christmas Day, but Gabriel rang the governor at his home and had our leave extended to the next day. Everyone kept drinking and dancing, while I sat in the corner bullshitting and doing cocaine with Gabriel's

327

brother. The seasons may have been reversed in the southern hemisphere, but that didn't mean you couldn't have a traditional white Christmas in Bolivia.

卌ll

After the Christmas celebrations came the New Year's Eve party. And on the following day, another special prisoner was transferred into La Grulla from the main prison. They moved Chapako into Chino's cell to make space for him. No one saw who the new prisoner was or knew why he was there. We were all too hungover to pay any attention. He was gone the following day. Later we found out why: he had been transferred to Chonchocoro for his own safety.

While the whole prison population had been partying, one of the women hadn't noticed that her six-year-old daughter was missing. When she sobered up the following morning and raised the alarm, everyone in the section went looking for the missing *niña*. They called and called. They looked in all the likely hiding places: under the stairwells, in the bathrooms, in the laundry, under clothes. They asked the other children. No one had seen her. The mother began to panic. They checked to make sure the *niña* hadn't fallen into the empty swimming pool. And although it was unlikely, they climbed up on the roofs to look for her there.

As word spread to the other sections, the whole prison population stopped what it was doing. Hundreds of worried people joined in the search. San Pedro was filled with the hysterical screams of the little girl's mother and the sounds of people calling her name as if she were a lost puppy. Still, they couldn't find her. The guards came into the prison and demanded that each prisoner open his door. They searched every single room, one by one, with a growing crowd following them.

When they finally found the girl, it was too late. Her tiny body was discovered in one of the inmate's cells. She had been raped, then strangled and left naked on the bed. The body was cold. The prison doctor sedated the mother and I finally understood properly about *la piscina*. The inmates began filling it with water and a mob went looking for the culprit, but he had already made it to the main gate and bribed the guards to be sent to La Grulla. That wasn't the only bad thing that happened. A couple of weeks afterwards, I got more bad news.

44
TERRIBLE NEWS

I guess it had all got too much for Abregon in Chonchocoro and he just snapped. At least, that's what I would prefer to think happened, but from the details I learned later, it seemed that he had the whole thing planned. And his girlfriend, Raquel, was stupid to have visited him, after what she had done. What did she think – that he would be happy to see her and want to give her more money?

It was Julián who broke the news to me and he did it in a very strange way. After Samir's escape attempt, all visitors were banned from La Grulla except those visiting the politician. However, Julián could get past the guards because he was delegate. He came into the cell block and knocked on my door very early one morning, even before the guards had let us out. I was barely awake, but I knew by the expression on his face that it was something serious.

'How much money do you owe Abregon?' he asked, after shaking my hand through the hatch.

'Nothing. I don't owe him a cent.' I stopped rubbing my eyes and looked at Julián. 'In fact, he owes *me* money. You know that.' I had never mentioned the Chilean stolen car deal to Julián because he didn't like to know about anything illegal that went on in his section. But he knew that Abregon and I were business partners and that Abregon owed me for something.

'Are you sure? People are saying that he left you all his money when he went to Chonchocoro,' he said, looking at me like I was a complete stranger. My mind started racing.

'He did. But I gave it all to his wife. Why are you asking me all this? You were *there*. You were my witness,' my voice squeaked. A wave of panic came over me. There was no way that Julián could have forgotten that amount of money, so why was he pretending not to remember? And why was he looking at me as if he didn't believe me?

'But you definitely haven't got any more of his money?' he asked me in an even tone.

'Julián, you were there,' I repeated, and that empty feeling in my stomach began to grow. 'You counted the money yourself. Don't . . . I mean . . . What, are you accusing me of cheating him?' Then a thought occurred to me and I felt my legs go weak: *What if Julián was the one trying to set me up?* He had been the witness for the loan contract with the Velascos. He had been the witness for when I gave Abregon's wife the money. He had been my witness at the police set-up. He had sat on my case at the discipline committee meeting. He was the one I relied on to send messages to Abregon. What if he had been against me the whole time? Who would ever believe my word against his?

'No, Thomas. I'm not accusing you of anything.' Julián's face relaxed. 'I'm sorry that I had to ask you that. I just wanted to make sure.'

'Make sure about what? Why? What's happened? What did he say?' I was in such a state of confusion that it took a while for his answer to sink in.

'Abregon's dead.' Julián paused. 'He died in Chonchocoro yesterday afternoon. I'm sorry, Thomas.'

'How?' I eventually managed to ask.

'Suicide. He hanged himself.'

I was still stuck on the idea that Julián was the one betraying me, so my first thought was that he had had Abregon killed and was trying to make it look like a suicide. But I was wrong. Julián had nothing to do with any of it.

Even though Chonchocoro was a maximum-security prison, it seems that prisoners were still allowed television sets. Abregon had cut the electrical cable at the back and had it ready when his wife visited him in his cell. He turned his stereo up loud and strangled her. No one heard a thing. Afterwards, he hanged himself. Julián had just been doing his duty to Abregon's family by asking me those questions about whether he had any money left over.

'Is there anything I can do?' he asked gently.

'Yes. Get my television back for me.' Julián looked at me strangely, thinking I might have been planning to do the same thing as Abregon. I wasn't. 'I want to watch the news.'

The guards couldn't find my TV, but Julián persuaded them to lend me theirs, which was smaller and black and white. They were probably using mine. The news reports said that Abregon had been depressed by the prospect of his sixteen-year sentence and had selfishly decided to take his young girlfriend with him when she visited him.

'Are you OK? Is there anything else I can do for you?' asked Julián when he visited the next day to check on how I was doing.

'Yeah. Call the governor. Get me out of here.'

I had been in La Grulla for sixty-six days when the governor finally signed my release form. The Velascos were released on the same day. They couldn't look me in the eye after what had happened with Abregon, but as far as I was concerned, the fight between us was over. The money didn't matter anymore, they could keep it. What I didn't realise was that our fight had barely started.

45
NEW CHARGES

When I was released from solitary confinement, the prison community was still recovering from the rape and murder of the six-year-old girl. Everyone was shocked and disgusted by what had happened and the whole prison was in shut-down mode. No one laughed or smiled for weeks. Inmates nodded sadly when they passed each other in the corridor. There were no parties. Children no longer played noisy games of soccer or hopscotch in the afternoons. Their mothers kept them locked safely inside the whole time. When they needed to go to the bathroom or to school, an adult always accompanied them.

For several days, photographers and television crews had been camped outside San Pedro. Journalists banged on the gates demanding access to the prison in order to film the children's living conditions and interview the families. The governor wouldn't allow them in. Instead, the journalists had to content themselves with filming the women and children leaving the prison each morning on their way to school.

Nevertheless, newspapers continued to run articles about how disgraceful it was that young children, who had committed no crime whatsoever, were being brought up in an adults' prison. The children were paying the price for their fathers' sins, they argued. A campaign called 'Don't Imprison My Childhood' was launched, with the aim of removing all children from San Pedro immediately. The campaign failed. Everyone agreed that it was dangerous for children to be in the prison; however, no one could agree on what to do with them instead. There were no government funds to look after them. Without parents supporting them, where would the children live? How would they survive on the outside?

Ultimately it was the parents, especially the mothers, who spoke out against the campaign. They knew that bringing their children up in a jail was far from ideal, but it was better than having them made into state wards or placed in orphanages. If the children were forced to leave San Pedro, their families would have no chance of sticking together. It was decided: the children were to stay.

For a long time, mothers continued to keep their children locked inside but the children wanted to be outside in order to play. Gradually, they were allowed out again, although they were supervised very closely. Everyone paid them extra attention and treated them even more like angels than before. The rule that inmates had to stand aside in the corridors to give right of way to children was strictly enforced. Babysitting rosters were set up for minding groups of younger children. Anyone caught fighting in front of a child was sent to punishment immediately, without right of appeal. No one would ever forget what had happened, but life inside the prison slowly went back to how it had been before.

$\cancel{||||}||$

Because of all the media attention focused on San Pedro, the guards became a lot stricter about every aspect of prison life. They carried out a series of *requisas*, mainly looking for weapons. During one raid, they confiscated all our knives, even my blunt butter knives, so that I had to use a fork and spoon to eat. The governor also placed restrictions on visiting hours. Only women and children with official permission slips could spend the night inside the jail. There was a complete ban on tourists entering. Officially, the tours didn't exist anyway, but the governor certainly didn't want photos of Westerners exiting San Pedro high on cocaine appearing as front-page news after what had just happened.

No longer being able to conduct the tours meant that my main source of income disappeared completely at a time when I needed it most. My financial situation was in ruins. I hadn't worked for over two months and I owed people who had loaned me money when I was in La Grulla. I decided to sell off the stock I had stored up in my shop. The only way to do this quickly was to sell everything to another shopkeeper at a huge loss.

I did manage to keep my restaurant afloat, but the tour business was never the same. Even when the media attention finally died off and tourists were allowed back in, I still wasn't able to run the San Pedro prison tours. During my two-month absence, the gangs had taken them over.

One of the reasons I didn't fight hard to re-establish myself as the main tour guide was Fantasma. In that year, he had his final court appearances before sentencing and he knew that he was going to be in prison for a long time. He told everyone that the devil had appeared to him and granted him a single wish. Rather than asking to be let out of prison, he said that he wanted to get his girlfriend pregnant. In the meantime, he became more and more violent. Rather than a suit and tie, Fantasma wore his designer sportswear and expensive sneakers to court. When reporters outside the court asked him whether he was sorry for what he had done, he replied, 'If I could, I'd do it again, motherfuckers.' On his way out of the court, he kicked at the journalists or knocked them out of the way and threatened to have them killed. Everything he did and said was reported in the media and read by the inmates of San Pedro. His girlfriend became pregnant and his reputation inside the prison grew.

The day of his final sentencing, Fantasma scratched, 'I will never repent' into the cubicle wall in the court bathrooms using his handcuffs. When the judge sentenced him to the maximum thirty years, he laughed and swore at her. With such a long sentence, Fantasma had absolutely nothing left to lose. Everyone avoided him even more, including me. This suited him well; by then he had developed strong ties with the guards and *taxistas* at the gate and he decided to take over the prison tours completely. I didn't protest. I didn't have enough energy to fight him. And to tell the truth, I didn't really feel like doing the tours anymore. I still felt very sad about Abregon and exhausted by my experience in La Grulla. Instead of the tours, I decided to spend more time on my own in order to stay out of trouble.

||||| ||

Gradually, the guards began allowing more tourists back into San Pedro. With the help of the gangs, Fantasma and the other tour guides continued to prevent me from running my tours, but every now and again, travellers came to the gates asking for me. My reputation had spread worldwide and these travellers had been told by friends back in their home countries to visit me. I wrote a letter of complaint to the governor saying that I was a foreigner and therefore should have the right to receive foreign visitors. He gave me a permission slip that allowed me to have visitors in my room. Many of the tourists didn't care about the tours, anyway; they just wanted to talk. I couldn't charge anyone for this, but many of them would buy me lunch or leave some money to help out with expenses. Occasionally, when the other tour guides were sick, I was called in to do the tours.

With my restaurant and the occasional tourist coming through the prison, I eventually managed to pay off all my debts. Whenever I had any spare money or leftover food from the restaurant, I would send it to Samir in La Grulla, where he was doing another ninety-day sentence. Samir continued to threaten to write a letter exposing the police he had worked for in the car-theft ring, if they didn't let him out. The police, worried about being implicated, had him transferred to Chonchocoro. I wanted to send him money there, but it was impossible. From what I heard, the police kept him in the isolation cells so that he couldn't communicate with anyone.

卌\\

I kept a low profile and managed to stay out of harm's way for over a year. I would have been content to patiently wait out the remainder of my sentence, but one morning during the *lista* my whole world was shattered yet again. The major asked me to stay back after we had answered our names. He was a friend of mine and I could tell that he had bad news for me. When everyone had gone, he looked at me like someone had died and handed over an envelope.

'This is from the administration office.' He stood by while I opened it.

The envelope contained an official charge sheet with the name 'Thomas McFadden' written at the top. At first, I tried to hand it back, thinking that there had been some mistake. But the major refused to take it, and held up his hands to say it wasn't his fault. I read further down the page and saw the names of my co-accused: Jorge and Jose Luis Velasco. We were being charged for the commercial trafficking of two hundred grams of cocaine.

At almost the same time as I received notification of the new charges against me, the other prisoners received the best news they'd ever had. A new law – *Extra Muro* – was introduced, which halved the sentences of most prisoners in Bolivia's overcrowded penitentiary system. Many became eligible for immediate release.

Ricardo came straight to my room and opened the door without even knocking, using the spare key I had given him. He had come to return it.

'Did you hear the news?' he said excitedly, turning on the light and slapping the daily newspaper on my table. It was open at the page of the article. 'We're out of here, *inglés.*'

Ricardo and Jack the Mexican were two of the lucky ones. And if it hadn't been for my new charges, I would have been leaving with them. Technically, my sentence was now over. In fact, owing to an administration error, my release papers had already been signed. However, since I had new charges, I was back in the same position as when I first arrived at San Pedro – stuck in prison until my hearing started, with no right to bail. And this time, I was innocent.

'What's wrong?' said Ricardo, producing a small packet of cocaine. 'We should be dancing. Let's put on some music.' It was the only time I ever saw Ricardo sniff more than two *puntitos* in one sitting. He did three to start off with. He jumped around and hugged me. I couldn't spoil his mood by telling him my own news right then. I did three *puntitos* too, then one more for good luck.

Apart from me, the only people who weren't celebrating the *Extra Muro* announcement were the poorest inmates. Being released wasn't automatic. Before having your release papers stamped and finalised by the administration, every prisoner had to pay *las costas del estado* – 'the costs of the state'. Until these inmates had enough money to pay for the water and electricity they had consumed during their imprisonment, they weren't allowed to leave.

卌ll

I was very sad that Ricardo was due to be released. I pretended to be happy for him, but I didn't want him to go. Ricardo had been like a father to me and I didn't know what I was going to do without him. He had also been extremely popular with everyone in San Pedro. The night before he left, we held a huge farewell party for him. Most of us were still a little drunk the following afternoon as the time to say goodbye approached.

Tears came to my eyes when he hugged me at the gates, but I held them back because I didn't want him to see me crying. It must have been hard for him also, leaving behind so many good friends. I had only told him the day before about my new charges.

'I'm going to miss you, *inglés*,' he said, giving me one final embrace and then picking up two of his suitcases. It had been four years since he had changed my name to '*inglés*' for my own protection. I no longer needed protection, but he had never gotten out of the habit of calling me by that name. The lieutenant turned the key and opened the gate for him.

'I'll come and visit you,' was the last thing he said to me before he walked out of the courtyard. The moment the gate clanged shut behind him, a cheer went up from the inmates gathered in the courtyard. The *taxistas* applauded, and even the guards patted him on the back as he passed them.

'*Chao, hermanos*,' Ricardo called back to us, dragging his heavy suitcases behind him.

A friend of Ricardo's was waiting outside the prison with a car to help him transport all his belongings. Even with his friend's assistance, Ricardo had to make two more trips back to the gate to pick up the rest of his furniture. San Pedro must have been the only prison in the world where an inmate arrived with only the shirt on his back but left with enough possessions to fill a house. I tried to find this funny but when I laughed to myself I could feel sadness sneaking in between the breaths of laughter and had to stop. Ricardo waved to me for the final time from the outer gates, but I turned away, not wanting him to see that I was about to cry.

I didn't cry properly until I was back in my room. I left the light off and I cried all that night. Ricardo had saved my life. He had taught me how to survive in prison. And he had been the best friend anyone inside or outside prison could ever ask for. I was happy for him, but a selfish part of me wished he hadn't been released. When one side of my pillow was soaked with tears, I turned it over and discovered a note underneath. I don't know how Ricardo had managed to get into my room without his key, but somehow he had.

My dear friend from *Inglaterra*,

By the time you find this letter, I will be a free man, living like a king somewhere in the streets of La Paz.

I can still remember the first day I met you by the main gates, holding on tightly to your blanket because you thought I was going to steal it. Do you remember? You couldn't speak a word of Spanish. And no matter how many times I told you, you could never pronounce *ají*. Do you remember the time Simón refused to sell you the beef?

I'm going to miss you, little brother. I have many good memories of our times together. I will never forget the look of shock on your face when you tried to sell me the stuff you had smuggled in and I refused because we already had tons of it inside. And that big smile you gave me when you tried your very first *puntito*.

The world needs to know the truth about this place. You're the only one of us brave enough to do it. You owe it to me and your other brothers in San Pedro. Stay out of trouble and keep your nose clean. Remember: *puntitos* only. Just like I taught you.

Te quiero mucho, hermano.

Ricardo

PS. You still owe me US$40 million from the bet.

‖

Ricardo had said that he would visit me at least once a week. He did come a few times, but only ever to the interview room.

'Why don't you come in and smoke some *ganja* with me, Ricardo?' I suggested each time he visited. 'Like old times.' But he always refused.

'I'd like to, *inglés*. But I can't.' He shook his head apologetically. When he saw how disappointed I was, he added, 'You already know why.'

Ricardo had told me he was afraid that one of the inmates might make him an offer to do some *negocios* on the outside. He had promised himself he would never go back to it, but he was worried that he might be tempted, if he came inside.

I think there was another reason he didn't want to step foot in San Pedro prison again – he wanted to forget the place entirely. On his last visit, Ricardo told me of a bad dream he had been having recently: he had come back inside to see his old friends, but when visiting hours were over and he went to leave, the guards wouldn't let him out. They told him he was still a prisoner and none of the officers would believe him when he said he wasn't.

338

'*Adios, inglés,*' he said, putting his hands up against the screen to say goodbye. By that time, the guards had placed wire gauze across the interview room bars so that inmates couldn't pass drugs through so easily.

'*Adios, Ricardo,*' I replied, matching my fingertips against his. I knew from his eyes and the way he said goodbye that he wouldn't come again. I think his telling me about his dream was also his way of saying that this was his final visit. Dreams like that may seem silly to most people. But if you've ever been in prison, you know they're not.

HH||

Once Ricardo had left, I felt very alone. However, because I now had new charges pending against me, I quit the tours completely and tried to avoid too many dealings with the other inmates. Instead of going out, I spent almost all the time in my room. The only prisoners I socialised with were foreigners, including a new arrival called Roberto.

Roberto had been busted for international trafficking at El Alto Airport. He was twenty-nine when he arrived at San Pedro, older than me, but I always thought of him as being younger, like a kid brother. He looked and dressed like a university student. He had glasses and black, curly hair and talked about star signs all the time. He read books on astrology and believed in destiny. I don't know why, but I felt sorrier for him than I did for all the others. It was probably because Roberto wasn't a real criminal. He wasn't even a proper drug trafficker. Well, not a professional one, anyway.

There's a rule that you learn in South America if you stay there long enough: if someone offers you a stack of money to smuggle drugs on to a flight, don't do it if the amount is anything less than two kilos. You'll be the sacrifice to get five other passengers through with the main shipment. If you're going to take the risk, then you might as well organise the whole thing yourself. That way, no one can set you up and you get to take all the profits yourself.

You're an idiot if you traffic drugs, anyway, unless you're prepared to face up to the consequences. Most people aren't. Prisons around the world are filled with stupid tourists who thought they could pay off their holiday or put down a deposit on an apartment back home by doing just one run. Statistically, their reasoning is correct; most mules do get through. But what if you are the unlucky one who gets busted? There are no credit points for having been a law-abiding citizen your whole life up until that moment. You get thrown in with the rest of them. So, if you're ever thinking of doing a drug run, before making your final decision you should visit the local prison where you'll be living if you get caught. And if you're in La Paz, you can even do a guided tour or stay the night as practice.

Roberto was one of those stupid tourists. The police caught him at the airport with a kilo of cocaine hidden in shampoo bottles. It must have been a tip-off; when cocaine is dissolved in liquid it's a lot harder to detect, so the cops have to be very certain in order to detain you just for carrying two extra bottles of hair conditioner.

Since tourists no longer stayed to party with me at night, I had almost stopped taking cocaine completely. However, once I was friends with Roberto, I started up again. Roberto wasn't a professional trafficker, but it was obvious that he had been taking cocaine for some time. He wasn't at all surprised to discover that you could buy drugs in San Pedro. He had started sniffing heavily within a week, long before he knew the outcome of his trial.

We began doing coke almost every night of the week, always staying up until daylight. I wanted to completely forget about my upcoming trial. With Ricardo no longer there to watch over me, we would sometimes keep sniffing even after the morning *lista*. Roberto wasn't at all what you would expect of an Italian. He spoke very quietly, sometimes in broken English and other times in Spanish, but his voice never varied and he never got excited about anything. The scary thing was that when Roberto took cocaine, it didn't seem to have any effect on him. His mood didn't change at all. He didn't get high or nervous. He didn't need to drink anything. He didn't talk too much. He just sat there at my table, doing more and more coke and smoking the occasional joint. I tried to cheer him up, but if anything, he seemed to become more depressed.

Roberto got five years and four months from the judge, but the news took a while to sink in. On the day he came back from sentencing, he didn't seem that sad. He told me how he had been thinking of getting back together with his ex-girlfriend. The way he talked about her, it was as if she was in the next room, not back in Italy, and that sorting out their problems was something that might happen quite soon. With *Extra Muro*, he'd be out after three years. But even that is a long time for a university student, even a philosophical one like Roberto. When you think about it, that's a whole degree.

46

MEETING RUSTY

Even with Roberto to keep me company, I got very lonely during that period without the tourists coming in to see me. Sometimes, when Fantasma was locked in La Muralla or La Grulla, the guards would call me to take a tour group. However, almost none of the tourists were allowed to stay the night. One of the only people who did stay during my fifth year in San Pedro was Rusty, a 25-year-old backpacker from Australia. He boasted to me that he had a law degree, although I didn't believe him at first. He didn't seem like a proper lawyer to me. For a start, he had hair down to his shoulders and dressed badly in dirty jeans and a T-shirt. Also, he laughed a lot and didn't seem to care that any of us were criminals.

Rusty thought he was pretty clever because he spoke more Spanish than the other tourists, but I knew straight away that he was genuine. During the official tour, I told the whole group about a Brazilian prisoner who had been bashed and brutally stabbed for being a suspected informant. The Brazilian's injuries were so severe that the guards sent him to a hospital outside the prison, but after the doctors stitched him up, he couldn't afford more treatment and his wounds became infected. Every one of the tourists that day promised to come back to San Pedro to drop off some medicine for me to send to the Brazilian, but Rusty was the only one who kept his word. In fact, he went directly to the hospital where the Brazilian was supposedly being kept, only to discover that he had been transferred to a cheaper hospital. Then he went to find the new hospital. When the police guarding the Brazilian told him he wasn't allowed to visit, Rusty bluffed them that he was an international human rights lawyer and therefore had the legal right to take some antibiotics to the patient.

The Brazilian later thanked me and told me how Rusty had stood in the hospital ward arguing loudly until the police gave in.

It seemed that Rusty wasn't afraid of the police. He would have made a good drug trafficker. For that matter, he wasn't afraid of the Bolivian inmates either. As soon as I told him that tourists used to sleep the night in San Pedro, he insisted on staying. That evening I took him to the inside sections to see the conditions of the poorer prisoners. He appeared to get along well with everyone, including the base addicts and the dangerous prisoners. Even Crack Cat purred when he picked him up.

The next time Rusty came into San Pedro, he had photocopied a colouring-in book and bought some marker pens. He organised a drawing competition for the little children in Alamos and handed out small prizes to the winners and made hot chocolate for all the entrants. I knew by then that he was the one who should help me with the book I had decided to write about San Pedro. He agreed to stay with me in the prison to conduct recorded interviews so that he could understand how the inmates lived.

I bribed the governor to get a permission slip that allowed Rusty to go in and out of the prison whenever he wanted. To avoid suspicion, I told everyone that he was my cousin who was here to visit because I had medical problems. I also explained to Rusty that you had to make the guards laugh in order to keep them happy. When the guards asked how he could possibly be my cousin, if I was black and he was white, he repeated to them exactly what I had told him to say: 'Thomas was born at night and I was born during the day.'

The only trouble with Rusty was that he didn't take things seriously enough. He thought it was fun to bribe the police, and he didn't seem to realise that I would be the one who would get into trouble if something went wrong. If anyone found out what we were doing, it wouldn't be hard for the police to get to me.

I didn't tell Rusty about my new charges, because I was sure the police didn't have a good case and I didn't want him to worry about me. However, maybe I should have told him in order to stop him from treating everything like a game. Rusty rented an apartment near the prison and I knew that he was partying a lot on the nights he stayed outside San Pedro. One time a whole bunch of tourists he must have met in a nightclub came to the main gate asking for 'el australiano'.

The guards sent them away, saying that there were no Australian prisoners in San Pedro, but they began to get suspicious about why Rusty was going in and out of the prison all the time.

卌ll

On the morning of the first hearing in my new trial, I told Rusty not to come in because I was sick. I waited at the gate with the other prisoners to be transported to court. The guards called our names, handcuffed us in pairs and put us in the transport van. My name was called immediately before that of Jorge Velasco. He had avoided me ever since the new charges had been laid and he panicked when he saw that the guards were about to handcuff us together.

'No. No!' he said, stepping away from the guard. He must have thought I would try to strangle him on the way.

'It's OK. *Tranquilo,*' I reassured him. '*No hay problema.*' I still hated the Velascos. They had tried to set me up and I knew they were responsible for having Abregon transferred to Chonchocoro. But there was no point in fighting. It wouldn't bring Abregon back and now that we were being tried together for the same offence, it was better for us to be on reasonable terms.

'*Vamos,*' ordered the lieutenant impatiently. Reluctantly, Jorge allowed himself to be handcuffed to me. We didn't speak the whole way to the court. Nor did he say anything to his father. I should have known by the awkward way he sat next to me that something else had happened to make him fear me more.

My lawyer visited me in the court holding cell just before the trial started. His name was Manuelo and he was a public defence lawyer. It was only because I was a foreigner that I was fortunate enough to get any assistance. I told him that I would pay him a bit myself, in order to make him try harder on my behalf. Sometimes lawyers didn't try their hardest in drug cases because if they won against a powerful *fiscal*, they might ruin their careers.

To start the trial, the *fiscal* stood up and made his opening address. For the sake of efficiency, the prosecution was to be done by joint trial, although we each had our own legal representative. The prosecution case against me was very weak, and until halfway through the hearing I felt confident that I would be let off. When the charges were read, I was asked to stand and Manuelo stated my plea: *inocente.* My defence was simply what had happened – that I had no knowledge of the drugs, was not inside the room where the drugs were found, had no money on me and had nothing to do with any of it whatsoever.

I knew the Velascos would also plead *inocente*. No one ever pleads guilty in Bolivia – if you admit to a crime, the judges give you a higher sentence. However, I couldn't imagine what their defence would be. There were two hundred grams of cocaine that had to be accounted for, and those two hundred grams had been found in their room. They couldn't deny it and, in fact, they didn't. Their defence was this: they had been acting under police instructions in a sting operation to catch Thomas McFadden, a known drug dealer in the prison, in return for the promise of an earlier release.

When the Velascos' lawyer said this, I was stunned. I looked at the Velascos in disbelief, but neither one of them would turn his head. I hardly heard another word of what was said by the *fiscal* because I was in too much shock. I kept staring at the Velascos. I could feel my muscles tensing up. Jose Luis continued to look directly at the judge, and Jorge wouldn't look at me either. The policeman at the front of the courtroom tapped his wooden baton to get my attention. He shook his head at me and tightened his grip around the baton. He knew that what the Velascos were claiming was untrue and he could also see what I was thinking.

This changed everything. The Velascos were supposed to be defendants like I was, but their defence turned the case into something completely different. Rather than being defendants, they effectively became witnesses for the prosecution in the case against me. I couldn't see how they could possibly prove that they were undercover agents, but that was what they were claiming. It was now their word against mine.

At the end of the hearing, the guard told me and Jorge to hold up our hands. He unlocked the cuff on my left wrist and handcuffed Jorge to Jose Luis. I got my own set of handcuffs. For the rest of the trial the guards used this same system; the Velascos were always put together, and I was kept away from them. They placed us in separate holding cells at the court. And whenever they could, they transported us in separate vehicles.

47
MONEY WORRIES

As soon as he came back into the prison the following morning, Rusty knew that something had happened. Usually, he sent a *taxista* ahead so that I could come and meet him at the gate once he had got past the security check. This time, I didn't meet him. He let himself into my room using the key I had given him, which had belonged to Ricardo.

'What's wrong?' he asked with concern, when he turned on the light and saw that I was still lying in bed. Then his tone changed when he noticed all the used tissues on my bedside table: 'Have you been up sniffing all night with Roberto again?'

I still didn't want to tell him about my case, even though I desperately needed money to fund my defence. I knew he wasn't rich. Besides, it was my responsibility to fix my own problems.

'No. I'm just tired, man,' I said, sitting up. 'I think I've got a cold.'

I was happy that Rusty was there with me, but not being able to tell him about what had happened with the Velascos made things very difficult. He didn't understand why I was in a bad mood. I also got sick very easily because I was so stressed, but he thought it was because I was taking cocaine. We had our first disagreement the following day when I asked for some money to buy cigarettes from the shop. He hadn't minded giving me money on previous occasions, but this time he refused, saying, 'I'm not a millionaire, you know.'

'Hey, man. A whole packet of cigarettes costs less than one dollar.'

'Well, if they're so cheap, why don't you pay for them yourself?'

'But Rusty, you've got to help me out here. I'm in prison.'

Rusty raised his voice at me for the first time. 'Thomas, I don't mind helping you out with your food and medicine. But I'm not here to pay for your drug addictions, OK?' I hadn't seen him angry before and I tried to calm him down.

'Hey, man,' I said, putting my hand on his shoulder. 'Let's not start a fight about one dollar, OK?'

Rusty jerked his shoulder sideways and pushed my hand off. 'What's gotten into you, Thomas?' Then he started lecturing me. 'Have you been doing coke today?'

'No. I promise I haven't.' He narrowed his eyes and looked at me like he didn't believe me. He knew that I was hiding something, so I finally decided to tell him the truth.

We sat down at my table and Rusty listened patiently. I had never mentioned the Velascos to him before, or the fact that I had been in solitary confinement, so it all came as a shock to him. When I finished, he didn't speak for a long time. Eventually, he said quietly, 'Why didn't you tell me this before?'

'I thought I could fix things myself. And I didn't want you to worry about me.'

He shook his head. My reasons for not telling him had been good, but he made it seem like it was because I hadn't trusted him.

'You should have told me. I had a right to know,' was all he said.

Rusty didn't stay angry for long, but I knew that this wasn't the right time to ask for his help with money. I was thinking about buying us a few beers on credit and bringing up the subject afterwards, but I never got the chance. Rusty told me he needed to leave San Pedro early that day to meet some friends outside.

'Hey, man. Aren't you going to stay tonight?' I asked. I really wanted some company.

'No. You probably should rest if you're not feeling well.' He put five bolivianos on the table. 'Here's the money for your cigarettes.'

When he left that time, Rusty shook my hand rather than giving me the usual hug. I could tell that he was disappointed with me for not being honest. Roberto came around, but I didn't feel like doing any coke with him.

卌||

Eighteen months before, I had been having the time of my life. Now, it was like someone was punishing me for every single crime I'd ever committed. Things started to go badly in every part of my life. Rusty and I were arguing. I had no money. I was doing coke every night with Roberto and not sleeping well. Ricardo had left me. And, worst of all, I was facing another prison sentence. I tried to concentrate on working hard to save up enough to be able to pay my lawyer and maybe send a bribe to the judges, but it didn't work. The restaurant business actually began to *lose* money. Although I never blamed him directly, I suspected that the reason was Mike.

When he took coke only occasionally, Mike was a good friend and the best worker I ever had. When he was back on it heavily, he cost me more money than he made. The restaurant ceased being profitable. I couldn't explain why. We had customers. I had done all the figures and worked out the profit margin on each dish. But the business kept going backwards.

'You're too generous. You give them too many fries,' Mike said, as I ran my finger over the accounts and scratched my head, wondering why I wasn't making a profit. Mike always did the cooking, but I was in charge of deciding on the menu and portion sizes. 'Look at those Bolivians. They are fat enough already. Stop feeding them so much.'

I was no longer in the mood for his jokes. 'Potatoes don't cost anything,' I snapped back, but Mike had an answer for everything.

'True, but the oil we cook them in is expensive. And the gas. Have you factored in the gas? I had to replace that valve, remember?'

'What valve?' I demanded. The main thing that annoyed me about Mike was that he didn't write anything down. Not orders, not money coming in, nor expenses. It was all recorded in his head. He also became angry quickly.

'Are you accusing me of lying?'

'No. I didn't say that. I just think we should write everything down.'

'It's all up here,' he said, tapping his forehead with his wrist because his hands were dirty. 'I haven't got time to write things down and I don't need to. My memory is perfect. Ask me any question.' I couldn't directly accuse Mike of taking drugs since he still claimed to be clean, but eventually we had a falling out over money. I had to get Sergio in to start cooking for me, but even then, the money I made barely covered my living expenses.

With the restaurant no longer so profitable, I needed to find another way of making money very quickly in order to bribe the judges. The most obvious way was to do some *negocios* with the other inmates. However, I was afraid of getting busted or being set up again. Besides, there was no real money in it. Ricardo used to tell me a joke he'd made up: 'Selling snow to a Bolivian is like selling ice to an Eskimo.'

Occasionally, tourists came in to visit me and I did consider selling cocaine to them. However, having Westerners take merchandise out of the prison was too risky; the other tour operators might tip off the guards at the gate. Besides, even if I sold coke at double the price I bought it, I'd still make next to nothing.

As I already knew, the real money was in exporting the stuff. In San Pedro, you could buy cocaine at three or four dollars a gram, and once it had arrived safely in any country outside South America, that same amount was worth more than a hundred dollars. However, since Abregon had died, there was no one on the outside I could trust to help me set up deals. I decided to do it on my own, but on a smaller scale, just in order to make enough money to fund my case and get by. I decided to send cocaine the old-fashioned way – by ordinary post.

People have been mailing small quantities of drugs in letters for decades. They put hash, heroin, opium or LSD in a letter and just hope it gets there. If the letter doesn't arrive, then that's the risk they were prepared to take: they simply lose the money they paid for the drugs. Or so they think – many people also get busted that way. My method was a lot cleverer and a lot less risky. It used the same principles I had used for packing the five kilos in Santa Cruz. I placed cocaine between two sheets of transparent plastic that were cut to fit exactly within the dimensions of a standard envelope, and then rolled the sheets flat with a bottle. I would then melt the four edges using a laminating machine, or by holding a hot guitar string to the edge. In order to prevent the contents from settling, it was best if the merchandise was slightly moist so that it would stick to the plastic. You could use any kind of spray to do this, as long as it wasn't toxic.

Finally, when I had made sure the whole package was airtight against sniffer dogs, I would wrap it in paper and insert it into an official-looking envelope, preferably one with a logo and a clear plastic window for the typewritten address. My favourite envelopes to use were the ones that Yasheeda had stolen from a local establishment and given to me as a joke, which read, 'With compliments, La Paz Hotel.'

In a standard-size envelope, I could fit ten grams. Anything more and it started to look suspiciously thick. However, ten grams were enough for the tourists to have a good time with. Most of them weren't doing it to sell, they just wanted to get their hands on some pure cocaine.

Obviously, there was always some risk involved; customs do have sniffer dogs and X-ray machines. However, with millions of letters from overseas being processed each day, they can't check every single item closely. Sniffer dogs are also very expensive to train and the authorities are more likely to concentrate their efforts on bigger parcels, or at airports and seaports. Why would they look for a few grams being sent by standard envelope, when there are tonnes of the stuff being smuggled in by plane and boat? And even if the cops found the envelope, they would still have to prove in court who was responsible. This would have been difficult, since the envelopes were usually addressed to a false name at an abandoned building or a post office box. Sometimes I would send it to someone's apartment, but always in the name of a previous tenant.

Of course, these precautions didn't make it one hundred per cent safe. The authorities aren't stupid. When they do intercept drugs, they often allow them through and then put surveillance on your house. The best way around that was to write 'Return to Sender' on the envelope as soon as you received it, and then leave it on your kitchen bench for a few weeks. The worst thing you could do was to ring all your friends and tell them to come around for a big party.

Customers placed orders for my special envelopes by phone or by email. Up-front payment was sent by telegraphic transfer in the name of one of the inmates' wives, who would pick up the cash and bring it to San Pedro for a small *propina*. I would then send the envelopes out to be deposited in a street mailbox. During the whole time I did this, no one ever got busted. A few of the envelopes didn't arrive, but I suspect that's because some of those customs agents had their sniffer dogs trained not to bark too loudly when they found something.

48
MY INTERNATIONAL HUMAN RIGHTS LAWYER

As the second date of my new trial approached, I apologised to Rusty for not having told him about the new charges and we made up.

'If we're in this together, Thomas,' he said, 'then I need you to be completely honest with me. OK? No secrets.'

I agreed, except for the part that we were in it together. He was there voluntarily, so he could go home whenever he wanted; I was the one who would do the time. Also, I didn't let him know about my plan to bribe the judges. There was no need to tell him about that just yet, because I hadn't raised enough money yet from my envelope scam. I could sense that Rusty was worried about me, but I knew better than to ask him for bribe money. Besides, I'd thought of another way he could help me, which didn't involve money, and he agreed to it.

That evening, I gave him my briefcase – the one I'd had at the airport with all my fruit juice company documents. He emptied it out while I made us dinner. When I turned around, I saw that he was probing around the bottom for secret compartments.

'Hey, man,' I said, astonished that Rusty could suspect me after staying with me for so many weeks. 'There are no drugs in there.'

But he was only joking. 'Hey man, you never know,' he said, copying the way I spoke. 'This is Bolivia, man. You have to be careful.'

For my next court appearance, Rusty was waiting for me outside the court. He had purchased a cheap suit and tie and some shiny black shoes. With his hair tied back in a ponytail and my briefcase in hand, he almost looked like a proper lawyer. He sat on one side of me and Manuelo, my legal-aid lawyer, sat on the other. The Velascos sat on the other side of the courtroom with their lawyers and family. We all stood when the three judges came in. Immediately, Rusty stood up and introduced himself as an international human rights lawyer who had been sent from England to observe my trial. When the judges asked him for documentation, he said he would bring it next time. The judges were thrown by this, but they couldn't say anything because the courts were supposed to be open to the public.

The hearing was quite short, but we learned a little more about the Velascos' defence. They intended to rely on their own witness statements, as well as a statement from someone in the FELCN that they were acting under instructions to catch me in the act of dealing. It was a dirty trick the Velascos were playing on me, but I knew exactly what I was going to do in return. It wouldn't be long before I got my revenge.

The guards were even more confused when Rusty and I returned to San Pedro together that afternoon, me in handcuffs and Rusty wearing his suit and tie. According to his permission slip, he was supposed to be my cousin helping me while I received my medical treatment, but now he had suddenly become my lawyer. One of the cheekier guards asked whether we were really cousins. By then, Rusty had worked out how to make the Bolivians laugh. Before answering, he looked at the guard very seriously.

'Every single one of my cousins is a doctor or a lawyer, except for Thomas,' he said, punching me in the arm as though he was extremely disappointed that I had turned out to be a drug trafficker. 'He's the black sheep of the family.' The lieutenant laughed so much he had trouble opening the gate.

Being my human rights lawyer also gave Rusty an excuse to take his dictaphone, laptop and micro-cassettes in and out of the prison. For my subsequent court appearances, he always took these to court to make himself appear more professional. The judges were afraid of being recorded, so when Rusty failed to produce any proof that he was who he said he was, they banned him from using the dictaphone and computer. After that, he had to take handwritten notes.

As soon as we got through the gates, I went straight to Orlando's shop. Orlando's wife worked as a legal secretary during the day. In the evenings and on weekends she supplied secretarial services to the inmates of San Pedro as a way of bringing in extra income to support their family. She had also leased various pieces of office equipment, including a photocopier. I qualified for the discount photocopying rate, since I needed one hundred copies of a single page.

Through contacts in the prison administration, I had managed to locate someone who knew a worker in the filing section of the drug court. He had told me more details of the Velascos' defence and I'd paid him fifty dollars for a copy of one specific page of it: the statement signed by both Jorge and Jose Luis Velasco testifying that they had been working in the prison as undercover agents with the FELCN drug police over a period of several months with the aim of providing information on drug dealing within the prison. The statement was entirely false. I knew it and they knew it, but the other prisoners didn't.

Across the top of each copy I wrote the word '*Buzos*' in thick red marker pen – our word for 'informants' – and then distributed them throughout every section of the prison. I stuck copies on walls, on noticeboards, under people's doors, and I handed the remainder directly to inmates as I walked around. In San Pedro, there was only one class of prisoner more despised than rapists and child molesters: police informants. I wanted the Velascos dead. However, when they got word of what was happening, they fled to the main gates and bribed the guards to be transferred to La Muralla. Even then, it was doubtful that they would survive long.

A few days later, Jorge went to the authorities. He feared for his life and asked to retract his statement. He told them the truth – that he and his father weren't really informants and that I had nothing to do with the two hundred grams of cocaine found in their room. For his own safety, he also told this to every prisoner he came in contact with. The Velascos began accusing each other of lying. I had done a good job on them; there was now a complete inconsistency between their statements, which put their whole defence in disarray. And with it, the case against me crumbled completely. There was no way the judges could convict me now.

꜔꜔ⅠⅠ

I wanted to celebrate my revenge against the Velascos immediately. I was actually looking forward to going to court for my next appearance. By then, I had completed four-and-a-half years of my original six-year, eight-month sentence, but with the benefit of *Extra Muro*, that was enough. I still had my signed release form from earlier in the year and as soon as the judges acquitted me of the new charges, I would be allowed to leave San Pedro. For the first time since Ricardo had left, I felt truly happy. I was absolutely one hundred per cent certain that I would be free in a matter of weeks. I went and bought two packets of cocaine to celebrate and sent for Roberto.

Earlier that week, there had been a rumour that the guards were about to conduct a surprise raid. The inmates hid their merchandise immediately, but when the guards didn't come on the night they had said, everyone began to relax again. I remained cautious, however, since they hadn't done a *requisa* for quite some time.

Roberto and I continued doing coke every night, but I made certain that we only ever bought one small pack at a time from my dealer, Comandante. I told Roberto that the safest place to hide any contraband was outside your room. That way, if the police came with dogs, they couldn't prove whose it was.

'And don't ever open the door without asking who it is first,' I told him. 'If the police knock, take as much time as you need to hide things. And spray deodorant in the air. If they get angry when you open the door, pretend that you've just woken up and you haven't had a shower.'

'OK, Thomas. I understand,' Roberto said, sniffing another line. But he *didn't* understand. Two nights later there was a *requisa* and he completely ignored what I had told him.

‖‖‖‖||

That evening Roberto knocked on my door as usual, but I was tired from the previous night's partying and wasn't in the mood to take coke again.

'I'm sorry. Do you worry if I only sit here for a very small time?' he asked. I just wanted to sleep but then I remembered how lonely I had been when I first arrived in San Pedro, so I let him in.

Roberto sat at my table sniffing lines and smoking *ganja* while I lay back in bed with the TV on, trying to stay awake in order to keep him company. Suddenly, word of a police search shot through the section. Doors opened and slammed shut as neighbours came out to warn each other. I heard feet scampering as inmates who were out visiting rushed back to their rooms to hide their contraband. Then the section lookout confirmed the rumour by sprinting through the corridors, knocking on all the doors and whispering, '¡Requisa! ¡Requisa!'

Roberto panicked. He quickly stubbed out the joint he was smoking and clumsily refolded his packets of cocaine and marijuana. When he stood up, he knocked over his chair and this made him panic even more. He looked frantically around the room for somewhere to hide the packets. However, he was in such a state of alarm that he completely forgot the advice I'd given him about spraying deodorant to disguise the smell and taking your time to find a good hiding spot.

'OK, Thomas. I see you later, *bueno*?' he said, depositing the two small packages in my open hand and racing for the door.

I was so sleepy that I hardly had time to realise what he had done before the police arrived at my room. They didn't even have to knock: in his rush to get back to his room, Roberto opened the door for them. When he saw the Devil Major right there in front of him, he let out a small cry of surprise. The major, who had his fist in the air about to knock, looked at him, equally surprised.

'*Scusi*,' said Roberto, forgetting his Spanish. He slipped under the Devil Major's arm, past the policemen and down the stairs. The major raised his eyebrows and watched him go. My fingers closed slowly around the packages. It was too late to do anything with them.

'A very good evening to you, *Señor* McFadden,' said the Devil Major, turning his attention back to me. The Devil Major always spoke very politely in front of his men, because he wanted them to think he was from the Bolivian upper class. He always wore a thick overcoat with stars on the shoulders to make himself look important. I already knew from what he did to Samir in La Grulla that he wasn't someone you wanted to catch you doing something illegal. He preferred to punish people rather than accept bribes.

'Good evening, major,' I answered from my bed, trying to be as respectful as I could.

'With your permission,' he said, bowing to me and wiping his feet before stepping onto my carpet. 'I take it that none of your wives are visiting you this evening?' he enquired courteously.

'No, major. I was just going to bed,' I said, sitting up on my mattress and trying desperately to think of what to do with the drugs. Luckily, the Devil Major was too busy being sarcastic to notice the look of panic on my face.

'Yes, so I noticed. Your little Italian friend was leaving in quite a hurry,' he commented, looking up at the ceiling to where Roberto's marijuana smoke hadn't yet dispersed. I saw the Devil Major's nose twitch at the smell. He didn't say anything, but the first thing he did was to inspect the contents of the ashtray. Fortunately for me, Roberto always made his joints by hollowing out a cigarette because it was very difficult to find rolling papers in La Paz. The Devil Major was disappointed not to find any evidence in the ashtray, but he knew that something had been going on and was determined to keep searching.

'Please stand in the centre of the cell, *inglés*,' said the lieutenant, who always stood beside the major, copying everything he did.

'Yes, *teniente*.' I threw the sheets back and bent down to get my slippers from under the bed, hoping I could flick the packets somewhere. However, the lieutenant was watching me too closely.

'Don't touch anything,' he commanded. He wouldn't even let me put on a jacket when I complained of how cold it was. I stood in the middle of the room in my pyjamas, holding the packets loosely in my hand so as not to look suspicious.

The police began their *requisa*. Normally, the high-ranking officers didn't participate in the actual search, but the Devil Major was so sure he would find something this time that he joined in. I knew it wouldn't be long before they would want to search me. When the major turned to look in my underwear drawer, I saw my opportunity. He had his back to me and the others were also busy going through my possessions. Because he was bent forward, the side pocket of his big coat was gaping slightly and I dropped the packets in just as he stood up and turned around.

The Devil Major hadn't seen what I had done, but he must have sensed my movement. He narrowed his eyes and looked at me suspiciously. I pretended that I had been looking over his shoulder, but he and the lieutenant knew from my startled expression that I was covering something up. To divert their attention, I glanced down at the ground when the major wasn't watching. I knew, however, that the lieutenant still had his eye on me.

'Lift your feet, *inglés*,' he commanded confidently, as soon as he saw me look down.

'What for, *teniente*?' I said, pretending to look worried that he had caught me out.

'Do it *now!*' barked the major. I lifted my right foot nervously and lowered it back to the floor, although slightly to the left of where it had previously been, so it was now touching my other foot. This made them more suspicious.

'And the other one,' he demanded. I lifted that foot also.

'Move back one step,' said the lieutenant, thinking I must have still been hiding something. I did as they ordered and once more they were confused and disappointed not to have found anything.

'We're finished here,' declared the major, trying to recover his authority. He turned to the lieutenant. 'Take this prisoner to the court-yard and search him with all the others.'

卌ǁ

It was a very lucky escape and I was angry with Roberto, especially since I had told him exactly what he should do during a search. He came around the next night to apologise, bringing a bottle of rum as a peace offering. After a few glasses, I forgave him. He was still new and it was his very first *requisa*.

When I told him what I'd done with the drugs, Roberto couldn't stop laughing.

'No. I no believe, Thomas. No is the true,' he declared, raising his voice and throwing his hands dramatically into the air. After a few more drinks and with no cocaine in his system, he had started acting like a proper Italian. 'I think you invent this story, yes?'

'I promise. On your mother's grave.'

'But my mother she is *Católica*.' He sat forward suddenly and shook his finger at me, pretending to be offended. 'You no talk about my mother like this way, please, Thomas.'

We did two more quick shots of rum and I also began to see the funny side. As we got more drunk, we began speculating on what might have happened after the Devil Major had left with packets of cocaine and marijuana in his pocket. Roberto was convinced that the sniffer dogs would have detected them and then the major would have had a lot of explaining to do in front of his men. I didn't agree.

'No way, man. There weren't any dogs.' But once Roberto got on to a subject, he couldn't let it go.

'Then perhaps his wife she will find the drugs when she is cleaning the jacket?' he suggested, leaning back in his chair and going into another laughing fit. 'He will have big problems in the home.'

'Maybe,' I said, trying to imagine what the Devil Major's wife would look like.

'Or maybe the wife she like the *cocaína*. Like my girlfriend in Italy she does. The *cocaína* is good for the sex, you know.' Roberto stood up in order to demonstrate. 'So this major he just put a little bit here on the end here,' he said, touching the front of his pants, 'and maybe some for her in the special place, and they will be very excited together. Making a lot of love. Very happy marriage. Lot of pleasure.'

'No, man, that major is a homosexual.' I was convinced that no woman would put up with the Devil Major.

'No. I no believe, Thomas. You are joking with me again. That homosexual major was the one who stole your hair machine.'

'It's true. They're all gay.'

'No.' Roberto put his hand to his mouth and gasped once more like a proper Italian. 'Is no true, Thomas. I no believe. How the country can get bigger then if all the Bolivian man is homosexual?'

For the next few weeks, I was happy and we had a lot of parties, especially when Rusty wasn't around. I told all my friends in prison that I would be leaving soon. With the Velascos retracting their statement and a 'human rights lawyer' observing the proceedings, I was totally convinced that my trial was over. It would have been, had it not been for the next surprise – the Velascos' chief witness.

49
WITNESS FOR THE DEFENCE

Before our next court appearance, Jorge Velascos changed his statement back, saying he had only retracted it because of threats made against his life by other prisoners. This strengthened the Velascos' case a great deal. I knew they had family connections high up in the drug trade, which also meant they would have connections among the drug police. I already knew that they would get one of them to act as their witness and I hadn't forgotten the warning that Chino had given me in La Grulla, either. Maybe they would use Jose Luis's brother, the FELCN agent. I didn't expect the testimony to be strong, however, especially if it only amounted to a family member backing up their story. Hopefully, my lawyer would be able to prove they were all lying.

On the day that the Velascos were to give full details of their defence, there was a new shock awaiting me. Their lawyer informed the court that the next defence witness was a colonel. My lawyer, Manuelo, looked down at his desk and picked up his pen. He seemed worried. Discrediting a high-ranking police or army witness would be tough. The Velascos' lawyer then mentioned that this colonel worked with the FELCN drug investigation unit. Manuelo closed his eyes for a few seconds. This would make it even tougher. We knew the *fiscal* would be of no help; he worked closely with the FELCN and he would probably know this colonel personally. I could tell that Manuelo was panicking, but as soon as I heard this, I tapped him on the shoulder.

'He's the brother,' I whispered to him.

'Who? This witness? Are you sure?' he asked disbelievingly. I nodded.

'I'm positive.' Manuelo seemed relieved to have some ammunition that wouldn't involve directly accusing the colonel of lying.

When the witness came in, I stopped breathing for a few seconds. It was Colonel Lanza! I stared at him in disbelief. I hadn't seen him since my arrest at the airport, but I recognised him immediately. It had been four-and-a-half years, but he hadn't changed. I kept staring at him, thinking it couldn't possibly be true. He looked calmly around the court. He even looked directly at me, but as soon as he spoke, there was no doubt.

'Yes. I swear,' he said, when the clerk of the court asked him if he swore on the bible to tell the truth. Next, he was asked to state his name.

'Colonel Mario Toro Lanza.' Manuelo panicked slightly and turned to me. He was worried because the colonel's surname wasn't Velasco. But it was too much of a coincidence not to be true.

'Brother-in-law,' I whispered.

When it was his turn to cross-examine, Manuelo asked Colonel Lanza detailed questions about the supposed undercover operation. But Lanza had already thought of almost every possible question and how to answer it.

'Who was in charge of the operation?' Manuelo asked.

'I was.'

'Who else knew about the operation?'

'I am unable to say. That's classified information.'

For some of the more specific questions, Lanza ran out of prepared answers. Every time he got into trouble, though, he always had the same escape route: 'It was a secret operation.'

My lawyer then asked why there was no record of this operation. He asked why none of the guards at San Pedro knew about it and why no one in the prison administration was informed, even when the operation had been completed. He asked why no phone call was made to external investigators once the operation had been 'successful' and why it took over a year to bring the charges. Lanza had a clever answer for those questions as well: 'It would have compromised the safety of the undercover operatives.'

At that point, Lanza also mentioned the great risk that the Velascos had taken in attempting to bring me to justice. He informed the court that it had come to his attention that I had deliberately exposed his operatives to grave danger by illegally obtaining copies of their statements and distributing them within the prison with the intention of endangering their lives. This was backed up by the fact that Jorge Velasco had been obliged to change his statement in order to save his own life. Lanza did a very good job of making the Velascos sound like brave police agents, and me sound like a calculating drug baron. He spoke confidently and looked my lawyer in the eye when he answered his questions. He was winning the battle until Manuelo pulled out his big question.

Pointing at Jorge and Jose Luis, Manuelo asked, 'And Colonel Lanza, would you please tell the court what is your relation to these two defendants?'

Lanza fidgeted for a few moments before mumbling an answer that no one heard.

'Could you repeat your answer, colonel?' Manuelo said, emphasising the word 'colonel'.

'I . . .' Lanza looked around nervously and tried to stall for time. 'I . . . I don't understand what you're asking.'

'It's not difficult. I'll repeat the question,' said Manuelo sarcastically, driving home his point. He had him now. 'What is your relation to the defendants Jose Luis and Jorge Velasco?'

'Why are you asking me this? I am a colonel in the Bolivian drug investigation unit.'

'Answer the question please, witness!' bellowed Manuelo. Colonel Lanza looked like he was finally about to answer, but the *fiscal* jumped in and saved him.

'Objection. The witness is not obliged to respond.'

'Why not?' snapped Manuelo, turning angrily to address the *fiscal*. His face finally showed the anger that had been building up against the prosecutor during the trial. The colonel was a witness for the defence, which meant the *fiscal* was supposed to be cross-examining him, not protecting him.

'By law, the witness is not obliged to answer that question,' the *fiscal* repeated, and quoted a statute. Manuelo argued strongly, but the *fiscal* shouted him down and showed him the statute. Even then, Manuelo continued to argue.

'The *fiscal* is correct,' interrupted one of the judges. 'The witness may decline to respond, if he so chooses.' Manuelo argued with the judge, but the other judges called for order and asked that the case continue. Manuelo glared at the prosecutor and slapped the table to show his frustration. But there was nothing more he could do.

As soon as Manuelo gave in, I felt a wave of anger surge over me. I was ready to yell out, 'But he's the *brother-in-law!*' I didn't care if there was a law preventing it. I wouldn't have cared if I got in trouble; once everyone knew that Colonel Lanza was a relative of the Velascos, they would know the truth. But Manuelo sensed what I was about to do and grabbed my knee.

'No! Thomas, don't do it!' he hissed. 'There's no point.'

I calmed myself down. He was probably right. Although they had different surnames, the judges must have known the colonel was related to the Velascos. Why else would he have wanted to avoid answering the question? I decided not to make things worse for myself, as I had in my first case. The judge at my first trial had never returned my Queen of England ring.

I later looked up the statute. It was a law designed to protect the identity of family members of witnesses who testified in drug cases. Whoever drafted it hadn't considered that the family members might be the ones on trial.

50
DESPERATE MEASURES

With Colonel Lanza against me, I knew that the only chance I would have of getting off would be to bribe the judges. I started looking around for some money immediately. The first person I asked was Rusty. At first he completely refused to help. He didn't say so directly, but I think he suspected that I was lying about being set up by the police and the Velascos. I didn't blame him for that – he knew I was a cocaine trafficker and that I sold stuff to tourists, so it must have seemed unlikely that I was innocent. I also knew he didn't have much money, but I tried my hardest to persuade him to borrow some.

'Look, Rusty. In a way I *am* guilty. I admit that I've dealt drugs in here many times. But this time I didn't.' He looked at me and nodded, but I could tell that he still doubted me. 'I swear to you on my life. If I had done it, I would accept the punishment.'

I even showed him the police facts sheet in order to prove that I was telling the truth. It stated that the police had found me outside the Velascos' room, but there was no mention of me possessing any cocaine or money.

'So you see, man, they didn't even get me with any drugs or money. I'm innocent. The charge just says I was intending to traffic. But there is no evidence.'

'Exactly,' said Rusty, as though I had just proven his point. 'There's no way they can convict you on that. But if you try to bribe the judges, then they'll think it's because you really *are* guilty.'

'Hey, man. You don't know this country. That's not how things work in Bolivia. The judges don't care if I'm guilty or not. If they convict a foreigner, it looks good for them.'

To end the argument, Rusty said that he would do his best to help me, but he still made excuses not to. He didn't believe me about being set up – until he got arrested himself and was told to leave the country. He almost ruined everything by being so stupid. I had to fix things with the governor to get him a new permission slip. Once I'd bribed the governor, Rusty was allowed back into San Pedro, but only on official visiting days and he could no longer stay the night. *He* was out of trouble, but *I* wasn't; there was now a misdemeanour report in the administration office that mentioned my name. I was worried that if the judges found out about it, it would affect my trial.

卌‖

The whole universe seemed to turn against me that week. It now looked like I would be convicted for the two hundred grams; Rusty got me in trouble with the governor; and then news came that Samir had died in Chonchocoro. Julián told me that Samir had killed himself, but I knew he would never have done that. I would have believed that he'd been shot in a fight with the police or trying to escape, but I knew that Samir would never take his own life. It took a while to find out what had really happened.

Samir had been kept in the isolation block at Chonchocoro the whole time, so that he couldn't communicate with the outside world. He kept trying to blackmail the police he had stolen cars for, but they stopped responding to his threats once he was powerless. Samir somehow managed to have a pen and paper smuggled into his cell. He wrote a letter that named names, dates and places. The letter never made it out because the police got to him first.

Before they killed him, the police tortured him for several hours, just as they had done in La Grulla. When they were satisfied that he hadn't sent out any other letters, they strangled him and hung the body from a rafter inside his cell. The cleaner found him when he was doing his rounds. There were at least three witnesses in the isolation block who heard everything that happened. At first, they were too afraid to say anything, but they made a pact to speak out together. A group of them contacted the media and told the truth about what had happened. Samir's death was reported in the paper, but it was only one of three suspicious deaths in Chonchocoro in a thirty-hour period. I didn't cry. I just felt numb.

After Samir was murdered, Rusty started to really worry about getting me out of San Pedro. He told me not to do any more tours, sell any more coke or take any more risks that might get me in trouble. He also agreed to help me look for money and began asking some of his friends for loans.

There were three judges sitting on my case. I sent a message to only two of them – enough to be found innocent in a split decision – asking how much they required. They sent back a message saying eight thousand US dollars, four thousand each. The figure wasn't negotiable, they said. It was a lot of money considering how weak the *fiscal*'s case was and that the judges must have suspected I was innocent. But I already knew that neither of these factors counted towards Bolivian justice. If you had money and knew people, you were innocent. If you didn't, you were guilty. It was that simple.

卌‖

Because of my trial, I had decided to stop taking cocaine. Roberto wanted to quit also. Before he was sentenced, he had believed there was some hope that his lawyers might get him off on a legal technicality. Now that had his sentence, he finally accepted that he was going to be in San Pedro for a while. We made a brotherhood pact: no more cocaine. We would quit together. If either of us was ever tempted to take some, he had to go to the other to ask for help and to find the strength to resist.

Before quitting completely, Roberto and I needed to have one final party, though. We bought five grams between us and stayed up all night doing lines and discussing the precise details of our pact. We both agreed it was unrealistic to think that anyone could suddenly stop forever, just like that. So, we changed the rules slightly: if one of us was tempted to take something, we could, but we had to tell the other first. We couldn't stop the other from taking it; the aim was to give each other support and be completely honest with each other. No matter what, we had to be honest, like brothers. Rusty was no longer staying in San Pedro, and right then, I needed a brother in prison. I felt very alone knowing that Abregon and Samir were both dead and that Ricardo wasn't coming back.

By the time the bell rang for *lista* the following morning, everything was settled. We stood and embraced like brothers, before walking down the stairs to the courtyard.

'I love you, my brother,' I said to Roberto, holding him close to me and squeezing his shoulder. It was an important moment for me because I knew we really had to stick together if we were going to quit.

'Me, too,' he said, hugging me back stiffly, slightly embarrassed by my sudden display of feeling.

Following the *lista*, we went back up to my room. We still hadn't finished the entire five grams. I couldn't have eaten breakfast anyway, so we kept sniffing until the whole bag was finished at around eleven o'clock. Immediately following the last lines, I kicked Roberto out of my room, drank two litres of water, smoked a joint and went downstairs to have a cold shower. When I came back, I cleaned my room, put on some nice clothes, smoked another joint, and then went to see the prison doctor. There was no point in lying to him, so I just came out with it.

'Doctor, I need you to help me. I want to stop taking cocaine.' He looked at me coolly, not at all surprised by what I had said.

'For how long have you been consuming?'

I counted back the time in my head. It had been almost four-and-a-half years since that first occasion on *la Noche de San Juan* – which was a long time, when I thought about it. I had never thought of myself as being an addict, but I realised that in all that time, I had never been without cocaine for more than two weeks, not even in La Grulla. The doctor informed me that there was no medicine that could cure me. I had to stop by myself and that would only happen if I really wanted to. However, he did offer to put me on a saline solution drip that was designed to flush the drug out of my blood system.

The doctor came to my room each day and put me on the drip for an hour or so. With the drip and keeping myself busy, I managed to stay away from coke. But Roberto didn't. He broke the pact. He made it through the first three nights OK, but on the fourth morning I saw him down in the courtyard and he waved to me to signal that we would talk later. But he didn't come to my room afterwards and when I saw him again that evening, he pretended he hadn't seen me and snuck off to his room. I knew that he'd had something to sniff. He must have been too afraid to say anything or too ashamed of his weakness. I wasn't angry, but I was waiting for him to come and tell me.

‖‖|\

Rusty was having trouble getting the money together. I continued to ring everyone I knew. I begged the inmates in San Pedro. I contacted all my old *negocios* friends in Europe, promising them a shipment. But none of them gave me a cent. I might have been able to set up a big deal, but that would have taken months to organise and the case was already coming to a close.

After the second-last court date, I sent another message to the judges saying that I couldn't get them all the money on time. They agreed to accept four thousand dollars between them. I tried all my contacts again, but the situation was hopeless. In fact, I had probably made it worse; now that the judges were expecting a bribe, they would be even angrier when I couldn't give them anything.

As the date for the judges' decision drew closer, we still had no money to pay them. I tried to stay positive by thinking about the many people who had helped me since being in prison. As the final court date approached, however, I became desperate. As a last resort, we sent an email to every tourist whose details I had, begging them to send any money they could spare, no matter how small the amount. I promised to pay it all back when I got out. Most of the tourists responded. Many couldn't afford to lend me anything, but some could.

All in all, with the money from Rusty's friends and the tourists, we got together just over two thousand dollars. I didn't want to send anything less to the judges than the full amount because I knew they wouldn't accept it, but Rusty insisted.

'Look, Thomas. We'll offer them half now and half when they let you off.'

'No, man. You can't do that in Bolivia. They won't trust that I'll pay.'

'Well, why should we trust *them*?'

'That's just the way things work. They won't accept half. You have to show them trust.' Rusty had been in Bolivia for only four months, but he kept arguing because he thought he knew better than me. He started giving me another one of his lectures.

'Thomas, listen. You bribed the colonel, he took the money, then betrayed you. You bribed him again at the airport, he took the money, then betrayed you again. You paid the lawyers, they took your money and then betrayed you. You paid the first judge, he took your money and then betrayed you. Can't you see a pattern emerging?'

'No. I've been here longer than you. I'm telling you, you just can't do it that way.'

'Why not? It's a business arrangement. And normally in business you pay an up-front deposit and then the rest on delivery. Bribery should be no different.'

Eventually I agreed to try his suggestion. I wanted to send the money to the judges with one of the inmates' wives, but Rusty was worried that it mightn't arrive. He said he would take it himself. However, the last time he had tried to bribe anyone, he had been arrested. As a compromise, he accompanied the inmate's wife and together they handed over the money in two separate envelopes. At first, the judges didn't want to accept it. They had already agreed to halve the original amount and now required the whole lot in a single payment. Rusty insisted, promising them that they would receive the rest before the day of the judgment, even though we didn't have it. The judges postponed the hearing date to give us more time. When we didn't get them the money, they postponed it again.

Three days before the final court date was fixed, one of my contacts in the prison received a phone call to say that the judges couldn't postpone the trial any longer. We still hadn't paid the outstanding amount. I kept trying everywhere and hoping that something would work out, but all my options were exhausted. The judges sent word that they had no choice but to proceed to judgment. I was done for. Rusty wanted to keep trying, but I knew there was no use. We had both tried every person we knew.

The night before the verdict, Roberto came around to keep me company. I tried to be friendly at first, because I knew that he wanted to help take my mind off my trial, but I was still angry with him for breaking our pact. Roberto had never come to see me to admit that he'd broken it. He had avoided me and I'd avoided him back. I didn't want to be friends with someone I couldn't trust. We were supposed to have been brothers.

'Do you want one?' he said, reaching for a CD case and holding up the phone card that he would use to cut up the lines of coke. I wasn't angry with him for wanting to take some that night. We both knew he had already broken our pact. Doing coke in front of me was his way of admitting it. At first I just shook my head and didn't say anything. Right then, sniffing cocaine was the last thing in the world I wanted to do. It had brought me nothing but trouble and the sight of the white lines revolted me. Why would anyone want to deliberately snort something so horrible up their nose?

'Are you sure?' he asked, unfolding the small packet he had brought along and tapping the paper so that some of it fell onto the CD case. I refused him again, but Roberto kept insisting, and I had to say something.

'I don't mind if you do coke, Roberto. But you didn't have to lie to me,' I said, raising my voice. 'That was the pact. How can I trust you now?'

Roberto apologised. He said he had been confused and that he hadn't told me because I wouldn't have understood, which made me even angrier.

'You don't need it, Roberto,' I told him. 'You think you do, but you don't.'

卌‖

I hardly slept at all after the argument with Roberto. Rusty rang my mobile phone about ten times. I didn't want to answer. He phoned up other inmates to send me a message: don't go to court. I should pretend to be sick so that we could delay in order to try to get more money. I had already considered that option. I could have cut myself and gone to hospital, but I knew that would only have put things off by a week, or two at the most. Delay or no delay, I would still have to face the judges' verdict.

I stayed awake until dawn, thinking about what would happen if they found me guilty. It had been almost five years since I arrived at San Pedro. My mind raced over all the things that had happened to me during that time. There had been many good times and I tried to concentrate on thinking only about them, but my mind kept returning to the suffering. I thought about Samir and Abregon, and the little girl being raped, and about the gang rapist's brains spilling out onto the concrete. I remembered all the sleeping pills I had taken when Yasheeda left me. I couldn't live through another five or ten years like that. And even if I could, what future would I have if I got out of prison ten years older? Then I thought of what my friend Sylvia, from the Anglican Church, used to tell me, and I started praying to God to save me.

In the early morning, when I was delirious from tiredness and from thinking for so long, I made a promise to God: if He let me go free, I would never touch or sell cocaine in my life ever again. When I got out, I would try to help people and do some good in the world. After that promise to God, I made another one: if the judges found me guilty, I would escape. And if I couldn't escape, I would kill myself.

51
VERDICT

I was barely awake the following morning when the time came for the guards to put me in the transport van. But I was calm. The money that Rusty had collected and that my tourist friends had sent from around the world wasn't enough but we had done all that we could. What happened from now on was no longer up to either of us.

Rusty was waiting for me in the corridor of the courtroom. He looked like he hadn't slept either.

'Didn't you get my messages?' he said worriedly, but my police escorts wouldn't let me talk with him. They led me towards the holding cell. Rusty followed us as far as they would let him.

'Don't worry,' I said to him. 'It will all turn out OK.'

Rusty wasn't reassured by this. He was convinced they were going to convict me.

The judges wouldn't look at me when they came in to read out the verdict. I was having trouble paying attention as they began the formalities of restating the charges and the evidence that had been presented to them. I only heard one word of what they said: *'inocente'*. I couldn't believe it.

'Gracias a Dios,' someone said loudly. Cheers went up on the other side of the room. I looked over and saw the Velascos hugging each other, still with their handcuffs on. Their lawyer patted them on the shoulder and smiled.

I was free! Suddenly, I had another thought and panicked: what if the finding of innocence only applied to the charges against the Velascos? I began listening intently to the rest of the judgment, but then Jorge Velascos winked at me and I knew I had got off too.

ⅧⅡ

The judges delayed another week before signing my release papers. In the meantime, I had to promise to get them the rest of the money as soon as I got out. They gave me a conditional release – I was free, but I couldn't leave the country. On the day I left prison, I had a big party. Giles and Sole, two tourists who had visited me many times, arrived with Rusty to help me pack my possessions. It wasn't as large a send-off as Ricardo had, but walking out through those gates was one of the happiest moments of my life. My legs collapsed from under me and I had to clutch on to Giles to stop myself from falling over. I never thought they would let me out of that place.

I left San Pedro prison the same way as I arrived – by taxi, without a cent in my pocket. Only this time I had my friends with me and the police had let me keep my possessions. There was Rusty, Giles, Sole and me. All four of us were squashed into the back seat of the taxi with our arms around each other's shoulder. The front passenger seat was empty. As we drove off, I felt like I should have been crying, but I wasn't. I had a sudden desire to turn around and wave to the prison through the rear window, but I stopped myself. I didn't want to look back. I would miss my friends in San Pedro, but I never wanted to see that place again.

What was I going to do? One thing was for certain: I wanted to keep my promise not to go back to trafficking. It was going to be hard – it was all I'd known my entire adult life – but I was determined to try. Apart from that, I had no real plans and I wasn't in a hurry to make any big decisions. Coming out of prison is completely overwhelming – when you're inside, it's like being frozen while the world goes on without you. But then they unfreeze you and expect you to fit straight back into the world, as though nothing had happened.

Anyway, I didn't want to think about these things too much. I owed Rusty a few drinks for his help and that's all I cared about right then. We were going to a bar to celebrate. After that, who knew where I would go? Maybe I could try to remake my life in England, if I could get the money together for a flight. One of the backpackers might be able to help me get a job somewhere. I might even look up Yasheeda in Israel. I wondered if she still thought about me once in a while. I hoped so. I know I still thought about her . . .

Thomas McFadden was released from San Pedro prison on 28 December 2000, having completed four years and eight months of his original sentence. He left Bolivia without paying the rest of the bribe to the judges.

Following Thomas's release, the San Pedro prison tours continued in spite of a new sign on the outside wall officially proclaiming, 'No Foreigners Allowed'. The principal tour guide was David Cordero, alias Fantasma, who worked under an assumed name.

The Bolivian government continues to deny that inmates are obliged to purchase their own prison cells.

Several hundred women and children still live inside San Pedro.

Acknowledgements

Rusty wishes to express his deep gratitude to Simone Camilleri, without whom this book would not have begun or ended.

Thomas also wishes to thank Simone, as well as Prisoners Abroad for their kind assistance during his imprisonment.